THE LETTERS OF CARL SANDBURG

THE LETTERS OF
Carl Sandburg

EDITED BY HERBERT MITGANG

Harcourt Brace Jovanovich, Publishers

SAN DIEGO   NEW YORK   LONDON

Library of Congress Cataloging-in-Publication Data

Sandburg, Carl, 1878–1967.
    [Correspondence. Selections]
    The letters of Carl Sandburg/edited by Herbert Mitgang.
        p.   cm.
    Selection of letters arranged to form its own biographical pattern.
    Reprint. Originally published: 1st ed. New York : Harcourt, Brace & World, 1968.
    Includes index.
    ISBN 0-15-150695-7
    1. Sandburg, Carl, 1878–1967 — Correspondence.
    2. Authors, American — 20th century — Correspondence.
    I. Mitgang, Herbert.
    II. Title.
    PS3537.A618Z48   1988
    811′.52 — dc19
    [B]   88-10907

Printed in the United States of America
B C D E

Introduction

"WRITING LETTERS TOO IS WRITING"

by Herbert Mitgang

Across the first six decades of the twentieth century, Carl Sandburg wrote the story of his life and aspects of his times in more than a score of books and in thousands of poems, essays, lecture-recitals on the platform, and pronunciamentos in the press.

Only one of his books, *Always the Young Strangers,* was an autobiography. It took him through his soldiering days in the Sixth Infantry, Illinois Volunteers, during the Spanish-American War. A short sequel, *Ever the Winds of Chance,* carried him through college and his early writing jobs; but he was not well enough to continue into his fascinating political involvement as a district organizer for the Social Democratic party. His creative years can best be discovered by reading the works themselves—especially *Chicago Poems; The People, Yes; Home Front Memo,* and the six-volume Lincoln biography—because almost all of his writing was stylized and self-revealing. "I lived with Lincoln during fifteen years of research and writing," Sandburg told me, "but I was never bored or lonely."

Had it not been for the letters Sandburg wrote, the starting-out years and those that followed when he became known up and down the land as a writer and performer would have been lost. These letters help to unfold the life story in his own words: the dreams and achievements as an author, the rare insights he gained by crisscrossing the country and getting to know the American people and landscape, his journalistic and political expression and identity, the friendships and adventures of a literary lifetime. This experience is unmatched by present-day American authors; few go beyond the boundaries of their mind and region.

It is seldom noted that for most of his working life Carl Sandburg was a newspaperman. Daily journalism schooled him and molded him. He raised his family and paid the rent with the wages earned by writing for the Galesburg *Evening Mail,* Milwaukee *Sentinel,* Milwaukee *Journal,* Milwaukee *Daily News,* Milwaukee *Social-Democratic Herald,* Milwaukee *Leader, Reedy's Mirror* (St. Louis), Chicago *World,* Chicago *Day Book,* Chicago *Daily News,* NEA (Newspaper Enterprise Association), and Chicago *Times.*

It was on his first major journalistic assignment that Sandburg got into trouble with the federal government. Some of the documentation appears in these letters. But

Introduction

it is a little-known fact (discovered by the writer of this new introduction while doing research in the 1980s for his own book, *Dangerous Dossiers,* under the Freedom of Information Act) that Sandburg had an FBI and an Army Intelligence file dating back to 1918. Today, his file reads like a comedy of errors.

Sandburg went to Sweden during World War I to write feature stories for the NEA. Because he had been a Socialist organizer, he had wide connections in labor and radical circles here and abroad. When he returned to New York all the notebooks, manuscripts, and books that he had gathered in a neutral country were seized. Much of this material referred to Finland and to Bolshevism in Russia, including the *Izvestia* files on the Soviet Congress that he hoped to have translated, and Socialist and labor publications. These marked him. Sandburg was accused of carrying "revolutionary literature" and, in addition, a ten-thousand-dollar draft on behalf of Finnish revolutionaries.

Eventually, Sandburg's papers were returned. His strong-willed editor, Sam T. Hughes, called the incident censorship and encouraged Sandburg to write what he pleased. Neither Sandburg nor his editor ever forgot the attack on their journalistic integrity. Nor did the government forget Sandburg. Seventy years later and more than twenty years after his death, a dossier is maintained on Sandburg at Army Intelligence headquarters and the FBI keeps a copy of this ancient dispute in its records. In later years, while Sandburg was writing and campaigning for causes and candidates he believed in, the dossier accusing him of being a courier for "revolutionary literature" was resurrected.

Before he is too enshrined—including by some of his modern academic detractors—it is helpful to an understanding of his lasting poetry and history to be aware that he also recorded the impermanent daily and weekly news. But he was a journalistic American with a large vision. Sandburg was in the direct line of two hobo newspapermen, Walt Whitman and Mark Twain, whose work is also better remembered in poems and stories.

Reporting worked two ways for him. In the city room he was regarded, in his colleague Ben Hecht's phrase, as "our Orpheus." On assignment he gathered a bottomless file of experiences for his poetry and historical writing. During long train rides, going from town to town between assignments, he observed and he wrote.

For a former Social-Democratic Party organizer in the Lake Shore and Fox River Valley District of Wisconsin, it was a natural step to become one of the country's first labor reporters. Strikes, lockouts, and boycotts were his daily fare; he listened to the grievances of teamsters and garment workers; from day to day he followed the fortunes of the Amalgamated Clothing Workers of America in its bitter struggle for recognition in Chicago. Even in his later years, when his correspondence dwindled and he had become a national personality, he found time to write cordial letters to union leaders. Sandburg would sign off, "Fraternally yours." Few poets, or even reporters, would do so today. "I planted a few soapboxes in the state of Wisconsin," Sandburg once proudly told me.

Sandburg was also one of the first movie critics. Harry Hansen, another former seatmate at the Chicago *Daily News,* recalled that his criticism confused theatre managers, looking for puffs and publicity, and sometimes moviegoers as well. Sandburg's reviews included sermons, vignettes, and homey philosophy about dreamers who saved their pennies for Saturday night at the picture show. Even movie criticism served Sandburg's research directly. In the early 1920s, he dedicated a long poem, "Without a Cane or a Derby," to Charlie Chaplin. Like the titles on an early Chaplin film, the words began: "The woman had done him wrong."

A pamphleteer at heart, Sandburg also served the Milwaukee and Chicago papers as an editorial writer. The banalities delivered on some editorial pages inspired him to set down what he called "Universal Parts for Editorials." Some of the interchangeable parts he kidded went:

> In considering certain events that have occurred recently we wish to quah quah and quah . . . And upon more rigorous examination there are not lacking traces of coo coo and coo coo . . . Neither can any satisfaction be derived from a permanent concept of hullaballoo and higgledepiggledy . . . And even the most circumspect of men may be drawn into the error of rotten rotten kill the umpire.

It was not until he was fifty-four that he could leave his newspaper column and the security of the Chicago *Daily News.* By then, in 1932, he was supplementing his book work—including the massive research on the four-volume *Abraham Lincoln: The War Years*—with guitar lecture-recitals. These continued until he was almost eighty years old. But he returned to newspaper work in 1941, before the United States entered World War II, to do a weekly column for the Chicago *Times* syndicate called "Home Front Memo." He felt that the place to be "during a time of world chaos and storm" was in the newspapers.

While covering race riots in Chicago, Sandburg decided that the most detestable word in the English language was "exclusive." He explained that the word implied that "you shut out a more or less large range of humanity from your mind and heart." In this respect, Carl Sandburg, as journalist, poet, and man, was not exclusive.

This selection of Sandburg's letters is arranged to form its own biographical pattern. A detailed chronology pinpoints specific highlights and publications. Notes have been added after many of the letters as background and explanation of correspondents and circumstances at the time of writing. In the choice of letters from several thousand that are available, I followed these criteria: progression of Sandburg's life and career; significant literary history and friendships; poetic language and thoughts that make letters interesting in themselves.

Stylistically, the aim has been to preserve the integrity of the original letters, which are printed in full. For the sake of consistency and clarity, the following editorial principles have been applied: places and dates all appear at the top of the letters, with a locale or date added in brackets when they were not part of the original letter; first or second names and some abbreviations have been added or spelled out within brackets. Sandburg's wordplays have been retained even where apparently inconsistent. He frequently used a personal shorthand (dropping vowels); where clear, words have not been spelled out or explained. Where of no editorial significance, some slips of the typewriter in spelling have been corrected to avoid what may seem to be typographical errors. For the most part, personal punctuation and abbreviations appear as he wrote them. As a poet, Sandburg employed language in his own way—even in letters.

It is fortunate that, while pursuing one of the most productive writing careers, he still managed to keep up his personal correspondence, for the letters explain a great deal about his life and works. I have deliberately included letters of a nonliterary nature, which may seem less than world-shaking, in order to show Sandburg's many friendships. A democracy of spirit can be revealed in a letter to a secretary as well as to a Presidential candidate (such as his admired friend, Governor Adlai E. Stevenson of Illinois).

I began to bank Sandburg reminiscences in the course of talks with him in New Salem, Galesburg, Springfield, Chicago, Gettysburg, and Flat Rock, N.C. Recollections by Carl and Paula Sandburg in the course of various conversations at the family farm, often in the cheerful presence of their daughters, Janet and Margaret Sandburg, unearthed details only they knew. Helga Sandburg provided several early letters. Margaret Sandburg is the main authority on the life and works of her father; her research and detective work tracked down clues for letters all over the country.

Scores of individuals and holding institutions contributed personal letters, whereabouts of other letters, missing dates, facts about events long forgotten. Their names are listed in the acknowledgments, together with those who provided other assistance. Less than a handful of persons could not bear to part with their Sandburg letters; some of these turned up in carbons or from other sources. The major letters—and the main turns and interests of Sandburg's life—are represented here.

"The delay in replying to you was partly that I seem to delay all letters," he writes here to critic Malcolm Cowley, "and the longer I live the more difficulty I find about answering letters, partly on account of time and partly because writing letters too is writing."

Writing letters too is writing.

That is the nature of this book. At the core of this selection of letters is his writing; within the core, Carl Sandburg himself.

Flat Rock, N.C., 1968
New York, N.Y., 1988

Chronology

1878 Born January 6, Galesburg, Illinois, first son of August and Clara Sandburg, Swedish immigrants. Baptized Carl August.

1891 Leaves school after eighth grade. Works at various jobs, including newsboy and milk-delivery boy.

1892 Works as shoeshine boy in barbershop.

1894 Takes second milk-wagon job.

1896 Visits Chicago for first time.

1896 Sees Robert Todd Lincoln at fortieth anniversary of Lincoln-Douglas debate, Knox College, Galesburg.

1897 Rides boxcar to Iowa, Kansas, Nebraska, Colorado. Works on railroad section gang, as farm hand, dishwasher, and at odd jobs.

1898 Serves as apprentice to house painter, Galesburg. On April 26, enlists in Company C, Sixth Infantry Regiment, Illinois Volunteers. Serves as private in Puerto Rico during Spanish-American War. Returns to Galesburg. Enrolls as special student in Lombard College, Galesburg.

1899 Appointed to West Point in May. Fails written examination in grammar and arithmetic. Enters Lombard College in September. To support himself, serves in town fire department. Becomes business manager of the *Lombard Review*.

1900 Works in summer selling Underwood & Underwood stereoscopic photographs, with Frederick Dickinson.

1901 Editor-in-chief of the *Lombard Review*. With Frederick Dickinson, edits *The Cannibal,* the Jubilee Year Book.

1902 Leaves college before graduating to wander over country, selling Underwood & Underwood stereoscopic photographs. Arrested for riding rails without ticket, serves ten days in Allegheny County jail, Pittsburgh.

1904 Returns to Galesburg. Writes articles for column called "Inklings & Idlings" in the Galesburg *Evening Mail*. In December has first poetry and a few prose pieces published in a booklet by Asgard Press, *In Reckless Ecstasy*.

Chronology

1905 Becomes assistant editor of *Tomorrow Magazine,* in Chicago, which also publishes his poems and sketches.

1906 Becomes lyceum lecturer on Walt Whitman.

1907 Publishes "A Dream Girl" in *The Lyceumite.* As associate editor of *The Lyceumite,* in Chicago, writes the series "Unimportant Portraits of Important People." Asgard Press publishes *Incidentals* in November. Delivers lectures on Whitman and Bernard Shaw at Elbert Hubbard's Roycroft Chapel. In December becomes organizer for Social Democratic party.

1908 Goes to Wisconsin as district organizer in the Lake Shore and Fox River Valley district. Asgard Press publishes *The Plaint of a Rose* in January. On June 15 marries Lilian Steichen, schoolteacher, also a Socialist. Speaks for the Socialists at a large chautauqua at Marinette, Wisconsin. Campaigns through Wisconsin aboard "Red Special" with Socialist candidate Eugene V. Debs during Presidential campaign. Writes pamphlet *You and Your Job,* published by Social Democratic Publishing Company, Milwaukee.

1909 Lives in Appleton, Wisconsin, from January to April. Moves to Beaver Dam, then to Milwaukee, where he becomes advertising copy writer for Kroeger's Department Store. Later in the year becomes a reporter for the Milwaukee *Sentinel,* the Milwaukee *Journal,* and the Milwaukee *Daily News.* Writes "Letters to Bill" and tuberculosis article for *La Follette's Weekly Magazine.* Tours Wisconsin (forty-five cities) with "flying squadron" of Anti-Tuberculosis League.

1910 Father dies March 10. Emil Seidel, Socialist mayor of Milwaukee, appoints him to post of private secretary. In August resigns to become city editor of the Milwaukee *Social-Democratic Herald.* Works for Victor Berger's *Political Action.* Asgard Press publishes *Joseffy: An Appreciation.* Socialist party reprints *You and Your Job.*

1911 First child, Margaret, is born June 3. Three articles, "The Man and the Job," "Making the City Efficient," and "My Baby Girl," are published in *La Follette's Weekly Magazine.*

1912 Writes articles for Victor Berger's Milwaukee *Leader.* His article "Where Is My Girl To-Night" appears in *Woman's New Idea Magazine.* Contributes two articles to *The Coming Nation.* Moves to Chicago in September. Joins Chicago *Evening World* staff briefly.

1913 Goes to *The Day Book,* Chicago, then *System,* a management magazine, for which he sometimes writes under the pseudonym R. E. Coulson. In December goes to the *American Artisan & Hardware Record,* writing under the pseudonym Sidney Arnold.

1914 Returns to *The Day Book.* Has some poems published in the March issue of *Poetry: A Magazine of Verse.* Wins Helen Haire Levinson Prize for best poems of the year. Moves to Maywood, a suburb of Chicago, in the fall.

1915 Writes two articles on "That Walsh Report" and three on "Fixing the Pay of Railroad Men" for *The International Socialist Review. Reedy's Mirror* publishes article on Margaret Haley.

1916 Has four poems printed in *The Little Review* in April. *Chicago Poems* is published by Henry Holt. Daughter Janet is born June 27.

1917 Covers labor conference for the American Federation of Labor at Omaha, in July, and Minneapolis Labor Convention. Joins Chicago *Daily News* in August. "The Four Brothers," first published in *Poetry,* appears in Chicago *Daily News* in October. Publishes article, "The 8-Hour Rail Drive," under pseudonym Jack Phillips in *The International Socialist Review.*

1918 Quits Chicago *Daily News.* Goes to the Chicago *Evening American* for three weeks, then joins Newspaper Enterprise Association. Does series of ten articles on "Books the Newspaperman Ought to Read" for *Pep,* an NEA magazine. Goes to Stockholm in October. Daughter Helga is born November 24. *Cornhuskers* is published by Henry Holt. Returns to New York before Christmas.

1919 Assigned to NEA offices in Chicago. *Reedy's Mirror* publishes "Baltic Fogs" in April. Rejoins Chicago *Daily News* as labor reporter; is later appointed motion-picture editor. Shares Poetry Society of America prize with Margaret Widdemer. Harcourt, Brace and Howe publishes *The Chicago Race Riots.* Covers American Federation of Labor Convention in Atlantic City in June, and the Gary, Indiana, steel strike, where he goes with William Allen White. Writes series on shop-steward system in the garment industry. Moves to Elmhurst, a suburb of Chicago.

1920 Gives lecture-recital at Cornell College, Mount Vernon, Iowa. *Smoke and Steel* is published by Harcourt, Brace and Howe.

1921 Shares Poetry Society of America Annual Book Award with Stephen Vincent Benét.

1922 Publishes first book for children, *Rootabaga Stories,* and a new volume of poetry, *Slabs of the Sunburnt West,* both brought out by

Harcourt, Brace and Company (later Harcourt, Brace & World), the publisher of the rest of his major work.

1923   *Rootabaga Pigeons,* his second book of stories for children, is published.

1926   *Rootabaga Stories* is published in France by F. Rieder & Company, Editeurs, as *Au Pays de Rootabaga,* translated by Leon Bazalgette. Magazine serial rights to *Abraham Lincoln: The Prairie Years,* called "The Unfathomed Lincoln," are bought by *Pictorial Review.*

1926   Two-volume *Abraham Lincoln: The Prairie Years* is published on Lincoln's birthday. Buys summer cottage at Tower Hill, Michigan. *Selected Poems,* edited by Rebecca West, is published by Jonathan Cape, London. Mother dies in December.

1927   Publishes a collection of folk songs, *The American Songbag.* Buys five-acre lot in Harbert, Michigan, on which to build large year-round home.

1928   Is invited to read as Phi Beta Kappa poet at Harvard. Receives Litt.D. from Lombard College. In spring, moves into new house at Harbert. Publishes volume of poetry, *Good Morning, America. Abe Lincoln Grows Up* (the first twenty-six chapters of *Abraham Lincoln: The Prairie Years*) is published.

1929   Receives Litt.D. from Knox College. Publishes biography, *Steichen the Photographer,* and book for children, *Rootabaga Country.*

1930   *Potato Face* and poems for children, *Early Moon,* are published.

1931   Receives Litt.D. from Northwestern University. Sister Martha Goldstone dies.

1932   Leaves Chicago *Daily News* in May. Publishes biography, *Mary Lincoln: Wife and Widow* (with an Appendix by Paul M. Angle).

1934   Lectures at University of Hawaii.

1936   *The People, Yes* is published in August.

1938   *Lincoln and Whitman Miscellany,* an essay, is published by Holiday Press, Chicago. Sandburg is awarded the Order of the North Star by the King of Sweden.

1939   Four-volume *Abraham Lincoln: The War Years* is published.

1940   Wins Pulitzer Prize for history. Is elected to American Academy of Arts and Letters. Delivers six Walgreen Fund lectures at University of Chicago. Receives Litt.D. degrees from Harvard, Yale, New York University, Wesleyan University, and Lafayette College.

1941   Essay *Bronze Wood* is published by Grabhorn Press, San Francisco. Receives Litt.D. from Syracuse University and from Dartmouth

College; LL.D. from Rollins College. Grandson John Carl is born December 3.

1942 Writes weekly column for Chicago *Times* Syndicate, commentary for U.S. government film "Bomber," foreign broadcasts for Office of War Information, captions for *Road to Victory* (Museum of Modern Art, New York). *Storm Over the Land* (excerpted from *The War Years*) is published.

1943 *Home Front Memo* is published. Granddaughter Karlen Paula is born June 28.

1944 Publishes *The Photographs of Abraham Lincoln* (with Frederick Hill Meserve). Brother, Martin Sandburg, dies April 7.

1945 Moves to Connemara Farm, Flat Rock, North Carolina, in late fall.

1946 Birthplace at Galesburg, Illinois, is dedicated. *Poems of the Midwest* (*Chicago Poems* and *Cornhuskers* together in one volume) is published by World Publishing Company, Cleveland.

1948 Publishes novel, *Remembrance Rock*. Goes to Hollywood to help in planning it as film. Receives LL.D. from Augustana College.

1949 *Lincoln Collector: The Story of Oliver R. Barrett's Great Private Collection* is published.

1950 Receives Ph.D. from Uppsala University, Sweden. Publishes *Complete Poems,* which wins Pulitzer Prize for poetry. *The New American Songbag* is published.

1952 Receives American Academy of Arts and Letters gold medal for history and biography.

1953 First volume of autobiography, *Always the Young Strangers,* is published. Attends Carl Sandburg Day banquet in Chicago, January 6, on seventy-fifth birthday. Receives Poetry Society of America gold medal. Publishes *A Lincoln Preface,* which was intended for, but not published as, a preface to *The Prairie Years.* Receives Tamiment Institute Award for *Always the Young Strangers.*

1954 *Abraham Lincoln: The Prairie Years and The War Years,* a condensation of the six volumes in one, is published. Receives scroll from Civil War Round Table in New York.

1955 *Prairie-Town Boy* (a version for children of *Always the Young Strangers*) is published. Writes prologue to *Family of Man,* a volume of photographs selected by Edward Steichen, published by the Museum of Modern Art, New York.

1956 Is paid $30,000 by the University of Illinois for his manuscripts, library, and papers. Receives Humanities award from Albert Einstein College of Medicine, New York. November 18 is proclaimed

Carl Sandburg Day in Chicago. The first of sixteen schools named after him opens in Harvey, Illinois.

1957 *The Sandburg Range,* an anthology of his work, is published. Carl Sandburg Elementary School opens in Wheeling, Illinois.

1958 Is made "Honorary Ambassador" of North Carolina on March 27, Sandburg Day, at a luncheon in Raleigh, North Carolina. Sister Mary Johnson dies July 29.

1959 Delivers Lincoln Day address, February 12, in Washington, D.C., before a joint session of Congress attended by members of the Supreme Court, the Cabinet, and the diplomatic corps. Goes to Moscow with Edward Steichen under State Department auspices for "Family of Man" exhibit. Meets Ivan Kashkeen, Russian translator of his work. Travels to Stockholm for Swedish-American Day and award of Litteris et Artibus medal from King Gustav. Carl Sandburg High School opens in Orlando Park, Illinois; Carl Sandburg junior high schools open in Mundelein, Illinois, and Levittown, Pennsylvania; Carl Sandburg Elementary School opens in San Bruno, California.

1960 Goes to Hollywood as consultant for film "The Greatest Story Ever Told." Publishes two paper-bound volumes of poetry, *Harvest Poems 1910-1960* and *Wind Song,* poems for children. Carl Sandburg Elementary School is dedicated in Minneapolis. Carl Sandburg Junior High School opens in Elmhurst, Illinois. Receives citation from U.S. Chamber of Commerce as a Great Living American "for lasting contribution to American literature."

1961 *Six New Poems and a Parable* is published by the University of Kentucky Press. Carl Sandburg elementary schools open in Rockville, Maryland; Pontiac, Michigan; Rolling Meadows, Illinois; Springfield, Illinois.

1962 Designated "poet laureate of Illinois." Writes Foreword for *To Turn the Tide,* a book of John F. Kennedy's speeches. Carl Sandburg Elementary School opens in Joliet, Illinois.

1963 *Honey and Salt* is published on January 6, his eighty-fifth birthday. Receives International United Poets Award as "Hon. Poet Laureate of the U.S.A."

1964 Receives Presidential Medal of Freedom from President Lyndon B. Johnson.

1966 Carl Sandburg Junior High School opens in Glendora, California.

1967 Dies July 22 at his home in Flat Rock, North Carolina. Carl Sandburg Elementary School opens in Littleton, Colorado. Carl Sandburg Junior College opens in Galesburg, Illinois.

THE LETTERS OF CARL SANDBURG

1898

1 | TO THE SANDBURG FAMILY

Co. C., 6th Regiment
Springfield, Ill.,
May 1, 1898.

Dear folks:—

I don't feel much like writing a letter, as I may be with you again in a week, because [Gov. John R.] Tanner has ordered that no one who has enlisted since the 15th will be admitted to examination for the U.S. Army, though it may come out all right yet.

There is many a young fellow here learning to appreciate home.

The first day I was here Andy Tanning & I went through the Capitol building & enjoyed the fine view from the dome.

As far as my health is concerned, don't you worry. I can pick out lots of boys here whose only ailment is homesickness.

To-day, I am writing to home, to Vic & to John, so you must excuse writing.

Geo. Martin of Knox College is also writing for the Mail, so I am going to write only once in a while. That letter Thursday was almost all from me, but there is no earthly use of 2 reporters in one co. & if I write once a week to Home, Mary, Vic, John and N. Henderson St., I will be kept busy.

Yesterday, we marched 5 mi. & some of the boys were pretty tired. About 7:30 last night, we were called to quiet a disturbance at the gate about ⅛ of a mi. from our quarters. We got there three minutes after we received the call.

Well, give Martha & Esther my kisses & love to all.

C.S.

P.S.:—Send this letter to Mary & tell her I will write Mon. or Tuesday.

C.S.

Sandburg was sworn into the Army on April 26, 1898. His tentmate was Andrew Tanning. Vic and John Sjodin were friends; John later organized the Galesburg local of the Socialist party. His sisters

1900

Martha and Esther were at home. Occasionally, he contributed to the Galesburg Evening Mail. *On July 25, Private Sandburg noted in his diary: "Sight Porto Rico . . . threw shells around vicinity." By September 21, 1898, Sandburg was home from the war. Mary taught at Bishop Hill.*

2 | TO MARY SANDBURG

Sheffield, Ill., July 8, '00 [1900]

My dear sister:—

You will please excuse this paper. I am at present engaged in filling the orders for 'scopes and views which I have received (or taken rather) in this town and vicinity and when I get through I'll have a more pretentious stationery. From all that I can see at the present I will come out of this delivery with some cash and a stock of views which can be used throughout the season and be disposed of before school commences. However I am becoming such an enthusiast over stereographs that I may keep all I have over at the end of the season.

Well how do you like Normal? I have a mental photograph of you boning physics in the atmosphere of the past week. However it's much cooler this morning.

I have a most congruous boarding place here; a private house, cultured people, two clever daughters, books and music. John Cleveland, principal of the high school, boards here. He attended Knox one year and is also a graduate of Normal.

I have received letters from a number of my friends and have answered only those from the Big Six and home so far, but I'm going to get in touch with the Mail office to-day.

There are lots of Danes about here. It riles me to hear them talk for it sounds just like Swedish but I can't understand it.

Well now sister dear don't cram too hard on your studies. Just get the fundamental principles and when you want to use them look up the details. Regretting that I put this letter off so long I close with love.

Charlie.

1901

Beginning in the summer of 1900, Sandburg joined his friend Frederick Dickinson as a salesman of Underwood & Underwood stereoscopic photographs, or stereographs.

3 | TO MARY SANDBURG

> Plymouth, Mich. Sunday.
> [Circa summer, 1901]

Dear sister:—

Your letter duly received. I am glad you are trying to use the vacation as it should be used and I hope you won't try to do any more picnics, parties and trips than you think will add to your reserve power. That trip to Minnesota would doubtless be of great help to you but some persons can make a trip like that one endless piece of mind-friction, worry over tickets, baggage and connections, fear that something worth seeing will be missed. Ergo, nerve is lost and you are not what you were. For example, from Berrien Street to Ann Arbor, I might have worried over an umbrella I had taken along. Kept it in mind with such constancy that I would have taken it off at Ann Arbor instead of letting it ride on to Detroit. The thing is gone and heartsick bitter longing shall not recover it. Make it a peaceful, quiet meander to Minn., letting Lillie H. alone with her ideal(!), eliminate any haunting fear that something terrible is going to happen, and you will be better, dear. (Just looking over your letter, I see you have started before this reaches you. When you return, see if I was right.)

You say G. [Galesburg] is for you a synonym of despair and disappointment. It might be another word for uncongeniality and lack of appreciation but despair is quite strong. If you are expecting a full, complete and just estimate of your work and influence anywhere on earth, your hopes are askew.

I believe you are strong enough to read Hubbard, that you are able to throw yourself into work with such spirit that earthly phantoms can not mock you. There is talk of love and art and beauty, but there is no joy compared to that of doing a work however small and doing it well. I hope you get the full gist of Hubbard's meanings and that if a sadness comes over you in reading him, it is not tinged with bitterness.

It is now well nigh certain that Dickinson and I will not go to the Pan-Americ [Panama], our territory has been too well gone over by other agents. However, we expect to go to Detroit.

I received a letter from the Fra containing fine bouquets and good wishes anent the Cannibal which we sent him. Well, be good to yourself. With love,

Yours truly,
Charlie.

The Sandburgs lived on Berrien Street, and Lillie Holmes was a cousin and neighbor. Elbert G. Hubbard published The Fra *and was known as "Fra Elbertus" or "the Fra."* The Cannibal *was the Lombard College annual; Sandburg was one of the editors of the fiftieth-anniversary edition.*

4 | TO MARY SANDBURG

[East Aurora, New York]
Friday night. [December 26, 1902]

Dear Mary:—

Here we are right in the heart of that vast organism known as New York. What a week! what a week! To traverse four states, to converse with such souls as Elbert Hubbard and Lee Fairchild, to see the mightiest material works of America—these subways, bridges, railroads, buildings,—If I had not met these calm, simple, seeing souls that see it all for the best, I'm afraid my brain would be in a whirl.

I have canvassed the situation a little today—enough to make me feel, dear sister, so hopeful for the future. You see, thru the men I know here—Fairchild, Hampton, Hasbrook, McConnell— I have letters that are bound to get me a hearing and consideration such as one without the same could not possibly get. More about this later!

I found Fra Elbertus at the R. [Roycroft] shop last Wed. p.m. We had a little chat, I showed him a Nov. Thistle, he remembered The Cannibal,—and showed me over part of the shop himself, one of the illuminators, a girl, doing the remainder. Then they left me a while to browse around among their masterpieces of book-making in the Reception room. I forgot to tell you the Fra said I must stay for supper. Just before supper, I went with him to deliver two Xmas turkeys, I carrying one and he the other. At supper in the "phalase", as they call it, I sat between the Master and the Roycroft physical director. Following that they had a short vaudeville. At 8 o'clock, a party of six of us, Hubbard, his son, Bertie, the Red One (Lyle Hawthorne), "Rudolph" and the physical director (a splendid specimen) and your humble brother went out over the plank road out of town two miles and back. I asked H. to sign a Chi Touque booklet when we returned. He brought down a deluxe "Book of the Roycrofters" and signed it "to C.A.S. in loving token of his little Jo[urney] to Sun Shop, E.H. Dec. 24th, '02" (the abbreviations my own).

I went away from that place with a kind of a lump in my throat and a gladness in my heart, about it all, only this,—when future generations weigh in the balance the life of Elbert Hubbard, they will pronounce him one of the greatest men the world ever saw.

Fairchild I will tell you about in another letter. Wizened, bald-headed, red-nosed,—a sweet, gracious, witty soul that to meet is to love. He has put me next to a cheap room in the house where he puts up. And invited me to the Pleiades Club Sun. eve.—a gathering of literary "guns."

This is more "myselfness" than ordinarily, isn't it? Now I must get some sleep to be fresh for the foray with fate tomorrow. Adios, good noble sister. Write me at Gen. Del., N.Y. City. Good-night.

Charlie.

1903

Hubbard's Roycroft Inn was chapel, boardinghouse, and communal enterprise. The Thistle, a little magazine in New York, was edited by Lee Fairchild, a Lombard graduate.

5 | TO MARY SANDBURG

Vineland, New Jersey,
January 19, 1903

Dear Mary:

Your cheerful letter from Rockville came to me here. I have moved as you notice above. "I have become a name for always roaming with a hungry heart." I could have had several things in N.Y. far better than anything I could get in Galesburg, but I believe I'll stay with the U. & U. [Underwood & Underwood] another year—perhaps less—and see what happens.

You ask about the Fra's private troubles. His private secretary the last two years, Lyman Chandler, has allied himself with Wilshire's Magazine in N.Y.—not because of any dissatisfaction with H. [Hubbard] but to work for Socialism. He and I were quite chummy in N.Y. H. admits the child of the Moore woman is his (he is no Nyblad!) Now if you *know* the man, you won't damn him—is all I have to say. His affair with his wife has nothing to do with the other case; she is not dissatisfied with his morality—the Moore case is an old one. The divorce suit is the outcome of their weariness of not being true mates. So, [missing page]

There are so many things to say and so little time to say them, maybe you like this, not altogether disassociated from Time:

Soft Pleasure sat her by Youth's side
    And pointed down the lane to Time.
"Come let us kill him now," she said,
    "He comes so weary, 'tis no crime.

Wine, Dress, and Midnight Balls in host
    Were called to knife him as he passed.
"Take that," "And that,"—they drove their steel—
    And thought that Time had breathed his last!

8

But Time, unhurt, passed noiseless on
  Till subtly still, he came once more,
And marked sweet Youth with shrivelled skin
  Sans hair, sans teeth, pale to the core!

I have read K's [Kipling's] "Vampire" and Zola's "Money" recently, perhaps that accounts for the above. I wonder what Mrs. Whipple will think of it. I wish you would send me some of her verse.

I am dubious about Arthur D's opinion of Nell T. as quoted by you—"there never was such a girl." It might apply to many a frill-bound fool. Yet if he means it as to complexity of character, he comes near it, tho I wouldn't make such a sweeping, inclusive "never." Do you see?

At what behest does my quondam friend, Louva Millard, withhold from me her words of cheer? I have not heard since early November.

I had a splendid letter from Mart, in which he enclosed a note from ex-Supt. Clark that shows superb work on Mart's part. He is climbing and if his health only lasts, I won't place bounds as to where he will end. I am beginning to understand better how busy he is.

I made a number of friends in N.Y. and also met a number of old ones, so that now, to run in there will be almost like a visit to Galesburg. Take Dickinson out of Chicago and I would say I feel more at home in New York. Albert Britt is in N.Y., an associate editor on Public Opinion. I spoke of Stoneberg to him—he thinks for sure that S. is a "queer" one, has him gauged about as I have—a brilliant intellect, impassive, self-centered, fettered by heredity and custom.

I shall send you before long some books and magazines I want you to keep for me. Also a bundle of papers written to me alone, for no other person's eye, to open them would be sacrilege. These I ask you to keep for me. For now, good-bye, dear sister.

                                                        Charlie

*The Reverend Carl A. Nyblad, minister of the First Swedish
Lutheran Church in Galesburg, was sued by a housemaid who*

accused him of fathering her child. Philip J. Stoneberg was principal of the Bishop Hill school.

6 | TO MARY SANDBURG

Millville, N.J., May 19, 1903.

Dear Mary:

Your note containing "stern", "neglect", etc. came to me to-day. You perhaps know of other periods in my life when I was undergoing experiences that I considered developmental to a high degree—and which time proved to be such—but which at the time, I did not think would interest you and of which, I therefore did not write. You haven't a great faith in stereographs and their future in education, nor do you see clearly that I am passing thru a sort of apprenticeship in salesmanship and dealing with people. I could go into some world-old work at or near home that would reflect more honor on the name Sandburg than that in which I am engaged now. But it takes time for big results— And I hope this is an explanation that explains that sometimes, "I am doing a work and cannot come down", in which I hope I am not a second Jonah. Don't think I have any Stoneberg dignity that's been scratched— I am a fool, but I know which way I am going.

During the last three months, I have let a great deal of letter-writing lapse. I will not let correspondence, or anything else that is not eternally vital, rob me of the sleep or recreation that I must have if I am to have health, do my work, and carry on my studies. So if you understand me, you will always cut out the "neglect", "stern", etc. And may the good Lord always be kind to the soldier from the Philippines in his uniform of blue that he may find his appeal to patriotism ever effective, but your brother wants no charity and is working no graft, and some day when he is working near you, you will watch his methods with surprise and pleasure. My problems and difficulties are enough without intensifying them by writing them to anybody. So you can depend on it that of all the good-cheer, happiness, sympathy, love, or whatever in me is worth your having, you are getting all I can give without hurting myself in a way you would not care to have me. And believe me always truly

Yours with deep brotherly love,
Charlie

7 | TO MARY SANDBURG

Grove House
Vineland, N.J.
June 10, 1903

Dear Mary:—

Your welcome letter at hand. I am glad to think of you as free from the duties that you attend with such conscientious devotion. Take my advice this vacation and get all the open air you can and as much contact with optimists as possible. Wasn't it fine of those Rockville people to show their feeling with tokens? Such keepsakes and ornaments have added value. I wish you could have got Bluffton. Get in correspondence with them next year. Such a town and such people as there are there you would like it better even than R. Where does Louva go next year? Back to V.? Will you see each other this summer?

Irish waitress this morning, "Steak and eggs." "Eggs." "Fried?" "Yes." "Both sides?" "No, only the outside." Biff! bang! And with a batter of wheat cakes, I repelled the sullen, mutinous boarders.

Some day I'll get newsy, but I haven't anything to tell you just now. Good luck to you, dear girl, and love from

Charlie.

P.S. Tell Mart I think Lillie Ericson got aniceman.

Mary would have preferred to teach in Bluffton, instead of Rockville. Louva Millard was a friend of the Sandburgs; Lillie Ericson was a neighbor. Sandburg deliberately made "a nice man" one word.

Vineland, N.J., June 22, 1903

Dear Professor Wright:

Yesterday is past and I hope you had a splendid midsummer night's dream. I felt more like I wanted to be back in Galesburg a few days than I ever have, upon receiving good word from you and Fairchild. The latter is both corn and roses, you are steel and gold, and I would like to have been an Ariel and gone along with you a-fielding, saying nothing, only listening.

If you are to be anywhere near Philadelphia this summer, by all means let me know. Phila. is worth seeing—it helps turn time backward so you can have a look at colonial America. There are two Delilahs and four Cleopatras here in Vineland—also several Salomes who will have my head if I don't move soon, so about the 4th of July, I expect to move. There are many interesting aspects of life about here. A little East is a settlement of Italians who have made the sandy wastes smile in a way that makes me think the immigration problem *can* be solved. To the woods and the fields and the open air with them, where old-world appendages can disintegrate.

I am going to send you two late efforts, asking you for a frank opinion about them. Whitman, Shakespeare, Joaquin Miller and Kipling have haunted me into these, and tho I like them in a way, I feel that they lack something, and I ask you for a designation of which way crudity lies. Your range is so great—from "Ebb-tide" to "a tail and toe" is a far cry, both are good—that I think you understand these.

"Friday" writes me, after a lapse of five months, that he is in a machine-shop in Chicago (Melrose Park) where they "make the machines that can the canned foods that you and a million others, more or less consume." [Harold] Metcalf who is there this summer says Chicagoans tell him he is foolish to buy books when he can buy beer with the money.

That modern literature is not on the wane, is demonstrated in this month's "New Metropolitan", to my eye. "The Carver of Pipes", and "The Men Who Swapped Languages" are near standard.

Again, try to swing down this way if you are East this summer, as it will do my soul good. When you write next, would you give me Fairchild's N.Y. address? My thanks to Mrs. Wright and best regards to her.

Sincerely yours,
Sandburg

P.S.:—Those lectures, I would I had the time to give them a careful study. Some day I shall give them a thorough study as they contain stuff I want and can't get elsewhere.

> *Professor Wright, who strongly influenced Sandburg's writing and political outlook, sent him poems by mail. Howard Lauer wrote a witty column for* The Lombard Review *under the pseudonym "Friday." He, together with Sandburg, Dickinson, Metcalf, and other students, had been a member of Wright's Poor Writers Club in Galesburg.*

9 | TO PHILIP GREEN WRIGHT

Grove House,
Vineland, N.J.
7-14-[1903]

Dear Professor Wright:

I am glad our correspondence is a little mixed, and answers to questions and questions themselves, etc. are a bit shuffled. For we are not young ladies or golf players, preening in our monogrammed card receivers, checking each call or note before replying and pigeon-holing.

My old Kumrad Dickinson joined me on the 3d. Being young and not very full of days, we have been rejoicing in the days of our youth. I may be poetic with him, but I must conserve—there must be no exaggeration. He may be practical with me, but he must be cautious—with a welcome eye to roses. And while he is not a biscuit, nor I a hyacinth, being true cannibals, we smell and eat of each other. While he knows summary processes, subpoenas, interdictions and assumpsits, I know "behavior lawless as snow flakes, simple as grass."

We have looked up Addicks' record thoroughly and are going into Delaware in August. Mayhap we will see something of the barter of birthright. We have caught the cereal craze and will before long experiment with diet. Dickinson has suggested that we make bi-weekly reports to you, as you may utilize them in economics. So after we leave here, you may expect some postal cards.

And Professor, after long and patient practice, we are now able to see stereoscopically without a stereoscope, that is, the right eye sees the right point and the left eye the left point on the stereoscopic card, and the effect is that sense of perspective, distance, vista, depth, space, which is the invariable concomitant and distinguishing characteristic of binocular vision. You have seen a small boy after wearying of wading or swimming? I have been wading in the literature of stereoscopy and vision and sometimes cannot refrain from splashing with the terms.

In one corner of the dining room sit Prof. Wilson, who wrote the series of Wilson readers and other books, a D.D., and several others who have not only browsed and munched in libraries, but I am afraid, sometimes gorged. Across their breakfast table words stalk rampant, while logic laughs, and the fuzz of split hairs are blown about in every eye. Scholarship is run amuck when it thinks it defines subconsciousness and then labels that as Soul. Culture, like madness, can run off of a steep place and be drowned in the sea. Let us pray that books may always be a light on life that makes us wonder and be children in beautiful mystery, rather than we should think learning (not wisdom) is life.

I know you understand me and I feel better.

If you do come East this summer, we hope you can make Philadelphia. Dick and I would be delighted to meet you there.

Thank you for your criticism of my "stuff". The great, long-suffering—yet also wheedling, babyish—public shall have a chance at it one of these years. Big Baby that it is, I don't want its smile, but I would trim its heart's garden of a few weeds and grow therein —perhaps roses, perhaps cabbage.

After writing to *you,* I can almost always say, "I did not know I knew that." Adios for this time, senor.

Sincerely your friend,

Sandburg

Professor Wright taught, among other subjects, economics, hence the suggestion by Sandburg's salesman-companion, Fred Dickinson. They also watched the political fortunes of James Edward O'Sullivan Addicks, of Delaware, accused of trying to buy his way into the U.S. Senate.

10 | TO PHILIP GREEN WRIGHT

Grove House,
Vineland, N.J.
Sunday [Circa early August, 1903]

Dear Professor Wright:

Yesterday Dickinson and I took a little run into the City of Brotherly Love (pretty name, isn't it). About the only incident worthy of record took place in the restaurant where we had luncheon. Each table had four chairs and every table's quota of chairs was full but one. There being at this table two strikingly handsome gentlemen, we seated ourselves there preparatory to ordering substantialities of something. Behold tho, the man opposite me spoke up quickly, "Pardon us, but we would like this table for ourselves. I am Howard Chandler Christy and this is my friend, Richard Harding Davis." "No!" I said, "the devil!—we too crave your pardon, but I am the Maharajah of Mysore and this is my friend, the Nizam of Hyderabad!"

D. [Dickinson] & I have been doing some brisk work canvassing from house to house here. When one has the right swing and enthusiasm, it is not unlike hunting, a veritable sport. To scare up game by preliminary talk and to know how long to follow it, to lose your game thru poorly directed argument, to hang on to game that finally eludes, to boldly confront, to quietly circle around, to keep on the trail tireless and keen till you've bagged some orders, there is some satisfaction in returning at night, tired of the trail, but proud of the day's work. "Peddlers Three" is good—a consummation devoutly to be wished. Perhaps one of these summers we can arrange something of the like.

The Whitmanish lines in your last run thru my head often. They are expressive of what I have thought but could not say. (Emerson was right that, "Expression is half the man.") They have a sweet, devil-may-care charm, and I rank them along with lines of his, such as those describing the cowboys, "Behaviour lawless as snowflakes, words simple as grass." On "The Dreamer", the mercury simile is striking and beautiful.

Hoping that you meet many examples of the smile that won't come off and that you are placing a proper estimate on the sour faces of publishers whom you are to eventually bring around, I am

Sincerely yours,
Charles Sandburg

"The Dreamer" was a poem by Wright, and the title of his first book of poems.

11 | TO PHILIP GREEN WRIGHT

[Dover, Delaware]
[Circa August, 1903]

Dear Professor Wright:—

I wrote to you nearly a month ago at your Galesburg address and have heard nothing from you since I received the postal inquiring as to Friday. I am writing this to find out the status of our correspondence,—whether you have failed to receive mine of July 22nd, whether you have received it and answered, and answer gone astray, or whether you are just busy. I imagine the swirl of Chicago is not without attraction for you.

We are now located in that little town that has been the scene of a political battle at which "all the world wondered" and wonders,—the practically open attempt of Addicks to buy this whole state, to subvert the legislation by money. Openly, there's the rub. Politics is not a matter so much of intelligence, as honor, here.

Dover is about of the Southern type of city, and gives opportunity for study of the race question on the ground where the race question arises. I have trimmed myself on several points where I thot I was cocksure. The negro slum that is fastened like a cancer on almost every southern town *radiates* its sensuality and shiftlessness, and the degree of this radiation is what is serious, what impresses the newcomer.

Here is a quatrain that resulted from Zola's "L'Assommoir"—there are others, this is the best, what must the others be?

I stood me near the mart and watched them flow
To worship gold and all the things that glow
And force; and no man came away and smiled
And softly said, "I have enough, I'll go."

'Twas haste and rush, "The day is passing fast,
And maybe we'll not get enough to last";
The sun we use is growing dim these days,
The stars are by another glint surpassed.

The fools who laugh at those who booze and scrap—
Have they as yet put on compassion's cap?
Have they been lashed by Circumstance till they
No respite found but in Oblivion's lap?

To no more know! The dread unrest of thot,
Regret and memory all set at naught!
An ounce of booze is worth a pound of wail;
They cry, they hie them where the booze is bought.

I do not know that it might be the worst
For all of us to have an awful thirst;
But woe to him who knifes the man ahead
That he may be the one who gets in first!

It would not be so bad to long for booze
And fondle bottles damp with precious ooze,

Could we but queer the green-eyed snakes who leer
Across our way whene'er we hear, "You lose!"

I do not gild my words with attic salt,
You think; and yet that's surely not my fault;
I would be fresh as winds that sweep the sea
And pack my words to last like God's basalt.

Charles Sandburg

12 | TO MARY SANDBURG

Dover, Del., Nov. 27. [1903]

Dear Mary:—

Yesterday was Thanksgiving—not quite so full of memories of a meeting with a sweet sister as a year ago. It is a year and I have not yet done anything for your material favor at that time.

Between now, and then, as I look back, it has been the most ragged, glorious, tempestuous year I have ever known. All the infinite variety of zig-zagging hopes and plans I have had, it would have been impossible to write. It is enough to say that literary aspirations were what knocked my financial hopes. And because you have been true to me, all thru college-years and this year, never complaining unjustly, and because you trust me, even tho you don't understand me—this is frankness—I am sending you this stuff. I am not presuming by this to raise your estimate of me, but it should make you feel that I have not wasted days, and that I have not advanced rearward "in point of development. Jesso! Jesso!"

I have no duplicates of these sheets I am sending, so I ask you to take care of them. Some of them, Fairchild and Wright and Edson say, are publishable. You may do as you like about Mrs. Whipple reading them.

I leave here next week for Portsmouth, Va., and expect to leave there on Christmas day for home. I may stop with Dickinson a day or two in Chicago, but I confidently expect to be home on New Years day. Then we will have some days packed with pleasure. We will have to swathe Mart in good-cheer, after his grinding Xmas season.

Yours lovingly,
Charlie.

P.S.—I have never heard from you ever a word about the songs I tell you appeal to me!

Anyway, I am sending you Tosti's "Goodbye", one of the most popular of the classics here in the east. If you already have it, you ought to have told me! There.

C.

Lee Fairchild was a poet, and Charles Edson was the editor of a college student paper, The Automobile. *Sandburg had printed some of Edson's poetry in* The Lombard Review, *when he was editor. Sandburg and Dickinson were on a sales trip in Delaware.*

13 | TO MARY SANDBURG

[Dover, Delaware]
[Circa December, 1903]

Dear Mary:—

Here is the skeleton of an oratorical stunt performed before the Y.M.C.A. of Dover last Sunday. It is a little scrambled—or shook up raw with milk, as you please. Anyway maybe you care to know the evolution of my religious ideas. And I thot maybe the Mother would like to look it over.

I thot I would make my Xmas remembrance in "views". Sent a box with a Rome Set, and book, for you, and a Yosemite, Niagara, Is Marriage a Failure? and a few miscellanies, as a combination Yule-tide thought for Mama and Papa, Mart, Esther and Martha. If I remember right, there is a 'scope at home, and I am waiting to get an exceptionally good one to send you for use in Rockville.

Possibly you've heard of U.S. Senator Frank Allee here. I landed him for an order yesterday. I have also done business with the Governor and the Sec'y of State. Canvassing is like being a

Swede—you can squeeze pride or shame from it. People never guess my nationality, and among new friends, they guess every one but the right one when I talk my cradle-tongue.

Did business with the Catholic priest here and at his invitation stroll around to his library for a chat occasionally. Am going to attend the 5 o'clock mass Xmas morning. I see a good deal of ministers.

I'll be back West sometime before Summer, I think, and want to get through Rockville and see your friends. It's a pity tho to have to tell them I am a canvasser, just a solicitor, one who changes persons' minds. Here is a C.S. nugget from Emerson, "Not he is great who alters matter, but he who alters the state of my mind."

Frankly, if I had been a canvasser all the time, I would have a thousand banked now. But I have been a canvasser only about ¼ the time, a scholar, a poet-taster, an athlete and a social lion (or cub) the rest of the time.

What mood is this to-night, when I ask you to look not only on the good, but on the badnesses of me? It's trust, if you know. But it's mighty hard when living a life packed with variety, to take up a pen and make it walk around on the paper and tell you what's what.

Well, when this reaches you, you will have had Christmas, but —Happy New Year!

Your loving brother,
Charlie.

P.S.—Will you see the Roycroft stuff for the last two months forwarded here?

14 | TO MARY SANDBURG

Dover, Del., Jan. 18, 1904.

Dear Mary:

Here I am yet all the while, trying to butt in on the ineffable, zigzagging toward the ideal, and every now and then sending my smile crashing thru some sour face and splintering the gloom behind it. You see, when canvassing, I so often run against an icy exterior that I have to challenge, defy, slap, coddle, calm, enjoin, exhort, thaw out and warm up, that I believe I am evolving a small-sized *aura*. I find that people think about as highly of me as I do of myself, so I am begetting a self-respect that borders on conceit. You don't mind my making such confessions, do you?

Mart wrote that he is dissatisfied with the Adams and still has that desire for a business of his own. He has such energy and a certain cleverness, I think, that I have written him that I couldn't think much of anyone that would slip into one place and stay there for life, and to just keep his eyes open and drop the Adam's any time his judgement says it's wise. He says, in effect, that he will want encouragement from you and me in order to do it. What I want to impress on him is that his own careful decision made according to his own desires and ambitions should guide him. Mart has an integrity of character, and also a charm of manner, that are requisites in business. But whether he has that keenness of judgement necessary for winning, time only can tell. I think he can only learn anyway, by floating this raft out and trying to navigate.

I see Esther is learning all the cogs and rackets of Lombard life. From the pictures she sent me, I thought at first she might be a model of Christy's. She has beauty without doubt, and she also has a wit I like. I am proud of her and very hopeful of her. Martha has a daring, piquant, half-elfish face that wins me. The arch of her eyebrows and the mischief of the smile, as tho "if you try to catch me, I'll run," I am going to watch with interest—and love.

Would you please send back that bunch of manuscripts, sister? They aren't much, but "he who abstains is taken at his word", and one can't do more than submit them.

I'll write you longer next time. Here's love to you, from

Charlie.

Martin Sandburg worked for the Adams Express Company. Howard Chandler Christy created the illustrations of breezy and beautiful American cover girls.

15 | TO PHILIP GREEN WRIGHT

Dover, Del., Feb. 11, '04

Dear Professor Wright:

I have thru innate interest given the subject some thought, and have read Harry Thurston Peck on the subject I refer to, i.e., "The Psychology of the Printed Page." And hereafter if I'm going to judge of the merits of two writers, they must both be read in the same typographical garb. Why, after that piece from the Asgard Press came this morning and I had looked it over several times, I thought I was in a class with Browning, Tennyson, Milton, et al. The getup of the thing so economized attention, permitting the discriminatory faculties such power of focus, that as I grasped the content of thought, I felt I must indeed have had a favored niche in the boudoir of the Muse. Now I am sure tho, and I shall never dogmatize on work which I read in de luxe print.

But here's an idea, you know I've studied advertising:

ASGARD PRESS ANNOUNCEMENT

COMPLACENCY: AUSTERITY.

By Keats Yeats Sandbrough

Two bits of blank verse for two bits!!

There's many a truth that's spoken in words. I wonder how a little limited edition of this thing—say 100 copies—would go among Lombard and Galesburg people; copies to sell at 25¢ per. I would think that about half could be sold among L. [Lombard] people and the other half in G. [Galesburg]. I think an arrangement could be made with the Review management by which it would have a per cent on amounts realized in exchange for advertising space. And notices—review paragraphs—in the Mail and Register, and display on the newsstands or book stores would undoubtedly dispose of some. I would demand one copper for each copy sold—I would put holes in them and make a bangle which I would dangle just to hear the jangle. 'Twould be a pitiful mutilation of "the mainstay of commerce", a spoilation of "the life-blood of business", yet a fitting expression and most proper token of the attitude of poetry toward money, symbolizing the spirit's disregard of biscuits.

Now if I were to offer a suggestion—unasked—as to improvement in any further work the Asgard Press may essay, I would say that maroon cord might be better—might harmonize more—with cream paper than blue ribbon. Blue, I think, is well with white. This may be only a personal liking.

I am delighted that you should choose to put a literary effort of mine into such a charming and delectable environment of paper and type. Needless to say I shall treasure it.

I dislike to intrude on your time, but I do wish my mother might see a copy of this. Naturally, I want to carry this one I have, and once in a while show it to one of the Blessed. So would you see that a copy is left with her for a little while?

I was going to say something about our possibilities for participation in the arts-craft movement, but it is getting late. I shall write in a few days in that regard, and others.

And now, "may all the gods go with you and smooth success be strewn before your feet."

Yours sincerely,
Charles Sandburg

The first Sandburg booklet of poems, In Reckless Ecstasy, *was printed by Professor Wright's Asgard Press in Galesburg.*

16 | TO PHILIP GREEN WRIGHT

Dover, Del., Feb. 17, 1904.

Dear Professor Wright:

You say in your last that this proposition regarding a College for Adults haunts you and will not let you alone. I know what the feeling is. A scheme clear in its fundamentals, but misty and varying in the details, is rooted in my subconsciousness and recurs to my mental vision at regular periods. This scheme tho, has pertained to a publication which should be bold, reckless, joyous, gleeful, yet sometimes sad and austere and mocking, in dealing with socialism, "New Thought", sexology, and themes on which I have decided convictions. I had thought too, that this publication might in some way be allied to an institution in which useful articles were made, and so made that in the process, the sense of beauty would be gratified, or the emotions of love and reverence moved. I would expect too, that such a movement would be hailed an imitation, and ridiculed like any imitation. But in time, there would appear on its products, manual, artistic and literary, the impress of the individuals connected with it. If it was to be only an imitation of Kelmscott or Roycroft ideas, it would it would not die (having never lived), it would merely cease, as scores have done. A certain individuality, a stamp, seal, mark, or impress which would be a composite of the personalities engaged in the work, would have to characterize everything issuing from the place, or people wouldn't buy, and all would fall flat.

I hope in time we can make a try of it. After I once settle down intent on such a scheme, I will eat shame and poverty, washing them down with cocktails made of gibes, jeers and scoffs, to make it a go.

Have you ever met one John Sjodin in Galesburg? He is an active socialist, a very earnest "red." His father was well acquainted with the Chicago "anarchists" and John is as violent a non-conformist as a law-abiding man can be. He is a painter by trade, but an agitator by profession. If he was lazy, he would be a bomb-thrower, but he manages to eke out his bitterness and hatred at the end of a paintbrush. So he does put some love and reason in his propaganda work. Well, he is *crafty,* in the obsolete sense of the word. He and I printed a little paper once. He used to bind books just for fun and has a nimble brain and deft fingers. I don't know but he would be a valuable man in an undertaking such as you are contemplating. Anyway, if you find the time, look him up and talk with him. He has some eccentricities of genius that you will find interesting, whether there are further results, or not.

I must close now. Time will give us more light on the project. Time—Byron called it the tomb-builder—but Byron never knew anything but the pleasure of being sad. If he could have hoed potatoes and built wood sheds part of his time, he would have dashed down yon Samian cup of sweet melancholy. "That word which the finger of God has traced on the forehead of every man— Hope"—will stand us in stead.

Yours sincerely
Charles Sandburg

17 | TO PHILIP GREEN WRIGHT

Smyrna, Del., May 15, 1904

Dear Professor Wright:

From now on, I eschew all literary effort and lay up treasures for my kingdom in England. I am sending you herewith one more poem, "Charles XII." He was my namesake and his career has always had attraction for me. If I ever do anything in biography, I think I would like to write him up. He is an anomaly among conquerors, and all-in-all I don't know but that I would as lief have been him, as pudgy, epileptic, paralytic Sam Johnson, who said he was fit only to "point a moral and adorn a tale." I have also culled from my "scraps" some "Wayside Talk" which I believe would give balance and add flavor to my volume. It will help to more accurately represent personality, and the more I read the more do I think that the nearer a man can come to portraying all the varied sides of what is bright and choice in his own individual soul, the greater an artist he is.

I have been thinking that we may put our volumes on the display stands of stores in Chicago to begin with and in accordance with the sales there, we will "invade" other cities. Of course there should be some sale in Galesburg and among Lombardites.

If "The Underlings" and poems of similar trend can be brought to the attention of the leading socialist magazines, I think they will get favorable reviews, reprints, and comment, that will constitute effective advertising. "The Underlings", if my editorial sense is at all correct, will be reprinted in scores of papers. It is pessimistic, gives me the shivers, "makes me mad" and turbulent, but it is so absolutely true, it may go hand in hand down the corridors of time with "The Song of the Shirt", "The Man with the Hoe", etc.

Do you know tho, I have a little misgiving about the title "Dreamer" for a volume. The exquisite irony of the poem of that name will be seen only by the elect, and the propriety of the title of the book would appear only after reading the poem. Socialism is pressing forward so strongly before the public that the title "The Socialist and Other Poems" might be more fetching. Then again, it might be advisable to change the title of "The Entrepreneur" to "The Captain of Industry", tho possibly the latter does not so correctly designate the character dealt with. Then you could call the volume "The Captain of Industry and Other Poems." Everybody is thinking about the captain of industry—the rank socialists want to squelch him, the wise ones want to win him over to run the cooperative commonwealth, while Republican and Democrat both want to get into his pants pockets for campaign funds.

Only the select few know that the true dreamer is the great doer, and the fine significance of the phrase as a book-title would be lost on many who will buy and enjoy, yet not appreciate to the full the import of your words.

Your assumption that any prestige gained by these books will be a help in advancing any "arts-craft" establishment we may institute is certainly correct. All persons whom we interest we should perhaps keep a record of, as they will constitute a basis for the clientele of patrons we will need for whatever wares we may make.

I am clipping and saving any rare, but not generally known, pieces of literature I come across. For instance, this "Rain" which I enclose, I rank classic. For rhythm, it equals Poe's "Raven". Then Senator Vest on the dog is widely known, but in de luxe form may sometime prove popular.

There were other matters I was to speak of, but enough for the nonce. I have read your old favorite "Tartarin of Tarascon" recently. I don't wonder you had a feeling that Daudet was your "other self". There are paragraphs that have a touch identical with your description of you and Thorpe repairing the water-pipes, and the plumbers' ukase. May fair winds blow on the sails of your projects! and the joy of life ride high in your heart.

Yours fraternally,
Charles Sandburg

"Charles XII" was included in Sandburg's volume, In Reckless Ecstasy. *Professor Wright's book,* The Dreamer, *included "The Underlings" and "The Captain of Industry."*

18 | TO PHILIP GREEN WRIGHT

Haddonfield, N.J., May 24, 1904

Dear Professor Wright:

During the past few weeks, I have been breaking away more and more from the habit of writing. My tendency is now more toward oratory. To-day, I cleared out my letter file—some of the "stuff" I would not read to anyone except in self-burlesque. But I have thought that here and there may be a stroke worth preserving and I am sending you these things to learn your opinion of them if you will be so good as to vouchsafe the same—I still have about the same attitude toward you that I had when I came to Lombard a seasoned soldier and a raw scholar writing "100 words" on rifles, Spaniards, canned beef, etc.

What you may consider worthy among these, please file away as I have no other copies. They may be of use some day if we start a periodical.

Yours fraternally,
C.A.S.

19 | TO MARY SANDBURG

Haddonfield, New Jersey,
June 2, 1904.

Dear Mary:

I don't know what you think of me by this time, good sister. It's been a mazy path I've been treading—mix-ups and windings around in all sorts and conditions of men and women. To say again here that the faith is strong in me that we will some day be chummy again and walk, and talk about the things that have happened to me that didn't get into our letters, to say that again is not useless, I hope.

As Mart has probably told you, the plan is for Dickinson and me to go to England this summer. Also, the chances are that by fall-time, I will have a book published in de luxe style. Prepare yourself for those who will extol and laud—and those who hoot and smile and deride.

I was in Walt Whitman's old home last Sunday, and on Memorial Day threw a rose in his tomb at Camden.

Some way I feel as tho I am not doing as much as you had expected me to—that I have fallen short of the standard of achievement you had your eye on for me. Whether or no, tho, never forget that you have a big corner in my heart, and that I look on you as one of the blessings and inspirations that has entered into my life.

Yours lovingly,
Charlie.

20 | TO PHILIP GREEN WRIGHT

Haddonfield, N.J.
June 14, 1904.

Dear Professor Wright:

The English trip is off—Dickinson will probably be in G. [Galesburg] before long, and apprise you of our plans. We will locate somewhere in the West and I will join him this summer. This makes it a certainty I will drop in on The Asgard sooner than expected. You certainly have a good variety of styles of type, from the showing made by the Commencement "program". Commercial printing as "hay for Pegasus" is good. The old hoss has had too much moonshine and star-dust.

You know I once figured on my suitability for the camps of theology?—but didn't want my economic independence in the hands of any religious sect whatsoever? However, I can pray, as witness enclosure. Seriously, haven't I as much right to make such utterance as Stevenson, Van Dyke, or Frank Bishop, gesso.

If Galesburg is on my way when I make tracks 'cross the country for Dickinson, I will stop off. Otherwise, I will be in in the fall. I want to have some long talks with you in the fall, or when I do arrive, which may be before then. I want to get your opinion on the advisability of certain moves that are up to me in this game I am playing with the World, "which is wise, being very old."

Faithfully yours,
Charles Sandburg

21 | TO PHILIP GREEN WRIGHT

Haddonfield, New Jersey
July 4, 1904

Dear Professor Wright:

Your letter received on this glorious day wherein we celebrate political independence and industrial servitude. If you listen real closely to the scream of the eagle you will note a little moaning quaver of regret—that's for the wings clipped by High Finance.

I spent the day with men and maids in the woods; did a stump speech; recited Shakespeare; impersonated a nigger preacher; and lived The Querulous Life to the full. I have a splendid idea in my head tonight, which if worked out would be a great literary hit. But if I started to develop it, it would mean 1:00 or 2:00 a.m., and when I woke up tomorrow, I would feel more like a man of thought than of action and business. I often deny myself and the world this way.

Sorry to hear of your blood-poisoning. Big, rude, incomprehensible Nature doesn't seem to care when she intrudes and makes a man writhe and wince for a slight inattention to Her, even if the man is engaged in trying to save the World.

Asgard Runes is good, and should be effective with the Well-read—Asgard suggesting the highly finished urbanity, breadth, suavity and criticism of Southern Europe, and Runes, if I am correct, the Norse men, with bowels, pulses, battle-axes, and "blonde, curly hair." Inasmuch as such stuff as we write can only be rightly understood by the well-read and broad-lived, "those who have gone up the heights," who prefer a wild rune to a fragile rondeau baked in a library, I should think Asgard Runes would be fetching. However, if after a time, we get polemic and "scrappy", twist the tail of conventionality, grab social and political fallacies by the scruff of the neck and throw them to the outer whirlwinds, key part of our stuff a little lower so to catch the upper strata of proletarians, we may change it to:

STUFF
A Magazine for the Mob

or something like that. Next year, I am going to have more time, and will do up some hot screeds on various phases of society, and government.

As to sealing the Runes, it would be a unique feature and add interest, especially to those sent thru the mails. But it may not be advisable to place them in book-stores in such shape, as many persons, like myself, like to open a periodical, poke around in it and sort of taste of it before buying. This point tho, could be overcome by having a few with the seals broken for inspection.

I enclose another prayer. This one I shall possibly rearrange slightly and previous to Xmas have the Asgard, if time permits, run off a few hundred in de luxe style—heavy cards—for holiday trade. It will be—like the whole Asgard movement—an interesting little gamble.

Well! success to you in all these noble efforts you are making. Even if you should not succeed, there is a little crowd of us ahead of the age, who would understand—and rather fail sublimely than succeed by present standards.

Yours for the Better Day,
Charles Sandburg

22 | TO PHILIP GREEN WRIGHT

Freeport, Ill., Aug. 2, 1904

Dear Professor Wright:

Not until this morning did I see aught of your Foreword. You see for the past sixteen days I have been on a starring tour. Unshackling myself from all the conventions and elegancies, and swinging clean to the extreme of Bohemianism. I wandered across Pennsylvania along the beautiful Susquehanna, past the coal mines and along mountain-sides whence I could look down on smelter-works in lurid lights much like the pits of hell—by orthodox descriptions. At Pittsburg, I was captured by railroad police and sent to the Allegheny Co. Jail where I put in ten days. The warden gets $.50 per day for each prisoner he is (supposed to be) feeding; and as said feeding does not entail an expense of $.05 per day, if only enough prisoners that can't make a howl may be obtained, why he can shake the plum tree and fill his own pockets. The charge against me was "riding a freight-train without paying fare." For breakfast, we had a half loaf of bread, and a cup of hot brown water masquerading as coffee; for luncheon a half loaf of stale bread again, —soup on Wednesday & Saturday; for dinner—but there was no dinner. How can we sleep on a big, heavy dinner? I was thrown in a cell with a young Slav who didn't know forty words of English, and a gray-headed Civil War veteran. It was a lark on the whole, and I think gave me new light on the evolution of a criminal. We will talk it over sometime this fall.

I came on to Chicago in the same style, then made a change and came on to join him of the white hair and deckle-edge audacity —Dickinson.

The Foreword—what shall I say? Am I falsely proud when I

say it pleases me immensely, or am I right to think it measures me true and "hits me where I live?" Let it go. Biography and criticism is ever a grope for the lost chord, and the greatest success is only a reach and never a grasp. Yours is a deft little skit that surely should be a help to a reader. I enclose it and will mail trusting it is not too late in arrival. Will write later re other points you mention. A little over a year and a half ago, I sent you two or three poems written by a lady who left me on the back-track. She was just such an elusive sprite as could pen the Skating Girl and the Rose-Queen. So don't mar the serenity of her wedlock by merging my stuff and hers. In more haste than usual,

Faithfully yours,
C.A.S.

23 | TO ESTHER SANDBURG

Orangeville, Ill., Oct. 12, '04

Dear Esther:

Tell Mart and mother for me that all of the things I asked for and which they kindly sent, have safely arrived. A new man was in the express office here and tho I got out two other packages, the poor, forgetful brute neglected to give me the one first sent.

I am writing this especially to you, to ask you to see if you can find a bunch of manuscripts which I sent to Mary last winter and which she took home. She writes me that you know where they are. Now all of these that you can find—if you can find any—I wish you would deliver to Prof. Wright. He will be glad to see you and you will like him, I am sure, if you can understand him. He looks a little serious and severe, but he has a big heart and I think will like you, and you will enjoy a talk with him. He has printed a little volume of his poems lately, for which I wrote a foreword. If you go, you might ask him for a look at it.

I enjoy your letters—I can see by them you are getting to be a young woman. I have your picture on a mantel in my room and am sometimes asked if that is my sweetheart. And I say, "Yes, but that picture don't give any idea of her—she has such a quiet, witty way about her." There now, don't hug that compliment too closely —it will smother. But I do have hopes for you, Esther, and I hope I will be able to do something toward your having some courses of study at Lombard. Always keep your hope high—and smile, smile no matter what comes, as mama does.

You didn't say boo about that clipping I sent you, whether you thought it was too deep or whether you rather liked it. Now, do write me,—and give my love to the whole household. And I am

Your loving brother,
Charlie

24 | TO PHILIP GREEN WRIGHT

Freeport, Ill., Nov. 22, 1904

Dear Professor Wright:

Your letter was addressed to Orangeville. That place and myself are sundered apart for good and always. Where I am there is a Latin Quarter—generally—but in O., there was neither aspiration nor discontent—God, the Devil, the competitive system, everything was all right. That's very well in a way, but above it I would prefer the canny, restless, turbulent spirits of the Pittsburg jail. Will o' the mill, calm, serene, wise with the wisdom of the tempted, is one man, and Dogberry, the judge, asseverative and thick-pated, is another. Will you sit down with me and we will rail against the world and all our misery.

Spoke to a vast audience that marshalled twenty shining faces Sunday. Good practice, tho. I had made preparation and had no trouble to consume an hour, and could have bombarded the ramparts of capitalism a full hour more. I have been working on an article I am going to submit to some conservative magazines, and if not acceptable to them, I think it will be to some socialist periodical—4000 words.

Will you be so good as to send me proof-sheets which you are done with? I give you my word I won't fire back any alterations of any sort—I'm just curious as to type, arrangements, etc. There are always some sheets run off which are not quite suitable, and I would take pleasure in having a look at such.

The political situation is gratifying. The advance of the socialist was pleasing, and to see Parker and the bushwhacking gang back of him eat crow, raw, feathers, feet, bill and all—shades of Pluto! I am afraid I gloated.

It seems to me there are going to be some great times on the political firing-line. There is some splendid blood in the Socialist party, and they are such reckless zealots, that I feel that whether I ever get even a dim glimpse of a co-operative commonwealth, I shall certainly witness some grand assaults on capitalism, and as sure as our blood is red, there will be a recession of some sort from the present arrogance, and bland, easy assumption of the powers that be. This is possibly more poetic than fictitious, but in a letter a man can't pile up the facts on facts that he thinks back his convictions. I don't particularly enjoy dealing with the sinister, the pathetic, and the execrable as one must do in socialist propaganda, but so long as these easy-going, complacent people will stand idly by and be expropriated, there is nothing for it but to taunt them with portrayals of conditions,—sting them with facts, as it were. I used to think there was a tinge of the sardonic in the socialist, but it seems now to be only the twisted smile of Gilliat as he opens his knife and calculates for the eye of the devil-fish. These people who talk of snipping off bits of the tentacles!

I go to Aurora this week, and expect to take the trolley now and then over to Joliet, where there is quite a bunch of Lombardites. So strange will those faces seem, and yet old and familiar. Since I left New York, except for Dickinson, and Dr. Lee in Philadelphia (who's fighting the devil with water) I haven't seen a face I knew before I left home. I will surely be tipsy with camaraderie Xmas.

Please send along such scraps as can't be utilized in the book you are building.

May sunshine and peace and the gold of manhood keep coming your way.

Yours fraternally,
Charles Sandburg

1904

Sandburg used "fraternally" in signing his letters to political allies and union friends. The reference to Gilliat is to the fisherman in Victor Hugo's The Toilers of the Sea, *a lonely romantic who had a terrible fight with an octopus.*

25 | TO PHILIP GREEN WRIGHT

Aurora, Ill. Dec. 8, 1904

Dear Professor Wright:

I was happy to have a look at advance sheets to-day—the happiness that possessed me was clearly the unconscious kind—I did not spoil it with "I am happy—so happy." Those old pennings I had not seen for months gladdened my eyes in such garb as you present them. The Plow-Ox: Spanish Bull seems to me now a bovinization of The Proletarian: Karl Marx if you will allow a gangway for the simile. A man's merits and faults come to him with more clearness when he sees his writings in print. But, I have been asking myself, what under the sun is literary achievement? "Hamlet" which I regard as the drama incomparable and which render the critics hoarse in articulating appreciation, Charles Frohman comes forward to say is mediocre, and an ultra-fervid class-conscious scribbler in Wilshire's Magazine says the Avon immortal was an aristocrat, and for all his boasted universality, he never understood the great underworld of men. I talked with A. M. Simons this week and he was so sorry that Jack London and Upton Sinclair couldn't flaunt before their readers a more rigid, more Marxian Socialism. Of essayists, I rank Hubbard highest among contemporary writers, but among literary artists, I place London even above Tolstoi. London, the coal-heaver, the gold-hunter, the tramp, the war-correspondent, keep your eyes on him, Professor. He bids fair to outclass anything in all America's literary output.

I came across a curious little specimen of a reckless ecstasy today in Maeterlinck's "Wisdom & Destiny". "Would Carlyle have desired to exchange the magnificent sorrow that flooded his soul, and blossomed so tenderly there, for the conjugal joys of his happiest neighbor?" I think with its context it is a beautiful sentiment, but

I am afraid it is lost on those practical people who would like to ask how anything could blossom tenderly, if at all, in a place that was magnificently flooded. But Maeterlinck does not mind—"The Intruder" frightens him not.

I shall be interested to see what you choose for the remaining pages of this book—also to see how many pale, timid arms venture to exchange their shekels for what it has to give them.

I have been rioting in social functions here and in Joliet and in Chicago but have called a halt now. Was almost persuaded to go to a U. of C. dancing party to-night. If I could only meet The Ideal Woman, I believe I could pull myself together and set the world by the ears. As it is, I shall continue to prepare my cocoa myself, sew on the trouser-buttons, and be an itinerant salesman, a vagabond philosopher-poet, and most unworthy descendant of Leif Ericson. I have silenced quite effectively the super-buoyancy of a young coquette at the house where I am rooming by telling her she reminds me very much of my first wife!

I anticipate some delightful holidays—in fact, I don't know if I keep my expectations too high and fine for this earth. Anyway I hope you and I can go up on some high place and have a view of potential Eldorados and Mississippi bubbles. Au revoir.

Faithfully yours,
Charles A. Sandburg

P.S. Will return "sheets" within one or two days.—Also enclose "The Street Speaker."

The sheets were of his In Reckless Ecstasy. *A. M. Simons was editor of* International Socialist Review. *The woman who was to turn out to be his ideal, Lilian Steichen, was a senior at The University of Chicago when Sandburg decided not to attend the dancing party.*

Aurora, Ill.
December 19, 1904

Dear Professor Wright:

Partly because I feel it will not be entirely uninteresting to you, partly because by writing about it, I may stumble on some new phase of the thing, partly because there are only plow-oxen about me to whom I may talk. My situation is much that of Lord Macaulay— long before he was a lord. He felt he could do great work as a writer, but to do anything fine and distinctive, he would have to have leisure, and at that a leisure unhampered by routine duties and devotion of effort to attaining competence. He was subsidized—he submitted. If I had cared to, I could have gone up from election-judge into some sinecure requiring no worry—except about speaking your mind. I am not a suffering martyr, by a long way. I am getting many fine thrills and quavers out of life. And I am doing it without having become a he-strumpet and bartering my honor for political pelf.

But I see myself approaching a parting of the ways. There was a time I could equalize my attentions to business and to literature, but of late the latter has been drawing me away from business. And the time I have given to books and reflection has given me a conviction that if I had the leisure I could produce several essays and studies that would be welcomed in the literary world. The Norse heroes, for instance,—Gustaf Vasa, Gustavus Adolphus, Charles XII and others—have not been represented with vividness, with a "living touch", set up before readers with their "blonde, curly hair", mocking blue eyes, and terrible fervor, as they deserve—they have not been sympathetically or fully (as far as may be) interpreted. Voltaire comes close to the heart of Charles XII, but he does not leave with a reader an adequate conception of the noble self-denial, and the sublime self-confidence of the man. Now, this scheme—that of giving a more correct and vivid portraiture of these men and their times—is getting such strong hold of me that I've either got to carry it out completely, dropping all business completely, or I've got to postpone it, not touch a hair of its head—not lust after it so much as to press my lips to the rosy cheeks of its bonnie head— and get down to business and acquire such a fund as will last me through. It seems to me, too, that if I could carry this out as I plan, and instruct and entertain the public, get its ear, show it that I am a self-contained individual, still "in love with enraptured life," that what I would subsequently say about the need for a social and industrial revolution, would be more quickly and attentively heeded. So I am thinking about formulating a vow, and on New Years Eve to stand on a stack of bibles, lift my right hand toward the vault of heaven and let the gods know by wireless that they may strike me with epilepsy, then paralyse me and disembowel me if I during the coming year entertain for a moment a dream of writing anything but letters, and orders for goods.

Good-by Arcadia! You blue-misted shores, you land of green arbors and purple grapes and waving grain! I'm going out on the breast of the Great Sea, where the winds break the beams and spars as I would twist a toothpick. Farewell, you libraries! Adieu, you Companions with whom I have gone hand in hand, and to whom I leave distended with eager ear—Adieu, you Souls who have lived and speak, tho dead—Fare ye well!

There—I am better. But I do not know of anything great and vital in literature that was done between-whiles. The great writer just fondly and madly forgets the whole scheme of human existence except where it touches on the theme at hand. I know Mrs. Stowe did "Uncle Tom" when the housework was done, but what egregious distortions of human kind, Eva and Tom are! And Roosevelt, the all 'round man, the litterateur incidentally—"this great Gawd Blud" could rage out his entire contribution and the world would not be poorer a great thought, handsomely said. To preclude further a splenetic coruscation, I shall quit here, as Friday has it.

I am brushing up on my Swedish and when I carry out the fore-mentioned scheme will do a good deal of reading in the original. I have said it before, but I've got to say "Out! you books and pad and pencil," in earnest now, or Destiny will hammer me into one of those short, lean, pale wretches who make a profession of literature, unceasingly perambulating with manuscripts, most miserable of all wage-slaves.

When I arrive in G. [Galesburg] I'll show you the Socialistic mss. I wrote in Freeport—I had thought to have it type-written and sent to magazines, but the places where it can be improved are increasingly numerous. Once in a while, and by a natural genius, a great, good work is penned off-hand, but as for me, I haven't got the habit yet, and so the co-operative commonwealth, the immortality of the soul, the Swedish Captains, the quiet thrill of a good book, and all the little delights of a scribbler who sees his stuff in print—they shall be trampled under my feet while I fight for economic independence. Up Guards! and at them.

There's no one else I could have rambled around and been so free to chat with to-night. I arrive in G. next Saturday evening and will see you then or sometime Sunday, when you may inquire about any of the gleeful expostulations herein. I enclose a mediocre effort, executed amid angry lightnings of self-reproach. Well—happy days!

Sandburg

27 | TO MARY SANDBURG

St. Charles, Ill.
[Circa March, 1905]

Dear Mary:

I am at a queer place in my life and feel all sorts of things buzzing merrily or snarling viciously about me. Badger, the Boston publisher, has written me that he has noted my work in To-morrow with much interest and will give "immediate and careful attention" to any material I might care to submit. It's new to me to have publishers write that way.

So I expect to put in about a week or two at home in April revising and type-writing about thirty-five poems of greater or less merit and length. I have been writing when I felt the mood and business has gone to the dogs.

Good-luck to you in all your comings and goings over there in the "Gas Belt." If you are ever passing thru Indianapolis, or are going to run down there sometime, I will give you a letter to Ann Coleman—different but as great in a way as Louva—I believe you would enjoy her and she you. Good-bye for this time,

Yours lovingly,
Charlie.

Early in 1905, Tomorrow Magazine, *in Chicago, began to publish his poems.*

28 | TO MARY SANDBURG

[Galesburg, Ill.]
April 14, [1905]

Dear Mary:—

I have been firing off a lot of stuff the past week here—just fixed a bunch of sixty poems now and am going to fire them at the tribe of Barabbas—make them go through them anyway, and put them through the exertion required for a turn-down. I am dabbling a little in politics and don't know but I may be back on the fire-department. Nothing certain though.

If you knew with what fine expectation they await your home-coming you would smile. Kate and Mart and Mama and Esther, all of them. And I too. Good-by for now.

With love,
Charlie

29 | TO ESTHER SANDBURG

[Chicago]
April 5th, 1906.

Dear Esther:

I have a letter from Prof. Kimble this morning in which he asks for the return of a book, The Theory of Business Enterprise. I am not certain whether I have the book in the main part of my baggage which is at Aurora, or not. I rather think tho, that it is at home.

Anyway, will you please look on the shelves and see if The Theory of Business Enterprise, by Thorsten Veblen, is there and if it is, see that Prof. Kimble gets it. If you can't find it, let me know at once and the next time I go to Aurora I will get it.

Everything is coming along as well as I could wish here—I have spoken in public several times and feel that I am improving along lines I would like to be better in—Have gained six pounds in weight.

Have met a number of men pretty well known over the whole country and almost believe that the nearer you get to a Great Man the smaller he looks. A Great Man is like a mountain and looks grandest from a distance.

Give my love to Martha Sandburg and tell her "muckels". Give my love to Mary, to Mamma, and Papa.

Yours affectionately,
Charlie.

30 | TO REUBEN W. BOROUGH

Aurora, Ill., Dec. 19, 1906.

My Dear Borough:—

Under separate cover I'm sending you a copy of a folder announcing my lectures. You have some idea of my theories. The Whitman lecture embodies them quite fully, and I want to ask you if you can refer me to a club or individual in Fort Wayne (provided you're there now—I'm sending this on a chance) who would make arrangements for a lecture there.

The terms on which I will come are these: I furnish circulars, window cards and pay for newspaper advertising. I receive 50% of the receipts after my hotel & railroad expenses are paid. If receipts do not cover expenses, I foot them myself, thus involving no one else in risk.

Write me about the field there, tell me also about your own work. I want to have a long talk with you sometime—we have much in common. I want to meet another youth who throws his poetry into loose, disarrayed rhythms, and lets rhyme go hang. You'll do other things than poetry, too, I judge from your recent story in the I.S. [International Socialist] Review. Let me hear from you.

Faithfully yours,
Charles Sandburg.

Reuben W. Borough was a reporter for the Journal-Gazette, *Fort Wayne, Indiana. He and Sandburg contributed to* Tomorrow.

31 | TO PHILIP GREEN WRIGHT

[Chicago]
12-29-'06

Dear Professor:

I've gone in with the Lyceumite here as assistant editor and advertising man, Barker and I being in about the relations of Dick [Fred Dickinson] and I on The Cannibal, Managing Editor & Editing Manager. A number of men were after the place, and as I was asked to take it and got a good proposition, meseems I will cut out vagabonding a year or so. I'm permitted to fill lecture dates occasionally tho this must not compete in any serious way with our bureau advertisers.

I have a date in Rockford at the Church of the Christian Union, Sunday eve. Jan. 6. If you get my window cards done, or part of them, by Jan. 2, please forward 50 of them immediately to

Robert C. Bryant
205 Mulberry St.
Rockford, Ill.

This is a kind of try-out affair, they paying my expenses and if it's a go, we have a bigger one later in the year.

A strong review of The Dreamer will appear in the next ite [*Lyceumite*]. I'm working up a live series to be called Unimportant Portraits of Important People, one each month with a ½ page cartoon. Am getting in with all sorts of platform people—when I get a thorough footing and the right opening will be able to throw some printing toward Asgard. Your Xmas greeting was a pleasant "Hello" to meet.

Had dinner with Humphrey yesterday.—He was surprised that he, a food crank, had not yet found that crowded haunt of food cranks, the Physical Culture Restaurant.

Here all good wishes, and the hope that in the coming year all your buds of hope will breed and fertilize and criss-cross, so they finally bloom as at a Burbank touch into consummations of beauty.

Yours faithfully,
Charles Sandburg

Edwin L. Barker was editor of The Lyceumite. *Alton Packard and Ross Crane drew the cartoons. Albert Humphrey was a professor at Knox College and a friend of Wright and Sandburg.*

32 | TO ESTHER SANDBURG

[Chicago]
[Circa March, 1907]

Dear Esther:

Your note was good to see. I am glad to see your enthusiasm in your piano work. If I should try to say something short and to the point that tells what seems to me is necessary to make a success as an artist of any kind, a musician as well as anybody, it would be this: Work and love, love and work. Live as your soul tells you you ought to live. Listen to what others have to say, good and bad, about what you ought to do and then do as your own soul, your own heart, your own self tells you. Thank God if you're not satisfied with your work. And don't worry. Go after big things. Tackle the delicate and subtle compositions, and tackle smashing and tremendous ones. If you don't play them to suit yourself or anyone else, you will have more power and skill just because you tried. Love the people you meet and do the best you can for them with all the heart and head you have, but don't allow anything big or anything petty, no combination of troubles of any sort to drag you away from your ambition or discourage you. Believe in yourself in the right way and then it will be easy enough to believe in others. Think yourself a piece of God's finest stuff and you will think better and do more for all others.

All this is much like preaching, but the reason I have written it down for you is because I think you show promise of being an artist, a pianist of more than ordinary talent. And I know that if you work in the right way and get the right ability, I'll be able to put you in the way of good things before the public. No amount of pull on my part would do any good if you didn't have the ability to charm and move people. Do you laugh and love and cry and swear—and learn to let it all out at the end of your fingers along the keyboard.

There are all sorts of piano stunts that could be worked up and be a "go" before audiences. I've been to all sorts of concerts, vaudeville performances, etc., and I know the public wants piano playing, that it will go wild over the right kind of a piano performance, a little series of pieces that mingle the classics and the homely, loveable folk-song airs. You needn't show this around. Just put it under your hat and work and love. And sometime before next summer is over we will get together and if you can really raise hell with a piano and make people sit up, there will be something coming your way.—Last of all, don't let your work wear your health down. Of all things, get out into the sun and pure air every day, and walk in the mist when it's cloudy. Vitality, bounding, exuberant health, is a characteristic of every artist worth hearing.

All of it, Esther, with love,

Charlie.

P.S. Kiss the mother and all at home for me. Tell Mary I got her letter and think her picture the best ever yet.

P.S.—Let me know what days Miss Hein is in Chicago & where I could see her. I want to have a frank talk with her about you.

Esther Sandburg (later Mrs. Arthur Wachs) was one of Sandburg's two younger sisters.

33 | TO PHILIP GREEN WRIGHT

[Chicago]
May 2, 1907.

Dear Professor:

Down with the trusts! A combine of bureaus whom the Lyceumite was knocking bought the Lyceumite and are going to use it in their business. I was tossed out of the deck like a dirty deuce. If I did not enjoy a scrap I would be crestfallen, undone, down and out.

Next week I go down in Indiana booking courses for the Midland bureau, also booking myself wherever possible. Have good prospects for getting dates for myself as a single number in Terra Haute and Fort Wayne, and several Michigan cities where Reuben Borough is in on the ground floor with radicals.

Frank Bishop's precious girl-child tore the pictures from about a dozen of my heavy circulars—I will want a number to replace those and during the course of the year will find use for a hundred or so more of them, if you will run them off. I am having a little folder run off here, to be an accessory to the large folder, some words from people who have heard me.

The printing of the Careless Essays will depend on my success in Indiana. I will write you from the gas belt how things go, whether the oil wells run well, etc. Next Sunday I lecture in Rockford on Blunders of Modern Civilization.

If you have any of those heavy folders left, will you send them to my house address? Otherwise address me care of the Chicago address above.

Here are all good wishes to you. I hope you will let me know when you are to be in Chicago at any time, as if I am in at that time, we can get together and talk about the world, which is full of a number of things.

Sandburg

"Careless Essays" became Sandburg's second book, Incidentals. *The title came from the line "Life is more vast and strange than any-*

thing written about it—words are only incidentals." Frank Bishop was a Lombard friend who had been on the basketball team there with Sandburg.

34 | TO REUBEN W. BOROUGH

Marion, Indiana
May 17, 1907

Dear Rube:

Some hatless runt of an individual got away with that proud, natty Stetson of mine—I was in the reception room talking with [W. H.] Sanders and when we came out lo! the sky-piece was neither here nor there. Again lo! Also, hell, and Dam.

Please send me that boxed-up black Fedora. I figure on your getting this Saturday and if you get the hat to Adams Xpress office before going to sleep Sat. night or Sun. morning, it will reach me at Marion Monday morning. Otherwise, I will have to push on wearing a golf cap and you know I don't play golf.

Here's hoping you're all to the good, lad—

Sandy.

35 | TO REUBEN W. BOROUGH

Hinckley, Ill., 5-30-'07.

Dear Rube:—

Does it convey anything to you to be told that I am in Hinckley? Yet that is where I am—such is the fact. Tonight both God and I know where I am—yesterday only God knew I was to get here.

Green-crested hills surround the town and white roads lead off into grey, mysterious distances. I will be in dire peril of tossing off a poem or two.

Hinckley! Isn't it musical? So like Barbizon and Heidelberg.

The town has been thoroughly evangelized this winter—I am plotting a hot socialist speech the night before I leave.

Be a good lad—throw off a short epistle for me once in a while

—tell Mance I think of him—forward my mail—and curse the [Chicago] Examiner for its outright falsehoods about Triggs. Can you remember all these?

Yours in comradeship,
Sandy.

Alfred W. Mance, a middle-aged harness maker and ardent worker for the Socialists, was a friend of Borough and Sandburg in Chicago. Oscar Lovell Triggs was a professor at the University of Chicago and editor of Tomorrow. *He was the victim of slanderous attacks by several newspapers, not only the* Examiner.

36 | TO REUBEN W. BOROUGH

Hinckley, Ill., 6-4-'07

Dear Rube:

In a separate envelope, I send you a short story, the only one I have in recent days felt some confidence in. If you will typewrite it and fire it to The Cosmopolitan, any returns that may come of it I will go half with you on. You will be gambling—it is a long shot, but just think—we will find out what now only God knows!

Here are some things written for The Daily Socialist editorial page, if they can be used. If not, will you keep the Mss.?

I am sending Wilshire's [Magazine] a MSS., a discussion of Kipling's Sons of Martha. I have fairly weltered in ink down here, haven't been out with sample case at all. It is so quiet here. I think Heaven is like Hinckley, with you and Mance, each with a woman he loves, as citizens.

Will you ask them to put my name on the sub list at the office, saying I will be in by July 1?

My good landlady says she see by the papers that the socialists was likely to break out agin—aint it awful?

Good-by for now, Rube. Let's have a word from you.

Yours,
Sandy.

P.S. Run with or without my illustrious name this editorial page gore. Don't run all 3 at once!

37 | TO REUBEN W. BOROUGH

Hinckley, Ill., 6-9-'07.

Dear Rube:—

Will you see that The Daily Socialist reaches me here? I haven't
received any copies as yet. I hope the militant and aggressive little
sheet is still alive. And if any of my stuff has appeared let me see
how it looks. Wilshire writes me that in the Aug. or Sept. number
he will print some stuff I sent him discussing Kipling's "Sons of
Martha". I enclose the letter for you—it is irony—a taunt whose
smile is almost a leer.

Stereographs—they are not pictures but actual photographs
made by a double-lens camera that duplicates reality—are going
well. I expect to hit Chicago, from present looking, about June 22.

I went to church yesterday and listened to a goddam oleaginous
preacher deliver that old stale discourse I have heard forty times
about the conversion of Saul of Tarsus. He began and ended like
all of them, describing Tarsus and the road to Jerusalem and the
shaft of light that was a knockdown to the saint, all with such a
mass and class of unnecessary detail that I am sure he didn't believe
it himself. Then I went to a ballgame—poor playing but it was sincere and therefore refreshing. Then I went out in the woods and
meditated whether a little woodpecker issuing from its egg and sur-
veying the world from the top of a walnut tree would come in the
category of an Immaculate Conception.

Tell Mance that when he dies I will lay a sword on his coffin
and say that he was a good soldier in the war for the liberation of
mankind. I will do the same for you. I hope you can do as much
for me. We are the Three Musketeers.

Yours fraternally,
Sandy.

Gaylord Wilshire was the publisher of Wilshire's Magazine, *and
a Socialist. The line "I will lay a sword on his coffin" refers to
Heine's words: "When I die, lay a sword on my bier,/ For I have
been a brave soldier in/ Humanity's war for emancipation."*

1907

[East Aurora, New York]
July 6, 1907

Dear Professor:

I really expected to find your good face awaiting me at the Shop here. To be frank & emphatic, we are having a hell of a time.—Lyman Chandler, who is artist, connoisseur & business man, & hasn't much to say, thinks The Dreamer is par excellence.

They are sort of crazy here about the lecture on Whitman I gave yesterday. You know I have dreamed & welded & prayed & laughed with it & for me & for the audience it was an occasion. They drew out of me my best. Mr. and Mrs. Hubbard say I have "a world-beater." The crowd caught things right on the wing all the way through & when I was done & had seated myself & was talking nothings with somebody Hubbard grabs me by the arm & pulls me to the front again—they were clapping & yelling for an encore. For the tribute as far as approbation is concerned I don't care any particular dam, but that I now am sure I have trained my powers, so that they can be of *service* to men, pleases me.—It will get me a number of dates next winter.—Since I left the Lyceumite, I have changed it from a strong literary lecture into an oration, & I know now that I have a winner.

Let me know where you are & what doing. I will probably leave here within a week and locate somewhere in southern Michigan.

I have learned a great deal about the workings of the scheme here. I have had access to reliable sources of information & have got a perspective on the past & present of the whole of it such as few have gotten.—Thru it all of course, my liking for John [Sjodin] doesn't diminish—

You won't pass around this effusive message—if Humphrey comes your way, let him see it—I am terribly busy or rather filling the days very full. While I was writing, Hubbard tells me that an insistent demand for more of my stuff dictates that I go on for at least a half-hour talk tonight.

Yes let me hear from you. I wish you were here to give them a Morris talk—the emphasis is a little too strong on New Thought.

Yours faithfully,

Sandburg

Address the Inn here,—it will be forwarded.

William Morris, the English Socialist and poet, had founded his own printing enterprise—the Kelmscott Press; Elbert Hubbard's Roycroft Press was patterned after it. In addition to the Whitman lecture, Sandburg also spoke on Socialism at the Roycroft Chapel, on July 13, 1907.

39 | TO REUBEN W. BOROUGH

East Aurora, N.Y. 7-16-'07

Dear Rube:—

I expect to locate in Homer within five days. I will take passage from Buffalo to Marshall, arriving in your town Wednesday or Thursday. If I don't find you in, I will write you from Homer. Philip Green Wright will stop off at Homer a few days, maybe weeks.

Buggies have a historic mission, no less than capitalism and socialism. Here's luck to you, old pal.

Yours faithfully,

Sandy.

Homer, Michigan, was twelve miles east of Marshall, where Borough was working for his father, a manufacturer, selling buggies.

40 | TO REUBEN W. BOROUGH

Chicago, Illinois, Aug. 19, 1907.

Dear old boy Rube:—

Back again in the whirl and the roar. I write a weekly letter for the Billboard, the Chicago stuff, and will write most of the

Lyceum matter for the Opera House Guide. Will also do occasional assignments on The Musical Medium and the Signs of the Times, the latter an ad journal. The work has a good deal of variety, you see, and I have access to all the theatres, and my time is to a certain extent, my own. Just so I get the work done, it doesn't matter when I do it.

I have an essay on Modernity in Verse, a Bibelot, treating of Henley's poetry. You will like it when you have time for it.

Saw Bill Haywood—he looks very much like presidential timber, a Whitmanic type—raw, strong, canny, and yet with the flavor of romance that we want in our heroes.—Be good, Rube. You will hear from me again soon. Let me know where you move when you move—keep the fires of the ideal burning in you—you are one of "the great companions."

With love and regard,
Sandy.

William "Big Bill" Haywood helped to found the Industrial Workers of the World (I.W.W.), joined the Socialist party, but was ejected for advocating violence.

41 | TO PHILIP GREEN WRIGHT

Chicago, Aug. 22, 1907.

Dear Professor:—

I came up here from Homer a few days ago to take a job helping edit this new lyceum publication. I write also the weekly letter for The Billboard, summarising the Chicago theatrical situation. It is twenty per week and I can do my work any time I please just so I get it in. I am in the office part of the time, tho no regular hours. You must let me know when you come back this way and I will meet you. I go to Spring Lake next Sunday and will write you on my return from there. With all good wishes,

Yours fraternally,
Sandburg.

1907

The new lyceum publication was The Opera House Guide, *a monthly that united* The Lecturer, The Lyceum, The Platform, *and* Chautauquas.

[Chicago]
Sept. 11, 1907

Dear Professor:

Under separate cover I shall send you to-morrow, the copy for Incidentals. I have typewritten them and given them headings. Order entirely with you.

I am enclosing here a booklet that comes nearer a model of what I want than anything I have seen. And one of this size will be enough to learn the selling value of my stuff, while its publication can hardly be anything but an advantage from an advertising standpoint. Of course, it will make some enemies and I will hear a lot about "irreverence" but if we can get people to reading, curious to see whether it is irreverent or not, we will have accomplished something.

The Holbrook-Barker Co. are going to book me for their Chautauquas next summer. I give them my Chautauqua time exclusively and their premise is that I will have thirty dates at $50 per date, minus their commission of twenty per cent and my expenses. We haven't signed anything but I am pushing their game in The Guide, and I know that if they have any season at all, I will share their luck. I am working on a new lecture, Bernard Shaw: Artist and Fool, which I am sanguine of.

I talked to Holbrook about what you have. I told him you would find five dates for expenses and following that you could make terms in accordance with your value as a Chautauqua card. I told him you could outclass a good many of the attractions that are drawing big money that I would write you and let him know within a week. Booking for next summer will begin very shortly. You have got better stuff than the most of them on the platform, and eventually should get a number of dates at Chautauquas every summer. Have you thought any about getting out a circular? It would be a big help.

My lecture on Civilization I am changing some and shall title The Mob, and use in it The Cry of the Underlings. I don't know quite where to class myself; after my Whitman lecture at Joliet, a Methodist preacher and a presiding elder felicitated me and said I sure had power—ye gods!

> Yours faithfully,
> Sandburg

Sandburg first met "Hurry-up Harry" Holbrook while working for The Lyceumite. *He was the subject of the second "Unimportant Portraits of Important People" in* The Lyceumite. *Sandburg's lecture was finally titled "Civilization and the Mob."*

43 | TO REUBEN W. BOROUGH

Chicago, October 5, 1907.

Dear Rube:— Yours from Fort Wayne came to me. I'm glad you're keeping hearty and aggressive—you sort of get your laugh, that ringing robustious mirthfulnes of yours, into your letter, and that counts.

I am out of the Guide office. I was offered the editorship, but it would have meant going to Cincinnati, preclusion from other work (lecturing). I couldn't have dictated policies & what the hell is an editorship then? I made them a price but they couldn't see it.—Have sold five weeks of time lecturing, beginning February 1, contracted with a reliable independent manager. Am going to try out a little scheme the next few weeks. It has big possibilities and I am game. Lecture at Manitowoc under auspices & for benefit of Daily Tribune there, a workingman's paper. It's a socialist town, you know,—the mayor and aldermen—& I expect to learn things there.

What are Mrs. Bradley's initials & what her address? I am going to write about the proposition she spoke of one day when we were together.

Since I saw you I have fallen in love and fallen out again,—the mote just dancing through the flame—with a crack violinist, a reader, an amateur palmist, an actress, a chorus girl, a newspaper woman, and at present don't know what I'll do about a live pundit and poetess.—If I had no work 'twould be dangerous.—Incidentals is coming fine, have just read proof on 25 pages.

Be a good boy. Give my best to our fine-hearted people at home.—Here's my hand.

Yours
Sandy

Chester Wright, editor of the Daily Tribune, *Manitowoc, Wisconsin, later became secretary to Samuel Gompers, president of the American Federation of Labor. Wright and Sandburg were friends.*

44 | TO REUBEN W. BOROUGH

873 Jackson Blvd.,
Chicago, Ill. 11-6-'07

Dear old Boy:—

The world moves, destiny keeps shifting the scenes of the Great Drama and in mysterious ways. If I "don't come around as often as I useter", you know why.

I had a great time up in Manitowoc and learned many things. Will probably do some work for the S.D. (Social Democrat) party in Wisconsin before long.

Glad to hear the buggy sales are coming along well. You mention the probability of your being on a farm. On the land a man is safe & comes nearer being one soul and body than anywhere else under present conditions.

I hope you won't mind the liberties taken with your name in my new circular. Yours is the only one that is entirely a fabrication. I am a ready liar in a good cause and will bicker until the cows come home on the question of whether there is any absolute truth expressible.

Be a good boy. Let me know what parts of the country you're in. Our ways may cross.

> With love
> Sandy

The fabrication appeared in a folder containing flattering comments about "Sandburg on the Platform" attributed to "Rube Borough in the Marshall (Mich.) News." It said that Sandburg was "tall, lean, proud, strange. . . . Epithet, denunciation, and eulogy leap and pour from him. . . . There are times when Sandburg means what he says, absolutely."

45 | TO PHILIP GREEN WRIGHT

> 873 Jackson Blvd., Chicago.
> November 13, 1907.

Dear Professor:

If you have 100 Incidentals or as many as 250 made up, will you let me have them by Saturday morning, the 16th?

It will be interesting to see how soon or whether any orders come in for The Plaint.

You certainly did things on the printing end—everyone who has seen a copy speaks of the originality and harmony of paper and type and form.

On the 21st, I am lecturing in Green Bay, Wis. ($15 and I pay expenses!) I want to send some copies up there to be placed in stores. I am going to put some in the stores here and think I will make the price after this, 15 cents the copy.

I was astounded getting a letter from Alber, editor of Lyceumite and Talent, saying he would have a review and excerpts in his December number. Have sent a copy, with letter, to Bernard Shaw, Brand Whitlock, and such likes. The scientific socialists are lukewarm but those who are not sure that socialism is inevitable, who understand the limpidity of the universe, are more favorable.

When I take up the organizing work in Wis., I believe I will be able to do some effective pushing of The Dreamer.

Yours as ever,
Sandburg

Sandburg's essay The Plaint of the Rose *was published by the Asgard Press in January, 1908. In the brief tale, a beautiful rose bush resembles people who are sheltered, while, below, a rose in the shadows pleads for a place in the sun so its beauty and soul can be expressed.*

46 | TO REUBEN W. BOROUGH

Two Creeks, Wis., 12-21-'07

Dear old Boy:—

I don't know whether you have heard of my latest "graft" or not, but if you haven't it will have a tinge of surprise for you. The last three weeks I have been up in this country as Social Democrat organizer in the Lake Shore & Fox River District. Have been rounding up dilatory locals, trying to put new spirit in them. Am at present on a three-day trip, barnstorming at crossroad halls. Population here: 74.

There's just about expenses in it but I am learning a lot, and don't feel that efforts are useless. One word for straight socialism now counts for more than ten maneuvering opportunist words. It's the only program that will rouse the stupor of the masses.

I looked & looked for the letter you wrote me, having that Los Angeles girl's name and address—Miss Bradley's chum. Let me have it again. I want to see what sort of a letter a socialist woman can write.

Brand Whitlock liked Incidentals, wants me to speak on Whitman in Toledo. Will probably be there sometime in January. So please let me know your whereabouts most of that month.

Mance is organizing up in Canada. On the move all the time. The Three Musketeers are scattered!

Give my love and holiday greetings to all your people, the whole Borough household.

As ever yours in brotherhood,

Sandy.

"Two Creeks" was Sandburg's way of saying Two Rivers. Laura Bradley was Borough's fiancée, and the Los Angeles girl was a Socialist friend of hers. Brand Whitlock was a novelist and reform mayor of Toledo.

47 | TO PHILIP GREEN WRIGHT

Manitowoc, Wis., January 2, 1908
[Sandburg wrote 1907 in error]

Dear Professor:—

The work and thought you have given The Plaint is in evidence. It is simple and direct—a literary composition conveyed as clearly, strongly and unaffectedly as type and paper can carry it. This cover design outclasses all the others you showed me. Mrs. Wright may be proud of it.

The one that appeals most strongly to me of the three you sent is the one with the red rope and black-type title. The cord is just the right thickness for the book, and you get harmony of weight between cover and inside, as you did with Incidentals. I enclose a dollar for as many copies of The Plaint as come to me for that amount.

At present there is practically only expenses in this job of organizer, but by spring I ought to have the district in shape to pay me from $50 to $75 a month and expenses, with chances continually growing of getting a few well-paid weeks of lecturing thru the winter.—I shall order the Social Democratic Herald sent you for ten weeks. I will have notes about this district each week.—Barker has been tossed out of the Bush Temple management. This, with Mc-Carahan of the Billboard, and Robert Towns of the Judge Co. are three bright instances of good, able men "doing their work the best they can", who thru intrigues, jealousies and fears, suddenly found themselves down and out, without slightest warning. They are almost ready for social-democracy.

These Wisconsin socialists are different from most that I have known. They have very little use for the theory of a social and industrial cataclysm, the proletariat stepping in and organizing the co-operative commonwealth! They know that a collapse is ultimately inevitable, but they know that a genuine democracy will not follow unless they have been trained and educated by actual participation in political and industrial management before the crisis arrives.

Ely says, "Socialism is better than the best presentation of it". Bear this in mind when you read this leaflet. It was run in the Tribune here.

Yours as ever,
Sandburg

48 | TO LILIAN STEICHEN

Oshkosh, Wis.
2-21-1908

Dear Miss Steichen:—

It is a very good letter you send me—softens the intensity of this guerilla warfare I am carrying on up here. Never until in this work of S-D organization have I realized and felt the attitude and experience of a Te*ach*er. With those outside the party, I am an Advocate. But those within the organization have so much to learn, and to show those who have intelligence what to do, and to get the hypercritical into constructive work, and to give cheer to the desperate and rousal to the stolid—sometimes I know just what it is to be a Teacher.

I see you employ the exclamation point as freely as I do!—You chip away at an idea in sculpture-fashion. You leave the thing unfinished and half-put, neither neat, correct, discriminative, nor scholastic! I indict you as fellow felon!

The Dream Girl is millennial—formed in the mist of an impressionist's reverie. Millennial, and at this time, impossible. But, my good girl, she is not of the leisure-class, as we know the l-c. She is a disreputable gypsy, and can walk, shoot, ride, row, hoe in the garden, wash dishes, grimace, haggle, live on half-rations, and laugh at Luck.

You remind me of two types of women—seem to sort o' blend the two in your cosmos. Actresses of the modern school of repression, Fiske, Kalich, and Ashwell. And the Russian revolutionist!

Am going to send you The Plaint of a Rose. It was written as and marks the half-way point on the journey "from Poetry to Economics." A protest and justification of the universe!

I shall plan to be in Milwaukee the last days in March and one or two in April, and will hope to see you then. Will tell you then about some of the curious and interesting phases of the work up this way. Will also make some inquiries of you, pertinent and quasi-impertinent with reference to democratic art. One can't lecture on Whitman or Shaw without attaining facts and convictions.

I will forgive you (out of inborn generosity and largeness of nature) for writing such a long letter, provided, as hereinafter stated, that you repeat the offense! And don't forget your exclamation points!

Charles Sandburg

P.S:—Am going to have the district headquarters here from now on. My permanent address will be

248 Wisconsin Ave.
Oshkosh.

P.S: P.S:—Once in my callow days and for many years I thot Oshkosh was like Heaven, Nirvana, Sheol, the North Pole; mythical, imaginary, fictive, and hopeless of attainment.—But here it is! Bustling and populated, stern and real, a factual entity stretching away from my window with lands, bldgs, laws, and noises!

Lilian Steichen, who was teaching in Princeton, Illinois, first met her future husband at Social Democratic party headquarters in Milwaukee, toward the end of her Christmas vacation in 1907. They were introduced by Elizabeth Thomas, the secretary of party leader

Victor Berger, whose editorials in the German party paper Miss Steichen was translating into English. Miss Steichen had written to acknowledge an earlier letter in which he had enclosed his leaflet "Labor and Politics." In her letter of a week before, she made reference to The Dream Girl: "My hope is that socialism will gradually create an environment favorable to the development of such a Millennial Dream Girl. But meanwhile under capitalism your Dream Girl must be a leisure class product." The actresses are Minnie Maddern Fiske, Bertha Kalich, and Lena Ashwell.

49 | TO PHILIP GREEN WRIGHT

Manitowoc, Wis., Mar. 20, 1908.

Dear Professor:

Enclosed is .50 in stamps—please send a copy of The Dreamer to Lilian Steichen, Princeton, Ill., along with Runes, etc.

Just arrived here from the lumber districts and Fox River towns. Your good letter greets me. The New Zealand enclosure is from a Whitman lover who wants to know whether my lecture is printed. To such I send the Manitowoc Tribune report.

I shall eventually get more of a material compensation for my work. Never had such luck as the past winter, along that line. Have lots of hope and—a number of chances yet left for ringing the bull's eye of fate.—You write calmly and with quietude but under it I know is the poet of you, sub-Vesuvian. I hope we can get together a few days next summer, neither of us having work nor bad colds!

Sometime the Wis. Social-Democrats will be doing things in a lyceum way. That talk you made before the Fairview High School some years ago was the best I've seen of your spoken discourse.

Am head over heels in work up here. It's merely a choice of what handles to take hold of!—All luck to you, old heart.

Fraternally yours,
Sandburg.

Forwarding address now,
248 Wisconsin Avenue,
Oshkosh, Wis.

1908

Sandburg wrote the introduction to Professor Wright's book of poems, The Dreamer. *As Social-Democratic organizer in the Lake Shore and Fox River Valley district, he was constantly on the move in Wisconsin.*

50 | TO LILIAN STEICHEN

Manitowoc, Wisconsin, March 21, 1908

Dear girl:—I will look for you on the 4:45 P.M. at the C.M. & St. Paul station on Friday the 27th. I expect to have everything cleared up and be ready for anything that can happen, gallows or throne, sky or sea-bottom! Yours Thoughtfully alias Paus'l will be dictator and mistress of ceremonies. You will announce the events and the gladiators will gladiate like blazes! The joy-bells on high will clang like joy. Motley will have vent and psalms will be sung and three or four peans will go up to the stars out of pure gladiosity.—I believe you asked about my cussedness. This is some of it. I am cussedest when I am glad, and so are those around me. Admonish me gently to behave and I may or I may not. For what ever is in must come out. That is the snub and sumstance of expression and great is expression.—I promise tho, that while we are on the cars and respectable people who pride themselves on demeanor are about, I will not, "Rah! rah rah!" nor sing "The mother was chasing her boy round the room" with all forty four verses. / Thus much is certain. The honorific norm of dignity shall have recognizance, all it wants. —As we pass triumphantly, we shall leave the leavings.—Haven't had anything, never touch anything. Just glad, L.S., just glad, that's all! that's all!

Well, what do you think of a paper on Love—from me—me going in on this age-old subject and grappling, juggling and tossing the theme like the strong man at the circus with the iron balls. You started it! You started it! That will be one answer to any reproach you may utter that I pontificate unduly.—Honest tho, I rather like it. A few months of rest and then some retouching and it may compete with Virginibus Puerisque, etc.

So interesting a brother you have! The letter gives me a glimpse

61

of him. "My tricks and carelessness" how naturally that drops from him—with those he loves confessing a little waywardness, knowing they love him for it.

Will you bring along and wear once that Graeco-Gothic white thing you have on in that picture? Just frinstance!

When you rebuke me on the gibbosity of this letter—for these are awful babblings—and chide me for gayety that spills and splashes—I shall take refuge in the authority of your Richard Wagner, the man who wrote operas occa. Rebuke not too rebukingly for Wagner is explicit on the point. I will quote it on the way out of Brookfield.—

To Her Thoughtfulness alias Pausl—

from
C.S.*

* Such as he is.

This letter was in response to an invitation from Miss Steichen to meet her family at the little "farm" at Menominee Falls, when she was home for the spring vacation. It was at the time of this visit that they decided to marry.

51 | TO LILIAN PAULA STEICHEN

[Two Rivers, Wisconsin]
Monday [April 20, 1908]

At last I have found it—a book tt comes near expressing my socialism. "Hurrah for Jaurès!" I knew he was much to the good but I had no idea so great oratory, with so fair logic, serious facts, & sublime sentiment, was in the world-movement anywhere. His oratory I know of scarce anything else to compare with—& his written papers, they please me. He has *sentiment,* Paula. Sentiment!

In so many, so sadly many, socialist souls, the facts of science buzz on the window-pane and the roses of sentiment never flower. Good-will, something of faith tt is fine, this Wis. movement has, but the sentiment, ardor, flowing, glowing enthusiasm of Jaurès—not yet.

1908

Who in the American movement has dared to write on the topic, "Moonlight"? J. is the only sclst writer, aside from C. S., who matches you, Lilian, in exclamation points!

Jaurès! The S-S greets you!

In this letter to Miss Steichen examples of Sandburg's shorthand appear: tt for that; sclst for Socialist. The S-S stood for Sandburg-Steichen. Jean Jaurès (1859-1914) was a French Socialist who sided with Dreyfus and, as a journalist, helped to expose the case. After his visit to the Steichen farm, Sandburg began calling Miss Steichen "Paula," inspired by her family's nickname of Paus'l.

52 | TO LILIAN PAULA STEICHEN

[Two Rivers, Wisconsin]
Thursday night—10 P.M. [April 23, 1908]

Back from a long hike again—sand and shore, night and stars and this restless inland sea—Plunging white horses in a forever recoiling Pickett's charge at Gettysburg—On the left a ridge of jaggedly outlined pines, their zigzag jutting up into a steel-grey sky —under me and ahead a long brown swath of sand—to the right the ever-repelled but incessantly charging white horses and beyond an expanse of dark—but over all, sweeping platoons of unguessable stars! Stars everywhere! Blinking, shy-hiding gleams—blazing, effulgent beacons—an infinite, travelling caravanserie—going somewhere! "Hail!" I called. "Hail!—do you know? do you know? You veering cotillions of worlds beyond this world—you marching, imperturbable splendors—you serene, everlasting spectators—where are we going? do you know?" And the answer came back, "No, we don't know and what's more, we don't care!" And I called, "You answer well. For you are time and space—you are tomb and cradle. Forever you renew your own origin, shatter to-day and reshape to-morrow, in a perpetual poem of transformations, knowing no goal, expecting no climax, looking forward to no end, indulging in no conception of a finale, content to move in the eternal drama on which no curtain will be rung. You answer well. I salute you to-night. I will see you again and when I do again I will salute you for you are sincere. I believe you O stars! and I know you! We have met before and met many times. We will meet again and meet many times."—All this time I was striding along at a fast pace, to the music of the merry-men. The merry-men, I forgot to explain, ride the white horses and it is the merry-men who give voice to the ecstasy and anger and varying humor of the sea. The tumultuous rhythms of the merry-men and a steady ozone-laden wind led me to walk fast and when I turned from the sea, there burst on my vision, the garish arc-lamps of the municipality of Two Rivers. So I turned to the sky and said, "Good-by, sweet stars! I have had a good companionship with you to-night but now I must leave starland, and enter the corporation limits of Two Rivers town. Remember me, O stars! and remember Paula down in Princeton, Illinois! and if any agitators appear in star-land, let them agitate—it will be good for them and for all the little stars." And as I plodded down a narrow street fast past the hovels of fishermen and the tenements of factory workers, I quoted from the bare-footed, immortal Athenian, "The gods are on high Olympus—let them stay there." Yes, let the gods who are on high Olympus stay where they belong. And let us turn to the business of rearing on earth a race of gods.

There—it's out of me, Pal. It was a glorious hike. I shall sleep and sleep to-night. And you are near to-night—so near and so dear— a good-night kiss to you—great-heart—good lips—and good eyes— My Lilian—

Carl

P.S.P.S.S!—No, I will never get the letter written and finished. It will always need postscripts. I end one and six minutes after have to send more. All my life I must write at this letter—this letter of love to the great woman who came and knew and loved. All my life this must go on! The idea and the emotion are so vast it will be years and years in issuing. Ten thousand love-birds, sweet throated and red-plumed, were in my soul, in the garden of my under-life. There on ten thousand branches they slept as in night-time. You came and they awoke. For a moment they fluttered distractedly in joy at stars and odors and breezes. And a dawn burst on them—a long night was ended. God! how they sang. God! the music of those throats—such dulcets and diapasons of song as they sang! I hear them & I know them. These birds want freedom. These imprisoned songsters are all to be loosed. But I can let out only one at a time. Each letter, then, is some joy till now jailed—but now sent flying—and flying and flying!—at the touch of release, called out by the woman who came.

So Paula, you have letters and letters to come—and we will send birds, love-birds with love-songs flying out over the world. We cannot live the sheltered life, with any bars up. It is us for the open road—loosing the birds!—loosing the birds!

Jesus wept, Voltaire smiled, William Morris worked, the S-S flung the world twenty-thousand beautiful, vibrating, fleeting, indomitable, happy love-birds singing love-songs swelling the world's joy. Even so.

53 | TO LILIAN PAULA STEICHEN

[Two Rivers, Wisconsin]
Friday, May 1, 1908

Paula dear,

I'm going to send you clippings like these from time to time—facts, jokes; plays of wit, short things notable for the simple and direct—put 'em all by—use 'em as you can—An incident, a little story, here and there in a speech, rest both audience and speaker.

I go to Appleton tonight and give my "The Poet of Democracy" to a literary society out on the edge of Appleton—about 30 people of all sorts—mostly indecisive types, "sober and industrious"—the kind the local newspaper says of, when they die, "He was respected in the community and loved by all who knew him. He was kind to his mother."—A sort of deviltry possesses me at times among these—to talk their slangiest slang, speak their homely, beautiful home-speech about all the common things—suddenly run a knife into their snobbery—then swing out into a crag-land of granite and azure where they can't follow but sit motionless following my flight with their eyes—It will be fun at Princeton—I know the stuff will hit

Magill—He will bat his eyes once in a while but he will keep awake! —listening to the man just suited to You!!

I've a lot more of [Bernard] Shaw than [Robert] Blatchford in me. S. is for the centuries, will be remembered with Diogenes and Epictetus. B. is for the decades, will be remembered as a mellower William Lloyd Garrison who fought a good fight and uttered for the average.

And Paula sweet, while the M.A.S. (Mutual Admiration Scty) is in session—S. stands to B. as you stand to May Wood Simons— the S.S. is hill-born, knowing not only all the crops, seasons, and flowers of the valley, but things higher up—stars out on the horizon-rim not seen from the valley—the S.S. is hill-born.

We will both change, and change mightily as the years pass, but all these "assembled parts" of ours that are so much alike will only forever go forward in ever better team-work and -play. I must catch a car!

Love and love—"I throw you a thousand kisses"

Carl

An earlier Whitman lecture was titled "An American Vagabond." "The Poet of Democracy" was his lecture on Walt Whitman. Robert Blatchford wrote Merrie England, *a Socialist book. May Simons, who wrote for the* International Socialist Review, *was the wife of A. M. Simons, its editor.*

54 | TO LILIAN PAULA STEICHEN

[Appleton, Wisconsin]
Saturday [May 2, 1908]

Paula—if you are asked "What is Circumstance?" tell them it's a laundry catching fire of a night and your losing your three best shirts—first time I've been stung that way. Snow on the 1st of May and such wind as brought out only a wee 10 of us to the school-house last night—that was Circumstance, but an Old One. So we called off the Lecture and I took a chair and told them about socialism for 40 minutes and there was a crossfire of questions and answers and they made me feel just a bit sorry for writing to you so about them yesterday. Real souls!

I told Comrade Fox, aside, tt one of the Three Great Facts of Life was to happen to me this summer, apprising him that aforesaid Facts are: Birth, Marriage, Death. He said he knew I had been born and also tt I was not going to die. Then, "Go on, Sandburg, I didn't see how I was going to make it when Hope and I started but when you begin, everything comes around allright." They have a beautiful little home—an extraordinary pair. He's a mail-carrier. I make my home with them when in Appleton.

At the house Fox speaks of a sudden, "Hopie, do you know, there's going to be a Mrs. Sandburg this summer." "Good!" was the instant rejoinder. "And she's a school-teacher, too", whereat he went on in further description of You, whom he has never seen.—This little group (they are three) have a tent in the orchard in the summer—they live on the edge of the town—So we will live out-doors, and work up the Appleton local for a week or more this summer. —Lynn Joseph, a young lawyer at Green Bay, married before he began his law-course at the U. of W.—took bigger chances than we are—so the Green Bay movement will say, "Hurrah!" And [Chester] Wright at the Manitowoc Tribune hasn't turned 25 yet and has been married 2 years.

And James Larsen, a Whitmanic old sea-captain at Marinette, the leader there, is tt combination of poet-philosopher I know will give us blessin'! This beforehand. Afterward, they'll all just smile and say, "No wonder they put out to sea, in such a boat!"

Just saw The Sordid today—a trifle too abstruse for Vanguard readers—nothing about "the means of production and distribution"! —no defiance. The Socialists are too prone to like a man who makes them ejaculate, "Don't he give it to 'em, though?" Uncork the invective!

Paula—I would like to have been with you between acts. We would have analysed Shirley and her "My father's honor—won't you save my father's honor?"

And Paula—on the trolley between here and Appleton I want You—You—to love the purple hills with. They stand up from the shore of Lake Winnebago, hazy and blue-misted—the deeps of me vibrate tremendously to the filmy beauty of it—and I want You—just to be with about it—so—

Good for Ed! And good for the S-S! The S-S has pictures too—how will our exhibition come out? We'll see—we'll see!

Will you send your April Vanguard to Joseffy, 16 Center Ave., Chicago? I'm sending the lone copy I have to Parlette. The copies are all gone at the office.

A few more weeks of The Lie—and then! I'm sending a five with this—it leaves me broke—but I can't raise money when I *have* money—and I'm going to try to have $50 or more for starting. We'll make a compact that all money from literature sales will go into the Baby-Fund—it should range around $15 or $20 a month and increase at that—and I'll turn over come dusk to you every once in a while if not twice, all that there is to spare over our material needs —if we ever save anything, ever have a good bank-account or not—that's up to you, after the stuff is once in—and the stuff will come in, eventually—we are about where Gaesjack was the day before he sauntered into Stieglitz the first time—so—

I now have a "Paula" envelope—all sorts of clippings on Woman and Economics going into it—to be used as you see how. *Plant* that fund of yours where it's absolutely safe—and it's not to be thought of except for last and unforeseen contingencies—call it the Desperation Fund.—The Baby-Fund will grow—and such a Baby! such a Baby as it will be—such a reckless cub—never to hear a "Don't"—learning fire by getting burnt—getting religion and ethics and love-powers from our kiss-in—never knowing *he's* or *she's* being educated—just living and unfolding—such a cub!

Good-bye—a kiss—for now—Paula

7!!! one by one the fingers go down.

Carl

George Fox became a close friend. "The Sordid" was a short essay, published in The Vanguard. *Ralph Parlette was a friend Sandburg met at* The Lyceumite; *Joseffy was a magician. "The Lie" meant that they were living a lie away from each other. Gaesjack was an affectionate family name for Ed—Edward Steichen, the photographer, Paula's brother. They were counting the weeks until the date set for their marriage; "7" stood for seven weeks before that date.*

55 | TO LILIAN PAULA STEICHEN

> [Wisconsin]
> Saturday [May 9, 1908]

Your last two letters to Oshkosh, the Schlgurville letters and the one here, just read!—and read again! What with yesterday afternoon and last night (it was 11:30 for the mother and me) and walking in to M. [Menominee] Falls this morning, and now all these letters and letterettes at the office, I'm all Kaflustrated—the air is all flying ribbons and clashing melodies, warbling birds, brass bands —Ess-esses! wild-circles!

If you could at this late day, swing the lecture, it would count. You see, the gigglers would sit up. The lecture was built in large part to handle a giggling civilization. *Magill's judgement* (!) would be vindicated. An after-interest would be intensified. It might mean return-dates—for one or for a course of three or so next year.—The gigglers are everywhere! The world is Princetonian!—They started when I opened at Hartford. I played them along, softened them into real laughter, and then took them off in a lonely place and hung shot corpses of their dead selves for them. Then I glorified life without giggling—and they gave me an encore—they applauded till I was led up for a final bow.—I made friends for us, when we go there for Socialism.

It's past recall, I guess, getting Magill around again. But if there's a fighting chance, try to swing it.

I will be needed in the convention—was elected 4th alternate— and don't know for sure about Friday or Saturday.—If I go down, I suppose I'll go on to Galesburg for a day or so, perhaps only a few hours.—All busy now, sweet, writing is a rush—will try to get you a note from the boat to-night. You! great great love-heart of a wonder—Lilian

> Carl

Mr. Magill was principal of the high school in Princeton, Illinois, where Miss Steichen taught. Carl and Lilian had hoped that he would agree to have Sandburg lecture on Whitman there, but, sev-

eral days before, she had written, "Mr. Magill is beginning to get scared about your lecture—not about what you'll say—but about the levity there may be in connection with the idea of my future half's giving a speech here!" Her family lived at Menominee Falls. The convention refers to the National Socialist convention, May 10, 1908, in Chicago.

56 | TO LILIAN PAULA STEICHEN

[Wisconsin]
Saturday Evening 6:30 PM
[May 9, 1908]

All ready for the trip to Chi again by boat. This is the 5th time I have made this trip—each time marking varied epochs. And never was life bigger, both with clash and conflict, but with the fine lure of beauty and far stars.

I congratulate myself I weigh 120 pounds more than ever! And the magic of fate!—I look with four eyes—I have twice as many wonderful dreams—and a strange new pair of hands that someway is not so strange and now fumbles around my head and cuffs me and thrills me with little touches.—

Paula—such scriptures as you send to me—throbbing letters—I can't take time to answer all as I want to—But You—You know. —Whenever I write you, meaning Lilian Steichen, as cognomens go, I want to emphasize it, put something into it tt will make it stand out like an electric sign in the night—you!!—so—It was "worth the money" to hear your mother call me "Carl"—You have been doing some sort of educating sure! Gave Berger the point of himself. Nothing direct between us in talk.

Edward Steichen is an artist. We all know our best selves, the selves we love. And he caught a self I pray to be all the time! By what wizardry of sight and penetration, he came to get that phase of me in so little a time, I don't know. It took more than eyes—it took heart and soul back of the eyes.

Such an "infuriating", "thrillingly", "awfully" Elsie Caskey!

There's education to know such a one. You were each other's pace-makers in cussing, I see—a divil—wild two o' yez!

At present looking, some of the Wis. delegates will not be at the convention all the time which will mean, I sit and vote and see and absorb and refrain from expostulation, muttering Paul Jones' "I have not yet begun to fight."

(Lights of red and white along the river flash into the dusk. The water repeats each of them instantly, as tho, "Hello! hello Night!" The materialities may not have a language but they seem almost to talk to each other.)

So I may have to be in Chi Friday and Saturday tho this is not likely. I will let you know as to the outlook. I think Princeton would be the better meeting-place, too. About Wed. or Thurs. we will know.

Miss Thomas is *so* good with me—as tho you had helped her see things—trifles of solicitude she never evinced before.—Is thinking about us. Murmurs a fear tt the district finances will not be large enough (she didn't say for what!) and intimates that I deserve more speaking dates outside the district.

We will do the best we can with what we have to work with. We will surprise them in increase of income. But always the literature sales go to the Emergency Fund—and if the rest is not enough, from elsewhere more will have to come.

Mrs. Gaylord phones things look dark with them now, "Win" being unwell, but they've seen worse, and she laughs in cheer and faith.

Such days! Oshkosh, Hartford, Menominee Falls, Milwaukee, the lake, Chicago and Princeton and you!!

The state convention is June 13—you know?

The prints will get to you Mon or Tues. The real Prince a few days later!—will see the Princess!

You're promoted from Duchess if you want to be—because you can *cuss* so.

It's almost dark, after the boat starts at 8:30, I shall walk and breathe for an hour and then turn in.—

I've got plans and details of plans for several things. We will talk about 'em.

Love to you—Paula—heart—love and love—and kisses on your lips and eyes—Lilian—

Carl

Sandburg and Berger did not always agree on Socialism. Berger opposed Eugene Debs, whom Sandburg favored, at the Socialist party convention. Elsie Caskey was Lilian's roommate and school-teacher friend. Mrs. Gaylord was the wife of Winfield R. Gaylord, a member of the State Executive Board of the Social-Democratic party, Wisconsin.

57 | TO LILIAN PAULA STEICHEN

Milwaukee—Wednesday
[May 13, 1908]

A wonderful spring day with the Spring Song everywhere— a tantalizing laziness over all—while I was in Chi the trees changed some and this morning on the avenues they greeted me with a little unusual haughtiness. We expect to make it up, though.

I am delayed some, in various ways; may not hit Sheboygan till to-morrow—for your messages there!

Several practical things to the advantage of the S. S. are on the move—also to the advantage of the S.D.P. [Social-Democratic party]!

Such hours as we will have with grass and trees and sky! Heart! 'Twas a bit like home, coming into the Northwestern station and seeing the ghost of you near the ticket window there where you passed me the rebuke beautiful.

"Hasn't it been beautiful?"

"No! *Isn't* it beautiful?"

Correct me on any tenses and my moods, Paula—

You!

Love and Love

To Lilian

Carl

1908

[Wisconsin]
Tuesday [May 26, 1908]

The malevolent Fate plotted darkly, but Paula was too quick.—
First, some other Fate mixed up with Fate No. 1 and your letter
of the 18th which should have reached me Sunday, was given me
yesterday.—And this morning, at 8:30 I get one that left your
dear hands only yesterday afternoon. You've got *despatch*—momentum—go—and yet you're not a hurrying hustler—You're a Wonder!
my thaumaturgist!

About the non-essentials—I like your picture of the wedding
doings at the farm—it would please your mother better probably
than any other plan—I had thought of our taking a car out to
[Carl D.] Thompson or [Winfield] Gaylord—get the knot tied
much as we might wash our hands at a wayside hotel—a few minutes chat—a stop and chat at T. or G., whichever lost the toss (!)
attend to business and greetings at headquarters and then ho! north-
ward!—But the farm picture is a lark, and so simply gay—that may
be best—I leave that with you and the dear Mother. If Joseffy has no
Chautauqua dates there, I will have him on hand, with the skull of
Balsamo, and the violin.—

My folks I shall calmly inform when it is all over. Merely more
of the unexpected which they regularly expect! Charlie has been so
queer in his tastes—they will look so and so at you when we go
to Galesburg one day! Gee! that will be fun—and downtown and
at the college they will look and they will find you baffling and only
sense something of power and beauty and wisdom and love—something as far-off and cross-textured as my poetry and warm and open
as myself. They won't understand you anymore than me—but they
will love you—yes, you will be good for them! A few, a precious
few, homely and yearning—so yearning—will understand. My
mother out of her big, yearning, hungry heart will hug you before
you leave and with a crystal of tears will find the soul of you. Mary
and Esther and Martha will all like you deep—but they have not

starved so hard nor prayed so vainly—they will get only sides of you. We should have a whole day with Wright (The Dreamer) of Asgard—he will do us a poem!

I shall save Green Bay and Marinette and Sturgeon Bay for The Honeymoon, inasmuch as we recognize some spectral validity in a wedding we must also concede a period of time immediately following a wedding known as a honeymoon. It is a shooting the chutes and at the bottom is The First Disgust. At the end of the honeymoon, they have found out which is absolute and to be obeyed. One subtly or outrightly domineers, the other similarly and synchronously submits—Or, there are sweeping northwesterly winds and storms in which this and that is torn up or broken down and flung windward while the wind whistles like anguish, despair and foiled hope. This condition, commonly known as hell, is followed by drought, monotony, a little dreariness, and then a capitulation to breakfast dinner and supper. Smiles are put on and taken off like wearing apparel. The hell-fires of revolt freeze over into strange, smooth, stupid satisfaction. Once a year on some wild night, the lurking rat of regret gnaws a hole into a calloused heart and tremulous lips give a cry, "Life cheated us! life cheated us! Something is lost! Something precious and wonderful is gone and will never come back!" But a little sleep, a little slumber, and a breakfast of buckwheat cakes and pork sausage and greenish coffee—and the gnawing is quiet for another year. The consolation is, "What does it matter? Everybody does it!"—Yes, we will call it a honeymoon and then we will have done with concessions to society. We will do our own christening and baptizing and if it ever comes to funerals, we're likely to call in Clarence Darrow the Agnostic or Father Vaughan the gentle priest who is bigger than the Catholic Church or a Xtian Scientist friend or just read a few lines of Whitman ourselves and let it go at that—living the calm and simple.—The district has so much of natural beauty, Lilian. That was one of the things attracted me up here. All nationalities are represented in it. You will find wilderness unspoiled in Oconto. You will find civilization at its best and worst along the Fox River—black, choking industrialism, and libraries, concerts, women's clubs, and art from Schumann-

Heink to 5¢ vaudeville. All big, pulsing, turbulent, panoramic! I have for it all the passion and enthusiasm Walt had for

> "Proud, mad city! my city!
> O Manahatta! My Manahatta!"

And all our efforts, dear, will be cumulative—the more we do the more we can do along any line. Our income will always be on the increase. Continued agitation and organization will familiarize us intimately with the various situations making us increasingly competent to advise, guide and direct the comrades. Loyal, wholehearted friends, like bitter, implacable enemies, will constantly multiply.—Such a trip as it will be, dear love-pal,—Mate—Woman! Sweetheart!—proud, beautiful Lilian!

Carl

Father Vaughan was the understanding priest who comforted Mrs. Steichen when her daughter broke with the Catholic church.

59 | TO LILIAN PAULA STEICHEN

[Wisconsin]
[June 5, 1908]

It's 4 o'clock, Paula, Friday morning. I have been plugging away since six o'clock last night—on the best thing I've done yet—the letter to Dear Bill—the homeliest, fairest, beautifullest piece of socialist literature, the nearest thing to Merrie England, yet done! Cuff the braggart, Paula!

A kiss to you—and now for sleep—

Cully.

You and Your Job *was written in the form of a letter to "Dear Bill." Robert Blatchford used this form in his book on Socialism, Merrie England.*

60 | TO LILIAN PAULA STEICHEN

Oshkosh—6/10/'08

Am staying over here because I had openings with the unionists. Was before the electrical workers last night and will have an hour with the trades council to-night.—I send along Miss T's letter. She's just a bit afraid I'm not up on fundamentals. So she explains that I am not headed nor' by east but nor' by nor'east!

O ho! Kitty Malone—3 days—3 days!—Oho! you'll be put to it—hard put to it again—no good to run nor dodge—you will find yourself surrounded so you can't get away—

Love—And Love—

Mickey

P.S.—I send an MSS—don't know just what it's worth—may send it to mags that pay for stuff bfr letting the Soc's have it. Enclosed is Three. And Kitty, Honorable High Turnkey of the Exchequer, Kitty, be careful how you give me money—I am "a son of fantastical fortune" and a spender. We will buy what we need. The rest goes into your hands. Now, having sent you all my money but fifty cents, I have incentive to hustle.

Soon—I see your lips and eyes again—and the Two of Us call out, "Look who's here!"

> *Miss T was Elizabeth Thomas, secretary of the Wisconsin Social Democratic party. Sandburg had given Lilian Steichen different names for various moods, and "Kitty Malone" meant a merry girl. In three days they would meet at the Wisconsin Social Democratic Convention, held on June 13 and 14, 1908. They were married on June 15, 1908.*

1908

[Oshkosh, Wisconsin]
September 9, 1908

Paula:

Will you go over that Dear Bill and get it in MSS shape for Kerr? So we can work on it together when I arrive on the 25th or the 26th?

I miss you—but it's just sort of abstractly—you are so near! Always! Always! For you, I find myself muttering gratitude and prayer of a kind—so utterly superb you are

Carl

P.S. Here's letter to Kerr with envelope. Send on.

The "Dear Bill" referred to the Sandburg pamphlet You and Your Job, *a letter on employment and the worker from a Socialist viewpoint. It was published by Charles H. Kerr & Co., of Chicago, which specialized in Socialist works.*

62 | TO PAULA SANDBURG

Manitowoc, Wis., 9/22 [1908]

Paula:

Your two big letters at Appleton gotten and taken and fed on. —Have just sent [Frederick] Heath notes on Fond du Lac Meeting, to be added to yours of last week. Heath is a slow one.—I am finding people like to see your name signed to stuff!—Have cancelled the date for Mishicot and will meet the Red Special tomorrow at Green Bay. Wish you could be along. Wishin' 'n wishin' lots O' things these days!—Am in Manitowoc the 24th, Kaukana the 25th; Oshkosh the 26th and 27th; Campbellsport the 28th; West Bend the 29th. Then for Menominee Falls and The Wonder-Girl!—I inclose Larsen's last letter. Write him, if time allows, mentioning that I haven't schedule made out but will make Marinette about the second week in October.—Here's the Kerr letter.—Next week the Physical Director takes charge again. And we talk over heaps of things.— Paula, I have actually got some of those letters answered, despite poetry, etc. Capt. Jack's Broncho Book is sure a buster. And [Robert] Ingersoll on Whitman is a precious thing, a treasure.

Always you're with me—dearest—such a wonder-girl. Turning pages we are, leaf on leaf together—Together!

Carl & Paula

Captain Frederick Larsen was a former Chicago alderman, and a Socialist leader, in Marinette, Wisconsin. The dates refer to the "Red Special" train stopovers when Sandburg campaigned with Eugene V. Debs, the Socialist candidate for President. The "Red Special" was the idea of Mahlon Barnes, Debs's campaign manager. It was a locomotive and sleeping car, loaded with Socialist literature and campaign material, and carried Debs across the country on speaking tours. The Physical Director referred to Paula.

63 | TO PAULA SANDBURG

Aboard Red Special—9/24, [1908]—Green Bay, [Wisconsin]

Paula:

All tumbled and hurried and dusty, here we are. The success of the Train has been understated, if anything.

Debs is superb. Crowded house, all kinds of enthusiasm.

Fine bunch aboard the Train. Lapworth, the Englishman is very interesting. He's Hunter's secretary, you know—has done much of Hunter's writing—so. Remembered Ed [Steichen] very well, and re-greeted me and congratulated, on learning of the June proceedings of You and Me. More later along this line!

Will sleep on the Train to-night—not very restfully, but hell, the revolution tingles and whirls around here.

Love and love to Paula—you!

Carl

64 | TO PAULA SANDBURG

[Aboard Red Special]
Sunday—Oshkosh
[September 27, 1908]

Dearest:—

I will make Granville, Wednesday—probably on the morning train—surely by the afternoon.—

Couldn't make Kaukana. Hope to get that letter here in the morning.—Your Oshkosh letter was forwarded to Appleton; they ignore your scribblings on envelopes!

It has been fight & fight lately—inside the organization.

Debs is superb. His face & voice are with me yet. A lover of humanity. Such a light as shines from him—and such a fire as burns in him—he is of a poet breed, hardened for war. Paula & I will see more of Debs.

I can't talk about myself or anything tonight. Think very cheaply about everything. I am going out into the mist and wind.— A throwback from over-reaching, being too serious, too deeply wistful—"wanting and wanting and always wanting."—

Carl

65 | TO PAULA SANDBURG

[Milwaukee, Wisconsin]
Tuesday night November 10, 1908

Owing to my suit case having gone astray temporarily, thru error of a new bell-boy, I leave here for Chi on the 9:00 instead of the 7:20.

Just had a long talk, and fried ham, with Thompson.—It has been this monkeying with platform work that has kept me from fully catching the organization situation. Oshkosh, Fond du Lac and Milwaukee, these two days, make me feel sure of the winter situation for Lilian & Carl—the S-S.

If you can work up a 10- or 15-minute talk in German on Socialism, also a 15- or 20- or 30-minute speech in English, we will enjoy some team-work in public once in a while.—Don't strain, but if the mood lures you, go to it, Paula.

Here is Wine—for the wine we did not have with the fried ham to-night—Here is Wine!—the dear, beautiful S-S vintage of 1908—You—

Cully

Carl D. Thompson was a national committeeman and a state officer of the Wisconsin Social Democratic party.

66 | TO PAULA SANDBURG

Chicago
Sat. night Nov. 21, 1908

Beethoven & Lizst tonight—and Paula was along every minute —her big heart thudding next to mine—like mad—S-S madness!— our duet!

Shall hear Lewis in the morning, Chaminade in the afternoon, Beveridge in the evening—some business Monday and then back to Wisconsin—Just as soon as I have some definite line on when I arrive in A. [Appleton]—back at The Rooms—back with Paula.

I will write.

Take care of yourself—dearest—wonder-girl—You—

Whenever the big things beat and whirl around me—I reach toward You—Paula is along—brave, passionate, seeing, with her own quiet magnificence—

—WINE—

Carl

Arthur Morrow Lewis was a Socialist speaker who lectured on Sunday mornings at the Garrick Theater in Chicago. Cécile Chaminade was a French pianist. Albert J. Beveridge was a politician and author.

1908

Darlington, Wisconsin
[November, 1908]

Paula dearest—

It has been nip and tuck and come and go—and always guarding the cold.—Have been up against forty different combinations, new ones every day, but now I am the best yet. Have been eating two light meals a day—seeing and hearing lots of things tt I am putting away for when the Snugglers are together again for love and chum-talk.

I must remember to send tt $30 by to-morrow. Will mail it to M. [Menominee] Falls. Mrs. Moore rather expected you in Monroe. They all remembered and asked about you.

That's a good suggestion about socks, Paula—Little Feet is so thoughtful far away about Big Feet!

Kisses and love—my girl!

Carl

On train to Brodhead
[Circa Nov. 28, 1908]

Dear Snuggler: The cold comes along fairly well. I ate 4 oranges Thurs. noon, milk toast and boiled eggs in the evening. Nothing more till this noon at Bdhd—About 150 out at Racine. The unionists very pleased. Dozing on trains and at the Globe yesterday afternoon I thought of forty different teasing beautiful things to write Snuggler but they have slipped out of my head. But they will keep!

I hope you have quit your kid talk for the time being. Don't say "besults" or "besponsible." It belongs only in the ritual of the Grand Secret Order of Snugglers—S. S.!

I got some playground slides of Martin at Racine so tt all told I have now a splendid series for lantern work.

Before leaving Bdhd I will mail you a money order so you can go ahead with the new nest. I hope you can get it fixed up by Xmas so we can go in the day after Xmas day and I can get ready for Mich. But remember to build up and keep well. You are "besponsible" only to Cully. On the next sheets is the route as finally determined.

Carl

69 | TO REUBEN W. BOROUGH

Appleton, Wis., Dec. 7, 1908.

Dear old Pal:—

Your LONG letter just at hand. Am going down with some mail and must send you this with it. So good and chatty a letter you send I must get this to you.

I am dated for Medina [Ohio] on December 14 and Douglas, Michigan, on December 16. Medina I have found on the map—over near Toledo. Douglas I am not sure about—I suppose it is the one over in Allegan County, near Grand Haven. Another date may be arranged for me—tho this is not probable. Looking over the map (I have not made out my route nor looked up time tables yet) it seems as though I will pass through or near Marshall. I shall make an attempt at stopping off at Jackson and seeing one Elmer Marshall there, who booked me for these dates.

I hope we will get together. Will write you my route so soon as I know. It will be fine to see you again—even if we can't go swimming and listen to the call of the wild.

Yours always,
Sandy.

70 | TO PAULA SANDBURG

Prairie du Chien, Wisconsin
[Circa January, 1909]

Dearest—the good little notes that fall into my hands at post-offices are so Paula-like and good to have—We are going to enjoy the next, I'm sure—I got Everybody's for Jan and am saving it for you. The leader article by Ernest Poole titled "The Blind Revolutionist" is one of the titanic, throbbing, kaleidoscopic and colossal things of American writings—

Levi Bancroft, president of the Wis. Senate, is to be chairman of the tub. meeting at Richland Center. I am interested to meet him and take his size.—And then, in a few days I will take Paula's size—my arms measuring Paula—Oho!

Carl

Sandburg lectured for the Anti-Tuberculosis League in forty-five cities through Wisconsin. Mrs. Sandburg also lectured in some of these places. In September, 1909, Sandburg wrote an article on tuberculosis for La Follette's Weekly.

71 | TO PAULA SANDBURG

[Milwaukee, Wisconsin]
Monday night. [Circa January, 1909]

It is 10:30—just in from Chi.—back again!—nearing Paula!—Paula in claspable and seizurable form!!

Ran across The Bear on 5th Ave., said he'd be going back on this train but he wasn't on. He looked tired & cussed freely & negligibly.

Had lunch with [Charles] Kerr & was instructed that I should post up on historical materialism from you.—Rodriguez & [Alfred] Mance & Haver at the Daily [Socialist] office.—And had a fine hour with Joe [Joseffy] at Steinway before leaving.

By to-morrow night I hope to write you when I arrive in Appleton. It will probably be Wed. night or Thurs. morning.

Kisses—and love—and love—dear eyes—and dear heart.

Carl

"The Bear" referred to Victor Berger. William E. Rodriguez was a Socialist who served as a Chicago alderman from 1915 to 1918.

1909

[Pittsburgh, Pennsylvania]
Monday night—12 o'clock [February 16, 1909]

Just back from Mars! You have been on Earth, but, have you been to Mars?

O the poetry and romance over this Pittsburg town! Slopes and hillsides dotted with electric lights twinkling bluish and flashing long banners of gleam along the river—and every once in a while we pass shadowy hulking sheds with yellow hell-mouths flaming—and the grim steel workers moving around like devils put to use.

Mars—God help Mars!—in the church where I lectured on *Walt Whitman,* they had last night just closed 3 weeks of rioting, drunken, emotional revivalism. They all listened finely and laughed in the right places, and the Methodist preacher was all aglow throughout, one of the inspiring auditors, but—Jesus wept—3 weeks! How could I overcome such a hoodoo in one night?

Just back here—such a glory-letter you send me—such plans you chant—such idolatry you cherish and evoke—

Joseffy has given me some fur stuff, *rare* quality, for a collar for *You.*—Oma got on at Granville and poured out a torrent of speech the way to Milwaukee. Is now a bit more adjusted to the "3 acres and liberty" idea. Is inclined to get an incubator and test the scheme herself before fully endorsing us.

My address will probably best be here, at the hotel, I come in and go out of Ptsbgh every day except Thursday this week!—Except to hit Chi. next Sunday. Wrote to the Spectator there. Have Thursday open here, will probably go thru some steel plant.

Love and love to Paula
Carl

*"Oma" and "Opa"—Luxemburg terms for Grandma and Grandpa—
were the names for Paula's mother and father.*

Appleton, Wis., March 12, 1909

To the Editor of the Mirror:

You are most naive and assumptive in running your finger along all American books of fiction, and picking out the lone, shadowy Hester Prynne as the only memorable woman in all our fictive art.

Have you never been through Frank Norris' "The Octopus," and come to know *Hilda?* She is a real, a vital creation.

In each of David Graham Phillips' novels, "The Deluge," and "Joshua Craig," is a living woman, an individual limned clear as in life.

We are in a bad way in some features of our art-life in America, but out of this melting-pot of the nations some things of worth are arising.

It was from *The Mirror* itself that I clipped, some two years or so ago, a poem by Bliss Carman, entitled, "A Lyric," beginning—

O once I could not understand
The sob within the throat of spring,
The shrilling of the frogs,
Nor why the birds so passionately sing
But that was before your beauty came.

I will put this in total against any alleged love-lyric in English for beauty, ardor, form, and the qualities going toward what you call a "perfect love-lyric."

But go ahead, Brother. The pages of *The Mirror* are as full of errors as the flowing talk of a healthy, normal, aspiring man. You lack the damnable gift of spinning delicate distinctions that lead a winding route to nowhere.

Yours, always,
Charles Sandburg

William Marion Reedy published Reedy's Mirror, *a liberal paper, in which he charged that America had achieved "mighty little literature, in more than one hundred and thirty years of nationality, writing and love-making." This is Sandburg's answer to the charge.*

1909

[Appleton, Wisconsin]
[May, 1909]

Dear Esther:

Just a little word to say I have thought of you and gay Martha Sandburg time and again since I last wrote you—more times than there are tulips and leaves on that tulip-tree in front of our house. The tulips are out in their glory now, I suppose,—kissing the south-wind and pouting at the north-wind. And they are awful gossips, —those tulips. Used to tell me all kinds of things when I sat in my room scratching my head for an idea for the [Lombard] Review. And they talk much more wisely than many girls do—try to have a chat with them and see.

A kiss to you and Martha, and one for Mamma—and Mary too, —she's home now.

Charlie.

[Milwaukee]
Monday 3 PM [June 7, 1909]

Paula dear: Have just come from Kroeger's. Will start in as ad-man Wednesday morning, at $20 per week.—

Don't pay rent for the next week till you hear from me. I will have word for you by the Tuesday night mail, as to what farther develops. It is a try-out at Krgrs. I don't know whether they will let their old man go this week or not. They may intend to try me while still holding him but I don't think so. They didn't like it that I had no references or previous experience in store advertising. Took me on my bluff!—It will be a better job than reporting.—

Only I wish you were here!

Carl

1909

Milwaukee, Wisconsin
Monday night [June 7, 1909]

Paula dear—

I wish I could say how long I will last with Kroegers as I could then tell you positively whether you ought to come on or not. But I can't say. I know I can fill the place better than the sorry has-been I follow. And I don't see where my fall-down can happen. The K. brothers rather like me personally and look for me to be a kind of a bright light around the place. They like my general build and style or they wouldn't have taken a man minus store experience. And I had a long talk with "our" printer—the man who heads the shop where Kroeger Bros. *and I* have our work done—and it seems to me I can swing the things allright and raise hell to the total satisfaction of my German-Jew chiefs. (Ach! a Swede married to a Luxemberger working for German-Jews in an English-speaking commonwealth where not even the streets are common wealth inasmuch as they belong to the automobiles). Having regained our breath after the interruption, we will to our mutton again.—

The chances are all that I will make good. But I don't feel warranted in asking you to pack in the terrific hurry that would be required to make the 4:55 from B.D. [Beaver Dam] Tues PM. And if you stay over Tues you are practically committed for a week's rent. So, I guess the best is for you to leisurely begin getting our stuff together, ready for shipping.—It may be tt K. Bros.' plan is to look me over between Wed and Sat night and if the looking is favorable, then fire the other man Sat. What I fail to see is how they can look me over if the other man is going to hold down the adv office, how they can test my work. If they fire the other man Wed. or Thur. or so, I will let you know—it will help us read the signboard of Things-that-ought-to-be-done. So. I miss you so, Kitty. And I want you so, Kitty.—But your dear great chum-heart is near me.—It was a dear letter I got here.

Take lots of sun and wind for yours, Girl—lots of the big open

—Big simple thoughts and big simple glories are yours. Keep them fresh for Paula's sake and for

Carl

P.S. I am down to $3.00 of cash—if you can send one or two dollar bills in your next letter, well and good. It may be skimping for me by Sat night.

77 | TO PAULA SANDBURG

[Milwaukee, Wisconsin]
Tuesday, 2 PM [June 8, 1909]

Nothing new, Paula dearest, tt makes me able to say when you should come on.—I've rented a room at $1.50 per week, midway between Kroegers and *our* printer, two blks from each, near Nat'n'l Ave., I don't know what street! Address me at Kroegers.—Yesterday afternoon and today I have been rambling over and back and thru all the dept. stores in the city, and buying armfuls of papers and studying ads and reading signs. Some phases of the job will be very pleasant, as I will be very much A Boss, as to when and how I do most of the work.

Went to the Majestic last night. I wished for Paula. There was one sketch Alicesque and Paula would have rippled. To-night I turn in at Beaver Dam hours and report at 8 in the morning.

To-morrow night I shall write you a note giving the latest, probably telling you to get here quick.

Ask about the U. & U. [Underwood & Underwood] express package. Find out whether they will hold it 60 days. Otherwise we will have to write U. & U. to instruct them.

The apart-days aren't for long now, that's sure. To Paula

Carl

78 | TO PAULA SANDBURG

[Milwaukee, Wisconsin]
Tuesday, Bulletin No. 2   6:30 PM.
[June 8, 1909]

They will fire the other man in the morning and begin taking their chances with me.—When you land here (at such time as fate decides you should land) we can both use the room I have now till we get another—there is a plenty thereabouts.—Delicatessens, dairy lunches, moving pictures, all kinds of things to keep Paula's eyes open.

Your letter (with Ed's enclosed) given me at the Globe. I wish I could have seen the comedy entitled "Mrs. Wms. Cow." If we didn't know them as we do I would pass the story on to some of the papers—so tragically funny!—I have walked six or more miles today. Had lots of good sun. Think I will have all the news I need for the start.—Maybe we are on our way to a little land and a living. Already we have much love and a little living. The little land we want will come—Paula dearest!

Carl

79 | TO PAULA SANDBURG

[Milwaukee, Wisconsin]
Wednesday night. [June 9, 1909]

Back from the first day with the store tt tries to please you. The dept. heads send me in the news from their fields. I edit this store news for a Bargain Circular issued twice a week. Four other days of the week there is copy to prepare for 3 dailies—also 3 weeklies—(all the weeklies Catholic!). I write what is to go on the window show-cards, I keep records of what advertising goes to the papers and how many inches each department gets in total. I am quite a cog in the machine if I make good. W.J.K. says when I have demonstrated this there will be from $1000 to $2000 a year in it. That is to say, they will either raise my pay or fire me within a few weeks. At present, I can't see how I would fail to make good. Not a part of the Kroeger Store publicity machine puzzles me—and I will improve some parts of it to good effect. It beats newspaper work of most kinds. The only fault is it may be a little hard on my eyes. But with Paula here and right living, I think not.

So I'm going to say: If you don't hear from me on the Thursday night mail at B.D. [Beaver Dam] then *come on* here! *Come on, Paula!*

If no countermand reaches you, no word tt some other course is better, then pack and skiddoo—flit from B.D. and get here as quick as you can—I'm looking for you—I want you—you are needed —you Wonder Girl!

Carl

I am rooming at 330 Hanover St. Ask for Mrs. Lahey—tell her who you are. I am home morning, noon, evening.

P.S. And Paula, this landlady of mine can TALK; speech flows from her like the waters of a perennial spring into a babbling brook; it is pure, ingenuous patter that gushes along with statement, proof, summary, repetition, paraphrase, asseveration, disclaimer, antithesis. Such inconceivable blarney about a battered brick house in a respectable neighborhood!—But (the plot thickens) I would like to see her matched against Oma. I will bet on Mrs. Lahey. She could subdue Oma! She would deprive Oma of all her laurels! Wait till you glimpse this discursive, proclamative, loquacious body.

Carl

80 | TO PAULA SANDBURG

[Milwaukee, Wisconsin]
Thursday noon [June 10, 1909]

Your letter with the Journals came this morning.—Come on, Paula!—

I am going to see the Journal man in a day or two. It can all be talked over better than written.—It is settled we will hold down Milwaukee a few months anyway.—Come on, Paula!

And lest you forget—Come on, Paula!

Carl

Special reductions!—Great Sample Sale!—By God!—Low Prices! Terrific selling!—Jesus wept!—Buy from us!—Quality, goddamn it, & prices, O Hell!—Sacrifice Sale!! Sacrifice! Great Offerings! Holy Mother of God!!! Buy of us—Purchase here—for Christ's sake!!!!!

81 | TO PAULA SANDBURG

[Milwaukee, Wisconsin]
Tuesday afternoon [Circa April, 1910]

Dearest:

It was good to hear you over the phone. I forgot to tell you that the S-S now have a guitar and there will be songs warbled and melodies whistled to the low Mexican thrumming of Paula-and-Cully's new stringed instrument.

The bungalow is all out of order. I don't eat anything at home and I am cultivating the philosophy of a lodger in a Furnished Room and I am sure it will be good for you and for me when you come back.

And speaking of "coming back", this is a very important matter and should not be neglected. Unless we have further communication, that is to say, no matter how our letters get crossed and mail service fails us, the Time is 9 A.M. next Friday, the Place is the St. Paul station, the Girl is Paula.

Carl

82 | TO REUBEN W. BOROUGH

Milwaukee, May 5, 1910.

Dear Rube:—

Your good letter here. Please remember the "Welcome" sign is out for you on the City Hall tower and remember that you ought to use your Wisconsin home, which is my house, just as I have used my Michigan home, which is your house. I will show you City Hall. The Wonder Girl will show you 200 fluffy chicks she has chaperoned out of eggdom.

> Yours faithfully,
> Sandy.

After the election of Socialist Emil Seidel as mayor of Milwaukee in April 1910, Sandburg became his private secretary. Rube Borough, reporting the Socialist victory, stayed at Sandburg's home.

83 | TO REUBEN W. BOROUGH

> Milwaukee, April 15, 1911.

Dear Rube:—

Many, many thanks for a word from you. Almost methought some terrible desolation had overcome you. The possibility of your coming here in case we get a daily sounds mighty good. There is hardly any doubt we will have one going during the campaign a year from now. We want it so well established when it starts that it won't be a drain but a help to the organization. You are just the kind of a man will be needed. We will make that daily an American institution!

Perhaps you know I was shifted from Seidel's office to the Herald at my request. The Herald has been weak, failing to present many of our strongest points. So I am a sort of administration editor, or S.D.P. publicity man, writing about a page and two columns a week—hurling the shrapnel into the Daily Liars, &c.

We expect to have a little red, babbling heir-apparent arrive this summer, June. He (or she) will constitute our vacation, probably. So it will be up to you and Laura to visit us, about August or so. More about this later. Be sure to write again.

> Yours always,
> Sandy.

Sandburg became city editor of the Social Democratic Herald, *the party paper in Milwaukee.*

84 | TO REUBEN W. BOROUGH

Milwaukee, June 3, 1911.

Rube:—

Arrived this morning—a girl and a wonder—everybody all to the good.

Sandy.

85 | TO WALTER P. STROESSER

Milwaukee, August 1, 1912.

Dear Comrade:

I am herewith laying before you certain facts to be used by you in such manner as you may judge proper, to correct misunderstandings that exist in regard to conditions that have obtained and actions that have taken place in relation to The Milwaukee Leader.

In the month of January, 1912, a committee was appointed by Newspaper Writers' Union No. 9 to draw an agreement, this agreement to be submitted to the management of The Leader with a view of having the organized news writers recognized on the same basis as the printers, pressmen, stereotypers, mailers and book-binders in Brisbane hall employed by the Social-Democratic Publishing company. Such an agreement was drawn, ratified by the union, submitted to the business manager. The agreement was not signed at that time the committee being told that it was not advisable. The spring campaign was beginning to rumble and as it got in full swing and every man on the staff had considerable night work during the campaign, the matter of a contract with the publishing company received no attention.

Early in May, another contract was drawn, to be submitted to the business management of the Social-Democratic Publishing company. The one big dominating purpose at that time was to get some kind of an agreement with the publishing company so that the union would be recognized and it could be said that the Social-Democratic Publishing company was operating a closed shop.

Though The Milwaukee Leader has received about fifteen thousand dollars in cash from the labor unions of Milwaukee and many other thousands of dollars from men who believe in the closed shop and who expect The Milwaukee Leader to maintain a closed shop, THE ABSOLUTE FACT IS THAT THE MILWAUKEE LEADER IS NOT TO-DAY A CLOSED SHOP AND DURING ITS EXISTENCE IT HAS NOT MAINTAINED A CLOSED SHOP. The Newspaper Writers' union No. 9 is a party of the International Typographical Union and of the American Federation of Labor and the Wisconsin Federation of Labor, besides having a delegate to the Allied Printing Trades Council and the Federated Trades Council in Milwaukee. The members pay dues and per capita taxes and the feeling was that the Newspaper Writers' union No. 9 was entitled to have a contract with the publishing company on the same basis as the other workers for the company who are organized.

When the contract committee was appointed in early May and a contract drawn to be submitted to the publishing company, NONE OF THE MEMBERS OF THE NEWSPAPER WRITERS' UNION EXPECTED TO HOLD OUT UNCOMPROMISINGLY FOR EVERY POINT IN THE CONTRACT. THE BIG POINT WAS THAT THE MILWAUKEE LEADER SHOULD NOT RUN AN OPEN SHOP AND THAT IT SHOULD RECOGNIZE A GENUINE AND BONA FIDE TRADE UNION.

The only raises in salary provided for in this contract were (1) that the police and district court reporter should be raised from $20 to $22 per week and (2) that the market editor should be raised from $18 to $22 per week. THE TOTAL AMOUNT OF RAISES IN SALARY PROVIDED IN THIS CONTRACT WOULD AMOUNT TO SIX DOLLARS PER WEEK.

One clause in the contract provided that two additions should be made to the staff of The Leader, namely, a news editor and a telegraph editor. Every other newspaper in Milwaukee has such editors and if a newspaper is going to have life in it and actually compete with other newspapers for the reading public, it will be necessary to have such editors. The salaries of these two editors would have amounted to $55 per week. THE MERE STATEMENT OF THIS FACT SHOWS THE FALSEHOOD AND THE MALICIOUS PURPOSE OF ANY PER-SONS WHO TRY TO SHOW THAT A SALARY GRAB WAS ATTEMPTED BY THE UNION.

IF THE CONTRACT HAD BEEN SIGNED BY THE PUBLISHING COMPANY EXACTLY AS FIRST DRAWN BY THE UNION, ONLY TWO MEN ON THE LEADER STAFF WOULD HAVE GOTTEN ANY RAISE OF PAY. THE TOTAL RAISE OF PAY WOULD HAVE BEEN $6 A WEEK FOR THESE TWO MEN, THE POLICE RE-PORTER AND THE MARKET EDITOR. THE FOLLOWING MEN ON THE LEADER STAFF WOULD HAVE KEPT ON WORKING AT THE SAME PAY AS BEFORE: NYE, WRIGHT, MORIARTY, OVIATT, GAYLORD, SANDBURG, O. SMITH, RHODES, AND HOWE. NO RAISES OF PAY OF ANY KIND WERE PROVIDED FOR SO FAR AS THESE MEN WERE CONCERNED.

THE STATEMENT WHICH HAS BEEN WIDELY CIRCULATED THAT THESE MEN WERE ATTEMPTING TO GRAB MORE SALARY FOR THEMSELVES AND WERE ACTUATED BY SELFISHNESS AND THEREFORE DO NOT HAVE THE SOCIALIST SPIRIT IS ONE OF THE MOST UNJUST AND VICIOUS SLANDERS THAT HAS EVER SPREAD IN THE SOCIALIST MOVEMENT IN MILWAUKEE.

At the time in early May when a contract was first drawn to be submitted to the publishing company, it was generally under-stood and it was the idea of the men on The Leader staff that The Leader's deficit was a small one and was not growing. The contract committee was not told and union members were not informed that a deficit of $15,000 existed in The Leader plant, until in June, more than three weeks after the first interview the contract committee had with the management. When it later developed that the deficit was $18,000 with probable chances of further examinations reveal-ing a still higher deficit, the general feeling among the members of Newspaper Writers' Union No. 9 was that all efforts at getting the union recognized with a genuine agreement should be dropped.

An important point that should have statement in this connec-tion is: THE FIRST CONTRACT SUBMITTED TO THE MANAGEMENT OF THE SOCIAL DEMOCRATIC PUBLISHING COMPANY CONTAINED NO POINTS BUT THAT THE UNION WOULD HAVE BEEN GLAD TO DISCUSS AND SOME OF THE DEMANDS WOULD HAVE BEEN GIVEN UP IMMEDIATELY, IF THE LEADER'S FINANCIAL CONDITION HAD BEEN KNOWN. THE FINANCIAL CON-DITION OF THE LEADER, THE FACT THAT IT WAS NEAR THE ROCKS, WAS NOT KNOWN TO MEMBERS OF THE LEADER STAFF JUST AS IT WAS FOR A NUMBER OF WEEKS ABOUT THE SAME TIME UNKNOWN TO MEMBERS OF THE SOCIAL DEMOCRATIC PARTY WHO WOULD HAVE PREFERRED THAT THEY BE INFORMED ON HOW MATTERS STOOD.

The individual socialists who have been victims of the salary grab slander which has been so widely circulated do not need sympathy nor do they ask for any action for themselves at this time for their benefit. These matters are cited for the good of the Milwaukee movement and The Leader in the future. This may, however, be the proper place to say that Chester M. Wright, during several months as city editor of The Leader, did the work of three men each day. C. D. Rhodes, as cartoonist, photographer, and special assignment reporter, did the work of three men during most of his time of service on The Leader.

A VICIOUS THING HAS BEEN THE HABIT OF SOME COMRADES TO MAKE HARSH CRITICISMS OF LEADER EDITORS AND STAFF MEN WITHOUT FACING THEM PERSONALLY TO FIND OUT WHAT THE ACTUAL FACTS AND CONDITIONS WERE.

IF THIS THING CONTINUES IN THE FUTURE, IT IS A SAFE PREDICTION THAT THE LEADER WILL COME FAR SHORT OF WHAT MANY OF THE LOYAL COMRADES ARE WORKING AND FIGHTING FOR.

Yours for Socialism,

CS

Walter P. Stroesser had succeeded Sandburg as secretary to Socialist Mayor Emil Seidel of Milwaukee. Victor Berger's Milwaukee Leader *was a Socialist newspaper which had its union and Socialist problems.*

86 | TO PAULA SANDBURG

[Chicago]
Thursday. [September, 1912]

Dearest:

To-night it is a rain song that's a-calling and a-calling you from The House. It is such a House we have here. During a rain as good as a wilderness.—I am going to bundle some Day Books and send on one day this week—sure. And, honest to God, I am going to write you one good first class letter one of these days—

just wait and see.—You and Marny [Margaret] call me back to the white blossoms that were singing all by themselves a wonderful soft peace this morning. This was their first real day for greetings of the season, a quiet summer opening without any advertising or any invitations but just a burst of hail salutations. They were all heavy with rain drops, sheer white and wild, the sun gleaming rainbows and prisms from them, a pathos of eager living in them. Again, so long for now, Sweetheart.

Carl

87 | TO PAULA SANDBURG

[Chicago]
Thursday [September, 1912]

Paula dearest:—

Now it is only a couple of days till we again maintain our establishment—huh!—a really truly home. And unless some over particular people rake up the leaves, it will be a fine yard for a homecoming celebration. It's been mystically wonderful lately, that backyard, with a half moon through the poplars to the south in a haze, and rustlings, always high or low rustlings on the ground and in the trees, a sort of grand "Hush-hush, child." And as the moon slanted in last night and the incessant rustlings went on softly, I thought that if we are restless and fail to love life big enough, it's because we have been away too much from the moon and the elemental rustlings. The more I think about Jack London and his John Barleycorn fear of the Noseless One and his intimations that Truth is too terrible to hunt down and face, I think he's had too much books and introspected himself too far as a genius. I like better Walt Whitman musing among "ashes of dead soldiers" and talking as tho he knows there is a thing he calls "love", which is a reality finer than "death"—I haven't got room here to work it all out. Sunday we shall go hand in hand. Love now from

Carl

P.S. The Ravenswood station agent says a train leaves Milwaukee 4 p.m., you transfer at Kenosha 4.45, and get off at Ravenswood at 6.25. Unless I hear otherwise I shall look for you on that train. He said that was the only one. If I hear there are others I will meet them, to grab you and Marny.

In 1912 Sandburg moved to Chicago, where he had joined the staff of the Chicago Evening World, *a new Socialist paper that folded by the end of the year.*

88 | TO WILLIAM LEISERSON

Chicago, Feb. 8, 1913.

Dear Bill:

Herewith you will observe I am knocking out a letter, shaping forth a communication to you, conveying salutations, and shipping by parcel post my wishes for you that all the gods of luck are with you and yours. . . Since the end of The World last December and checks for two weeks wages never cashed and tribulations various and unique at that time, I have been working for the Day Book. It's a Scripps paper, takes no advertising, and therefore tells the truth. Chicago, however, is unfamiliar with the truth, can not recognize it when it appears, so the paper is having a steady, quiet growth and seems to have large destinies ahead. . . My two girls, the one I married, and the one which came a couple of years ago, are both coming fine. . . We're hoping your co-operative arrangement is paying big returns already, that like the Prudential, it is Strong as Gibraltar, and like Sapolio, "Best by Test." . . One of these days when you are in Chicago let me know. Give my love to Fred King; I hope to get off a note to him this week. . . I'd like to write you something about the splits and cross-sections of the Socialist and labor movements here, but I wouldn't know just what phase of it could be given proper handling in a letter. . . Here's our blessings and good wishes.

Yours fraternally,
Carl Sandburg

1913

William Leiserson was a liberal and Progressive in Milwaukee; he worked in the Citizens Employment Bureau and was an authority on labor and management. Fred King worked with Professor John Commons on Milwaukee city improvement.

89 | TO REUBEN W. BOROUGH

Chicago, July 30, 1913.

Dear Rube:—

It is mighty good to hear from you, to know that you are still numbered among the strong whose grinders have not ceased from their grinding and whose silver cord has not been loosed. I wrote you the love of one poet unto another about a month ago and the letter, addressed to Vermont Avenue, Los Angeles, came back to the office here and was opened and read before it got to me. It had several blue cuss-words in it; I shall find it and send it to you.

The ramblings of Rube in the west sound good and match the sinuosities of Sandy. Here's the thumbnail autobiography.

I came to Chicago a year ago, was on the World, the old Socialist, until it went smash; then on the Day Book, an adless newspaper started by the United Press; and in March began with System.

I wrote the High Cost of Government series, two signed stories on accident prevention in the July and August numbers, and in September and October numbers will have "I" stories signed by W. C. Colson, a retail clothier who keeps country trade from going to the city. The facts in the latter give strong support to the theories of Edward Bernstein, the notorious "revisionist" who perpetually elicits the maledictions and sneers of Arthur Morrow Lewis, Marxian. . . .

You might say at first shot that this is the hell of a place for a poet but the truth is it is a good place for a poet to get his head knocked when he needs it. In fact, it is so good a place for a healthy man who wants to watch the biggest, most intense, brutal and complicated game in the world—the game by which the world gets fed and clothed—the method of control—the economics and waste—so good a place is it from this viewpoint that I think you will like it.

Any way, I gave your address to C. D. Murphy, head of the "How" book writers, telling him I know you can fill a place on his staff. . . .

We are getting to be quite a magazine city here in Chicago. The Red Book has a new editor, one who made Hampton's hum; the Popular Mechanics, and Popular Electricity, and some live trade publications; and others projected. Come on, Rube! It's a mighty good crowd here with the A. W. Shaw Company. Pay is better than in newspaper work and the more experience you have the more you are worth, whereas on the newspaper your experience often gets you nothing and only your legs and capacity to hot-foot keeps you on the payroll.

As you said in your letter to me, "You don't have to read this —I'm just getting it out of my system."

They know you here and they have an impression that you know the business game and have writing ability. I tell them you understand the selling, manufacturing, and cost-keeping ends of business in a practical way, from experience; also that you are some writer. Also I am giving you a certificate of moral character, good repute, sobriety, industry. I believe these things myself. I guess you can come on here if you want to take a job a little over what most of the reporters on newspapers are getting.

Tell me how things stand with you and whether you are nailed down to that coast country, whether you think a wage slave gets more out of life along the Pacific Coast than along the shore of Michigan. . . .

This letter has run so far now I've got to stop without putting over my home gossip. Lilian [Paula] sends regards. We are hoping the Four of Us can make up a gesellschaftsverein one of these days.

Sandy. . . .

1914

[Chicago]
[Circa July, 1914]

Dear Bill:

I send you herewith some pictures of extraordinary people. By close observation, you will detect a Superchild, also a Monkey that does almost everything but talk. . . I'm hoping you made your train all to the good. It was fine of you to stay over for a later train. . . When you're in Chicago again, try to make your plans fit for a night in Ravenswood. Bring along those pictures of yours and yourn. We may be able to give you a few pointers on the Superchild. And we may accept some pointers from you. . . Here are thoughts from our three to your three.

Sandburg

[Chicago]
[Circa December, 1914]

Dear Mrs. Moody:

A referendum in our house yesterday was unanimously for acceptance from you of One (1) Irish Setter, and I was placed under special instructions to compose a Song of Thanks for a Dog. In any event I shall get for you the Chippewa Songs among which is Song of Thanks for a Pony. The choice is for a dog of January, 1915, since you are so good as to offer such a wide range of choices. I shall try to reach you by phone re where the dog is to be seized for transportation to Maywood and a subsequent career as watch-guard and playmate for the wife and daughter of a Scrivener.

Yours faithfully,
Carl Sandburg

William Vaughn Moody was a Chicago poet. His wife, Harriet, bred and raised purebred Irish setters, and was famous for her hospitality to poets from all over the country.

1915

[Chicago]
Monday [March 20, 1915]

My Dear Harriet Monroe:

After that editorial of yours on The Fight for the Crowd, I must leave the Miss off in addressing you—for the same reasons that I don't like to call Tagore a Mister. This editorial I rewrote into a free verse form, parts of it, and sent on to Bill Reedy of the Mirror. It was you at your stormiest and is an authentic page of your autobiography.

This clipping on free verse has real drive to it. Please keep it for me as I must use it on the editors of the Scoop and other newspapermen here who have their heads all in a muddle about "new-fangled" poetry. I am finding the quickest way to convince them that free verse is worth while is to show them that Stevie Crane and other crack newspapermen did some terribly serious work in libertarian rhythms.

I hope to see you when the blue-misted Padraic Colum comes to town next Saddy.

Yours faithfully,
Carl Sandburg

This editorial, "The Fight for the Crowd," was published in Harriet Monroe's magazine, Poetry, *in March, 1915. In this she told of an "editor's night" at the Book and Play Club, describing "the difficulty of finding and winning over a public for art, for ideas, while the great headlong tolerant American crowd huddles like sheep in the droves of commercial exploiters." She also wrote, concerning Sandburg, that "Mr. Edgar Lee Masters, for example, told how the Spoon River Anthology was conceived nearly a year ago, when his mind, already shaken out of certain literary prejudices by the reading in Poetry of much free verse, especially that of Mr. Carl Sandburg, was spurred to more active radicalism through a friendship with that iconoclastic champion of free speech, free form, free art— freedom of the soul."*

93 | TO THEODORE DREISER

Maywood, Ill.
Aug. 9. [1915]

My Dear Mr. Dreiser:

Your good letter came today. It is fine to have because I have read The Titan well and on various beer-fests Masters has told me of your aversions to throwing the bull. I am writing fast here, just an acknowledgement.

I mailed to Masters at the Hotel Holley some forty or fifty additional poems, which should prove enough for any publisher by way of quantity.

I add one more which is enclosed herewith after its final shaping-over.

Yours faithfully,
Carl Sandburg

Theodore Dreiser had written to Sandburg after Edgar Lee Masters had shown him samples of Sandburg's poetry. "They are beautiful," Dreiser wrote Sandburg on Aug. 6, 1915. "There is a fine, hard, able paganism about them that delights me—and they are tender and wistful as only the lonely, wistful, dreaming jargon can be." Dreiser's novel The Titan was published in 1914. Edgar Lee Masters was then practicing law in the Marquette Building, Chicago. In 1914 Masters had written Dreiser that he was "going for a tramp in the sand-dunes with a Swede bard. He is a new find and I think has the right fibre."

94 | TO THEODORE DREISER

Maywood, Ill.
Sept. 1, 1915.

My Dear Mr. Dreiser:

Such a dandy letter as you sent along to me I can't so far think out any real good answer to. For the fellowship and the sentiment of it, the enheartening element, I haven't got the reply now. When you are in Chicago maybe you and Masters and I can go out for a single sacramental glass of beer, and square things. You see, I used to read Floyd Dell's book reviews in the Post here. Not as a duty or for information but for the swing to them. And he drove me to your novels. While working on traction and financial stories for the Day Book I have covered many of the old beaten trails of Yerkes. So I know the Titan from many angles.

On his return here Masters said he received the 50 or so additional poems which I mailed to him in New York, and he turned them over to the John Lane & Co. man with whom he was dealing. If there's anything I can do at any time to help the publishers make a book out of what is now in their hands, I shall be glad to do so.

Yours faithfully,
Carl Sandburg

Dreiser's novel The Titan *was based on the life of the public-utilities tycoon Charles Tyson Yerkes. Floyd Dell, Chicago newspaperman and novelist, had moved to New York in 1914 and became an associate editor of* The Masses.

95 | TO ALICE CORBIN HENDERSON

[Maywood, Illinois]
15th Dec. 1915.

My Dear A.C.H.—The rumors are that you not only survived New York but dented it in several spots and returned to Chicago triumphant. Every time Masters and I talk about going out to Lake Bluff we end up with a plan to have Lake Bluff moved closer to the loop one way or another. I hope you enjoyed my Pound stuff if you've seen it. Harriet has it. I told her I have the notes for a similar treatise or public love letter on you and Harriet M. as Modern Forces. Coiled inside the graphite of my pencil also is a disquisition on your poetry and your personal urge for the brief and poignant. I am slaving now to get a book into shape to send to Harcourt of Henry Holt & Co. He wrote me on your suggestion.

You were very thoughtful. . . . Reedy is to print an article he ordered from me on Margaret Haley and the Teachers' Federation. . . The garment strike is hell: it's like a voyage in a submarine with ventilation machinery busted. . . Regards to William Penhallow Henderson: he knows what I think about the picture he is showing at the Art Institute.: there are models from which no great picture can be devised. . . Miss K. Dudley comes off good. I have a feel about her pictures and wouldn't be surprised if her genius leaped into masterpieces. Lawton Parker's rendering of Jim Patten is the Hearst paper wheat gambler, overdone melodrama. . . So you see you have opinions and chit-chat here as well as sentiments and near-Yule wishes. . . Tell Alice the Little I hope she forgives me and I will rough house to her heart's content next time I see her.

C.S.

Alice Corbin Henderson was associate editor and co-founder of Poetry. *This article in* Reedy's Mirror *was titled simply "Margaret Haley." Margaret Haley, of the Chicago Teachers' Federation, was a battler for teachers' rights, and Sandburg wrote some articles about her in* The Day Book. *Miss Katherine Dudley was one of three Dudley sisters in Chicago, all of whom were talented. The editors of* Poetry *and the poets in their circle adopted the habit of signing with initials instead of full names.*

96 | TO ALICE CORBIN HENDERSON

[Maywood, Illinois]
[Circa December, 1915]

My Dear A.C.H.—

I shall phone you Friday or Saturday which day I can get out. It may be the missus can come along. It's a sure go for either Saturday or Sunday, pos-i-tive-ly. Will bring along some late wild stuff. . . Thanks for the Jap book. I feel like writing hokkus whenever I peep into a few pages of it. Perhaps, God help us, it will soften my style and render it more flexible. . . Also, I will bring along the Ezra Pound critique, what I have got done of it. . . The Day Book is smashing ahead, making its place. Many of the Best People who know all the other Best People are getting so they don't feel they know all that's going on unless they read the Day Book.

Yours faithfully,
Carl Sandburg

97 | TO HARRIET MONROE

[Chicago]
[Circa early January, 1916]

Harriet:

Use all of 'em. Splash with a Chinese Number. These and like things in Chinese poetry put me closer to the antipodean Chinks than anything else. I would rather have The Orphan than all of Dickens' Oliver Twist or Little Nell—and I would like to know where the genius of the soldier in a lonely place is better delivered than in Fighting at Lung Tou.

C.S.

Poetry published Chinese poems translated by Arthur Waley, whose work Sandburg admired.

98 | TO ALICE CORBIN HENDERSON

[Chicago]
Jan. 8. [1916]

Dear A.C.H.:—

I have sent to Mr. Harcourt some 260 poems, each one neatly typed or pasted on a sheet by itself, all of it paged, and headed by an index, and table of contents under the title "Chicago Poems". I wanted much to have you go over them before they went on but he had sent me two letters about the stuff. I am away behind in sleep, and work, and for peace of soul I had to get the whole thing

out of the house and off my mind. As the original "discoverer"
of the "Chicago Poems", and evocator of that title, and as it was you
who told Harcourt et al these poems were worth going after, your
suggestions on what should have gone into the bunch would have
been worth while. . . . You would have been a proper personage
to be present at the launching ceremony to pronounce prophecies
as the bottle was broken on the prow. . . Outside of The Missus at
home I'm not even bothering anybody else with the knowledge that
I'm trying to unload a book of poetry on the world. . . When you
think we can even up the score by service to you, let us know about
it.

Carl Sandburg

P.S.—I have six Bibelots of yours and a copy of Captain Craig by
Arlington Robinson. They will get back to you. . . Your poems in
the January magazine [*Poetry*] are lovely and finished things. It
is a blasphemous shame that publishers and public insist on bulk
in books of poetry, that the call is for big multitudinous Lorado
Taft Marches of Time rather than Paul Manship bronzes.

99 | TO ALFRED HARCOURT

Maywood, Ill.
Feb. 4, 1916.

Dear Mr. Harcourt:

Of the poems you suggested for elimination from the present
volume, all were left out from the manuscript of "CHICAGO POEMS"
sent to you, with one exception. That was "Murmurings in a Field
Hospital". That, I believe, has a present time value above that of
others.

You placed a question mark on "Dynamiter". I would say
put it in. I believe the backing for this book will come from the
younger, aggressive fellows, in the main. Without tying it up to any
special schools or doctrines, the intellectual background of it takes
color from the modern working class movement rather than old
fashioned Jeffersonian democracy. Anton Johannsen of San Fran-

cisco, who was the model for "Dynamiter" probably commands more deep and genuine affection than any other man in the labor movement. Even those who want to jail him like the heart and wit of him. Some of his implacable enemies have known the motif I tried to catch in this poem.

In "Buttons", I see where some folks might consider the phrase "by Christ" to be taking the name of the Son of God in vain. In this particular climax, however, I feel sure all readers with any true streak of religion in them will take this oath as the proper exclamation, a cry not lacking kinship with, "My God, why hast thou forsaken me?" It is the one oath in the book which has the best defense and justification.

I can readily see how the Billy Sunday excoriation may be accused of lacking the religious strain that should run through all real poetry. I saw clearly your points about certain words forming what might be taken as an irreverent contrast with the name of Jesus. And I made revisions that I believe put the Sunday poem in a class of reading enjoyable and profitable to all but the most hidebound and creed-drilled religionists. If necessary or important, which it is not, I could furnish statements from Protestant ministers and Catholic priests that this poem has more of the historic Jesus or the ideal Christ in it, than does a Billy Sunday series of exhortations. Mike Kenna (Hinky Dink) tells me that Sunday has bought stock in two Chicago hotels, one of them the Hotel Morrison, persistently notorious in Chicago courts for the studied and civilized vice, the commercialized night pleasure which is so much harder to look at than natural depravity. I used to lunch frequently with Sunday's Chautauqua booking manager, Harry Holbrook, and I know the opinions and convictions of those immediately around Sunday as to whether he is a salesman and crowd trickster or whether he is one sent from God. His own bunch privately admit that I have nailed his hide to the barn door and fixed him in correct historic perspective. There is terrific tragedy of the individual and of the crowd in and about Billy Sunday. He is the most conspicuous single embodiment in this country of the crowd leader or crowd operative who uses jungle methods, stark voodoo stage effects, to play hell with democracy. This is the main cause of the fundamental hatred which men have for Sunday. It isn't a hatred of Sunday so much as a flaming resentment against that type of human individual. The question is whether I have caught the values of it intensely enough. Such an apostrophe to Roosevelt or Bryan could not be tolerated because both of them are more or less pre-figurements of the average man, the crowd man idealized and envisioned somewhat. The only other American figure that might compare with Sunday is Hearst. Both dabble in treacheries of the primitive, invoke terrors of the unknown, utilize sex as a stage prop, and work on elemental fears of the mob, with Hearst the same antithesis to Tom Jefferson that Billy Sunday is to Jesus of Nazareth.

I am writing about Sunday at this length, Mr. Harcourt, because I want you to know what sort of foundations I see the poem resting on. When your letter came saying the Billy Sunday poem with some revisions would be used, Mrs. Sandburg commented on that first of all. Edgar Lee Masters asked first of all, "Are they going to print Billy Sunday", and getting "Yes" for an answer, said, "They are going after the soul of America."

If you think other changes are necessary to put across the Sunday poem, I'll co-operate. He is a type of crowd-faker the literature of democracy must handle.

Enclosed is what newspaper men call "personality dope". The newspaper sketch is by Chester M. Wright, editor of the New York Call. He and I have worked together on papers.

In two or three days I should find time to send on a "Who's Who" outline to you.

Yours faithfully,
Carl Sandburg

The Billy Sunday poem, "To a Contemporary Bunkshooter," was included in Chicago Poems. *So were "Dynamiter" and "Buttons," the first a labor poem, the second an antiwar poem.*

100 | TO THEODORE DREISER

[Chicago]
2/13/1916

My dear Dreiser:—

Nothing but the merciless jostling of a lot of jobs that had to be done has kept me from making proper and timely answer to your good letters. When I look at the two-fisted thickness of your last book and contemplate the efficiency of toil and utilization of time as a factor in producing the book, I rebuke myself that I ought to have found time to reply to you . . . I perform all tasks, except certain newspaper deadline assignments, slowly. I take my time at the joy-tasks as well as the wage-jobs. That's why some day I'm going to write a more accurately-gauged review of The Titan than any one who has touched it. I am part of the human mass which is background of that book . . . Henry Holt & Co. will bring out my poems this spring under the title "Chicago Poems." The one you asked me to send on to you is not to be printed. I shall mail it to you soon; can't lay my hands on it today.

—Masters and others will tell you I have a bum record, a criminal record, as a letter writer. So you'll not put me in the rogue's gallery of your memory.—When you're to be in Chi. I will drop all other stuff on my programs in order to hear you discourse over a glass of beer.

Yours faithfully,
Carl Sandburg

101 | TO ALICE CORBIN HENDERSON

[Maywood, Illinois]
March 25, 1916.

Dear A.C.H.—

I think I shall send you telegrams. You don't want letters with news and knowledge. You know all you need now. You've got layers of knowledge risen into stalactite cliffs, Arizona buttes, maybe New Mex. . . I'm sending a hello instead of news. Amy Lowell came and went amid the same sort of furor as last year, doing good work, with a brave air of a Cyrano de Bergerac facing life's inpulchritudes. . . Harcourt says our book will be out April 22. I will shoot one your way immediate. If you should come across the proof sheets amid your luggage send them back tho it's not important. . . I am having a holy picnic with some gnarled massive ones I hacked out lately. . . Say, you be a turtle, one of those big slumbrous idling fellows three hundred years old, satisfied with everything, people, politics, arts, and linear distance between the earth and Canopus. Go to it. Be a turtle six months, lady.

C.S.

Mrs. Henderson, in her reply to Sandburg's advice to rest because of her poor health, wrote: "If I knew as much as a 300 year old turtle, I might be as quiet and content."

102 | TO AMY LOWELL

[Chicago]
April 2, 1916.

Dear Miss Lowell:

A copy of Lao Tse went on to you. About ten per cent of it has poetic values of a style that ought to be more widely known.

I am still haunted by your "Six French Poets" and when I get my physical cosmos a little better reorganized, I'm going to do one real review of it. And if, in your conferences with publishers you see any opportunity to get your translations gathered into a cheap paper covered book, you will be doing a service to the many young fellows who are so busy in glorious living hunting the poetic sides of life that they haven't time to earn the money to buy big books in boards.

I am ready to serve notice on Walter Lippmann that a booby prize for aimless cleverness is due him. His nostrils are keen for the revolution everywhere except in literary style. In an electric

motor age he writes like an early steam engine. He defends or justi-
fies violence and sabotage in the labor movement while gesturing
desperately at identical tactics of non-conformity in the sphere of
action where new methods of reaching human thought and emotion are being daringly experimented with.

Enclosed is the "Alix" we spoke of. And there's some clipping
or other I'm to send you I can't find just now but will later.

And remember my "Six French Poets" is torn to pieces and
thumbed by separate pages over the street cars of Chicago, and you
were going to send another copy if the publishers were not bank-
rupted of the edition.

Also, remember that color-bearers invite sharpshooters, and
as you go further in ultimatums declaring your literary independence, there will be cross-fire.

Many, many lucky days!

Yours sincerely,
Carl Sandburg

*Miss Lowell was influenced by both French experimentalists and
English romantics, and was one of the drumbeaters for the vers
librists. She wrote to him: "The 'Mare Alix' is a delightful thing,
and you make me 'want to rub my nose against the nose of the
mare Alix.'"*

103 | TO WALTER LIPPMANN

[Chicago]
[June 21, 1916]

Dear Lippmann:—

Your Chi. convention story has the teeth and passion of democracy in it. When you write of actual contacts—when you do
real reporting—I get you. I get more hope from your cry of despair
about that convention than any of the masses of reasoning and
cool, clever assemblage of facts in much of your work. By this sign
of your cry of despair I know you are now strong for battling, even
futile battling. I have wondered about you. I feel safer. As a member

of the Amalgamated Secretaries to Socialist Mayors, I am free to write you this way.

Carl Sandburg

The basis for the letter was Lippmann's report on the Republican Convention of 1916 in The New Republic: "*. . . It was a gathering of insanitary callous men, who blasphemed patriotism, made a mockery of Republican government and filled the air with sodden and scheming stupidity." While Sandburg was secretary to Mayor Emil Seidel, of Milwaukee, Lippmann was secretary to Socialist Mayor George R. Lunn, of Schenectady.*

104 | TO ALICE CORBIN HENDERSON

[Chicago]
July 9 1916

Dear A.C.H.:—

It's a girl and perfection frog legs fastened to a perfection torso. Avoirdupois: 8.5 pounds. Wavy dark hair, this notably Northern French. Mother: 100%.—Here's much luck to you and Will and the Little Devil. If I had a Secy at my elbows perpetually I would send you written thots oftener.

C.S.

Now it's July 20—in the heat of some heavy fighting lately I delayed putting this in an envelope—Janet lost a half pound and gained ¾ meanwhile.

C.S.

105 | TO AMY LOWELL

[Chicago]
July 23, 1916

Dear Amy Lowell:

That's a pippin of a review. That you should find the stuff you did in Chicago Poems of art and writing craft and personality-expression, ought to be good coaching for me. I have, of course, a thousand points of defense or counter-offensive against the antagonisms you voice, and I'll get to those sometime with you. What you call "prejudice" may be "instinct", primal immemorial heart-cry, of hate. Also I admit I may blurt this hate as one gagged or tongue-tied and therein fall short of the articulate. I'm going to write you a long letter on this sometime, hoping to analyse some of my own motives in the matter, a thing I have not had time to do as yet.

We have a new daughter, Janet, who sends you her love.

Yours sincerely,
Carl Sandburg

106 | TO ALICE CORBIN HENDERSON

[Chicago]
[Sept. 16, 1916]

Dear A.C.H.:—

Our letters met, along in western Nebraska, I would guess. And in my letter speeding westward was an initial fulfillment of the wish in your eastward-speeding missive: provided as hereinafter stated, that what I enclosed in my letter was properly and factually POETRY.—Haven't asked McClurg's or Field's how the book is going nor heard a word from Holt's so October, the royalty month, has for us the joys of mining investors or lottery ticket holders. Which reminds me I would like to get in a poem the gayety of a group of Wisconsin German farmers at Sunday noon in autumn after Catholic church is out gathered around their beer holding a duck raffle.—Ezra Pound—yes—I am for him stronger than ever since this last sheaf in Poetry: he is so doggone deliberate and mocking and masterly in many of his pieces: that "salmon trout" like a "wafer of light" for instance: if only his letters and personal relationships had the big ease and joy of life his art has I would hit it off great with him.—Masters I haven't seen much of. In fact I'm off the literary, even the poetry crowd, lately. The why of it is all huge and mixed with me but I guess more than anything else I like my politics straight and prefer the frank politics of the political world to the politics of the literary world. The betting chances are all that I wouldn't have had any book out this year if you hadn't got busy last year.—From Adelaide Crapsey's book I get much of the repression, the reticences, and the quivering color points, of your work. Have you seen the book?—I have had a love affair with a dog this summer: Mrs. Moody gave me an Irish setter I'll swear has as immortal a soul as any of us: he's a marvelous listener.—Janet, the new kid, has her mother's hair and face whereas the other daughter, has mine: so the household is at a glorious standoff.

And this—will not this do for a Saturday afternoon's gossip? Rihakku?

Carl Sandburg

PS.—I've come across a big rare collection of Japanese prints you and Will will enjoy. A life insurance man now living in the south half of Frank Lloyd Wright's Oak Park house has some 250.

Mrs. Henderson had moved to Santa Fe with her husband, the painter William Henderson, and Santa Fe later opened a wide circle of friendships for Sandburg. The poem "Dan" in Smoke and Steel *was written about this Irish setter.*

107 | TO ALICE CORBIN HENDERSON

[Chicago]
[Oct. 9, 1916]

Dear A.C.H.—

Went over the proofs of [Edgar Lee] Masters' forthcoming book "The Great Valley" today. In power, range of pictures, play of motives, it will surpass Spoon River. It is a terrible book and will bring a hell's storm of censure. Its art, method and craftsmanship isn't up to Spoon River. But the size, vision and assertion of it are above Spoon River. It will be more than 300 pages, a big book in more than physical scope, free from the tone of respectable surrender there was to Songs and Satires. So I write you to know

E.L.M. is virile and alive and is going to crack the tribe of criticus about the ears this coming November and December.—Jerry Blum and Mrs. have gone to New York and are aiming for France; Theo. Dreiser and the Hyman girl have quit; Mrs. [Dorothy] Aldis is in hospital recovering from appendicitis operation; John T. Mc-Cutcheon is to marry Evelyn Shaw, daughter of Frances; the Roy McWilliams are due from France next week; and Harriet [Monroe] et al are wondering who to give the three prizes to next month.

Yours chroniclingly,

C.S.

108 | TO GEORGE FOX

[Chicago]
[Circa early 1917]

Dear George:

I have just been reading Hopie's letter to Lilian about Randall. Down under all the sharp pain that cuts now, I can see that Hopie is keeping her head and heart like a strong mother holding on to the foundations of things. A world that could produce a Randall can't be a crazy world. The last time I saw you, George, I remember how you surprised me into new thoughts about how time and all our clocks may be an illusion. I counted it an unfinished talk; what I got from you was not definite and clear but it was a hazy and yet deeply certain impression that the Unknown and Unknowable is close to us, in touch, all the time. . . With Janet and Margaret, I am ready for anything all the time. Every day I come home and find them alive I take as a day snatched from Death. I think too about how they die every week. The little fluff of a Janet we had a year ago is dead. The Margaret that was learning to talk three years ago is dead and replaced with an endless chatterer. . . Every beautiful thing I know is ephemeral, a thing of a moment. Life is a series of things that vanish. . . I had two brothers go with diphtheria and we had a double funeral on a bitter winter day when I was a boy. I buried a child that had not lived long enough to be named. And whenever I think about these who emerged into so little of life and then faded off, my head gets into all the big overtones of life: that hazy illusion of time and the clocks that you were talking about. . . We are all such little things. A day of life is a day snatched from death. And the only fool is the one who can prove that death is a blank nothing or something less than life. . . A world that can bring a Randall to life is a sane and a beautiful world and that death has taken him doesn't subtract from the sanity and beauty that brought him and kept him till he went. I'm sure it's something like this that fine strong mother instincts of Hopie are feeling for and rallying by now. . . Our love and thoughts are yours.

CS

George Fox was an old friend from the early Socialist days in Wisconsin. For a while the Sandburgs lived in one of the Foxes' back rooms. Fox was a Socialist, a mailman in Appleton, and later a museum curator in Three Oaks. The Foxes' son, Randall, had died of burns when a kerosene stove burst into flames. The Sandburgs had had a baby girl, who died in the process of birth, about two and a half years after the birth of Margaret. Mrs. Sandburg had chosen the name Madaline for her. The reference to the double funeral is to the death of Sandburg's two younger brothers, Emil and Fred, in 1892.

109 | TO AMY LOWELL

[Chicago]
[Circa June 10, 1917]

Dear Amy Lowell:

These enclosures contain in part some of the material I would present if I ever reach that "long letter" to you. In some paragraphs of Incidentals you will find my own viewpoint coinciding with yours in your protestations of a propaganda of violence in Chicago Poems. I admit there is some animus of violence in Chicago Poems but the aim was rather the presentation of motives and character than the furtherance of I.W.W. theories. Of course, I honestly prefer the theories of the I.W.W. to those of its opponents and some of my honest preferences may have crept into the book, as you suggest, but the aim was to sing, blab, chortle, yodel, like people, and people in the sense of human beings subtracted from formal doctrines. . . The typewritten notes enclosed were for my use in a Little Theater lecture. Incidentals was published ten years ago. Please slip them back to me when you are through with them as I have no other copies. . . The poem you may keep, if you like. It's one [Edward J.] O'Brien is to run in The Masque. It's up to you to tell me if I am violating confidences in showing a Masque piece to a fellow-masquer before it is published. . . The Missus and I will be on deck Monday bringing all we have of joybells.

Carl Sandburg

P.S.—In free verse today, Rex H. Lampman counts. He has written "Once Overs" and "Listen". They are 75 cents each and his address is Portland Hotel, Portland, Oregon. At his best he is more like some of your Six French Poets in blithe rippling. Though his work may not class as free verse it has singing power and makes pictures and has analogies to free verse. Anyway you must know about him and have him in your portfolio.

> *Sandburg's 1907 "Incidentals" was sent for Amy Lowell's book* Tendencies in Modern American Poetry. *"The Masque of Poets" was to run in* The Bookman.

110 | TO FANNY BUTCHER

[Chicago]
[Circa June, 1917]

Dear F.B.

Here's one O'Brien is going to run in The Masque of Poets in The Bookman—anonymous—so this is a literary diplomatic secret. . . And it was one sentence, not two, I meant in my note, wherein you epitomized Chicago Poems, getting the high contrasts of this massive, negligee town. . . And one of these umbrageous, halcyon days you must fix it for me to hear Sowerby. . . And the Missus, the heiresses, and the dog, we each and severally send our love to you.

Carl Sandburg

1917

F. B.—Fanny Butcher—was literary editor of the Chicago Tribune
*and one of Sandburg's early admirers and friends. Leo Sowerby, a
musician, later prepared some of the music for Sandburg's* The
American Songbag.

111 | TO AMY LOWELL

[Chicago]
[Circa late June, 1917]

Dear Amy Lowell:

It was good to get your letter. As I told you over the phone
when you were here, you have always gone better than fifty-fifty
with me. They told me at the Poetry office one day that you were
inclined to be discouraged about the middle west. The fact is you
have many quiet friends whose interest is never voiced to you. I
know an insurance man, collector of Japanese prints, and byway
sojourner in good things, who has read all of your work and takes
you as not only a personality but an institution. Laura Sherry, the
Wisconsin Players woman of Milwaukee, is one who suddenly
spoke to me the same things I have spoken to others about Six
French Poets.

Under separate cover I am sending a photograph by Edouard
Steichen. If it is used he is to be credited. And would you give instructions that it is to be handled with care and returned? Also, I
enclose a photo reproduction of a Steichen print for any use you
wish: it shows 5-year-old Margaret whom you must see on some
western trip.

Every once in a while I write something that I have an impulse to send on to you. I have several of this sort in my kit now
and as I get copies they will go on to you.

The Dynamiter came through a few weeks ago. A friend of
his had seen the Poetry Review article and sent it to him. He enjoyed it hugely. You and he are really kinfolk and sometime I'll
get the background of the whole thing across to you. . . Glancing
over some old and genuinely propaganda material of mine of ten
years ago, I got a sneaking suspicion that maybe you're right and

maybe I have struck a propaganda rather than a human note at times.

We wish you all the luck there is. And some of the poems that will be sent on to you are as a studio view of rushing joyous work that the sculptor wants to keep around a while and make changes in.

Sincerely,
Carl Sandburg

112 | TO MRS. WILLIAM VAUGHN MOODY

[Omaha, Nebraska]
[July, 1917]

Dear Harriet Moody,
From strong hills about Omaha
and singing bushes of prairie roses
I send you a Sunday afternoon greeting.
Luck and health to you.

Carl Sandburg

Sandburg was in Omaha at this time covering the building trade strike for the American Federation of Labor.

113 | TO HARRIET MONROE

[Omaha, Nebraska]
[July, 1917]

H.M.—
What shall it avail a man even tho he have a room with bath in Omaha since his heart is eaten with a loneliness for old companions?

C.S.

On the letterhead of this note to Harriet Monroe, the Hotel Fontenelle advertised, "Every room with bath."

1917

[Omaha, Nebraska]
July, 1917

Dear H.M.:

Big days—a great conference—Vachel [Lindsay] couldn't find enough boom-boom words to tell the story.—You must be interested in this [Herman] Hagedorn evolution.

C.S.

115 | TO EDNA KENTON

Chi.—Aug. 21, [1917]

Dear Edna:

Once more I can only send you *thoughts*. Whatever and wherever you are on the war is either right or terribly near right. Sometime I'll write you a real letter for the chatty, newsy one you sent me.

The Day Book was shut down. I start on the Daily News staff next week.

Carl Sandburg

Edna Kenton was a short-story writer who lived in New York City. The adless Day Book *was the E. W. Scripps paper edited by Negley D. Cochran. It was making a slight profit when it suspended publication, a victim of the war.*

116 | TO NEGLEY D. COCHRAN

[Chicago]
Sept. 12, [1917]

Dear N.D.—

Ben Hecht just back from Europe tells me that he had a talk with George Patullo and Patullo said at Cantigny he was four miles from the front and determined to move up and see the action while it was hot. He went two miles and met Col. Robert R. McCormick and McCormick said something like, "I'm going to the hospital. I'm all in. It's the first time I've had to go to the hospital since I've been over." Patullo said McCormick didn't specify any particular complaint except that he was "all in". He was not wounded. Patullo was sore about it, or rather just plain disgusted, says Hecht.

I send this on to you because I've enjoyed so much your satirical drives at this bird and because it's all pertinent to the latest move of naming a highway after him. I mean that everything comic about it hitherto is now all the more comic. We shall have to get you to write a book and Goldberg draw the pictures for it. SOME book that would be.

Always wishing you all the luck there is—

Carl Sandburg

Sandburg kept in touch with his former Day Book *editor, Negley D. Cochran, who had moved to wartime Washington. Colonel Robert R. McCormick was editor and publisher of his family's Chicago* Tribune. *Sandburg joined the* Chicago Daily News *in August, 1917, where one of his colleagues was Ben Hecht.*

117 | TO ALICE CORBIN HENDERSON

[Chicago]
Sept. 27. [1917]

Dear A.C.H.—

Next week about Oct. 3d or 4th, maybe the 2d, there will stop off at Santa Fe a pilgrim of the name of Alfred MacArthur, without kilties or insignia of his clan though very Scotch, one of the Chicago prophets and enunciators of Rabelais, professionally the general agent of a big insurance company but avocatorily a collector of Japanese prints, head resident of Frank Lloyd Wright's most original dwelling house, quite human but with stripings of the primordial brute. Feed him, tell him the news, and exchange your philosophy of life with him, and I think he will class up as a good bet in the way of a time-killer. Like Kipling's Zogbaum, he incorporates many stories and poems and in proper mood will give you the gist of libraries. He's on his way to California for a vacation and I told him he ought to play once at Santa Fe.

C.S.

Alfred MacArthur was the brother of the playwright and news-paperman Charles MacArthur.

118 | TO AMY LOWELL

[Chicago]
[Oct. 26, 1917]

Dear Amy Lowell:—

I'm more than glad about your book. The first and big thing about it is that it is alive and well free of the taint of the academic. Your thesis is stated and supported but not allowed to dominate and sap the human companionship quality. You make so interesting a book that I wonder how fate slipped me a ticket to be one of the six. To write my points of disagreement would be to wrack my head and write a book on my theory of the art of poetry. The clear sincerity and decisive personal viewpoint, its scope and challenge, give it the vividness required for war days. And your war apologia in the preface is a good lure at the front door. I will my volume to whichever of my daughters is most devilish.

Sincerely,
Carl Sandburg

Sandburg was one of the six poets in Miss Lowell's Tendencies in Modern American Poetry.

119 | TO ALICE CORBIN HENDERSON

[Chicago]
[Nov. 27, 1917]

Dear A.C.H.—

If you want to organize to stay out of Braithwaite's anthologies, I'm with you. Two with God are supposed to be a majority. If you know more than two, send me their names. A pathetic personage has been permitted to grow into a fungus mistaken for what it grows on. The popery and kaiserism of it, the snobbery, flunkyism and intrigue, I'm on to it. All I can do is put up with it, even as I put up with the British financial imperialist anti-Kerensky coloring of the news from Petrograd as it passes through London. I can only await a day of reckoning. "I see these things and keep my mouth shut." I hurrah with my hat off for the drive to your letter. . . . [Alfred] MacArthur got back a few weeks ago; said he was to see you but you and Will were away to Taos. . . . Your New Mexico songs are hauntingly beautiful. Your groups in back numbers of Poetry have for me the same irreducible glimmer that there is to Adelaide Crapsey's work and when you cash in if I don't write a better obituary for you than I did for Adelaide I'm guessing wrong. Meanwhile during this time that the Holy Ghost still possesses you, I hope to make some publisher see, SEE, you. Shall I write to Knopf and to Brown, the Four Seas man? I will plug in anywhere you say with any kind of a letter because I am not only for you and your poetry personally but I believe that there's a small but permanent public that will buy it when printed and that you ought to be a tradition and an asset worth any publisher's venture. . . . If I hadn't had so much work and war of every kind I would have been busy on this long ago. With Harcourt, it's all a gamble; sometimes he follows my hunches and then again he doesn't. I've absolutely gotten beyond trying to spot why or why not he does or doesn't do a thing. He is as temperamental as any prima donna but he's so strictly on the level, I have found, that after he says yes or no, I quit. . . . I can't write you about how the hell I've been going it lately. Only the last two months I began to be sure that I had a new book that would surpass and put it all over the first one. If I had the time to shape them up and go to it I'm sure I could sell some of them. But I think I'm lucky enough a dreamer to regularly connect with the payroll of a daily newspaper that reminds me of nothing so much as [Vachel] Lindsay's "proud respectable hearse". I have been among strikers in the coal fields, the American Federation of Labor convention, among pacifists, Sinn Feiners and

German spies, and there has been such a tumult in my head lots of times when I wanted to write you that I couldn't get to it. . . . Go write and dream more. Produce much: you are worth it.

C.S.

120 | TO AMY LOWELL

[Chicago]
[Circa December, 1917]

My Dear Amy Lowell:

I call your Tendencies the most human-and-alive book of commentary and discussion that has thus far come off a printing press in America. I would say this as readily if you had put some other guy than myself in to represent the "multi-racial" or any link necessary to your thesis. I see the book kicking up all kinds of pro and con talk. It has galvanized the ganglions of poetic chatter. By the time the verdicts and referendums have arrived to you on it from the Metropolitan centers and the back country, you will feel something of the exasperation at human gab and suspicion blended with literary politics which were part of the background for this piece "Reactions of Excessive Gossip" some months ago.

Would you be so good as to get your publishers to return the photograph of me which was used in Tendencies? It happens to be the only one we have; properly it belongs to Mrs. Sandburg and was made by her brother who is now Lieut. Steichen in France in charge of photographic war board.

I notice two of your poems are in a 10-cent pocket edition of the Fifty Best American Poems sold at the Woolworth stores. Also a dandy little edition of Whitman pieces, Memories of President Lincoln, is being Woolworthed. This is almost enough of a tendency to be worth a note in your next monograph. . . . I am off the suspended Day Book, the world's greatest adless daily, and am now writing editorials on the Daily News, the world's greatest ad sheet, bar none. . . . Regards! and luck and health!

Carl Sandburg

125

121 | TO FRANCIS HENEY

[Chicago]
March [2] 1918

Dear Mr. Heney:

There are two men in Chicago whom you should have in mind when you add to your staff in handling the cases of the packers. One is Robert M. Buck, former alderman, and the other is Harry Herwitz, former secretary to Charles E. Merriam, when the latter was an alderman. I think Neg Cochran would remember them as two who could keep a scent in the nostrils and follow a trail that's not easy to follow. Buck is bulldog stuff and in a career touching many seamy spots is known as a guy that can't be reached. Herwitz does not know I am writing this and Buck knows it only because I told him he was out of place in the kind of a respectable efficiency organization he is now working for if at this time you need real hounds. I notice the Christian Science Monitor gave a full report of your Iroquois club speech; if I had known about it beforehand I would have tried to get it for the News. You have already done a big job in Chicago; I don't hazard a guess on how soon results will come from it but when I hear a lawyer, a newspaper man and a business man, all in one day volunteer the belief that rope or a firing squad is wanted on the stockyards situation, I know the whole thing is on a different footing from a year ago.

Sincerely,
Carl Sandburg

Francis Heney was at this time investigating the meat packers, or, as Cochran called them, "food profiteers." Robert Buck was a labor man, and editor of The New Majority, *the official organ of the Labor Party of Cook County.*

122 | TO HENRY JUSTIN SMITH

On assignment in Minneapolis
[Circa March, 1918]

Dear Henry:
I find the scenery
along the Northwestern Railroad
in the Minnesota river bottoms
up to specifications.

Keep the hills
as they are.

And let the birches be.

These are my recommendations.
Do as you like about them.
Only remembering I send
a special prayer
for the birches.

I pray for all standing white memorials
of people I care for.

C.S.

Henry Justin Smith, editor of the Chicago Daily News, *encouraged literary pursuits by his reporters. According to Isadora Bennett, a young reporter, whose desk was near Ben Hecht and Sandburg, Smith used to say, "I don't want writers, I want fighters."*

123 | TO NEGLEY D. COCHRAN

Chicago
April 5. [Circa 1918]

Dear N.D.—
That was good preaching, being no preaching at all, and yet all there—the which you sent along. That about being good and wanting to make others good. As people and as a nation we've got something to learn and I don't see what the way is going to be.

This I am sure of. The uplift movement and the cut-this-out-be-cause-I-say-it-ain't-good-for-you all has a relation to the efficiency movement. That was one of the terrible things I saw being worked out at the System magazine. If workers had a five or six hour work-day I could reconcile myself to time and motion studies and a standardization reaching into workers' lives to the point where you could tell what any operative is doing at any minute of the day by consulting the card graphs of the efficiency engineers. I thought of Bill Reedy's protest against forcing the bricklayer to cut out that final pling of his trowel. The efficiency sharks classify it as use-less because it has no utility. It is the amen and the snatch of song with which the bricklayer says, "I'm happy" or "I don't care" as he finishes putting one brick of thousands of bricks into a niche it is to hold for years. "The right of the workers to control their own lives" was a saying printed and spoken much in the labor party campaign here and is a root impulse of bolshevism for all its zealotry that resembles prohibition. Mother Jones spoke of you the other day as "good" and also employed the word "noble". I said to myself she's about the only person in the country that could get away with that from you. She's a wonder; close on to 88 years old and her voice a singing voice; nobody else could give me a thrill just by saying in that slow solemn orotund way, "The kaisers of this country are next, I tell ye." I put this old lady past Galli-Curci. —I still owe you another sheet of letter on that one you sent me the other day and it will come along soon. That letter of yours was like one of these pictures taken from high on a airplane, a shadowy confused humanity way below struggling somewhere.

Sincerely,
Carl

124 | TO UPTON SINCLAIR

[Chicago]
4/7 [1918]

My dear Upton Sinclair:

When I can get to it I shall make a list of radical book shops—the eight or ten I suppose you mean. I am writing news and editorials on The Daily News and if I can bring your magazine into print I will do so. I'm glad about your war stand. It was just one more war, a clash of dynasties and junkers—now it's something else—a big gamble with the odds on the red.

Yours,
Carl Sandburg

125 | TO ALFRED HARCOURT

[Chicago]
May 3. [1918]

Dear Harcourt:

The book will be a real and an honest singing book when it gets to you. I have been holding off on sending it to you, because I have been working on it to accomplish what you call "tightening." Last fall I had a book I felt was as good in its way as Chicago Poems. The new book:

CORNHUSKERS,

is a bigger conceived and all round better worked-out book than Chicago Poems.—Your Trotzky book is liked by the Reds. Leslie Marcey of the International Socialist Review says Our Revolution has a sweep, vision and spirit that the Boni & L. book hasn't.—The public librarians' convention at Saratoga is putting me on for an hour July 4th to read The Four Brothers and anything else showing we have a nation worth fighting for.—Met [Robert] Frost and [Vachel] Lindsay last week. What with letter writing, lectures and being lionized I felt their minds were mussed up worse than the day-by-day newspaper worker.—Bill Reedy is getting to be enough of a dean of middle west literature to be represented in a book. But there I go with another random hunch for you, having seen none of my frequent ones get from you "the nod of inward approval."— Regards and luck!

Carl Sandburg

126 | TO SAM T. HUGHES

Maywood, Ill.
July 15, 1918.

Dear Sam Hughes:

It is a go. On hearing from you that you can finance the stunt, I will begin packing for Stockholm, and looking up Chicago ends that have connections in Eastern Europe. I was more than glad to get your letter. It goes both ways.

Sincerely,
Carl Sandburg

Sam T. Hughes was editor-in-chief of Newspaper Enterprise Association (NEA). On July 11, 1918, he proposed to send Sandburg to be correspondent in Eastern Europe, with headquarters in Stockholm.

127 | TO SAM T. HUGHES

Chicago, July 23, 1918

Dear Sam:

Passport authorities want a statement from you why you send me to Stockholm. Recite for them that I am 40 years of age, was born at Galesburg, Ill., and have lived all my life in the United States, except the time for an expedition to Porto Rico in 1898 as an enlisted soldier with the Sixth Illinois Volunteers, that I am a newspaper man and for the past six years have been continuously in active newspaper work in Chicago: that I am leaving a position as editorial writer on the Chicago Daily News, the world's largest afternoon newspaper, to go to Stockholm for the Newspaper Enterprise Association, which serves [320] newspapers with news stories and descriptive articles and has a circulation going to 4,500,000 subscribers, being the most extensive service of its kind in the world. Tell them I have co-operated actively with the American Alliance for Labor and Democracy, which is the loyalty legion of the American Federation of Labor, and that the alliance gave wide circulation to my war poem, "The Four Brothers." Make me important as hell. Make it look as though there ought to be brass bands and girls in white dresses strewing flowers on my pathway to the steamboat slip.

The time that I get this statement may affect whether I sail Aug. 10 or Aug. 24. Sailing of The Stockholm has been postponed from Aug. 3 to Aug. 10 and unless red tape and officialdom are worse than usual, the passport ought to be ready easily 72 hours before sailing Aug. 10.

I go to Galesburg, Ill. this afternoon to get my mother to swear I was born when I was. They might take a week by mail, for such an affidavit. In Thursday's morning's mail I expect your statement which with birth affidavit, will go forward with application for passport. The passport will then be mailed to any point I designate. I am told it will probably come along within 7 to 10 days from date application is sent from Chicago.

I figure on leaving the Daily News Wednesday of next week. Mr. [Charles] Dennis, the managing editor, said I was "specially fitted for the Stockholm post" and Julian Mason of the Evening Post was tickled. It seems to me I've got to hunt up some sort of live copy and stories or some good friends will be sore. My hunch is that I will find several Big Stories.

This letter is terribly personal. But so is getting a passport. They want to know every mole and scar on a guy's frame. And he has to go get mugged and hand in three pictures of what kind of a pickpocket he looks like.

Sincerely,
CS

128 | TO AMY LOWELL

[Washington, D.C.]
Aug. 5, 1918.

Dear Amy Lowell:

I go to Stockholm, Sweden, soon, sailing set for next Saturday, to run a news bureau for the N.E.A. I may write a true poem of the

Ocean, and one of Rocks, Pines and Fjords, and dark thoughts and lighted whimsies of the winter under the short Yule days. Though I expect to come back in a year or two and go to Brookline and tell you the ins and outs of vast actions, if my luck went the other way, I want you to know I have counted you friend and counselor. And I hope the years will be kind so that we may better speak some of the things war and work have not let us have time for. . . I shall remember you to Gustav Fröding and Selma Lagerlöf and write you sometime from over there of your friends whom I am sure are there. . . If this gets to you and you want to send me a two line note for the steamer, address it to Henry Holt & Co., 19 W. 44th st. . . In all events, luck and regards!

Your
Carl Sandburg

Gustav Fröding was a Swedish poet who wrote exquisite nature poetry in lyric form. Sandburg's poem "The Way of the World," in Good Morning, America, *was written after the manner of Froding. Selma Lagerlöf was a famous Swedish novelist who wrote a fantasy for children,* The Wonderful Adventures of Nils.

129 | TO PAULA SANDBURG

[New York]
Wednesday Night. [September 4, 1918]

Paula Dearest:

Just gave a third reading—and the first real quiet reading to your good-by letter. There were tears in it and a big gladness and a stronghearted woman—my pal—in it.—What we are having is only a breath of the world storm. We will hope that resolves and consecrations enough have been born out of the millions of separations, enough for the remaking of a world.—What with your line about Janet waving, and Margaret's dear note, and the Shewolf's kiss too, it all tugs at me tonight. I got the warm kiss of your calling me "Buddy" at the finish. What we know is that all the chances are in favor of our sitting under our own cherry tree some day and talking about the year Carl went away and the Third Child came. (No Indian name. Maybe "Mary Illinois" if it isn't John Edward.) And when I say God keep you and God keep you I mean it in its oldest and deepest way.

Your
Carl

Sandburg signed with NEA and began to wait—for months—to get his passport. The "Shewolf" referred to Oma, Paula's mother. The Third Child, or "Mary Illinois" here, was born in November and named Helga.

130 | TO PAULA SANDBURG

[New York]
Saturday [September 7, 1918]

Dear Paula:—

I'm saying over again everything I ever said about your being The Best. I see Men and Wives and Men and Women—and so often the wife or the woman hasn't been The Best for the man—and the general run of 'em haven't got *Mind*. I talked with John Reed and his wife last night, Louise Bryant, and she was the first I've met in a long while with something like your range, your head and handling of things. Only, you've got Janet and Marge on top of all this woman has. I can see how you and I would have fitted in Greenwich Village and how we had GV in our "organizing" days. I scribble idly because I like you a hell of a lot.

Carl

131 | TO PAULA SANDBURG

[New York]
Sunday. [September 8, 1918]

Dearest Paula:

Here yet—a leaf in four winds. The day I go two or three weeks from now I'll wire you just for fun.

The day John comes cable me, if all signs show me to be at Stockholm—cable to whatever my postal address is—whether it's John or another little sissenfrass.

Wrote Epictetus for Pep today. Expect to do Rodin and one on the City Directory, and then no more of that for months and months.

The more I look it over the surer I am that we know this world we're living in and all its human trends. Only those breaking pre-war roots and taking risks and being buffeted and lonely, can know.

Carl

"Sissenfrass" was a Steichen term for a little girl, used affectionately. But the Sandburgs had chosen the name already for a prospective boy. Epictetus's Encheiridion *was the ninth in the series for* Pep Books a Newspaperman Ought to Read. Rodin's Art *was the tenth. The one on the City Directory was not published.*

132 | TO SAM T. HUGHES

[New York]
Sept. 12, 1918.

Dear Sam:

A Red Cross man tells me he has waited seven weeks for passport. His backing is bankers and the war work crowd. A Y.M.C.A. man has waited six weeks. I think our national war machine is tightening up on all passages, every form of non-combatant transport that has possibilities for enemy communication. If it takes a Red Cross man with gilt-edged backing more than seven weeks to get to France where enemy communication is difficult I reason I'm going to be patient over delays in getting to Stockholm, the nest of spy nests. All reasons for this tightening up are given added force because of the known enemy desperate efforts to plug our transports through a U-boat raid and because our offensive warfare is at its height. I am willing to accept without protest, and to understand that it's stripping to fight the war through to the shortest possible finish, that the war department forbids circulation of Fred

Howe's book, "Why War", and the censorship prohibits further printings of Barbusse's "Under Fire" and further advertising of Ellen LaMotte's "The Backwash of War." I can see how the government in doing this is reflecting the mood of the country, which is to get the war won and done with the Hell with any chafferers and gabbyjacks who get in the way. I can even see how it might be reasonable, a reduction of hazardous contingencies, for certain authorities to rule that no man of ex-socialist connections and with known bolshevist friends, should be permitted at this time to go to Stockholm. Before I accept any such decision, however, I am going to arrive at some explicit understandings and locate responsibility. I am not going to get excited about any angle of it. I am as willing to be misread and misunderstood as Woodrow Wilson. I know that some of the most portentous facts of the war are not in the foreground at all now. Chester Wright showed me an Associated Press dispatch the other day telling how the Allied troops engaged the Bolsheviki somewhere near Vladivostok, the item ending with a statement: "The American troops did not participate." From forty angles I get it that Wilson is refusing to be pushed into certain drastic imperialistic moves, with the lines of policy much like that in the tangled watchful-waiting Mexican situation.

While in New York I have kept away from the Socialist and I.W.W. bunch, though I have had occasion twice to be thrown into the company of Jack Reed and both times got a lot of good pointers on how to travel, utilize aspirin and saccharin, and permits for supplies to be obtained from the Swedish embassy at Washington. In the matter of association, [F. W.] Kerby here being a dues-paying Socialist party member, and [J. W.] Duckworth a neo-pacifist, and both of them suspicious of Wilson and voicing their suspicions, and both being accredited and open sustainers of the Liberty Defense League, a remaining pacifist bulwark, I am sure this one association is as complicating and implicating as any of recent record. I enclose a reprint of The Four Brothers from the Richmond Evening Journal. This makes probably thirty daily newspapers, outside of the labor papers using the American Alliance for Labor and Democracy service, and several magazines, that have printed this thing in full. Clarence Darrow asked the National Security

League to issue it as a pro-war propaganda pamphlet. I merely point to this record. I am never going to brag of my patriotism, like a virgin of her chastity, or a chorus girl of her shape.

I start for Washington in a day or two. I may have one or two of the strongest banks in New York backing my claim for a passport. Francis H. Sisson, vice-president of the Guaranty Trust Co., was my first city editor. Though we don't agree on economics, he knows my word is good if I pledge him that while the war is on I won't make a move that will affect the solidarity of the allies or the morale of the U.S.A. in war.

In Russia, the Terror is on and all who have issued from the hot breath of it have their nerves gone fliv and can only gibber a disconnected story. I'm going into chaos when I go, Sam, and I'm going to wear the same physiog and try to take it all from week to week like a game I played once with a small town ball team against a champeen big league bunch.

Chester Wright says that if [Samuel] Gompers were here he would press for the passport. Altogether, it seems to be a matter of finding where it's hung up and who's assuming to hang it up and why.

Sincerely,
Carl

In the foregoing the word "say" means what do they know that's news, actually doing, or fairly sure to happen?

Regarding salary, I will try it at first with a 50-50 division between the wife and myself. That is $50 a week would be paid her and $50 to me. And if living cost, such expenses as meals, room, railway fare, telegrams, all expenses that ordinarily go on an expense account, should go above $25 a week, I am to draw on you for it. All inquiries I have made so far indicate I ought to be able to get along on $25 a week. I was brought up on herring and potatoes, and my forefathers lived on black bread the year round, with coffee and white bread only on Easter and Christmas. So if I have to revert— O very well.

I have made this memoranda of our conversation regarding salary, merely in the event that you should be bumped off and your successor not have it as a matter of record.

The length of time which will appear necessary for getting the passport will determine when I leave the Daily News.

Henry J. Smith, news editor of the Daily News, goes on a vacation this week. He is going to stop off at Cleveland and look over your place. He is the fellow I was telling you about, whose mental and spiritual mechanism repeats regularly with a hunch that he ought to be with the Scripps organization. He is too slangy, abrupt, direct, simple and human to be able to function properly on the News. This is not "plugging" in any sense. I merely affirm that you ought to know H. J. Smith and his ways because some day he might fill a hole at some vital salient. He is as individual and indigenous an American as Mark Twain, George Ade or Ring Lardner, and is up to them in personality and writing, only he prefers newspaper work.

And about my being with the N.E.A. permanently, well, I know that if destiny so spake I would rather go down with Petrograd cholera while working for the N.E.A. than any other newspaper organization I know of.

Sincerely,
C.S.

133 | TO THE EDITORS OF CHICAGO NEWSPAPERS

[New York]
[September, 1918]

To the Editor:

Will you kindly inform your readers that it is impossible for one man to do all the work and have all the excitement connected with my name recently in Chicago? It is unfair to myself as well as unfair to the Dr. Karl F. M. Sandberg, who is a member of the propaganda board of the communist labor party, to not only misspell his name but to spell it like that of the undersigned. Dr. Karl F. M. Sandberg is a graduate physician whereas I am a journeyman newspaper writer. Dr. Karl F. M. Sandberg is a member of the communist labor party whereas I am an independent in politics. Dr. Karl F. M. Sandberg was a candidate for lieutenant-governor on the socialist ticket in the last campaign and it was a daily experience for me then to meet voters who said they had scratched their tickets for the first time in their lives in the belief that the under-signed would make an excellent executive head for the state of Illinois. Moreover, in his vocational writings, Dr. Karl F. M. Sandberg is an economist who writes complex analyses of our banking and money systems, assuming the critical ability to wreck and reorganize all our dominant financial structure, whereas my writings are more about smoke and steel, moonlight, women and babies rather than finances as such. Furthermore Dr. Karl F. M. Sandberg writes only the purest English while I take a header into slang if I feel that way. With such diversities as these in personal backgrounds why should the two be tagged with the same name?

Carl Sandburg

134 | TO PAULA SANDBURG

[New York]
Friday, September, 1918

Paula:—Sometimes I wonder if I'm alive or a lizard on a high rock watching a smoky salty misty stupendous drama. Take care of John: he may see great days never known to our eyes.

Carl

135 | TO PAULA SANDBURG

[New York]
Saturday. [September, 1918]

Dearest Buddy:

Hurrah for the kitchen fire, Janet yelling, and the luck of everything. Until one has had a stovepipe break like that one never knows how to properly watch the habits of stovepipes.

Supper tonight and a stay with the Wrights.

I hope I get the exemption without going to Maywood, because a day stay, and the brief spitty smacky kisses of Janet would be a pain. When I come back to Maywood I want it to be for YEARS.

I am wiring MacArthur and McFeeley to see you and to co-operate with the local draft board on getting an exemption. A Spanish war veteran with a wife and two children, 40 years old, ought to make an easy and immediate decision for the board.

Your letters are beautiful. Out of my tumults I try to get one a day to you, one of some kind, sometimes just a Hello My Buddy.

Carl.

136 | TO PAULA SANDBURG

New York
Saturday, September, 1918

No letter in three days from Paula to The Lizard.—One page proof had "dreams of money" instead of "honey". If I were like the printer in this case I would absently write to you as Money.— Lucky I've been on the ground for this proof-reading.—I could easy worry over Maywood today . . but . . it would spell a finish.—The Sphere of London runs a page review by its editor, Clem Shorter, going the limit for Chi. Poems, saying he loves a dedication to "wife & pal". Going to be an English edition of Chi. Poems.

The Lizard

137 | TO PAULA SANDBURG

[New York]
Sept. 23, [1918]

Buddy:

You certainly scribbled a letter the other day. The war industries board will get after you as a paper waster and you will have to get a permit before you can write a letter to Carl unless you write smaller with less space between lines. . . This is a certainty: If Paula can't be counted on to find all the ways of sending supplies to an American cit. at Stockholm, nobody can. . . I'm wondering what luck will be with the draft board, whether I get a telegram from MacArthur to-night. . . I'm sure you have little idea of what

I have been learning in New York, the resignation and humility and obedience of the infinitesimal human unit in the world storm. When I see the boys in their allwool coarse uniforms and hobnailed trench shoes clampety-clamping and slouching leisurely along the sidewalks, on their way, ready, I can't rebel or be restive over anything fate is handing me or us. . . I get the whole length of the thrill you write about attaching to Stockholm. And I'm glad you know it. You knew it wonderfully when I first spoke of the thing. . . I've started to write you about New York days and people sometimes and then feeling it would take a book, I rung off. Maybe we will sit under our own cherry tree some day with John plucking our shoe strings and I reel off the gossipy things that didn't get written. This is a cheap dream like all dear dreams and I'm going to buy one every day even though I haven't got a permit from the war trade board. . . Holt's advertise Cornhuskers in this weeks New Republic as out Sept. 26. . . From the tone and vitality of this Big Letter today I know John will be a Holy Terror.

Carl

138 | TO PAULA SANDBURG

[New York]
Sept. 24, [1918]

Dearest Paula:

You certainly got quick action on the exempt certificate. I give you a hug on that. It would have been hell to go home for two hours—instead of for twenty years as it should be and will be. Now the way seems to be clear for a getaway next week. I wire you before I go on the ship and leave a letter to be mailed you after I sail. Talked six hours with A. M. Simons last night and enclose memo on it. File this. Dinner with [Alfred] Harcourt today. We are getting to be quite pals. The dine was at Columbia Univ. club. Have eaten at Harvard club and Yale with other Parties. Getting to be very quite-so. All the fat I've put on, which is not a much, will be needed in Stockholm. . . As I said once before: Love, regards, hope, everything.

Carl

1918

[New York]
Sept. 27, [1918]

Dear ACH:

When you hear I've sailed—and it's only when I'm gone you can be sure I'm going—write me c/o American Legation, Stockholm, Sweden.

Tell me if Night's Nothings Again gets over. And don't show it to anybody, because I may repeal all its statutes and cut off all its heirs and assigns.

Just got the Sept. Poetry a few days ago. Masters is getting a sicker man all the time. In June he thought he was "all gone, all in" and went to Dr. Frank Billings, being told he was near 100 per cent physically and the trouble was psychic. I wonder whether Homer would have rebuked any one of the seven cities who claimed him as their own born boy.

The new book, Cornhuskers, is out next week.

New York tries to live more life than is livable and it plays hell with the population which is sleazier and snivellery than in any similar compass of American territory.

As I said before—love, regards, hope—everything.

CS

[New York]
Oct. 2. [1918]

Dear Alice:

Thanks for the Wood book. It's real.—I'm going to write Pound from Stockholm that he may hope and hope on that now I acquire a continental suavity.—There's a Big Wind blowing over Europe. Maybe I will write The Song of the Big Wind.—Sometime I shall see how it goes trying to warm myself when the Northern Lights are Playing their mystery pieces, trying to warm myself with

141

Pictures of the adobes where you are and how the sun never fails there.—Whenever you see ice think of me, please! while this Stunt of Folly is on.

Yours,
CS

141 | TO AMY LOWELL

[S.S. Bergensfjord]
Oct. 10, 1918

Dear Amy Lowell:

Those last two letters of yours made good steamer letters—for the time when the sea fills the circle of horizons—and one bird or one fish—is news.

Please send that Shorter article from The Sphere. I read it hastily at Holt's and noted that you had opened his view.

Next time I may write you about icebergs seen—and fjords—and what headway I made on a Sea Poem! "I am a son of the sea and the Sea's wife, the wind."

Please send me one of those good letters:

c/o American Legation,
Stockholm, Sweden.

I hope to see Ellen Key and others and shall tell them you are one of those so good as to vise my credentials. (Cornhuskers was published the day after I left New York.)—Luck and health to you. As ever.

Carl Sandburg

Clement Shorter of the London Sphere *was a great admirer of Sandburg and had written an enthusiastic article in that paper on* Cornhuskers. *Amy Lowell, on hearing from Sandburg about his new job in Stockholm, had written to him: "You mention Gustav Fröding and Selma Lagerlöf, but what is the matter with Ellen Key? She is a fanatic, of course, but I think a most interesting and intelligent one." Actually, Sandburg saw none of these people, for the war news and conditions kept him fully occupied.*

[S.S. Bergensfjord]
Oct. 17, [1918]

Paula:

The captain says we reach Bergen this afternoon. Had an hour of sun yesterday, the first in six days. High seas four days and everybody foggy, soggy, loggy. I ate my heart for being lonesome for you and Maywood and thoughts of the little ones. Been sleeping 10 to 12 hours a night, and eating such as I don't expect again in many a day.

A N.Y. Eve. Post man, R. Long, formerly Asstd. Press man in Russia, was aboard and other good talkers.—Seems it will take about 6 weeks for news correspondence to get thru from Stockholm to our papers.—We have had brief wireless bulletins daily on the ship, all indicating the war goes well and the Kaiser will get his.— Enclose plenty clippings of what you think I might like to hear, when you write.—Send chewing gum, a little, in package. It will help digest fish and potatoes.—Send reviews of our book, if anything good or bad, is printed.—The boat rolls and I pray you make sense out of this foggy soggy letter.—I have your last letter with me. It was an ideal steamer letter.—We are glad it is the fifth and not first winter of the war.—Send Ed's address.—Have had daily salt water plunge bath.—Passed one iceberg.—Passed the Newfoundland banks on a clear afternoon. They thrill grimly. The Christianafjord, a sister of this boat, stranded off Cape Race July 15 last year and 1100 passengers were unloaded, 40 motorcars dumped in the sea and tons of typewriters. We are carrying 13 first class, 3 second, and 1 third class, total of 17 passengers. Sort of like a special chartered boat!—Kiss the kids—All looks good ahead. A kiss to you and all the love there is.

Address: American Legation, Stockholm, Sweden

Your
Carl

1918

Kristiana den Oct. 24 1918

Paula:

I cabled a 165-word story last night which may be a hello to you.

C.

P.S.:—Landlady here is a nut pro-German and curses Wilson all over the map.

Stockholm 10/28, [1918]

Dear Paula:—

These are big days. Looks like I have five or six fierce months of it and then home. Correspondence goes so slow from here that I will cable more than first expected. You will have that advantage over me that you know what I'm doing and who seeing while I can not know who of you is best and worst.—Had to pay $20 import duty on tobacco, & glad to do it & have some real American nicotine. —When I get home I will talk & talk for you—impressions. Lucky I know some Swedish for getting around & most of all for reading papers.—A thick note-book to bring home!—Love to the homey-glomeys & you—all prayers for you and the littlest one.

Carl

Stockholm, Nov. 1, [1918]

Dear Buddy:

Nothing to report, absolutely nothing till I get back home again and we sit in the swing in the back yard and talk. That is, Stockholm and eastern Europe are all such a blur and a chaos now that nothing in the future seems much of a certainty except that a circle of expeditions will get to the bolshevik soviets and wipe them off the map. A New York Evening Post man I came over with says the war will be over soon in every way and "then the old universal human muddle will go on again."—There was a thrill about seeing the soil of Sweden, setting foot on it, and hearing the speech of one's forefathers spoken by everybody and on all the street signs. And the Norway waterfalls are a memory to keep. Much that is homelandish here. But . . . I look forward to when I can go home and have the everlasting youths tousling my hair and giving me spitty smacky kisses. I want to go ahead on that Homeyglomey book. I have seen enough sophistication and ignorance to last me a good while. . . With a lot of love,

Carl

146 | TO PAULA SANDBURG

[New York]
Friday [December 27, 1918]

Dear Buddy:

The Authorities loosened up to the extent of one suit case of stuff today, a few things much wanted. They still hold all Swedish and Norwegian socialist and labor papers, also a mass of Russ pamphlets, books and newspapers. The Scandahoovyan papers had lots of dandy stuff—but I guess we're glad enough we're alive. They did let go two Russ things very good, the 3-vol. Klyuchevski history of Russia and the Izvestia files on the Russian Soviet Congress last June. . . Busier than a cranberry merchant these days. American and British Intelligence officers and an assistant district attorney spent three hours asking questions.

"Which group do you personally favor, the Liebknecht-Luxemburg Spartacans or the Ebert-Scheidemann government?"

"Well, I can't say I favor either of them."

"Huh—well, who do you favor? Why are you so reluctant?"

"If I favor—as you put it—if I favor any one group, it is the Haase-Lebedour Independent Socialist group."

"That is not answering our question strictly. As between the Ebert-Scheidemann group and the Liebknecht-Luxemburg group, which do you favor?"

"I would rather answer that question by saying that I regard Liebknecht and Rosa Luxemburg as honest fanatics while they lived and martyrs now that they are dead. And I have no other opinion than that Ebert and Scheidemann are crooks and will never establish a stable government in Germany."

So it goes. . .

Your
Carl.

Sandburg's baggage was held up in New York after three months abroad as an NEA correspondent. Karl Liebknecht and Rosa Luxemburg were German Socialists who had founded the Spartacus League. Both were violently opposed to war, and they wanted a soviet form of government in Germany. Friedrich Ebert and Philipp Scheidemann wanted a democratic constitution, though not a republic. They were moderate Socialists. Ebert was chancellor and Scheidemann vice-president of the Reichstag; the republic had been proclaimed by Scheidemann on November 9, 1918. Increasing anger and bitterness on the part of both sides led to the murder of Liebknecht and Rosa Luxemburg on January 15, 1919, while they were being conveyed to the Moabit prison.

147 | TO SAM T. HUGHES

[New York]
Dec. 31, 1918.

Dear Sam:

I handed over to the military intelligence officers yesterday the two drafts for $10,000, payable to Santeri Nuortava, and a copy of my letter to you last week with its statement of the purpose of the drafts.

I have gone over this whole matter with Frank P. Walsh, formerly of the War Labor board, with Frank E. Wolfe, director of press service of the American Alliance for Labor and Democracy (which is a division of the Committee on Public Information and financed by the Committee), besides members of the War Labor board. They all feel that my course has been aggressively pro-American and that some sort of definite action must be taken to stop the free and easy propagandas and communications of royalists and imperialists in this country, if a mass of people like those of Finland, subjugated by Prussian machine guns and howitzers, are to be denied rights of communication.—I hope to get full clearance for Cleveland and a long talk with you this week.

Sincerely,
Carl

One of Sandburg's news sources in Stockholm had been the Soviet agent Michael Borodin, who gave him revolutionary literature and $10,000 in drafts for a Finnish agent in the United States, Santeri Nuortava.

148 | TO SAM T. HUGHES

[New York]
Jan. 17, 1919.

Dear Sam:

District Attorney Mathews was in court today, they told me from his office today. I expect to make an appointment with him to-morrow. Capt. Trevor of the Customs Military Intelligence, told me over the phone that the entire disposition of my case is now in the hands of the district attorney.

You recall that just before leaving Cleveland I wrote an article for you on the present hysteria of Europe, a touch of "the daffy", nearly everywhere. I find this corroborated in an editorial in The World yesterday leading off with a quote from some European paper to the effect that most of Europe is suffering from a case of shell shock. The quality needed now for the solutions of the hell's brew of problems to be handled is, says The World, "patience." I have been going along on this theory. My ten days in the middle west, with my own people, with my old neighbors and associates whose fighting and working in the war was 100 per cent, has convinced me not only that my record for Americanism comes clean. The whole affair is much more serious than that. In substance, if the district attorney here chooses to bring this matter to a jury trial, the issue is whether I have read American theory and practice of democracy clearer than the military and naval intelligence officers at the Port of New York and at Christiania, and the United States District Attorney.

The charge against me in case of trial would be that in carrying funds from Norway to the Finnish Information Bureau in the United States I violated the Trading with the Enemy act. This would mean that it is un-American for us to act against the best interests of the present Mannerheim government in Finland. What is the Mannerheim government? A regime established by German guns and bayonets, crack Prussian battalions brought from the western front into Finland at the height of the drive on Amiens when the military situation of the Allies was at its most desperate pitch. For whom was I carrying funds? For those who fought the Mannerheim government, for the imprisoned and starving whose friends and kinsmen died by tens of thousands under the machine gun and shell fire of Prussian guns. Who is the chief beneficiary of the course of official conduct followed in my case? Who but the royalist Mannerheim government which in early October decreed through its parliament that the Prussian Prince Frederich Karl should occupy the throne of Finland?

The farther the matter were carried before a jury the more evident would it become that the prosecution was representing interests alien and inimical to America. The evidence would be overwhelming that the socialists of Finland took a different course from that of the Bolsheviks of Russia in establishing a republic; that they had a peaceful and legal majority in the Finnish parliament and that this properly constituted assembly was sabotaged and its will defeated by the connivance and violence of pro-German imperialists and ex-Russian royalists. The latter have now free entry and free communication with the United States. Their propagandists enter our ports with no embarrassing search and seizure, no halt in their duties and purposes. These, who had their authority established by German howitzers and flammerwerfers only nine months ago, they carry funds and bring literature here and are subjected to no challenge under the Trading with the Enemy act. Such challenge in my case was reserved for one who holds an honorable discharge from the United States Army of 1898 and whose loyalty is a matter of record from the day we went into the war, and whose allegiance to France and England was spoken the day the Great War started. Clarence Darrow and N. D. Cochran will recall that I was not neutral but pro-ally from the start.

Day by day the retention of the Russian "revolutionary literature", which is NEA property and which was brought in under instructions, becomes more preposterous. Of the total of stuff printed in the Russian language probably less than a half can be construed as "revolutionary". Of this more than 75 per cent has already been printed in publications in the United States and is now in the public libraries and has been on sale nation-wide at newsstands.

Sincerely,
Carl

Jan. 28, 1919

I, Carl Sandburg, do hereby consent that the Military Intelligence, of the War Department, the Bureau of Investigation, of the Department of Justice, or the United States Attorney for the Southern District of New York may retain in their possession or in the possession of any one of them all of the books, pamphlets, newspaper clippings, magazines, magazine articles, manuscripts and other similar material brought by me into the United States from Christiana, Norway, on or about the 25th of December, 1918; and I do further consent that any of the agencies above-named may allow any department or agency of the United States Government to have free access to the said material and to use the information contained therein, and I do waive any and all rights that I may have to protest or object to such retention and use of the said material.

It is understood that all the said material will be returned to Mr. Sandburg, providing an investigation by the United States Attorney or any of the other above-named departments shows that the said material if published or otherwise used, would not constitute a violation of the Espionage Law or any other law of the United States.

Sandburg turned over the material, signed the statement, and the charges were dropped.

1919

[New York]
Jan. 30, [1919]

Paula:

Every day action and action. The world turning over. A new thousand years beginning. For some weeks I felt the result in the balance, democracy defeated, checked, smothered, put off a long while. Now I can see a democratized earth on the way in about th same vague outlines that men a hundred years ago could see a republican earth on the way—and by democracy I mean in*dustrial*. Always so far just as I am about to have doubts of Wilson he comes through. He certainly understands the impossibilists among the reds—and the frequent testimony from all sides that he is an "enigma" is a certificate of some good stuff in him. Terribly big days. . . Always I have loved watching storms. And this world storm with all its shadows and pain and hunger has its points—I'm for it—just as I have no criticism of all the waste and afterbirth gore that go with a child born. . . Write me Cleveland after getting this.

Carl.

[Cleveland]
Tuesday [February, 1919]

Dear Buddy:

I'm glad you've been a translator and know the work by which exactitude is arrived at. I've been on a document today—and what with getting it right maybe I've missed the train that ought to carry this to you on Wednesday. Well, it's a homelike gang around the office here—different from New York—50 per cent nearer home and headquarters. And then, I hope to be home Saturday night, anyway sometime Sunday. The czarina letter is going big and they feel I'm a good investment, which ought to mean the three of you have a good investment. . . . A wild world, with the news from Belfast and Glasgow.

Carl.

Sandburg had brought back with him from Europe the czarina's last love letter to the czar.

151 | TO PAULA SANDBURG

[Washington]
Feb. 25, [1919]

Paula Dearest:

I got in here today—and not a line from you in sight. And as there wasn't a line in Cleveland I haven't had a line from you since I left home. Where do you think I am? Or have you quit me? Or are your hands full of trouble? Has the flu come to Our House? Or are you working for the United Charities, or taking up bridge, or welcoming veterans home?

Honest, I miss your notes when they don't come.—Ain't much news. Here maybe two or three days, then New York about two or three days, and then I hope to be through with this all-over-the-map stuff.—Kiss Mary softly once for me.

Carl.

The new baby girl, born in his absence on November 24, had been named Mary Ellen, after a friend, but Sandburg was enthusiastic about Swedish names when he returned, and the name was changed to Helga.

152 | TO WILLIAM MARION REEDY

[Maywood, Ill.]
March 14, [1919]

Dear Bill:

I hope this comes under the wire in time. Some day it will get into the histories that the White Terror of this period was a hundred times more cruel than the Red Terror. See the two in our own country. Debs says something about the war or the government being worse than criminal and gets ten years. Rev. Geo. Simmons after being staged by the Overman senate committee as a witness speaks in New York and as the Kansas City Star reports him he employs directly the words, "criminal" and "pussyfoot" and "bolshevik" to characterize Woodrow Wilson, naming W.W., and the Rev. Simmons gets by without prosecution, which I don't suggest, but without any of the editorial heckling and hazing which might be in line with our official declaration at Paris to support no Russian counter-revolution.—The Mirror has not begun coming to Maywood, Ill. yet.—AND I hear [John] Hervey wrote a crack review of Cornhuskers for The Mirror. If you can slip me two or three I want it. I suppose you're getting The New Majority, labor party paper of Chicago. They are Mirror fans running it.

Sincerely,
Carl Sandburg

Sandburg sent Reedy an article about his experiences in Finland, entitled "Baltic Fogs," for the Easter issue of Reedy's Mirror.

153 | TO SAM T. HUGHES

[Maywood, Ill.]
April 5, [1919]

Dear Sam:

That sitting in with the editors and showing 'em how you get your editorials ought to count. It hit me strong. The suspicion of propaganda these days is much alive. Editors with intelligence enough to brighten their editorial page generally have a curiosity about where an editorial comes from. Indicating who wrote an editorial lets the editor in further on the service idea.

I enter the claim that our story about the inside fight of the socialist party is precisely the sort of a story that all the live newspapers of Europe would consider worth a cable or at least correspondence. I think everybody who has read the news of the I.W.W.

convictions, incarcerations and releases would like to hear what they're going to do when they get back in Chicago and what these demon-demons read on the scrolls of prophecy for to-morrow.

I have just received a mass of stuff from a friend in the bureau of ethnology at Washington. She has lived two years among Sioux Indians (following two years among Chippewas) and has a raft of legends and Indian lore. I think kids and grown-ups, Murricans and Melting Pots have a curiosity about the folks that owned this country before we took it away from 'em. So I'm going to turn in a series of five or six and we can try out the appetite of the nation for it.

Carl.

154 | TO LOUIS UNTERMEYER

Maywood, Ill.,
April 10, [1919]

Dear Louis:

It was a book hard to keep in perspective. The only window you shut down and pass on in too much of a hurry is the Others bunch. Wallace Stevens, for instance, holds for me repeated readings. The music of his lines and the dusk of implications in the phrases stays on and delivers its effect for me always in pieces like Thirteen Ways of Looking at a Blackbird and one, about the elephant's ear shrivelled and the leaves ran like rats, is autumn in city corners immemorially.

As I look it over I feel it a colossal work, a big job, representing experience and concentrated effort. You had to know a lot of live people to keep your interest so vivid, so running to the imagistic in the prose of its telling. And you had to center on the sheer labor of it.

I never got the real measure of Jimmy Oppenheim till this. I always felt a flame about him, a fine flame, but I didn't realize how fully he had worked it out. I've got to read him again and more closely.

The Masters and Pound sections, I suppose, represent a pretty general opinion and feeling. With both of them I feel their best work is as good as there is, by anybody. If I hadn't known Masters in days when he was about the best talker in Chicago and so wonderfully democratic and companionable, before some miasmic malady of fame hit him in the midriff, I think I would go along with every line you have written. With Pound I have the same complex (I knew I couldn't write this dam letter without a "complex" in it) the same complex as when one of my children won't do something good for it which it is told to do. Pound is genius of some kind.—The whole theory and practice of criticism is a hard business. I go in on it in politics, the labor movement; and I like to call a crook a crook; and drink beer or near-beer with pals. But in literature and matters that have to do with the intellectual, spiritual and artistic honesty of other people, I'm a good deal of a fliv.—You have done a red-blooded book. It has a maximum drive of constructive suggestion. When I try to analyze and get beyond my first statement that it's a hummer, I don't get far. There is a generation of young bucks coming along in this country; not afraid of facts or theories; preferring the new experiments to the old bunk; and they're going to eat up your book; in high schools and colleges, in public libraries.—And the foregoing is a hell of a sight more sympathetic comment than I've written on lithrachoor in a long while. I hope it reaches you lazying and lazying in the Jersey Mountains not caring a dam whether American bookdom is more important than the nearest young frog scraping a frogland chorus from his froggy throat. What we want here is the restoration and control of L. Untermeyer pep for the writing of the more and more books in his system.

As ever,
Carl Sandburg

Louis Untermeyer's Modern American Poetry *was published in 1919.* Others *was a poetry magazine edited by Alfred Kreymborg.*

1919

Chicago
April 10, [1919]

Dear Sam:

I've been slanting through a book just out called "Home Made Beverages" by Albert A. Hopkins. It tells about "the manufacture of non-alcoholic and alcoholic drinks in the household." I get a hunch from it that the boozefighters, the lovers of Omar and most everybody except the teetotal abstainers and holier-than-thous would sort of like to know all they can know about near-booze and all beverages that might possibly speak a language to the human system something like the speech of booze. Here's Friend Housewife. Her man's been stopping for beer to help his digestion and one way and another she knows his system has got used to ferments, ticklers, teasers and coaxers of digestion, faith, hope and fellowship. Friend Housewife would like to do all she can to provide her man with stuff to throw into him, not as a substitute for booze, but as an element in his metabolism and the proper coordination of his guts. When I had case beer in my house in Milwaukee I noticed I didn't care much for it when there was a plenty of lettuce, radishes and fresh cabbage slaw, especially lettuce. Of course, near beer will take care of much of this. The digestive upset. Yet there will be a lot of men restless physically and mentally with the real booze bazaars gone and these men and their wives would like to know what science says is good as a nerve food, bodily tonic and mental solace in place of the old stuff. The Hopkins book is published by Scientific American.

Galsworthy is sticking here several days yet and I hope to get one real interview.

Carl.

1919

Chicago
April 14, [1919]

Dear Sam:

The first week or so here I felt I wasn't getting the stuff. The last two weeks I have been getting into a stride of work that I can keep up indefinitely. What I am sure of is that if I'm not getting the news or feature or personality twist to the things I'm sending you and to what I'm picking out of the day's drift, then it's because I'm picking it wrong and sending it wrong; the cinch fact is that there is a steady stream of live NEA stuff here for use, and for use as "circulation builder." The Kernel Clark Bascom story, for instance, is a real news feature; if you don't run the first one I sent I'm going to send more because he and his talk are up to Henry Watterson; he's as vivid as Watterson but in harder luck. He is one nut, a colorful specimen and a characteristic specimen out of the physical speed and mental chaos of our day. Everybody he meets laughs with him and is half-sorry and half-glad about him; he is up to any of the queer ones George Ade ran in his Stories of the Streets and Town; if I didn't put him over it was because I was holding to NEA space decrees.—Yesterday I heard Prof. Starr in a picture lecture on the cave men and have him jotted down to be seen for pictures and stories besides one I've sent today on the cave man's preference for a fat woman. Then I went to the art institute and saw the Anisfeld pictures; they are vital and joyously loony and I'm wondering if there isn't a way to put 'em across; to give every NEA reader a substitute for a visit to the pictures, because they stop 'em all. Then I met my wife and we had tea with the Galsworthys at the Blackstone. They were just from Milwaukee and Peoria engagements. They feel a homelessness about faces and houses in America. I told him I saw a man leaning on a farm fence one morning in Sweden and it seemed to me the man had stood at that fence a thousand years. And I never have seen a man lean on a fence that way in the U.S.A. A little land for any and all people must be an essential of any program of democracy, as

G. sees it. The instinct for land is so deep and important that nations will not see prosperity nor the world peace till the common man has land on fair terms.—Then we went to the City Club, the going being good, and our ears in order, and heard Raymond Robins give a two hour speech and 40 minutes of questions and answers, all this covering ground not covered in his previous speech which took two hours and a half with an hour of questions and answers. The truth is that Robins is quietly raising hell and there will be results from these many long speeches. Used to be he couldn't thrill me at all; I suppose now it's because I think he tells more of the God's straight truth, more of what will in the long run go into history, than anybody who has talked or written on Russia in this country. The City Club or the New Majority will publish all his first speech; I'll send it on to you. He's been giving this stuff at big churches here to packed houses; at the home of federal Judge Carpenter and at the Casino Club to Art Meeker and all the plutes. I call it a big job of reporting he's doing. His main point is that while he considers the bolshies "economically impossible and morally wrong in social theory" he refuses to lie about or agree with the lies told about Lenin and Trotsky and their gang.—Among things ahead: I'm after an interview with a surgeon who performed 6,000 operations at the western front; going to hear Arthur Morrow Lewis on How to Know the Summer Stars; and Prof. Starr on the League of Nations, Lewis saying it's the best lecture bar none he ever heard. Then . . . there are business men I'm seeing with ex-pect-ta-tions. I notice The Trib today has the first cock fight story in years, clearly a follow on ours. So it goes. Tip me off if I'm too far from my base. But don't take me away from Chicago for awhile.

This may look like a funny letter. But you said put in the reactions.

Lot of talk around about how the Republicans next year will spring cablegrams between Wilson and Germany, and figures and documents on Hog Island and aircraft.

Sincerely,
Carl

Chicago
April 17, [1919]

Dear Sam:

The return of my letter thus criss-crossed was as good as a trip to Cleveland. Maybe I'd better try writing out my hunches and let those pass that you and Star knock down and work away on those you pin hopes on.

I know that "Who the hell is Galsworthy?" story, also the one about "Where the hell is Zanzibar?" and the one "What are Keats?" and "Is molasses plural or singular?" So I purposely started my story with the claim that whoever he is he is the most American Englishman who has come our way, followed by remarks about him that would be listened to with interest if spoken by any nobody on a street car. The interview hangs 20 per cent on Galsworthy and 80 per cent on what he says, ending with a barber shop quartet song that might stand by itself but gets fresh interest through getting the official O.K. of an upper class Englishwoman, even though we never heard of her. If a man's books are in every public library and if magazines pay him $200 a page and his name has been bawled noisily from the Hearst papers and he has figured in the Associated Press dispatches and on top of it all he is a foreigner whose spirit is kin to everything that's best about the NEA—and he then chooses to let loose comment that Bechtol would send from our London office—why, I'm going to send you the stuff. I'll grant there's a lah-de-dah angle to the guy that gives you some standing in court. BUT I'll bet you 80 per cent of the Omaha 6 o'clock trolley car riders would get his points and thank the paper that gave it to 'em. And Frisco the Jazz King tells me any man's a fool to count on getting more than 80 per cent of his audience. One person out of 100 undoubtedly thinks Bela Kun is a coffee but they would read an interview—80 per cent of the 100— if told he's the new Hungarian prime minister. I purposely refrained from sending you an interview with Gen. Wood, whom 80 out of 100 knew, because there was nothing but good-will political bunk to his talk.

I'm sure I'll be sending you stuff regularly because it interests me and I think there's a chance it might interest you but my bet is that you can it. Equally as often I'll send a story or editorial that I would argue for till the cows come home, being sure that by not printing it you are limiting the headway of the NEA. I can see you throwing away Kernel Clark Bascom but if you ditch the Galsworthy, then I'll feel your faith in the mob is too wobbly, you're out of the mob instead of in it. What NEA aims for is to get circulation and hold it. Not always is circulation made and held by the stories read by everybody. There are "the captains of the tens and twenties"—teamsters, machinists and crossing flagmen who would chew on Galsworthy's point that England may resist bolshevism as she did Napoleon, and talk about it as having been in such-and-such a paper. Of course, this makes no immediate enthusiasm among the egg-head editors. But across any length of time, a newspaper or a newspaper service has got to have this element to get its circulation rooted. Then too—and I'm going into this Galsworthy thing fully because it's typical—in vaudeville there's an act known as "classy"; they don't get all of it, all the art of it; but they do know they could get all of it if they had more time to be decently developed human beings; and they applaud half because they enjoyed the soft lights and the nice gowns and the elegant langwidge and the history and the mystery and the suggestions and half because they know they ought to get more of it and it's worth their time. Somebody said of Edmund Burke, "Meet him under a rain shed for a half hour and you might not discover he was a great man but you would surely say he is an interesting talker." I hear kids telling each other to read Robinson Crusoe not because it's a child's classic but because it's a "dandy" book. So I believe in playing certain stuff in newspapers that will get some folks just because it's interesting and others because it's classy and still others, the captains of the tens and twenties, because it's both. I guess I'll try to illustrate this with some action.

Carl.

Maywood, Illinois
May 6, 1919.

Dear Amy Lowell:

I enjoyed your New York Times letter . . . like watching Tom Marshall of Keithsburg shoot clay pigeons . . . you cite each demurrer and objection and then your evidence goes pling!

Your Atlantic poem goes far. I have seen men hanged and I know all the hanging poems and this beats out great and sure cadences. And two or three other things of yours in magazines the last year make me believe your book next fall is to be the best you have printed.—I wonder if you got the chief point of this analogy of you and T.R. It isn't so much that he was always making the front page as that he was always moving from one adventure to another.—I get the `impression definitely that you pull down high vagabondries out of life in spite of all New England heritages; you are a break from the N.E. tradition; I must hunt up a piece I have on Nathaniel Hawthorne for you; Mrs. Sandburg card indexes you as not modern American so much as old Elizabethan, modern French, and most ancient Chinese. When I get to flinging that portrait of you onto canvas maybe I shall have to use "Synchronist" theories and title it "Organization 4-11-44".—Anyhow you are always one of the good invisible presences at our house; you are one of those we name when we are specific in our prayers.

Sincerely,
Carl Sandburg

Chicago, May 13, 1919.

Dear Star:

I hope your temperament will thrill at these Vaux photos. I have been having a big powwow with Maj. Edouard Steichen, who is not only the world's greatest art photographer and impressionist painter, but was Chief of the Photographic Section of our air forces. He got the stuff I wired you from a high medical corps man at Brest. We're in line to get more peachy picts, provided your temperament gets fixed to these Vaux views as peachy.

The N.Y. Times ran a picture May 4 showing, I am told, American troops going over the top and one soldier, the only one in the bunch without a gas mask, clutching at his throat, gasping, falling. It was captioned by the Times as a photo taken from a German prisoner and supposed to have been taken by a German camera of our boys going over. The fact is, Maj. S. says, that the picture was framed up by American officers and widely circulated among men at the front to show the men that the fellow who neglects his gas mask has a hell of a time during a gas attack. So if the NEA wishes to correct the goddam N.Y. Times, opportunity yawns and beckons.

Enclosed is that book shop copy. Though this isn't the letter I was going to write you. Today is one of the days we work all day.

Can you send back the Vaux pictures. They belong to my wife and we all obey our wives in matters of this kind.

Carl.

160 | TO EMANUEL CARNEVALI

Chicago
May 17, [1919]

Dear Emanuel.:

If I were anything like a free vagabond I would have been to see you a lot of times. Whatever happens I hope things will shape up for me one of these days so I will have more time and you are one of the companionable spirits of earth that I will want to share some of the time with. I am just finishing up Mss. of "Smoke and Steel," a third book that will run over 200 pages, God help us all. I enclose two bluish maroons that represent hours of fate of recent days.

I wish you lonliness and strength for lonliness and a grasp of the secret that you are and must ever be one of earth's lonely ones, that if you become otherwise you are a goner, and therefore you will make the months and years register pleasure plus accomplishment only by learning to nourish your roots many years all by yourself. Companionships, yes, but only as a preparation for your lonliness, a stand-by and a memory for your creative hours. Your vision is one no one else can parallel. The foregoing has been known to every genius with daemon analogous to your own, who succeeded in hitching up that daemon and driving it. Possibilities, friends, for you, are legion. I am writing you exactly what I would talk to you if we were shackled together on a chain gang with no outlook for anything but hell for breakfast and ashes for dinner across years to come.

Yours amid long files of chain gangs
Carl

161 | TO SAM T. HUGHES

Chicago, May 20, 1919.

Dear Sam:

You're right, I guess. Your letter was exactly what I wanted you to send if you looked at it that way. I've seen you through months that tried men and my hat's off to you on forty and one things, your readiness to fight on certain specific human issues, your letters to the New York office on how to write to the plain people, your frank vision of your own job and the newspaper game. I never worked with a finer gang than the NEA staff, Star, Finley, Doc Rogers, Kerby and Duck, Miss Clark, Higgins, Tommy Johnstone and all. I never saw so little "office politics" in a place. And I know this is much your own spirit running through the team.

That I'm leaving the NEA applies to this time and now chiefly as to the payroll. When I go Cleveland way and stop off I'll look you up. And I hope when you're in Chicago you'll see me once in a while. I don't want to say I'm through with the NEA for good and always. When I stopped in to see you last summer on my way to Saratoga it was because I wanted a look-in on an American institution a lot more important than Harvard or the Smithsonian Institute. So I warn you I will sometimes send in suggestions just as any citizen does to a government he respects; and I may come in with a definite layout of work connecting me with the NEA again.

Where I go next I can't say now because I have not been keeping touch with other openings. Two offers were made me in February, to go to work then. I suppose a week or two will clear things up. You have been more than generous and thoughtful with me and you will never hear otherwise directly or indirectly from me but that you were on the level all ways with me.

Sincerely,
Carl

Sam Hughes had written to Sandburg on May 16, 1919, "I have to tell you frankly that you and NEA are not hitching well together. . . . You are a great writer—your poems are sufficient evidence of that. . . . Nevertheless I don't like to say the word to you that we are through. What do you say?"

162 | TO VACHEL LINDSAY

Maywood, Ill., May 21, 1919

Dear Vachel:

The California thing is way your best—a strong vast sardonic that will bring various meanings to varied people. In its farther implications it explains why nobody loves a fat man and supports the historic fact that lean races take what they want and a too swiney girth leads to hellangone.

Yours endlessly,
Carl Sandburg

163 | TO HENRY JUSTIN SMITH

Maywood, May 31, 1919.

Mr. Smith:

There never was a time when demand was so keen from a large section of the newspaper-reading public for scrupulous, sincere accuracy in the reporting of facts and statement of trends in that hydra-headed thing we call "the labor movement". Fifty-two members of the teaching staff of the University of Illinois have formed a local union and affiliated with the American Federation of Labor. An association of 5,000 engineers and office draughtsmen are to affiliate with the A.F. of L. Work is now quietly proceeding on formation of unions in two "white collar occupations" in Chicago and the completion of these organizations will be as curious and significant a development as were the launching of the federations of public school teachers and city hall office clerks.

Two or three times a week I can hand you a column or half-column of news items from the organized labor field, this not running as a department but having a lead story. On May 24 a special train left Chicago and the Indiana steel districts taking some 300 delegates to a national conference at Pittsburg of all trades involved in steel making, with a view to organization of steel workers nationally. A few days ago James E. Tobin, 20 years president of the boot and shoe workers' international union, and 12 years a vice-president of the A.F. of L., a close personal aid of Gompers, died. Chicago papers have had neither stories nor items chronicling these events.

Among stories worth while outside labor would be one listing the cities of the United States which have increased traction fares; the partial list I have seen is formidable and with amounts of increased fare would interest all who ride surface and "L" cars. Tactics of left wing or bolshevik-spartacan elements of the socialist party attempting to win control of the party machinery, are dramatic; the county convention May 18 was as rough-house as any old time old party convention. Samuel Hopkins Adams of Colliers is here in June to write articles on the Labor Party; there are angles of that situation that offer live stories—and I would add that with the Labor Party group the Daily News noticeably commands a respect as a news medium that puts it over all other Chicago papers.—On June 8, Glenn Plumb, attorney for the Big Four railroad brotherhoods, speaks at Carmen's Hall on a plan favored by the Big Four and the street car men's international and the National Public Ownership League, for ownership and operation of all railroads in the U.S.A.; big preparations have been made for the mass meeting and labor officials say it will have national significance; there is a fraction of the membership of the Big Four (whether it is majority or minority is not definitely known) which aims to bring on a rail strike crisis unless this plan is adopted.

I believe there are some big, live feature stories down in the steel and iron works towns, from South Chicago to Gary. What are superintendents and workmen saying about "Americanization"? How are the returned soldiers going to work and what does life mean now to the steel workers who went overseas?—Why have bank deposits doubled in most banks in Chicago the past year?— What will be the action about June 15 when large payments are due on Russian bonds held in this country?

I have spent two whole days talking with Maj. E. J. Steichen, chief of the photographic section of the A.E.F., and with two other men who saw front line service with the American forces. There are stories here, the first in America, on how Gen. Foch once held up all forward movement of the American army during 48 hours in which American airmen settled conflicting reports as to whether bridges were intact over the Meuse river, by taking photographs. There is fresh scientific value to this material, also action and adventure.

Mrs. Wm. Monroe of the Illinois Social Hygiene society says there are 2,500 defectives in Chicago and 10,000 in Illinois whose nerves went to pieces in their first weeks at cantonment camps.

Why shouldn't a Chicago paper print the first story on the Russian wives of American millionaire socialists in New York who are breaking away from their husbands, as in the cases of the Stokes and Wallings, where the wives are bolshevik and the husbands anti-?

Carl Sandburg

164 | TO LEW SARETT

[Chicago]
June 6, [1919]

Dear Sarett:

Glad to have your letter. We had a lot of fun home about that preface and hoped you would get it that way.

I'm going to see Mrs. Stevenson, head of the Pond office here, this week and ask about hopes and horizons. I'm started on building a show as will be a show and whatever you're telling Vawter will be vindicated from the drop of the hat and to the crossing of a T. What I am day by day more sure of is that this is a field where I will have to end up because . . . I'm trained for it. I'm going to keep my eye out for dates for the two of us next fall and winter.

May go to the A. F. of L. convention Atlantic City next week to stay two weeks and so sorrily missing you if you come on June 16, and leave before the 20th or 21st which is the latest date I'll be back. There's a chance I won't go in which case you must figure on an afternoon or evening with Mrs. Sarett and yours out at our place, such as it is.

And a lot of luck to you—

Sincerely,
Sandburg.

Lew Sarett was a poet and long-time friend of Sandburg's. He had written a poem about Sandburg, entitled "The Granite Mountain," which had just been accepted for Reedy's Mirror. *The preface mentioned was the one Sandburg wrote for* Many Moons. *The Pond office was a lecture bureau. Sandburg was about to return to lecture-recital engagements in addition to writing for the Chicago Daily News.*

165 | TO EDWARD STEICHEN

Maywood, Ill.
July 8, [1919]

Dear Ed:

What can we say . . . more than that we are all tied up closer to you and with you than ever before . . . and as fate deals the cards sometimes there is reason to say, "This is the worst of all possible worlds" . . . and my gnomic friend, the Irish philosopher on the steamship, was right about the spiders having forgotten some things we know because in the end the wireless telegraph and all our electric push buttons are useless or superfluous . . . Well, remember what you said about Chicago having no art at all and so being possibly a place worth trying out as a place to live in. I don't know whether any one ever called your attention to our class of murders out here. Editors and specialists agree that we are the best.—I have spent ten days in the Black Belt and am starting a series of articles in the Chicago Daily News on why Abasynnians, Bushmen and Zulus are here.—Come along sometime, if only to see Janet. She's got your own elusive way and she is a hunter of beauty and will be hungry all her life. She is your kin all over.—Paula keeps more beautiful forty ways than ever before and is worth your knowing more.—If luck can come from wishing, daytime and night-time wishing, you will have it from us out here.

Carl

These articles later were published by Alfred Harcourt's new firm, Harcourt, Brace & Howe, as The Chicago Race Riots.

166 | TO EDWARD STEICHEN

[Elmhurst, Illinois]
[Circa September, 1919]

Dear Ed:

Thanks for those Pershing parade pictures. The editors feel Pershing is already overplayed. But they are dandy picts and so we'll have 'em at home.

Great times moving from Maywood to Elmhurst. Paula is having the time of her young life. Be ready to look over some live branches of nieces of yourn when you come this way.

You're in our thoughts and speech often. And we're always wishing you all the luck there is.

Carl

167 | TO AMY LOWELL

[Chicago]
Sept. 26, [1919]

Dear Amy Lowell:

Your letter about the Chinese things came just in time to stop publication. Max Eastman has them and your straightaway reply wrecked the hopes of Max. I have so many orphans and stray dogs in my portfolio now that these will go in with plenty of companionable vagrants.

I am interested watching the onward sweep of free verse. Certain it is that never before such a turn toward a cultural value had so sure a hold on the young: I could write a book on the way this new trend is taking root. It is not an iconoclastic break with the Past; it doesn't move with hate for a dynamic; it's only that here's something they believe nourishes them better and all round has the attractions that connect with more of life. It's the Young who are our best friends.

The way Collier's weekly editorial hit you off has been the direct comment of Mrs. Sandburg about yourself from the first. You are no more New England than Popocatapetl. All regards!

Sincerely,
Carl Sandburg

Sandburg had sent Miss Lowell a note asking permission to print some poems which were made from translations by Florence Ayscough. She replied: "I am awfully sorry, but you cannot possibly print these poems without Mrs. Ayscough's permission, and I feel sure that she cannot give that to you at present. She is very particular about the way these poems are done, and we are doing a book together, as doubtless you know. She insists upon the slightest little thing going back to Shanghai to be gone over by her teacher, and I know she did not consider your renderings at all exact, although she thought they were very beautiful."

1919

[Circa October, 1919]

Dear Sir:

You ask me to belong to something. You wish me to join a movement or party or church and subscribe to a creed and a program. It would be easy to do this. It is the line of least resistance. If I have a fixed, unchangeable creed then I am saved the trouble every day of forming a new creed dictated by the events of that day. If I have a program and a philosophy and a doctrine, crystalized in an organized movement, then the movement is supposed to do for me what I ought to do for myself. I am a socialist but not a member of the party. I am an I.W.W. but I don't carry a red card. I am an anarchist but not a member of the organization. I belong to the modernists of the Catholic church but I have not made the sign of the cross with holy water in two decades. I am a Francis Heney Republican and a Frank P. Walsh Democrat and a Victor Murdock Progressive but I am free to vote any ticket or back any candidate I pick in the next campaign. I belong to everything and nothing. If I must characterize the element I am most often active with I would say I am with all rebels everywhere all the time as against all people who are satisfied. I am for any and all immediate measures that will curb the insanity of any person or institution that is cursed with a thirst for more things, utilities and properties than he, she or it is able to use, occupy and employ to the advantage of the race. I am for the single tax, for all the immediate demands of the socialists, for the whole political program of the American Federation of Labor, for the political and economic measures outlined in the Progressive and Democratic party platforms, and the trend of legislation and activity voiced by Woodrow Wilson in "The New Freedom", and I believe the most important correctives and the most imperative human rights collectively attainable at this time, are given in proportionate statement in the report of the federal industrial relations commission. I am for unrest, discontent, revolt and war to whatever extent is necessary to obtain the Russian Bolshevik program which centers on the three needs: bread, peace, land. Until the earth is a free place to free men and women wanting first of all the right to work on a free earth there will be war, poverty, filth, slums, strikes, riots, and the hands of men red with the blood of other men. I am against all laws that the people are against and I respect no decisions of courts and judges which are rejected by the people. I believe all property is sacred for which men have wrestled with the wilderness or in any way toiled with their hands or brains or suffered and exchanged their lives and years to create. I repeat that all property created by man's labor is sacred to me and such property should be protected, invested with safeguards and an automatic machinery of production and distribution whereby and wherethrough the man who works would receive the product of his work. In other words, the institution of property should be so ordained that no man should be granted ownership and title to property for which he has not rendered an equivalent, or nearly an equivalent, of service to society. Property is so sacred to me that I want to see it only in the hands of those who are able to take it and use it and make it of the greatest service to society. I believe that in order to attain an institution of property so ordained it is not so necessary to have a specific and detailed program of measures, policies and plans as it is that the people shall be strong enough and wise enough to take what they want and use what they need.

Any steps, measures, methods or experiences that will help give the people this requisite strength and wisdom, I am for. I can not see where the people have ever won anything worth keeping and having but it cost something and I am willing to pay this cost as we go along—rather let the people suffer and be lean, sick and dirty through the blunders of democracy than to be fat, clean, and happy under the efficient arrangements of autocrats, kaisers, kings, czars, whether feudal and dynastic or financial and industrial. I can not understand how the people are going to learn except by trying and I do not know any other way to honestly conduct the experiment of democracy than to let the people have the same opportunities of self-determination that belong of right to nations small and large, the same opportunities of self determination that are the heritage of a healthy child. In their exercise of the right of self determination I expect the people to pass through bitter experiences and I am aware it is even possible that the people shall fail in the future as they have failed in the past. Yet I cannot see it otherwise than that we are nationally and internationally a lot of hypocrites and liars unless we have [line missing] verse of this viewpoint I would write that the reputed wise men of the books, newspapers and platforms have often been only the unwitting mouthpieces of cruel and willful masters and it is not outside of reasonable prophecy for a man to say that the people may surprise those who sneer a perpetual despair at what the people would achieve in administration of government, industry, transportation and land. The republics of France, Switzerland, Australia, New Zealand, and the United States have been surprises in history and though the outcome of the great war can not be envisioned in the concrete workings of the surviving nations, it is conceded that political government is an institution that must pass from the hands of feudal and dynastic autocrats. That is, the nations of the world are now getting ready to do what France and the United States did in the nineteenth century in spite of those who sneered their despair at the people. The deep but quietly passionate affection that men the world over have for France traces in degree to the fact that France as a nation has loved the people and voiced the and fought for the aspirations of the people for self determination. It was a surprise of history when France overthrew the third Napoleon and established a political democracy instead of picking another crowned head. It was a surprise of history when the doubts, wranglings and conspiracies of the thirteen American colonies ended not with one more king but with a new republic. It was still another surprise when the United States fought a civil war sacrificing two million lives, the bloodiest war in history, [line missing] the majority rule on which democracy depends for life. It was still another surprise when the wronged and betrayed people of Russia refused to hang their czar. A Polish philosopher has written that humanity consists of mob at the top and mob at the bottom, at one extreme an ignorant, idle and incompetent leisure class, at the other extreme the vags, bums, down-and-outs, the rickety, mal-nourished, tubercular and anemic men, women and children of the slums. Our Polish philosopher neglected taking account of the vast section of people between these two mobs. I have a theory—with no authenticated facts to support it—that Jesus of Nazareth was crucified by the lower mob through a conspiracy organized by the secret diplomacy of the upper mob and therefore, the mercy of the Russian mob toward its former czar should stand as the classic instance rather than the crucifixion of Christ and the ride of humiliation on the rump of a jackass round-about the walls of Jerusalem. I wonder if I make myself clear in venturing to suggest that I am for reason and satire, religion and propaganda, violence and assassination, or force and syndicalism, any of them, in the extent and degree to which it will serve a purpose of the people at a given time toward the establishment eventually of the control of the means of life by the people.

Carl Sandburg

This statement of Sandburg's creed was in response to a letter from Waldo Frank in New York enclosing a translation of an Appeal which Romain Rolland sent to Sandburg as one of the "intellectual workers of the world." Rolland, author of the internationally famous roman-fleuve Jean Christophe, *had become interested in the emerging U.S.S.R.*

169 | TO JOSEPH WARREN BEACH

[Chicago]
Nov. 22. [1919]

Dear Beach:

Thanks for your good works. I felt that my own contribution was somewhat too hurried and didn't match up as well in the entourage and the melee as it would if I had had more time. But what is a poet with a family to do? When he has daughters who are fine tigresses and he wants 'em to grow up, he can't let his daily bread job slip away even for such glad ships of passage as Foolscap. It's in my bones I'll make Minneapolis in a year or so and I hope this time to find you in. I believe I wrote you that I was at a convention a year ago and phoned you but the word was you were on vacation. We are a-wishing you all the luck there is, all the time.

Carl Sandburg

P.S.—Just finishing a smoke and steel piece, about the length of Prairie. If you've done anything on the M. gas plant let me see it whether you're going to print it or not.

Joseph Warren Beach was a poet and teacher at the University of Minnesota. Smoke and Steel *was published in 1920. Beach later wrote a poem on the Minneapolis gas plant.*

170 | TO EMANUEL CARNEVALI

[Chicago]
[Circa early 1920]

Dear Emanuel:

Thank you forty ways for a living and vivid letter filled with as good laughter as you or anybody else ever laughed. Touches here and there too with a high spot of song. One with such a capacity for throwing the golden rings of the moon into the lake and hauling them up on the sands ought to go slow about doing anything except a few steady things of a set program of doing nothing in particular on odd days and nothing special on even days::$$1234567890—and a cuppa coffee. That is my advice to you. Melt the golden rings of the moon into a shield and write this advice on it.

If you ever learn to eat loneliness and like it half the time—and if you ever learn to be so deliberate that you capture so much as one half the dreams running across the disc of your consciousness —you will outrun and outdo any and all Latin artists I know of in these latter days.

I shall pray for feet and hours to make the dune journey. Just now all roads to the dunes are blind alleys with ash barrels and rat carcasses so far as I am concerned.

Go to it, kid. Eat your heart out and make yourself like it. Harden all that is brass in you and forget all that is not brass. The logs, swivel and protective case of the apparatus that enabled you to throw golden moon rings into the lake—all brass.

Pope of the Lake, Emperor of the Sand, for the Mass sung to my coming, I am going to write a Bible of requiem, I am going to execute a composition of music, a series of hosannah notations to be shouted with the throwing of moon rings of gold into the lake, the length of each hosannah to be based on the diameter of each ring thrown.

And I shall tell people that just now you are more than happy —happiness being only a negation of misery—that you are close to discovering mockeries and secrets of the earth—how when one has flown all of life flyable in a day it is time to drop down to place as next-of-kin with all things that know nothing, say nothing, and wait.

Yours for the gray gateways,

Carl Sandburg

Emanuel Carnevali, an Italian poet, for a time was an associate editor of Poetry Magazine. *He wrote an article on Sandburg, entitled "Our Great Carl Sandburg," which was published in the February, 1921, issue.*

171 | TO JOHN HOLME

[Chicago]

Jan. 3, 1920.

My Dear John Holme:

Wood handled the Gary situation fairly well. With the exception of a few personal manners and mishandlings by Col. Mapes. I doubt whether the Gary job could have been done better. The steel trust was after violence, some kind of a blow-up, something sensational. The nearest it came to this was Col. Mapes announcement that a nation-wide red plot was in the making with headquarters at Gary. This was more the work of cheap newspaper men than of Col. Mapes. You will be safe in saying there was a military administration at Gary that was somehow coolly and shrewdly managed from the top: that in similar situations it has almost always happened that the military permitted itself to be used, was outmaneuvered or tricked by the instruments and machinations of the anti-labor crowd, while at Gary I found the feeling general on both sides that the military was neutral.

The last figures I heard as to the race riot death toll was 35 negro dead and 20 white men. It may be a few, two or three, more or less on either side but that just about represents the score. The stories of many niggers being killed and hidden are bosh. It's a dam hard job to get rid of one corpse in a big city. Corpses stink. One stinks much, ten considerable, and fifty would be awe-ful.

Mr. Strindberg is glad to be able to do something for a glad and mucking Icelander who has an honest-to-God pride he came from a climate that would freeze the nose off a brass monkey. Mr. Ibsen wishes a happy year to you.

Sincerely,
CS

P.S.—If you want the backgrounds of the race riots, see Harcourt, Brace & Howe, 1 W. 47th St. for my pamphlet; it's a collection of the Daily News articles.—

John Holme, who worked for the New York Evening Post, addressed Sandburg as "Dear Ibsen."

172 | TO JOHN A. LOMAX

[Chicago]
Jan. 9, 1920.

Dear John Lomax:

There isn't a man south of the Mason and Dixon line who could reach in and get at me as you do in criticism of the general spirit of my race riot articles. I am sure that no other white man in recent years did so much for me to help me get at the way inside interiors of the negro human soul as you did. Your letter itself has big human flashes that make me very ready to say that I must have stressed some points wrong. You are representative of that part of the South, like Thomas Nelson Page and others, who start with the admission that the negro mind and soul have cultural values. I have not met any man with a keener sleuthing instinct than yourself for these wonderful, vivid singing qualities in the negro soul.

I know you would understand, if we had the time to go over all the evidence, that there is a prejudice which if it could achieve its desire would segregate, repress, and again make a chattel of the negro if that status could again be restored. Both north and south this prejudice was loosened with the end of the war and was given added impetus by the very physical hysteria of war. I believe that this prejudice, as sheer prejudice, runs deeper and wider down south than up north and that this is the basic reason why the southern business interests have completely failed in their endeavors to induce movements of negro population from northern points back south again. There is no place in the south that I have heard of where the negro has the freedom of ballot and the political equality and economic opportunity accorded him in Chicago and other northern cities. I did go out of my way, probably, in my writing, to throw a flashlight on discrepancies in the "democracy" of the ruling class of the south just as I also went out of my way to show the terrible shortcomings of the Chicago stockyards overlords, whose work and wages policy across the last twenty years must be counted as a factor in the production of hoodlums, white hoodlums. Whatever reflections I may have cast on the south, however, were merely incidental and cursory as compared with the direct indictment of the intelligence of my own home town for its lack of plan in housing, its economic discrimination, its collusion of police and gamblers by which negro crap joints exploit the negro workmen by wholesale. I want to thank you for writing that letter just as you wrote it. It has just the thing about it that used to make me go out of my way to look you up and learn new things worth knowing, when you were here.

Faithfully yours,
Carl Sandburg

John A. Lomax grew up on the Old Chisholm Trail and became one of the country's pioneer teachers and ballad collectors in the South. Later he and his son, Alan, helped to establish and develop the Library of Congress's Folk Music archives. Lomax had written Sandburg: "What the Negro wants, what his real ambition is is to have absolute equality. I do not blame him for it, I only know that he wants it and equality involves social equality."

[Elmhurst, Illinois]
Jan. 20, 1920.

Dear Alice:

This last poem has your own magic to it. The group lacked generally that final unbeatable lift to your best stuff. . . Sometimes I
think how in the afterworld you and Wallace Stevens, writing better poetry than the mass of the listed, printing and performing
poetry, will have your laugh. . . Great issues hang by an eyelash. I'm
watching and thinking and feeling. Moscow, Paris, Wilson, forty
great crossroads of history. And I'm trying to miss no time-bar of
it. Here and there realists who know; and here and there sleep
walkers who missed on the biggest guesses of their lives. Many weeks
I've talked, read and walked and thought with only short snatches
of sleep around dawn. The peak was passed this last week. The
chance for a plunge into a modern dark ages now is nil. . . I had a
card from Kathryn at Santa Fe, then heard of her later on the coast.
Give her my regards. I count her of good salt. . . The kids at home
are a tantalization of loveliness. And The Missus takes life all the
time with finer zests. We walked eight miles in fierce winter
weather last Sunday. . . The kids are a loan, only a loan, out of nowhere, back to nowhere, babbling, wild-flying—they die every day
like flowers shedding petals—and come on again. . . Well, I'm writing you my Peer Gynt heart today. . . You are alive and your voice
lives, that much I know from this Egypt song.

Carl

[Chicago]
Jan. 24, 1920.

Dear Mr. Baker:

I am enclosing herewith clippings of the two articles on the
men's clothing series which you missed in The Daily News. The
three articles which followed the first three have not been published.

If it were any other newspaper than The Daily News I would feel it was a case of suppression. But when I have worked hard and written scrupulously on a complex situation I feel that either I haven't gotten at the final vital points in it or else there is a surplus of similar material in the paper, when The Daily News doesn't publish it.

I was trying, in fact, to unload a whole book in a few news stories and so probably, was not well articulated. I would hazard the guess that the men's clothing industry has now the factors and elements that will be dominant in the thought of the country some years from now, perhaps five or ten years. This because in our country the two warring factors have not gotten at each other's minds, as here. They know each other whereas the combatants in other fields will not know each other till they have tried new strangle-holds. And of course, it must be set forth that the Amalgamated Clothing Workers in organization efficiency and social vision are farther along than anything in the country, while Hart Schaffner & Marx is in all-around quality farther developed than any shop or factory I know.

We are enjoying your series a lot. I wouldn't file a demurrer at any point in your bill of particulars.

Faithfully yours,

CS

Ray Stannard Baker was one of the early muckrakers and later a biographer of Woodrow Wilson. Sandburg first began writing about the Amalgamated Clothing Workers during their 1915 strike. He became a friend of Sidney Hillman and Joseph Schaffner, who had made a progressive labor agreement with the Amalgamated.

175 | TO PAUL L. BENJAMIN

[Chicago]
Feb. 13, [1920]

Dear Benjamin:

Thanks for your letters. As soon as ever I can get to it—I hope inside of a week, maybe sooner—I'll sling together the memoranda you mention. Biography is hell. Auto is worse. Still, my end of the job ought to be easier than yours. What I hope is that after a week of reporting the farmer-labor conference for the Daily News and the Survey, I'll be in shape next Sunday to get to this and have it in your hands on Tuesday.

> Faithfully yours,
> Carl Sandburg

Paul L. Benjamin was writing a series of articles for The Survey *on authors who dealt with social material.*

176 | TO CLYDE C. TULL

[Maywood, Illinois]
[February 24, 1920]

Dear Mr. Tull:

A note from John Lomax says among other things he expects to be in Chicago in April on business but is to give a recital for the University club. He is about the best authority on cowboy and negro songs in the U.S.A. and if you could get him I think you would enjoy an evening with him. Don't know whether he has the time or not.—I've been home four days sleeping nearly all the time, catching up on a heavy winter. I sent you copies of Pep, a newspapermen's magazine now defunct.—Will you thank the very gracious writer who did that review on my evening for the Cornell paper? It is seldom that I care to pass around any "mention" but there was a knack and an atmosphere to this. I would call it "creative criticism" if c.c. sends a man on wanting to do better and cleaner work than before.—My eyes are in a bad way, overworked, so I may have to send those manuscripts back without a reading of them. —When you are ready for me again I'll arrange to take a night train and meet all interested in newspaper work during the day, also any local clubs or college organizations, and in the evening read from manuscript poems not yet published and sing Casey Jones, Steamboat Bill, and medleys, the fee being the same as before. The western Pond bureau, overloaded with English talent, is out of business.—

Whether I get to Mt. Vernon again, make it a point to see me when you're in Chicago. And ask Mrs. Tull to send some of her work to the Poetry magazine.—Regards to Mrs. Tull and wishes for your patience with a dull letter.

Faithfully yours,

CS

Professor Clyde C. Tull, chairman of the English Department at Cornell College, Mount Vernon, Iowa, offered Sandburg $100 in January, 1920, for a reading of his verse.

177 | TO NEGLEY D. COCHRAN

Chicago
March 26. [1920]

Dear N. D.—

The congressional record doesn't have that LaFollette speech. At least, Buck and I can't find it. He moved an amendment to the Victory Loan bill providing that persons employing threats, intimidation or undue influence to compel others to buy bonds should be subject to fine and imprisonment. He filed affidavits from Nonpartisan league territory of people mobbed, slugged, etc. He shook his pompadour and said in a way that woke up sleeping senators that some day a mob might come "into this (the senate) chamber." He read statistics to show 65 per cent of the people of the U.S.A. "have no property except the clothes on their backs and a little cheap furniture." The latter description was often repeated. Then he argued the war cost ought to have been paid by taxing profiteers instead of selling bonds to people the profiteers had already mulcted. Passing on, he analyzed remarks of Carter Glass and his assistant before a senate committee regarding why the people could not be told beforehand what the interest rate on the new bonds was to be and from quotations and other material deduced that the government was close to methods that would be in violation of some of the blue sky laws. Once he went way up in the air on probabilities of revolution in this country, then caught himself suddenly and said with perfect calm, "I restrain the impulse to digress." He was interrupted by one senator who said he understood "15 per cent of the population of the U.S.A. is constantly in a condition of primary poverty, that is, lacking the actual necessities of life." Kenyon of Iowa made two or three interruptions showing sympathy with La-Follette.

And all the time they go on talking and talking here about your duty to come back and start an after-the-war Day Book. Nockels, Miss Haley, Buck, they all see it clearer now than ever.

The big drift is all for Thompson. His organization, the stiff fight he's given the newspapers, and the general public suspicion and resentment about "patrioteering", put him in the lead. Two Tribune men who have been razzing him tell me it's all Thompson. But there's a new soul growing in the labor movement and they will come out stronger and cleaner no matter what happens. .

Sincerely,

Carl

N. D. Cochran had written Sandburg on March 6, 1920: "I didn't happen to see LaFollette's filibuster speech in extenso; saw only the brief and unsatisfactory press association reports. I would like to see it, and if you have it, wish you would send it along." He also mentioned coercive tactics used in the Liberty Loan drive in Toledo.

178 | TO NEGLEY D. COCHRAN

Maywood, Ill.

March 30 [1920]

Dear N.D.—

Congressman La Guardia of New York, the Republican who beat Meyer London, was in to see Gen. Wood the other day. I talked with him in Wood's outer office. He said he was in Chicago to help Thompson win. He indicated he didn't care much about Thompson as a patriot but the big thing was to win Chicago with Thompson as an outpost captured for the 1920 campaign. So if Thompson goes over you can count on it as figuring in things nationally and as a pawn that Fred Lundin and the LaGuardias are playing with. With even a possibility of the Gen. Wood bunch being in on it. I sent the NEA a story on Wood but didn't know how to handle the big point. Wood had aphasia some time before he went to France, forgot his name and people's faces, for weeks couldn't rationalize. Republicans are afraid of the damage the story would do him if it's brought out in some positive way and they grin grimly about the proposition of electing a man president who, the doctors say, is liable any time to forget who he is, who you are, and whether tomorrow is yesterday. "The army is better than the people", says Wood in speeches here. His assumption is that the army is something separate from the people and superior to the people. The next step in the argument is logically that government and everything should be turned over to the army. This is a good Hun theory. Wood is busy with Jake Loeb and the new school superintendent Chadsey, on Americanizing the public schools.—My mother comes on a visit from a small town down state. She says everybody expects some kind of a big change coming but they don't know what it is. The churches are collecting more money than ever on the plea to the faithful that the church should be more strongly established than ever against what is coming.—I haven't seen the News-Bee lately but I know you can never pour out the real soul of you there as you did on the old Day Book and would on a new one.

There is a new deep solemnity coming over the labor movement of Chicago. The cynicism about existing government and morals is deeper than ever and their faith about labor doing something for itself goes deeper than I ever saw it before. They asked me for a slogan to write on a parade banner. I told 'em I couldn't do better than Ed Nockels who had just called out to somebody coming into the office: "The world is ours and we're on our way." There is a balance of forces about this new labor thing. They have each new next step thought out beforehand. It looks to me like they're going to grow and root deep and hold on till they run Chicago.

Am sending the NEA story about a big boat which is to load with booze at Halifax and anchor four miles out from New York after July 1 and supply cocktails to those who come out from the

United States by ferry and motor boat to get a drink. What will the drys do? Pass a law requiring passports for all who go beyond the three mile line?

Here's all wishes for luck and a lot of life to you.

Sincerely,
Carl

Major General Leonard Wood sought the Republican candidacy for president in 1920.

179 | TO LOUIS UNTERMEYER

[Chicago]
[Circa March 30, 1920]

Dear Louis:—

You're right about the S.O.B. Let it read, "crying, 'Kill him, kill him, the . . .' " deleting "the Judean equivalent" and "Son of a Bitch." I would never have put this in but that it's come over me clear the last two or three years that in a group killing of a man, in a mobbing, the event reaches a point where all rationale is gone; such a term as "anarchist" or "traitor" or "Boche" or "Englander Schwein" disappears and they babble hysterically only one or two epithets, in our language usually a tenor of "Son of a Bitch" with a bass of "Cocksucker." Since some of the finest blood of the human family goes this way poets and painters have a right to try to employ it or at least not kid themselves about what actually happened at Golgotha. Since I've tackled with men who were in the trenches and since I've seen race riots I am suspicious that the sponge of vinegar on the spear is a faked legend and what probably happened, if the historicity of Jesus is ever established, is that they cut off his genital organ and stuck it in his mouth.—The Black Belt is arming. Big strikes coming.—

Carl

For a poetry anthology, Louis Untermeyer had questioned a reference to Christ as a "son of a bitch" because, he said, it would arouse the Society for Suppression of Vice and church organizations and possibly kill the book.

180 | TO LEW SARETT

[Chicago]
April 12, [1920]

Dear Lew Sarett:

Your letters and Mss. are here. I am lugging several loads now and can't say when I'll get to that introduction but it can be only when I can go to it decently. I am willing to speed up in newspaper work, for my meal ticket, but in poetry and The Arts, I shall never be anything but a loafer. I could write a bluff introduction based on The Blue Duck alone and what I know from throwing ball with you but that isn't what we want. I hope to get to a thorough reading of the stuff and then write a page or half-page defi to The Public and The Critics. I may be a month getting to it. If that's too long a time to wait I'll shoot it back to you any time you say. In two or three cursory readings of the Mss. I have the hunch that it all balances pretty even, holds up throughout better than I expected. And when I see [Robert] Service and Edgar Guest outselling everything in the bookstores, and you know that this hokum is a pleasure to a lot of people, even though Prof. William Line Whelps and other highbrows might have their sensibilities mussed up a little, wotell!—put it in the book.

Yours fraternally,
Sandburg

"The Blue Duck" is the first poem in Sarett's "Mss.," which became Many Moons. "Prof. William Line Whelps" was William Lyon Phelps, of Yale.

181 | TO ALFRED HARCOURT

[Chicago]
May 8, 1920

Dear Harcourt:

Manuscript for Smoke and Steel is well shaped up now and we expect to register it and send it to you special delivery on May 10, from Elmhurst.

The lecture bureau stunt has an angle we want to hear from you about. We are advertising Smoke and Steel as one of the books I read from. And if anyone asks me which is the best one bet of my books I say Smoke and Steel. What we—Mitchell Dawson and I—want to know from you is whether you'd like to take on half the printing cost of these. The circular would then give its whole emphasis to HBH [Harcourt, Brace & Howe] as publishers and the high lights so far as possible to Smoke and Steel. We are figuring on mailing 2,000 copies of the circular during the next year to college and school people, women's clubs, all lyceum and chautauqua managers in the country—unless more dates come along than I have time to handle. I don't want more than 20 or 30 of the right kind. Cost of printing 2,000 gloss paper circulars plus 4,000 rather ordinary paper (though not newsprint) will be somewhat over $200. The cheaper ones are mainly for distribution in communities before a recital. Advertising window cards and hangers will also mention Smoke and Steel—and HBH if you wish.

I don't mean to imply that there is any claim at all on you to share in the expense of this. What I do know is that from time to time there will be a certain amount of books sold as a direct result of my platform work. Whether it will be enough to warrant your going 50-50 with us on this I can't say. I would say that from what I know of advertising outlay and its probabilities and gambles, it is as good a risk as any item among your appropriations.

I haven't written a letter in this lingo since I was on the System magazine but if you want to come in I think the going will be good for all of us. That Holt's went in $25 for a page in the Pond bureau circular on the Sarett-Sandburg Show, where the total circular cost was $52, doesn't indicate anything. Or that Edmund Vance Cooke and others say their platform work helps sales.—We believe we have a circular that will help get results but only the try-out will tell. As I said to you when you were here the aim of the circular is to prepare the minds of people somewhat on what they are to look for when they ask me for a recital. If they have it in black and white that New York, London and Paris are saying this stuff is really headed somewhere they are more ready to try to understand; they are more ready to practice that human intelligence which begins with a taking off of the ear muffs.

It's a book of smoke, high winds, underworlds and overtones, going to you. If you and Louie and Spingarn vote to throw anything out I'll stand for it—"you'll never hear a whimper outa me."

Sincerely yours,
Carl Sandburg

Mitchell Dawson, an attorney, handled the booking for Sandburg's lectures. Joel E. Spingarn, who helped to found Harcourt's publishing firm, was an influential critic.

182 | TO ALICE CORBIN HENDERSON

[Chicago]
May 10. [1920]

Dear Alice:

The [Gladys] Cromwell book has it over all others. I told Harriet [Monroe] so weeks ago and she gave me a duplicate copy at the office.

If [Edwin] Piper's edition of Barbed Wire published last year with some additions and changes over the book of the same title published the year before, could be construed as of 1919 I would hand it pennant and money and no regrets.

Sarett's Many Many Moons is of this year. I am telling him I don't know whether he's a crawfish or not. He has in his kitbag all the raw material of a Thoreau or Jack London. But he's thoroughly respectable, church-going believer in what-not, always springing important copy book spencerian script Chautauqua TRUTHS about making the world better, the hire life, blaa blaa. He is to me what America is to Ezra, almost. And why should any Jew be ashamed of Jewry and his blood?

Carnevali has been shaken with the Black Plague and boasts of it like wrinkled Latin beggars proud of their rags. . . I called on him at a sanatorium where Mitchell Dawson, Harriet and good friends had put him. "I have found out I don't need sleep; I haven't slept for a week." "You're a dam fool; you ought to have two hours a night anyway. Try counting the sheep as they go over the fence or a long line of wagons and cattle crossing a prairie." "I saw how sleep comes, the other night. A little stream of water starts at a mountain top and then it comes down and down and it all stops in a round pool." He is flame and genius. The hand of the Potter shook making him. I know Wilde and forty others better through this dago boy.

Mailed Smoke and Steel today. Those who holler propaganda will holler louder than ever at this. Smoke, high winds, under-worlds and overtones, mobs, hung niggers, and a finish:

Sing one song for me when I die.
Sing John Brown's Body or Shout All Over God's Heaven.
Or better yet, sing nothing at all.
 Death comes once, let it be easy.

Today I feel I won't put out another book of poetry in forty years. Anyhow before another of poetry I'm going to do a Kid book. They are the anarchs of language and speech and we'll have a lot of fun whether it's a real book or not.   Sometime in a year I expect to do platform work in the west and get to Santa Fe.

As to Starved Rock it isn't there with its writer. It lacks the sporting instinct and the dynamic illusions of the Anthology. Then too, one thick book a year is too much when it all purports poetry. Like you I can't talk frankly to Masters because he ascribes motives. Moreover, what he calls his "literary career" is the big shine of his life, what he lives on and for, and he doesn't like the people who interfere with his mystic circle of accomplishment.   Well . . . Thoreau looked at the clouds and said, "Thank God, they can't cut them down."

                                        Carl

The "Kid" book, Rootabaga Stories, *was published in 1922. Carnevali's illness was finally diagnosed as sleeping sickness. It left him palsied and he returned to relatives in Italy.*

183 | TO REUBEN W. BOROUGH

[Chicago]
July 12, [1920]

Dear Rube:—

Thanks for your greetings and news and all. It brings me a freshing waft from the days when we were going to take the world by the tail and fling it at Saturn. Or Canopus, I forget which. Any how, those were the good days and we are no worse off for having tried to stand on our tiptoes and drink from the brim of the Big Dipper.

Sometime this fall I may get a booking for the Pacific Coast. Just now I'm reading proofs for a third book, "Smoke and Steel." And during the next year I want to finish a book of kid stories, some real nut college stuff. It's a go so far with the kids I've tried it on.

We have three daughters, Margaret, Janet, and Helga; and a human zoo when the going is good.

Write me more newsy letters when the mood is right with you. We're always going to be neighbors.

Yours always,
Sandy....

184 | TO PAUL L. BENJAMIN

[Chicago]
August 7, 1920

My Dear Paul Benjamin:

You ask questions I could print a book or two in making reply. Read Louis Untermeyer's "The New Era in American Poetry" and Amy Lowell's "Tendencies in Modern American Poetry" and Marguerite Wilkinson's "New Voices". These, particularly the first, for criticism. And in poetry Masters' Spoon River Anthology, Untermeyer's "Challenge" and "These Times," Giovannitti and such writers in general as Untermeyer emphasizes, the point being that his view is much the same as yours and he deals at length with the very queries in your letter.

Will you pardon my delay in answering your good letter? I have had close-ups of race riots, strikes and other things lately, with a load of work. You write that "less time for journalism and more for creative work" would be good. True but I can earn a decent brick-layer wage the year round with newspaper work while three years sale of poetry would not keep my family six months. The Survey, for instance, which should three years ago have praised or damned Chicago Poems, hasn't mentioned it. I don't mean that it needs mention. I merely point to the fact that a volume boldly attempting emotional and art handling of the scientific material recorded in The Survey, goes without notice. Well, as adventurers in life, with me getting all their stuff and they getting none of mine, maybe the advantage is all my way . . .

Here's wishing you all the luck there is. And when you are Chicago way, phone me.

Sincerely,
Carl Sandburg

185 | TO CHARLES J. FINGER

[Chicago]
Aug. 26, 1920.

Brother Finger:

Far be it from me to do any Chubbian correcting of the way-ward and joyous errata of other writing men. I know how mistakes happen. But the fact is I am surprised at the number of good people I meet who are reading The Mirror and your stuff, and who base impressions thereon. I suggest you vamp over the following paragraphs into a Fingerian editorial:

THE TWO CHICAGO SANDB..RGS

There are two men in Chicago with names alike. One is Dr. Karl F. Sandberg, author of "The Money Trust", and member of the communist labor party. The other is Carl Sandburg, a news-paper man, author of "Chicago Poems", "Cornhuskers", "The Chicago Race Riots", "Smoke and Steel", an independent in politics and member of no party.

Karl F. Sandberg is under conviction for violation of the criminal syndicalist laws of Illinois but has not yet served time behind the bars. Carl Sandburg once served a jail sentence in Pittsburg, having been convicted of riding on a railroad train without a pass, but is not at the present moment in the status either of a martyr nor a malefactor of the law.

The two Sandb..rgs are both jailbirds, one prospective, the other retrospective.

The mail and telephone calls of the two often get mixed. Persons interested in revolutionizing banks and finance sometimes request Carl Sandburg, the poet, to lecture on currency, credits and fiat moneys, while Karl F. Sandberg, physician and communist, is sometimes asked to explain free verse and give a recital of the anapests and dythrambs thereof.

I've been looking for a sketch of Reedy I wrote for the Daily News, published some two years ago. If I come across it I'll send it on, as it had points pertinent now.

My work on the News is mostly editorials. Enclosed is one of Mirror school trends.

Fraternally yours,
Carl Sandburg

Charles J. Finger took over the Mirror, St. Louis, *after William Reedy's death. The sketch Sandburg wrote about Reedy was called "A Middle Western Man."*

186 | TO AMY LOWELL

[Elmhurst, Illinois]
September 2, 1920.

Dear Miss Lowell:
We are glad you came and that among our few traditions we have the added one for the south porch that you supped with us

there. Personally I had two regrets, one that I couldn't do more clever book inscriptions, and second, that the rainfall began and broke in so you couldn't get the last verse of This Mornin, This Evenin. The hunch is definite with me that your Indian book will come strong like Pictures of the Floating World. Your very latest work has a sureness of handling, a mobility of material. If we live another ten years it will be interesting to see how our eyes measure the outputs of now and today. Remember us to Mrs. Russell. And let us call you a good neighbor as well as joyous artist.

Sincerely yours,
Carl Sandburg

Amy Lowell had visited the Sandburgs in Elmhurst, and she sent back a poem, "To Carl Sandburg," which showed the pleasure she had had there. He then sent to her his "Three Notations On The Visit Of A Massachusetts Woman To The House Of Neighbors In Illinois."

187 | TO ALICE CORBIN HENDERSON

[Elmhurst, Illinois]
Sept 12, [1920]

Dear Alice:

There is nothing to write. There will be the largest unloading of cargoes of poetry this fall that America has ever seen in a season's drift. And there will be new spots on the moon, new specklings on the trout of the Milky Way, and fresh million mile wisps of fire on the older ribbons of the sun. Otherwise, there is nothing to write.

The old wriggling shirt-tail parade of death, the macabre of the minions of the nose-less folk, will go right on. And the psolmn asses of the arts of speech will go on parsing and conjugating. And there will be a slightly higher average of crucifixions and cutting of the entrails of such fools as do not understand rightly how to break the inhibitions of the race. Outside of that I think God's in his heaven and all's right with the world, barring exceptions.

Every day I meet new American nihilists. They have not formulated any philosophy of "all is nothing", but they offhandedly say and with a casual sincerity more terrible than oaths, that there is nothing much to believe in or live for. They are going on because the convenience of life is slightly more satisfactory than the inconvenience of death.

You wish a comic? Knopf after slipping Eunice [Tietjens] 300 beans wouldn't take the novel—but Boni & Liveright have tooken it.

Another comic? I am the cinema expert, the critic of the silent celluloid for the Daily News.

One satisfaction—the book of kid stories, tales of impossible villages, out next year, will be a hummer. Fifteen done and passed. These are my refuge from the imbecility of a frightened world.— Have ordered a Smoke and Steel sent you.—

Remember me to the Dudleys and to Winter. I don't see how a year can go by without my seing you all out there or some of you getting this way.

And . . . I was out in high winds along the Du Page river yesterday . . . blown red haws in yellow green river water among great grey roots of trees . . . and three hawks flapping hoarsely out of a big treetop . . .

Don Levine has gone to Russia again. Steichen is painting flowers near Paris and says if he keeps on some day he may do something worth looking at. Art Hickman is here soon and I expect my third interview with the king of jazz. [Vachel] Lindsay is in England under maternal chaperonage. The coal shortage and box car shortage have not improved in 60 days and next winter will see coal riots. And the more I think it over the better I like the Chinese poets and feel like reading them whenever a new prize winner appears in America. All messengers from Philadelphia I beg to tell Stork I know he is a poor fish.

Love to you and the gang.

CS

1920

[Chicago]
Oct. 20, 1920.

Dear William Allen White:

Of course, there was a deep quiet thrill for me in getting your letter about my book. I saw you keeping your footing and your head while so many were losing theirs in Europe in 1918 that, with all your other and older backgrounds, makes me read more than twice a judgement of yours in the cross-plays of American currents now.

Harry Hansen, editor of the D.N. book page, thinks Smoke and Steel ought to be bought and taken home by a lot of people. He and I have arranged a thumbnail review out of your letter. Perhaps it's unethical, as the doctors and lawyers say. But a one word telegram "Don't" from you will stop it in a whiff, or a letter from you will make any change. This is the thumbnail review:

"I have just finished reading Carl Sandburg's book, 'Smoke and Steel.' He has done a real thing. He puts America between the covers of a book. His verses stink and sting and blister and bruise and burn, and I love them. I am sending his book on to my boy who is at Harvard. I wish every student in America could read 'Smoke and Steel.' These verses are as good as a trip across America, vastly better than a trip in a Pullman or in a motor car, for they are American. If a European should ask me who is the best single hand catch-as-catch-can Greco-Roman poet in America worth reading, I would tell him to read Sandburg and 'Smoke and Steel.'"

Looking this over a last time I'm afraid it's too fine and personal a thing to be used this way. So we will count on a telegram from you saying. "Don't" as being the decent thing as against the other or bookselling thing.

And I hope and pray that when I get over into the half century years I will have the open mind and the ready heart that make you a certain rich man and distinctively rich in the state of Kansas.

Faithfully yours,
Carl Sandburg

1920

William Allen White and his Emporia Gazette *were greatly admired by Sandburg. White wired back: "Go ahead would have made it stronger if I had known you were thinking of publishing it. . . ."*

189 | TO AMY LOWELL

[Chicago]
Nov. 1, 1920.

Dear Miss Lowell:

Thank you for the Times review. Honest writing, all straightaway, it comes clear and clean with your own thought, your own impressions, in a rarely convincing way. At several points, on the use of 'stenog' as an instance, our variance of viewpoint and method is perhaps a good deal like that of some cubists as against impressionists. The use of 'stenog' was very deliberate and I feel like a painter whose good friend is calling out, 'Too much paint, boy, use your scraper, take some of it off.' That analogy or figure of digging a way through rock with a pocket knife was a poem. In this review and in the one of Chicago Poems there were several little Chinese poems scattered along. Why do I often feel in the stride and cries of your prose and your personal speech a play of thought and a vivid drive of words that a good deal of your poetry lacks, and which appears only in your topnotch best? I wonder if some shrewd one in later years will write it that I put in too many realities I was familiar with and you not enough. Your dying chestnut tree, your eye-glass millimeters that are as real, hard and beautiful as crystals (and 'millimeter' as a word has xylophonic value), your splendidly abrupt handling of the young lady who wished views on poetry from you along with her acknowledgement she had read none of it—the Chinese handle this stuff of life. I write this frankly to you because of the vivid, closely-woven prose, finely personal, in this Times review. Also, I believe it probable both you and I will in the next ten years surpass the best we have so far done.

Faithfully yours,
Carl Sandburg

P.S.—From our house and home we send all the wishes there are that you come through all to the good in health. Six months out of one year is hard luck.

They asked me at Beloit College about you for a lecture next spring. I told them they would be in luck if they could get you and it would mean a sure revival of interest among the slothful and the laggards if they should have you lecture and read. Incidentally, it's the kind of a place where the embers are burning, the way laid, and I believe you would enjoy them.

Amy Lowell reviewed Smoke and Steel *for the New York* Times.

190 | TO ALFRED STIEGLITZ

[Chicago]
Dec. 27, 1920.

Dear Alfred Stieglitz:

The only numbers of Camera Work that we have are the Steichen numbers and the Rodin number. Whatever numbers you can send us of those available to you will be kept, used, cherished.

Lilian Steichen is hardly able to believe that such good luck can happen as that we should add to the treasures we have from "291". If you should send any on to us please do not bother about express-age bill. Ship to

331 South York St.,
Elmhurst, Illinois

and if they ever arrive in this town they will be safe for a good many years.

That afternoon hour looking at Miss O'Keeffe's paintings and your series of photographs is still with me as a big hour. I went away shaken and soothed—and recalling that I had not spoken the word "miracles" in some years. You were fine and thoughtful to let me have that hour.

By express we have sent you my four books with the front fly leaf written on with wishes for you and yours.

Faithfully yours,
Carl Sandburg

1921

Stieglitz was the leading theorist of photographic methods in the United States. He married Georgia O'Keeffe in 1925, and edited Camera Work *from 1903 until his death in 1946. "291" was the Photo-Secession Galleries in New York. A famous Stieglitz photograph, "The Steerage," hung in the Sandburg home.*

191 | TO NEGLEY D. COCHRAN

[Chicago]
Jan. 25, 1921

Dear N.D.—

I'm just sending along greetings and all good wishes, for you. Once in a while lately I've been told I can write. I never hesitate about saying that probably the best single course of instruction I ever had as a writer was working along with you on the Day Book. I can never forget the way you spoke once about how other men came along and told you their troubles and you said, "They wanted me to live their lives for them." Sometimes I think that's what's the matter with civilization. Anyhow, I always count you a rich uncle who was good to me and for me. What Thoreau said of Walt Whitman goes for you: "He is democracy."

Sincerely,
CS

192 | TO ISADORA BENNETT REED

[Chicago]
Jan. 26, 1921.

Dear Isadora B.R.—

Thank you many ways for those songs. You know how to put 'em down. This whole thing is only in its beginnings, America knowing its songs. If you are ever changing your line of work and going on the stage with an act better let me give you my hunches on how to use some of these songs. It's been amazing to me to see how audiences rise to 'em; how the lowbrows just naturally like Frankie an' Albert while the highbrows, with the explanation that the murder and adultery is less in percentage than in the average grand opera, and it is the equivalent for America of the famous gutter songs of Paris—they get it.

Why, I don't even know any version of the old man and the oyster, not to speak of the Sullivan Island version. So I hope you'll send it along. And the group from Dr. Babcock.

Understand, a new song learnt is worth more to me than any Jap print or rare painting. I can take it into a railroad train or a jail or anywheres. And somehow I'm going to give you back kind for kind, song for song. . . Oh, this is what I'll do. The kid stories I'm working on now, I'm going to send you some of those. . . The call is strong from the Carolinas. Near Fort Motte, S.C. is a plantation, 500 black, 6 white people. . . We'll be down there one of these days.

Faithfully yours,
Carl

Isadora Bennett Reed, a former colleague of Sandburg's on the Daily News, *lived in Columbia, S.C., and began to send him plantation songs, which found their way into Sandburg's* The American Songbag. *Dr. James W. Babcock obtained many songs from Negroes at the state hospital for the insane in South Carolina, where he was superintendent. Sandburg often visited Julia Peterkin's Lang Syne plantation near Fort Motte, S.C.*

193 | TO DUBOSE HEYWARD

[Chicago]
Feb. 1, 1921

Dear Dubose Heyward:

Your letter here—listens good—"shy the teafights" is correct— you shall have the best in my kit bag. Last time I was in Charleston, 1898, buck private 6th Ill. Vols. bound for Porto Rico, sleeping on a cotton warehouse floor: and I wanted to see more of the quietly beautiful old town.—All luck to you in getting one or two more engagements that week. I plan arriving Feb. 14—(forgive pencil and writing on a train)—Thank you again for a good letter.

Faithfully yours,
Carl Sandburg

Heyward was head of the Poetry Society of South Carolina. His novel Porgy *was later made into the opera* Porgy and Bess *by George Gershwin.*

194 | TO PAULA SANDBURG

[On Southern California & Santa Fe train]
Sunday night [March 20, 1921]

Just left Santa Fe—new songs & new friends—now I can give a good long reading to your letter & think over every newsy love line. In weather you've had it all over me; snow and wind at Santa Fe like an Illinois March day.

What with the Hendersons, Mitchell Dawson and his bride, Arthur Yvor, John Curtis Underwood, it was a friendly place—tho not home.

I ride Santa Fe from Santa Fe to Trinidad, Colo. arriving there 3.10 a.m., waiting till 7 a.m. to catch the Colorado Southern & ride straight southeast across Texas 24 hours to Ft. Worth, another date Armstrong got while I was en route—Waco Wed. p.m. at Baylor U. & dinner that night with Prof. Armstrong—invitations made & accepted by telegraph.

The Hendersons were fine; their girl is a radiant simple genius; I hand it to her over all except our own.

About 10 days now—taking the last leg of the trip—Chinese things from Frisco & Indian stuff will come along to you—pay the express—a singing blanket—rain gods, animals for the kids—have kept well all along, every show a go.

Love to you, dearest—

Carl

195 | TO MRS. WILLIAM VAUGHN MOODY

[Elmhurst, Illinois]
Sept. 8, 1921

Dear Harriet:

We have lost our dog. If you get hold of a setter, sheep dog, collie, German police dog, mastiff, Danish bloodhound, or any dog spotted or unspotted that growls at strangers and is good to children —bring him along. Don't let dog thoughts interrupt your vacation. Of all the teeming millions in Chicago you deserve an uninterrupted vacation. But if anybody says to you, careless like, that they got a good dog you can have, and it does look to you like a good dog, call their bluff, copper the hund, nail the dog, sign a contract that there will be the best of care.

I am trying to get some final revised copies of some of those kid stories done next week and hope to send some on to you. Along about the last of October I hope your reading eyes will be in good form because there will be almost fifteen or twenty of these babies of literary destiny sent to you.

Your black-hearted renegade,
Carl

196 | TO WITTER BYNNER

[Chicago]
Sept. 9, 1921

Dear Witter Bynner:

A book for you, "Smoke and Steel", has gotten as far as this office, has writing in it for you, and will be packed and go on to you one of these days. It goes slow in these things because we have our living to make—and we are doing a book of kid stories. You must believe, however, that this will be a case of the mills of the gods grinding.—I have suggested to John Farrar he should have the Best Poems editor each month classify poems as the journeymen egg inspectors do—fresh firsts—ordinary firsts—miscellaneous—checks—dirties. Why not?

> Faithfully yours,
> Carl Sandburg

Bynner was one of the leading young poets in the newly founded Poetry Society of America. John Farrar was editor of The Bookman.

197 | TO A. J. ARMSTRONG

> [Chicago]
> October 13, 1921

Dear Dr. Armstrong:

It is good to have your note about four months of "days off". While you sojourned in Europe I travelled in a Far Country of make-believe, writing a child book. The book will come short if it is not enjoyably impossible. The titles of two episodes, tentatively written this week, are: (1) The Home of the Ivory Ax Handle (2) Never Kick Your Slipper at the Moon.

You inquire about my plans. During the coming year I am going to stay on as photoplay reviewer or movie writer for the world's greatest afternoon newspaper, finish the book of child stories, make revisions and rewritings of a fourth book of poetry, besides filling platform engagements. The enclosed circular came off the press last week.

You were thoughtful and more than kindly in arrangement of dates for me last March and April. If your time should permit of similar work this year I would be pleased to have a week or ten days in Texas or states near Texas under terms and conditions that seem to you wisest all 'round. I am in correspondence with New Mexico, Kansas and New Orleans people who ask about my schedule.

With all good wishes for you and yours, I am

> Faithfully,
> Carl Sandburg

P.S.—I trust that a Bibelot mailed to you came to your address okeh. It is of keen interest to any one who has gone deeper than the surfaces of Browning.

Armstrong, a professor of English at Baylor University, had a keen interest in Robert Browning, was a collector of anything connected with him, and had made Baylor a Browning center, with lectures on him and a collection of Browningiana established at the Baylor Browning Library, now the Armstrong-Browning Library.

198 | TO CLYDE C. TULL

[Chicago]
Nov. 15, 1921.

Dear Clyde Tull:

Thank you. I didn't think either of us could get off letters of the length of those two in that exchange.

The kid stories are now in such shape that I can bring 'em along and read three or four in a program. Then I have a new guitar bought from a man who had it eighteen years; it may run right along with the new mandolin you are proud of. Anyhow I'll offer you two great ballads: Stackerlee, and Jay Gould's Daughter—both classics—each a child on the doorstep of the neglectful parents, Mr. and Mrs. American Culture.

And if you can let me know well enough in advance I must plan to make a two day stay. I want to canvass the English Club for songs and give them anything I have out of 11,000 miles going between the two coasts since we last met. A twenty minute talk about the making of movies, with a questionnaire afterward, might be worth while.

The poems by Jewell Tull have wing whirr and are elusive as light.

Faithfully yours,
Carl Sandburg

1921

[Chicago]
Nov. 23, 1921.

Dear Older:

I'm just sending you greetings—and a clipping of stuff about a man as stubborn as yourself. I know this will interest you and John Barry.

Steffens, Fay Lewis and I toasted your health with ice water a couple of nights ago.

Please remember me to Mrs. Older, to Miss Wells, and that fine gaunt lad who showed me the way up the mountain.

Faithfully yours,
Carl Sandburg

Fremont Older was editor of the San Francisco Call, *for which Evelyn Wells also worked. Sandburg, after telling Older that he wished to see the sun rise from the top of Santa Clara mountain, had slept one night there. Jack Black, a former burglar who was now "going straight," and was a protégé of Older, had shown him the way up.*

[Elmhurst, Illinois]
Thursday [November, 1921]

Buddy:

If I can make it on Saturday or Sunday to the Foxes and Three Oaks I will.

Or if you should say that the battling with Margaret is hard then I would shelve things I'm working on and come up.

Harcourt says it is important to have the second Rootabaga book ready for illustrators this winter, if we want early copies next year so salesmen can have them to show to the booksellers in the summer. So I am rounding out the book in shape for you and May Massee the last weeks in October.

To-night it's a free show at the Medill School of Journalism. I am writing at home just before starting. Out of the window I can see the wild ruddy face of Helga with its wonderful curves. She is at the sand box. For hours those kids have been talking and laughing out there. I am only living in the present with them, which is what I am going to do with Margaret. The worst is to come and if it doesn't come what we get is so much velvet.

Helen Williams came for a visit yesterday, dropped in on the way back from Glen Ellyn. She is coming again soon when you are home. We had a long talk at Oma's after supper.

Kisses to you and Marge—then for the train and the show—

Carl

Paula Sandburg had taken Margaret to the Battle Creek Sanatorium, where she was being treated, by fasting, for nocturnal epilepsy.

201 | TO MARGARET SANDBURG

[Elmhurst, Illinois]
[November, 1921]

Dear Margaret:

This is only a little letter from your daddy to say he thinks about you hours and hours and he knows there was never a princess nor a fairy worth so much love. We are starting on a long journey and a hard fight—you and mother and daddy—and we are going to go on slowly, quietly, hand in hand, the three of us, never giving up. And so we are going to win. Slowly, quietly, never giving up, we are going to win.

Daddy

[Chicago]
Dec. 7, 1921.

Dear Witter Bynner:

That Boston or New York date, whichever it is—the earliest one I'm due for—is Feb. 1. So, any date you can pick up between Feb. 1 and the last Thursday in January will be welcome. With me, it isn't merely a matter of tying up my dates in a straight schedule. I have, also, to watch my newspaper job and not stay away from that beyond a certain limit of consecutive days. As between the newspaper work and the platform I always discriminate in favor of the former.

It was good we had that talk on your stop-over. (Business of looking over your letter again.) (This communication is an answer to yours and I mustn't drift into railroad depot talk.) As between two gypsies, I'd be glad to go on the P.S.A. [Poetry Society of America] program if there were any one or two engagements that would bring $125 between Jan. 25 and Feb. 1. If in some town or two towns three, four or five organizations clubbed in for that amount, it would cover certain remorseless inevitables that I have to match my time against.—There are P.S.A. people who don't understand I am a loafer and a writer and would rather loaf and write, and pick a guitar with the proper vags, than to deliver spoken exhortations before any honorable bodies wheresoever. I know you understand that.—If it should turn out that my Boston booking agent or any direct leads should connect me with dates in the interregnum between Jan. 25 and Feb. 1, I am then your huckleberry for any stunt you call for. I can't ask you to make a guarantee. And so the thing stands. You are fine and thoughtful and this is put to you all straight.

Faithfully yours
Carl Sandburg

Witter Bynner wrote a poem on Sandburg which was titled "The Iron Cat," a short time before Sandburg went to Santa Fe to lecture. It was first published in a Santa Fe paper, March 11, 1922.

1921

[Elmhurst, Illinois]
[Dec. 16, 1921]

Dear Margaret:

You asked me often when the stories would be ready and printed in a book for you. I am able now to vouchsafe the information and knowledge to you that this event will probably be realized in September of the year 1922, which is the year beginning on the first of next January. The title of the book will be "Rootabaga Stories". It was understood that I should let you know as soon and at the earliest possible moment I should know.

A great magician who performs strange, fantastic marvels with mysterious paraphernalia has promised us he will be at our house on Christmas Day, when you are expected to be home.

Stick to it with that strong will of yours—set your teeth—listen to your mother—and you will win the battle you are fighting. Your mother tells me you are a wonderful sleeper, that you are making a grand fight, and everything looks like a gay and merry Christmas. The fat, fat gobbler of a turkey is ready, and though you won't eat any of it probably, you will enjoy your sisters eating, and you will enjoy drawing a picture of it. I showed your letter, the one signed "Yours forever", to several people and they said you are a very much alive girl. Harcourt, our publisher, liked the pictures you made at the end of it.

Yours forever too,
Daddy

On the back of this letter a note to Paula Sandburg:

Buddy:

This goes both ways—

Carl

The great magician was Sandburg's old friend Joseffy.

204 | TO PAULA SANDBURG

> Sevenels
> Brookline
> February [7], 1922, Sunday night

Buddy:

This is it—where we live the higher life—and tell all about it when we get home. Mrs. Russell gives me a good line from a letter of yours 'I married a slow man'.—Luck to you, dear battler—

> Carl

205 | TO PAULA SANDBURG

> [New York]
> Sunday night [Feb. 14, 1922]

Dearest:

Raw weather and a raw throat—show going well enough—but it's a fight against the bla bla and lah de dah—Got a grand interview with Fox; first newspaper man to have an hour with him; first to tell him that for good or bad he's more important than Yale & Harvard put together. The Meadville, Pa. date seems cinched, going there from Detroit on Feb. 15.—Harcourt says *3* fairly tall books will be *5* times as effective as *1*—see?—Vanity Fair will pay $50 for the [Charlie] Chaplin poem. Windy City and another group will be sold.—I miss you, the kiddies and Crow Hut and hope the weeks go fast till in April I can settle down to the main work again.—

> Carl

1922

[Elmhurst, Illinois]
Feb. 22, 1922

Dear Mrs. Perry:

Did I ever thank you for those vivid shimmering castanets? They light up a room. The growing young wildcats will learn how to use them. Sometime I shall do a story about a town in the Rootabaga Country where the money is all castanet clicks; they count out and pay castanet clicks in all their dealings; the poets are the bankers; and sometimes there are blue rabbits no number of castanet clicks can buy. Something like that. It is all rather in the air like the Village of Cream Puffs in a high careless wind.

Faithfully,
Boll Weevil

Sandburg occasionally used one of his favorite folk songs as his signature.

[Chicago]
Feb. 28, 1922.

Dear Alfred:

I get no sign from you that you receive such a scrawl as I send you about one Julia Peterkin, Lang Syne Plantation, Fort Motte, S.C. I find I have two letters with manuscript enclosures that I have had around for months and not acknowledged. The reason I send you a smudge memo about her work is that I am sure sometime she will be rated as a sort of Turgenev of the plantation niggers. The best of it is as good as the best in American literature, some of it subtle and simple as good Chinese poetry. She ain't no author at all but she has a few thumbnail things that will be kicking around when Edna Ferber and Fannie Hurst and Mary Roberts Rinehart are lost monickers. I am sending her a carbon of this letter as a memo to send you all her manuscripts for your once over, to see if you don't figger out a book by a southern woman who believes Lincoln was the bastard child of John C. Calhoun yet who knows the nigger heart like a loving artist.

And so today—

Carl

Julia Peterkin was a specialist in the life and language of the Gullah Negroes of South Carolina. Her book Green Thursday *was published in 1924, and her novel* Scarlet Sister Mary *won the Pulitzer Prize in 1929.*

208 | TO HARRIET MONROE

[Chicago]
[Circa June, 1922]

Dear H. M.

These register with me. Those I have excluded, eliminated, also register, but are lacking in the compression and directness of these. I think Madam Sherry has much more to say than most of the published and accepted poets, but when she gets lost midgesture and quits trying to say anything at all she is more effective than the writers who fit into Gladstone's category of the gentleman who "is lost in the exuberance of his own verbosity."

Carl Sandburg, Emergency Associate Editor, Poetry.

209 | TO ELLERY SEDGWICK

[Chicago]
June 30, 1922.

Dear Mr. Sedgwick:

Your letter, after careful reading of it, has me hesitating about whether to say briefly that I am tied up in work that I enjoy keenly, that the work is assured of enough of an audience now so that it will stand or fall on its own merits, and there is no importance attaching to a presentation of it and allied contemporary works.

There is no need to rehearse for you the facts of the industrial revolution that has changed the terms of life for the human race the last 150 years. It is not strictly true to say, "Everybody goes everywhere and hears everything nowadays." But if there is ever a history of culture and arts reporting this last century and a half, it will have to take account of the terrific acceleration of contacts of races, peoples, nations, cultures, arts, directly traceable to the shrinkage of the frontiers that no longer are frontiers because transport and communication connect human thought and feeling across such vast areas. We are in the first decade of human history in which men such as Wilson, Lloyd George, Charlie Chaplin, Einstein, speak, and reach with what they have to say, to the intelligent minorities of the peoples of the globe.

It is a time of confusions. Particularly in America is it a period of chaos, in the economic America that hurls forms and images of new designs so rapidly and changefully that artists who honestly relate their own epoch to older epochs understand how art today, if it is to get results, must pierce exteriors and surfaces by ways different from artists of older times. Something of this is operating among writers, painters, sculptors, musicians.

If I find the time during the next year to put this viewpoint into an article, I shall submit it to you. The case is stated in implication, and with other derivations, in my two books, "Smoke and Steel" and "Slabs of the Sunburnt West."

Carl Sandburg

Ellery Sedgwick, editor of The Atlantic Monthly, *and other editors frequently asked Sandburg for magazine articles. But most of his writing time was confined to his books and the Chicago* Daily News.

210 | TO G. D. EATON

Chicago, July 11, 1922

Dear Eaton:

Of course, there is this: When I wish to be lucidly, unmistakably understandable, communicating the feeling of thought to be communicated with a 100 per cent perfection of communication, then I never make the mistake of picking any feeling or thought or song or picture or rhythm or nuance or echo or overtone unless I am absolutely sure that it is communicable, that it can be put on the wires and sent across so that it is lucid and unmistakably understandable. You know I can write for the millions, if I cared to. It has been necessary for me to keep my feet off pathways stretching straight up into an Art Brisbane job. How do you know but there is a theory or feeling held by some artists that the important thing is not whether a projection urging itself inside of an artist is understandable to others. If the artist does not believe that the depths, crypts, cross-lights and moon wisps that haunt him and make his life will be answered to by some others if he registers them in the briefest, most powerful and appealing form, to him. Life is terribly short, succinct. People are gabby, artists gabby. The accusation of not enough is better than too much.

Carl Sandburg

211 | TO G. D. EATON

[Chicago]
July 14, 1922

Dear Eaton:

Art must be understandable, have explicit meanings, be definite, tangible, explicable? No. It must communicate something—yes—and yet it may only shoot a rocket around a dim rim of the *in*communicable. "Two Humpties" fails with you now, and yet, next year or the year after you may find a clear thin silver sliver of laughter shooting around it. And you'll say, if shown the longer explicit version from which the surplus-age was stripped, that it has a theory, design, and feeling. The difference between the two of us on what you call the enigmatic pieces may run into something serious. Of course, you may find that art delivers most to you when you require it shall be explicit with no mockery or mystery. For me, it is a test of a work of art whether it has the elusive, the incommunicable, the blue jay blue and the gray mouse gray running up the canyon walls. And .. as Anna Christie says, "We're just a lot of poor nuts .. and we get mixed up .. and nobody is to blame." .. It may be sad or gay that there are muddleheads who enjoy being misunderstood because they have seen that every great work of art seems to those who get nothing from it to be a joke or a fake or a pretense.—There is no judgement possible except from the *positive* approach; I know what is good for me by what gets to me and what it does for me.—"This is the perfectest hell of it, that all of them think right well of it."—Just what did Anna mean? "we're just a lot of poor nuts."—?

Faithfully—
Carl Sandburg

212 | TO ALFRED HARCOURT

[Chicago]
29 July, 1922.

Dear Alfred:

Thanks for the [Frank] Swinnerton article. All he says is true; most authors are ignorant on those points and temperamental as pedigreed dogs off their feed. Beyond all Swinnerton's points, of course, is a big angle as subtle as the technique of the sixth sense and the feeling for the fourth dimension or the picking on the first day of the winner of a six day bicycle race. It involves the instinct that tells a publisher which and when. Of two pitchers with the same equipment of curves and speed, the one winning the most games is the one who knows which and when.

If we can get stores like Brentano's and McClurg's to fill a show window with rutabagas and cream puffs for a display of Rootabaga Stories, I don't know whether it would be worth while. If a half dozen big rutabagas and a dozen cream puffs surmount displays at Xmas shopping time, I don't know whether it will help people to peep into the book or whether the peeping would make 'em want the book. But sometimes I think the projection of the physical or pictured rutabaga and cream puff (nix on liver or onions) might connect people with what is simple and real in the book.

Would a 3-compartment cardboard display rack be any good—each compartment filled with copies of Rootabaga Stories—No. 1 marked, "For People Five to Ten Years of Age"—No. 2, "For People Ten to Twenty Years of Age"—No. 3, "For People Twenty to 105 Years of Age"—and would the impress of the point occasionally that the book is "For People from 5 to 105 Years of Age" help cinch the idea that the book is for all ages?

Do we want some reviewer to say, "This book is better than goat glands"? I am going to read the stories at book stores in Chicago and sometimes in other towns. I'm going to talk cold turkey with booksellers about the hot gravy in the stories. I may even say, "Do you realize that Mr. Harcourt is seriously considering at a later period publishing pocket editions of these stories, to be placed in selling cases in drug stores with guarantees and testimonials that the book is better than nuxated iron and its tonic and healing properties are assured by the editor of the Journal of the American Medical Association, who has tried them on himself and his children?"

The people I showed Miss [Ellen] Eayrs' [the future Mrs. Harcourt] paragraph in the autumn book list announcement to, all liked it. Mrs. Sandburg, May Massee and the Sinclair Lewises at a dinner at May's last week, all voted it "spiffy".

Why not send a copy of "Smoke and Steel" to the editor of The Fort Dearborn Independent, Detroit, Mich.—the Ford weekly—with a note telling him this is a book with a poem on page 242 on the "New Farm Tractor" and in the piece titled "Boy and Father" beginning page 39, the Ford flivver is mentioned and not as a comic instance?

Please slip me back this clip from the C.S. Monitor. Why not tell the writer of this editorial that Rootabaga Stories is the answer to his final point?

Don't answer these questions. Use whatever hits your "which and when" savvy. Take care of yourself. Let me know if there's anything I can do to join up with your work.

Carl

213 | TO ROBERT FROST

[Chicago]
[Summer, 1922]

Dear Robert

. . . if you hear anything from A. J. Armstrong at Baylor University, you will make no mistake about co-operating with him on any plans he may have for bringing you south. I had some engagements under his direction last winter and found him just the kind of all round worker I believe you would enjoy taking up with. At Dr. Armstrong's own school they not only read a man's books before he arrives but they buy them in record-breaking numbers. His interest in you is a sure one and they have a way of looking after you that gets to your heart.

Hastily—
Carl Sandburg

214 | TO LEW SARETT

[Elmhurst, Illinois]
Sept. 3. [1922]

Dear Lew:

That was a bird of a letter you sent on six weeks ago. A Box of God letter.

I told 'em to put you on the book page list and they said you were already there.

I read The Box of God for the third time one Sunday this month. And I put it way high. I know I can reread it for years and it will have the freshness, colors and singing winds, tangs of the bitter wild and the wildly sweet. It has a tang I caught from Bliss Carman's work fifteen years ago and has captured and held that tang more strongly. I know you are going to write swinging and vivid words and music out of woods and waters and their people.

Sincerely yours,
Carl

215 | TO WITTER BYNNER

[Chicago]
5 September, 1922.

Dear Hal:

Be sure to let me know when you come this way. Gene Debs wants to see you too. He is at a sanatorium just two blocks from where we live and is making nice headway.—I suppose you have noticed that progress and justice are on the boards these days. Among railroad trackmen they want 100 per cent Americans at 23 cents an hour.—You'll find it a good vacation day to look up Gene. He is a living Chinese poem. He is not so much an agitator and organizer as he is an artist, adventurer, and sun-treader. His vibrations are the same as Shelley, only higher voltage.—Until I can get to making a copy of those poems owed to you and to Alice Corbin, I can't send 'em on. What with accidents and acts of God it's been a slow summer.—Come on, and collaborate on a spectric poem apostrophizing this country, with an opening and recurrent line, 'Stuff your guts, America.' Everywhere the ad and the proclamation is to eat, eat well, and eat the proclaimed goods.—Excuse me, I didn't start to write a Book of Jeremiah.—Take care of yourself; make your throat new; bring all your foolish songs along.

Carlo

"Hal" Witter Bynner spent part of 1922 with D. H. Lawrence in New Mexico. Eugene Debs was at the Lindlahr Sanatorium in Elmhurst, Illinois, where Sandburg often visited him.

216 | TO MARGARET SANDBURG

[Elmhurst, Illinois]
Thursday [September 22, 1922]

Dear Spink:

We are all thinking here that you are a very much alive girl, and very strong, to be able to write such letters as you do, after more than a week of fasting. Your handwriting stands up as though your fingers and fists are good for many long, steady, hard fights and struggles. But then you are now one of the champion, long-distance, unconquerable and invincible fasters of the United States—you are a veteran—and since Uncle Ed pinned the Legion of Honor cross of France on you, I don't know what further honor and acknowledgement can be made. Everything here at home is elegant, hunky dory, up to snuff, 100 per cent and first class. Only when you and mother get back, it will be more so—see? I suppose you understand I am coming up to see you at the end of the fast—and I know it will be a good time for the three of us and maybe I ought to include Dr. Conkling and call it the four of us. Maybe you will show me that parrot; if you do, let me see it when it is taking a bath like you write about. Well, inside of a month you shall have your two special autographed copies of "Rootabaga Stories", and you can tell Dr. Conkling there will be one for him. Here is love to you and your mother—from—

Daddy

Margaret Sandburg—"Spink"—was back in the Battle Creek Sanatorium. Edward Steichen actually gave her his Legion of Honor medal for courage.

217 | TO PAULA SANDBURG

[Elmhurst, Illinois]
Thursday. [September 22, 1922]

Buddy:

Janet and Helga coming fine; Ed took some particular looks at their legs and said their legs are more than perfect; that should be final.—Oma shook hugging Ed, in the house, then rallied and from the porch waved a grand gay good-by.—Pooch learns; we can get him so he won't give long vocal performances; but he will never learn to stop his passionate enjoyment of scaring people by rushing them with his terrible eyes and teeth; he must have seen himself sometime in a magnifying mirror so that he imagines he is six or seven dogs in one.—Kitty Whispers seems to have many thoughts about the creche and the layette.—It is rich luxury to walk around the house and goddam any ghosts I please and nobody hears, nobody is bothered, the echoes are musical.—The reports could be endless. The book grows. You and your Marny, and mine, are missed all over the map.

Carl

218 | TO PAULA SANDBURG

[Elmhurst, Illinois]
Tuesday. [September 28, 1922]

Paula Dear:

On second and later thoughts that is a hummer of a letter for Dr. Hoffman, says about all there is to say and says it right.

I am going to shape up my work so I'll be with you at the time the fast is ending. The only date I have about that time is a talk, an "address", to the Medill School of Journalism, Oct. 5.

The mortgage is being watched and going nicely. Edith called today, was disappointed on hearing you were not home, then picked up on hearing I was. She asked for a reference; I wrote out a to whom it may concern that she was loyal and efficient, her leaving us was caused by outside family affairs, and she is an exceptional cook. Lina handles the kids wonderful. Oma is okeh except for pains in the left leg. The race relations stories began today on the front page. I have written 32 letters in three days, four full pages to Harcourt today. He says the book will get a full page with pictures in the New York Times.—Get a lot of sleep. Kiss the kid for me. With love—

Carl

Miss Eayrs is due this weekend.

Kitty Whispers is frisky and friendly even tho she's going to have kittens. Rhoda is growing, is a good pal of the kids.

1922

[Elmhurst, Illinois]
[September, 1922]
Tuesday 1 a.m.

Dearest Buddy:

Every day and some days every hour the thoughts go to you and the little battling one.

Worked on Rootabaga (books), revises Saturday night, coffee at 12, till 4:30 Sunday morning. Breakfast with Miss Eayrs and talk till her 10 p.m. train. She's going the limit.

$208 from the Designer today. A letter from the metropolitan mag says two poems, bring $75.

Helga & Janet blooming miracles of good will, mirth, health.

Unless something drastic happens I'll make Battle Creek next Monday for a two or three day stay—

Carl

[Elmhurst, Illinois]
Wednesday. [Circa late September, 1922]

Dear Paula:

The main regret of the day is that you couldn't be here to see Janet and Helga. They never were better. Their laughs ripple. Janet has color, is growing. And Oma was gay today. I am going to get tickets to "Lightnin'" for Oma and Lina at a matinee some afternoon next week when I will stay home with the shiners. Margaret's letter to Lina today made us all feel she has big and deep vitality. That a girl fasting six days could write so keenly of so many things and in such a handwriting, was testimony. I am deep in the final rewrite and shaping up of the second Rootabaga book. A check for $65 came from Holt's for rights to use eight pieces in

Percy Boynton's anthology for Ginn & Co. A check for $10 came last week for right to use the Billy Sunday poem in a MacMillan anthology of "The World's Great Religious Poetry." Kitty Whispers is gracious and friendly and I am betting on the kittens having one or two we want to keep. Mona languishes; she was washed in sand today, Helga scrubbing her with a pear she called soap; Alice B gets shinier. While Rhoda tops 'em all; the chances which were one in five that we would raise her I now put at one in three. Such is news from your old empire and domain of days. There is love from all, includin'

Carl

221 | TO ALFRED HARCOURT

[Chicago]
23 October, 1922.

Dear Alfred:

You can get from the letter today to Ellen Eayrs some of my feelings about the book you've made of "Rootabaga Stories." There has been so much genius employed on making books look gay that I doubted whether we would have anything more than average. Now around our house we walk with the lift of those balloon pickers, over that jacket and frontispiece, and then over that quiet blue cover with its corn yellow lettering.

And now to a matter of a kind that I won't bother you about maybe again in a lifetime. We are buying a lot next door south of us in Elmhurst. If we don't get it somebody else will and we will have a house we may not care to look at slammed close to us. The price is $2,300, of which $1,300 must be cash down, the rest time payments. We have paid $200 earnest and borrowed $500 and need $600. If you can find this $600 it will go into good land. It has two marvelous sugar maples in front. At the rear it has the biggest incomparable lilac bush in northern Illinois. It is the only place I have ever found glow worms. I spaded it all and raised sweet corn year before last. Our cats have their kittens there in special sunny lying-in corners. So you see we know what we're getting. And all we need is $600 spot cash greenbacks of the national government. The man who owns the lot has notions; now he'll sell and now he won't; and this week is the first time he has been in a selling mood and would talk prices.—If you don't have $600 available would you wire me collect? And I know you'll understand that only a very special situation would let me bother you like this.

Sincerely yours,

Carl

Alfred Harcourt sent Sandburg a check for $600 as an advance royalty for Rootabaga Stories.

222 | TO FANNY BUTCHER

[Richmond, Virginia]
November 19, 1922

Dear Fanny—

If you look close here you can see foot tracks of Rootabaga pigeons. What I tried to tell you over the phone was that your review was as young and careless and easy as I wanted to make the book itself. It was a winsome piece of writing to send out to your big audience.

Carl

223 | TO EUGENE V. DEBS

[Elmhurst, Illinois]
19 November 1922

Dear Gene:

You will always be close to us. The only way we can decently remember you and what you left with us here will be a certain way of living it, maybe dying it.

And some day I hope to get the strong truth about those hands of yours into a poem. It's only a hope but I'll try for it and learn something.

My signature goes for the whole bunch under our roof. As you went away out the front door one of them said, "He's a big rough flower."

With you it isn't really a good-by because you are still here.

Carl Sandburg

224 | TO ANNE CARROLL MOORE

Chicago
20 November, 1922.

Dear Miss Moore:

Sometime we should have a good long talk as I am sure each of us has worth while questions to put. I am enclosing a clipping from the Metropolitan magazine which has to do with any answer I would make to the query you put to me before the audience at the Library. Some of the Rootabaga Stories were not written at all with the idea of reading to children or telling. They were attempts to catch fantasy, accents, pulses, eye flashes, inconceivably rapid and perfect gestures, sudden pantomimic moments, drawls and drolleries, gazings and musings—authoritative poetic instants—knowing that if the whirr of them were caught quickly and simply enough in words the result would be a child lore interesting to child and grownup. Something like that. . . . Sometime we'll have coffee and go farther on this.

Faithfully yours,
Carl Sandburg

1923

[Chicago]
Sept. 20, 1923.

Dear Alfred:

I am sending this to you in case Ellen has left for the west. This seems to be the final bunch that ought to have Rootabaga Pigeons. I don't know whether I found time to send you corking reviews some of these people did of the book last year; Bookstugan had one half Swedish and half English. Hal Cochran is an old Day Book pal of mine and tells me to send him any story we would want to go out in the N.E.A. service which goes to some 420 papers now; so I'll leave it to you to send him this enclosure along with a picture.—Sometimes I think the Lincoln book will be a sort of History and Old Testament of the United States, a joke almanac, prayer collect, and compendium of essential facts.—There is a man in Springfield who makes a specialty of selling Lincoln books and the works of Illinois writers; he told me to tell you he would want some Rootabaga Pigeons; you can reach him at H. E. Barker, Art Store, Springfield, Ill.—I notice Beveridge tells us Lincoln had a right to his melancholy but it is "difficult to understand why he made a public show of it so frequently;" he will give us an Arrow Collar biography.—You haven't written me a line in a long while. How goes it? Luck to you.

Yours—
Carl.

While working on The Prairie Years, *another juvenile book for Harcourt was in the making—*Rootabaga Pigeons, *published in 1923. After seeing the beginning sections of* Abraham Lincoln: The Prairie Years, *Harcourt responded, "We've had not more than one or two books in this shop as good as this piece. . . . You're just the boy to do this—to understand Abe and make him real." Albert J. Beveridge was writing a Lincoln biography at the same time; it was published a year after he died, in 1927.*

[Chicago]
October 15, 1923.

Dear Hal:

There ain't silence at all. I write you many letters, riding on the cars, watching the moon arch up an east window I work at, but the letters don't get onto paper. The Vildrac book is a lovely work; the status of art and poetry in America is somewhat indicated by its reception; the need for the literal, for surfaces that impinge, is terribly definite. I wonder if the ignorance of our intelligentsia isn't more at fault than the apathy of the mob.

Please tell me who the man was, and what the place and occasion was, that gave you that Lincoln poem-sketch, the man who makes such a picture of Lincoln as an old farmer. That is a great poem. Lincoln breathes through it. It is the best explanation there is of why he wore whiskers.

Shall send the poetry contest bundle soon. You and Alice [Corbin Henderson] are the only ones who ever drafted me for this low-down job. Love to the both of you.

Carl

227 | TO WITTER BYNNER

[Chicago]
Nov. 2, 1923

Dear Hal:

Answering your earlier letter later. You are right that it is an inaccurate and unjust characterization that places you as an "always tactful and graceful gentleman." I did not see any of this copy before it went to print; I told them I didn't have the time for the work and to take me off. If I had had any chance at stopping such a commentary on you I would have done it; the sentence is wrong in wording and tone; and the rest of the sketch or evaluation of you lacks the stature and stuff I would want there. I think I can understand how they may be back where I was once; it seemed to come across me rather suddenly that you had a terribly stubborn streak in you, the peaceable hell-raising Quaker who wouldn't shut up; they could kill him with an ax first. There is this one advantage in this occurrence; you are ten times more dangerously effective if as you approach they believe you are a tactful and graceful gentleman.

Faithfully—
Carl

Bynner answered: "Your later letter answering my earlier letter later than your answer to my later letter, more than eased my irritation. You're some doctor."

228 | TO ALFRED HARCOURT

[Chicago]
Dec. 8, 1923.

Dear Alfred:

I don't know whether I ever answered that long handwritten letter of yours. It was good to have. What you mention will all be easy enough; if you can stand two days for a going-over of the manuscript I'll ask three if you can stand that. The wife and friends are saying the job will kill me if I don't slow down. BUT it's exactly the kind of a job that with me has to be a spurt job; if I had one of those retentive efficiency memories that took a never-let-go grip on names, dates, places, actions, I could slow down—One thing I'm sure of; the biggest part of American history has all to be rewritten; and it will be done. William E. Dodd is the surest big-range bird I've found. I told him you would be the best gun in New York for him to know. He's going to look you up sometime. His publishers of his "Life of Jefferson Davis" have tried to get the copyright from him, but he's holding on to it. He's writing now on a five volume work on PLANTER culture and INDUSTRIAL culture, a massive outline of the two groups about which most of American history centers. Luck to you. So long.

Carl

229 | TO CLYDE C. TULL

[Chicago]
Feb. 16, 1924

Dear Tull:

Your letter was like the grimace of some Chinese masks, pains with laughs—the most Rootabaga letter I've had in a year. It had the flicker of that old legend about the two jayhawkers starving on the prairie; they shot a crow, cooked it and while eating one said, "Do you like crow?" The other, "I can eat it, but I don't hanker after it." It will be good to sit with you and Jewell and talk about what the flying and the crying of the high geese in the air means this year—

C.S.

230 | TO AMY LOWELL

[Chicago]
March 25, 1924.

Dear Amy—

If there would be any chance to have a stenographer copy the letters of William H. Herndon to Truman Bartlett in the Massachusetts Historical Society archives, I wish that could be done. The stenographic bill I would take care of. . . For one thing, the letters are not of vital importance, and I already have their essentials from other sources. . . Mr. Ford sends a fine letter about it. The only regret is that the dam family can't decently cherish their father's or uncle's fame by telling the whole world to come and photostat till the cows come home. . . Two friends send me a clipping from the Xtian Science Monitor, with talk of yours, like a window flung open to the azure. Remember me to Mrs. Russell. Great good luck to you.

Faithfully,
Carl Sandburg

231 | TO ALFRED HARCOURT

Elmhurst, [Illinois]
Aug. 3. [1924]

Dear Alfred—

About three weeks ago we had Abe make his farewell speech at Springfield. And as the book now stands, he is crossing the state line of Illinois into Indiana, leaving the prairies, starting to grow whiskers. It is the end of the smooth-faced Lincoln, of the man whose time and ways of life belonged somewhat to himself; he is no longer a private citizen who comes and goes, but a public man who must stay put.

Now in these three weeks as I have been getting thoroughly into the civil war stuff, I find that what I would be doing to now go on with a compressed handling of Abe in the war, would be to really tack on another book, of different style. Also, to work out the series of portraits of Abe in the war, as I have already sketched them, would run the book beyond the limits of even the big single volume that I had expected would hold what I planned.

So, I am working on shaping up the manuscript now finished. It is a book, of a unity, an entity. You can title it—

LINCOLN THE WESTERN AMERICAN
LINCOLN THE PRAIRIE MAN
THE PRAIRIE LINCOLN
THE WESTERN LINCOLN

It wouldn't quite do to call it "The Smooth-Faced Lincoln" or "The Pre-Whiskers Lincoln", but it delivers the Lincoln who knew the time for whiskers, who has the Chicago Daily News readers buffaloed so that it is a remark in the art department, "Oh hell, the people don't want to see Lincoln without whiskers." So we won't call the book, "The Well Razored Abe."

As the script looks in the loose now I would judge there will be about five or six sections of the size of one of the two you now have. I hope to get it shaped up and bring it on before September 1st.

It is mighty good to have your note. Tell me how the above looks to you.

Faithfully yours,
Carl

P.S.—For another title I would submit ABRAHAM LINCOLN AND HIS PRAIRIE YEARS. And as I glance through the manuscript I doubt whether I can get it smoothed out and decently organized by September 1st, but it would probably be wise to get on to New York about then and go over the layout with you. I was going to write you about a month ago, that I had been throwing drops, outdrops, slow straight balls and wild pitches, and the last innings of the book would have to cross the pace into spitballs and high inshoots near the chin. But the last innings will have to wait. A man can't write the Gettysburg speech and the Second Inaugural, and make the portraits of Lee, Stephens, Sherman, without tears, wet or dry.

P.S.S.—The Catholic World for April or March had a general article on books for children, in which was a paragraph saying both the Rootabaga books ought to be in every nursery.

232 | TO ALFRED HARCOURT

[Elmhurst, Illinois]
Sept. 8, 1924.

Dear Alfred—

I have been off the main job, mostly sleeping, lately. The smoothing out and finishing up of the thing will take weeks yet. One thing I am sure of, and I had my doubts at first about whether it could be done. The book marches; it has good Second Wind;

the last is better than the first. As soon as I get certain changes made the part tacking on to what you have will be sent on to you. . . One more point. A lot of material, some unpublished letters, old newspapers, Mrs. Lincoln's jewels, and such were opened in a bank vault for me by a man who seldom shows them. He brought out a poem of Walt Whitman's, a long one, "A Carol of Harvest," unpublished, written in 1867, one of the sweetest, sanest, surest things Old Walt ever did. I'm writing, or going to write, a one-page preface for it, and he promises he is going to see you about publishing it the next time he goes to New York. His name is Oliver R. Barrett; he has in this same little bank vault unpublished poems by Thackeray, and others, not to mention 600 letters Charles Dickens wrote to a woman. Why don't you take a run out h'yer? . . Luck and health to you.

Faithfully yours,
Carl

The great Barrett collection later became a Sandburg book, called Lincoln Collector, *published in 1949.*

233 | TO EUGENE V. DEBS

[Elmhurst, Illinois]
Oct. 18, 1924

Dear Gene:

If you hadn't stayed so long you wouldn't have left such a big lonesome spot. We can nearly see a ghost in the doorways where you came in and went out. Take all care of yourself. When the book —in which you have collaborated—comes out next year a copy will go to you. And sometime I hope to see you in Terre Haute.

Faithfully yours,
Carl

234 | TO PAULA SANDBURG

[Mt. Vernon, New York]
Nov. 16, [1924]

Dearest Paula—

After hanging around Ed's [Steichen] place all the time while in and out of New York, I have now settled with the Harcourts in Mt. Vernon, to stay till Thanksgiving, at least, . . . The cuts came out perfect. . . . The Mss. as now figured runs over 300,000 words. . . Ed was pleased with your photos; the one of Debs and Helga he thought a hummer, forty ways. . . Take care of yourself. . Sing a little sometimes. . . And sleep a lot.

Carl

The big "Mss." was The Prairie Years.

235 | TO MARK VAN DOREN

[Chicago]
Dec. 26, 1924.

Dear Mr. Van Doren—

That is an interesting question you are to have a symposium on. It involves those terrible questions: What is Art? Who is an Artist? I'd rather have that one little poem of yours on how daring and improbable is man, than the whole symposium you'll get. Just now I am sewed up with work, overloaded, or I would like to tackle a contribution. The subject is terrific; it runs into movies, radio, education, standardization, the Lincoln Memorial, Gutzon Borglum, the box office success of Griffith's "America" and the failure of his fine "Broken Blossoms", the psychology of vogues, the quarrels of artists about art, the greeds for expressions of personal critical tastes and divisions into great, greater, and greatest, the endless jargon of undefined bluff terms such as "persons of discrimination," "modern standards", "authentic values". A good deal of an argu-

ment can be made that the volubility and satisfaction of the in-
telligentzia or highly book learned and art versed people is harder
to look at than the beefy apathy of the crowds.

Sincerely yours—
Carl Sandburg

Mark Van Doren was then literary editor of The Nation, *which
printed some of Sandburg's poems.*

236 | TO MAY MASSEE

[Chicago]
[Circa 1925]

Dear May:

That's That is a duck, a darling and a darb of a book. First
because of the way it says what it has to say, second because of what
it has to say, third, because it knows where to stop and say no more.
It is truer than life because it is more fateful than fate. It is what
the country needs because it's so young and the country is so old.
It is sweeter than the beeshumming and as subtle as the cream
rising in a cool crock of milk.

Carl

May Massee was editor of The Booklist *of the American Library
Association in Chicago, and then she became editor of children's
books at Doubleday and Viking.*

237 | TO L. W. PAYNE, JR.

[Chicago]
March 12, 1925.

Dear Flummywister—

And the Ides of March brought your annual letter. Your average is three across three years. This one being one in two years is
a biennial. But the batting average is still one a year. This one

belongs alongside "Songs of Vagabondia," and border ballad collections, only it's more mysterious and got happier feet and cooler, shrewder eyes than most border ballads.

On March 23d I am due in Tucson at the university there. As my schedule looks now I don't know whether I would be able to jump over to Florence before or after Tucson. If I could make it I would like to hear you sing those songs you write about and listen to you talk the way special golden cockroaches talk. And if I can't make Phoenix maybe you can get to Tucson; and if you can't then all causes of science and poetry will have to wait.

Take all care of yourself. It seems to me you are growing all the time, and if there is any arc of flight you decide to take in life, you will take it and the minions of hooddoo and vooddoo will have a hard time stopping you. Thank you for so living and singing a letter.

Stackerlee

L. W. Payne, Jr., was at the University of Texas. The signature "Stackerlee" came from a folk song.

238 | TO AMY LOWELL

[Greeley, Colorado]
March 17, 1925

Dear Amy:

Thank you for the Keats. I have read it and he is no longer "a figment of a pigment" but a British citizen and a living wisp that clipped out of God's thumb and index finger a few moments. It's an enduring piece of work many will thank you for.—I am on the last long mile of the Lincoln. Ain't it hell the way a book walks up to you and makes you write it?—Don't you feel almost predestinarian?—A love of a dedication to your book: remember me to her: love to you both—

Carl

Amy Lowell produced a two-volume biography, John Keats.

1925

239 | TO CLYDE C. TULL

[San Diego, California]
March 25, 1925.

Dear Tull—

I am wedged in with dates in a peculiar way this year and I hope you can find some day that Feakins says is available between April 9 and May 7. If we can make the connections this would be the sixth year at Cornell and not a year skipped. If extra copies now expected have arrived in a couple of weeks, I would bring along a copy for you and Jewell of the French translation of Rootabaga Stories; it was done by Leon Bazalgette, and published about six weeks ago. His introduction deals with my verse and you will be interested in his handling of the Corn Belt. . . It is toil and toil finishing up the Lincoln book; so many details have to be watched. But I think that you and some others like you will say it is about time some cornhusker had done this kind of a job.

Faithfully yours—
Sandburg

240 | TO PAULA SANDBURG

[Commerce, Texas]
April 4, 1925

HARCOURT WIRES BOOK SERIAL RIGHTS SOLD TO PICTORIAL REVIEW FOR $20,000. FIX THE FLIVVER AND BUY A WILD EASTER HAT.

CARL

241 | TO ALFRED HARCOURT

[Chicago]
April 13, 1925.

Dear Alfred—

This is the first time I've understood something about the emotions of holding the lucky number in a lottery. Prof. Armstrong of Baylor College at Waco wired your telegram to me at Commerce saying, "I have received the following telegram does it mean anything to you." I replied, "Thank you for sending a telegram with news equivalent to falling heir to a farm." . . I was glad book publication was thrown to a farther date because in a job of that size and kind we can then be surer of where it needs sandpaper. . . I'll be in New York May 7, and later will have two or three days with you. Meanwhile I shall send along those illustrations with captions; surely inside of a week, that is, before April 20. They would have been finished up two or three weeks ago, only, I have been doing two new chapters of the book, two that are among the best, one on the pedigree and the other on the smutty story teller; I wondered if they were too politely done and put it up to Sherwood Anderson who said I left out just the dirty stuff that wasn't significant. . . You got a fine half-tone of the ax handle; I didn't expect it to be so good; it's a luminous page.

Write J. Frank Dobie, Agricultural College, Stillwater, Oklahoma, and get his promise to let you see any book script he gets ready. He had an article in Country Gentleman two months ago on "The Trail Boss", which I'll mail you in a day or two, has the Zane Grey fanatical enthusiasm about that country, without Z. G.'s bunk. . . Only on this my third trip across the desert and the semi-arid belt have I begun to get the feel of it. I thought of you often, and sometimes with a hunch that you ought to get out to Arizona and California at least a week a year. . . . Well, some evening in May we'll have good talk again. Remember me to Ellen. And tell Paul I have several keen puns he had never heard. Luck and years to you—

Carl

P.S.—This man Robert Littell on the New Republic has been doing some humming stuff the last three or four months. One skit after another with unusual quality.

[Elmhurst, Illinois]
2 September, 1925.

Dear Mr. Beveridge—

Your telegram came to me at Bread Loaf Mountain but as my appointments shaped themselves while in the east I could not find time for the visit to Beverly Farms.

Your regrets, expressed to various persons in various cities, that my work will not be "authentic", may or may not be dissipated on publication of my Lincoln book next February. (The Pictorial Review serial will contain but 45,000 of the 320,000 words of the book.)

Twenty-two years ago I was reading speeches of yours through and through; I heard you twice in extended addresses; I was five feet from you as you sweltered through hours of the Bull Moose convention; I have read books of yours; some day in a series of sketches I am going to write about you. . . This, while you know nothing essential of me. Though you cannot yet spell my name you assume that you know whether I may be a trustworthy chronicler. Perhaps I should also say that there are no suppressed chapters in my Lincoln of the character of those of your Marshall, also that whatever adverse commentaries may be made on my Lincoln they will be of an order different from those made by McLaughlin on your Marshall.

The issue that you have raised, in private conversations, implies your belief that your writings are to be "authentic" and mine *not*. This may run back to a personal habit of yours of speaking freely or loosely, in private conversations, or it may involve an antagonism as to method, a chasm in points of view as to presentation of materials. In either case I have the advantage of you that exists between two men where one has the familiar facts that enable him to understand and measure the elements of sincerity in the case. It would be gratuitous to point out that your own character will get written into your Lincoln work, in degree, as inevitably as it did in your Marshall.

Sincerely—
Carl Sandburg

1925

Sandburg, responding to the criticism of Albert J. Beveridge, the statesman who was writing a Lincoln history of his own, referred to Beveridge's 1919 Life of John Marshall, *which received a Pulitzer Prize.*

243 | TO JACOB ZEITLIN

[Elmhurst, Illinois]
Sept. 15, 1925.

Dear Jake—

Every poet should have his turn at barbering the lawn for some nabob such as Doheny. . . Harcourt is holding me down pretty strict on the number of review copies for the Lincoln book, but I shall surely put you and Stanley Babb on the list. . . Remember me to Edythe. . . Luck to you but remember it's hell to be a poet and if it isn't you're not a poet. . . And go on picking up songs. You'll never be searched for them; they'll never get you into trouble. . . All luck and health to you. . . If you see Frank Wolfe tell him that hell must be necessary or there wouldn't be so much of it through all the centuries.

Faithfully—
Carl

Jacob Zeitlin, a poet who had written to Sandburg that he was "barbering lawns for E. L. Doheny," became a rare-book dealer in Los Angeles. Frank Wolfe was an old and close friend who had migrated to the West.

244 | TO IDA M. TARBELL

[Chicago]
Sept. 26, 1925.

Dear Miss Tarbell—

Page proofs of my Lincoln book are being sent to you. It may be that you will read them over for what they are worth, and that sometime this fall we can talk about them. Yourself and Oliver R.

Barrett are the only persons receiving advance sheets, as you are the two who have helped me most, which I believe is made clear in my preface.

> Faithfully yours—
> Carl Sandburg

Ida M. Tarbell's Early Life of Lincoln *preceded Sandburg's books by a quarter of a century. Before the turn of the century she had tramped the Lincoln countryside, interviewing those who had known him.*

245 | TO FANNY BUTCHER

> [Chicago]
> Feb. 4, 1926.

Dear Fanny—

That was a superb valentine you handed me publicly. It smashed all formulas for book reviews and made its own style, driving in its own independent brass nails of persuasive discourse, written eloquence. I have never had a book review that I am so sure so many people read more than once and took as testimony to be deliberated over. It was as though you had had some fun with that line on the last page of Smoke and Steel: The peace of great phantoms be for you.

> Faithfully yours—
> Carl

Fanny Butcher's Chicago Tribune *book valentine for* The Prairie Years *employed the phrase from the last stanza from "Smoke and Steel": "Yes, the peace of great phantoms be for you."*

246 | TO IDA M. TARBELL

> [Chicago]
> Feb. 9, 1926

Dear Miss Tarbell—

Write Mr. Barrett at Strauss Bldg., Jackson and Michigan Blvds., Chicago. He wants a letter from you for his collection—and says he will unlock any or all vaults at your bidding when you arrive this month.

So good an ending paragraph to your letter coming today—so fine from one so long a friend and helper.—Barrett and I talked long this evening about how much less of *fresh glint* there would be to the Lincoln legend without your work. Luck and health—

Faithfully yours,
Carl Sandburg

Ida Tarbell had written to Sandburg saying that she would like to see the Oliver Barrett collection and asking if he could arrange it for her, adding, "I am hugging your book to my heart."

247 | TO L. W. PAYNE, JR.

[Chicago]
March 26, 1926.

Dear Payne—

I am glad you wrote your impressions and suggestions as to a "sequel" of the Lincoln book. Whatever I may undertake in the way of a "sequel" will not start for five years and may be of so different an order that it won't be thought of as a sequel. The vague distrust that you feel is one I have myself; I know precisely what you mean. . . The review was a big, vivid piece of writing, and I thank you for that and so kindly a letter. . . I am going to be in and out of Chicago a good deal this spring but I hope luck will be our way so that we can have another evening as "loophounds."

Faithfully yours—
Sandburg

248 | TO CLYDE C. TULL

[Chicago]
April 3, 1926.

Dear Tull—

Friday, the 23d, is okeh. I am writing Frederick hoping the 24th is good with them. Unless I hear otherwise from you I shall count again on zigzagging by trolley to Geneva, Ill. and then being hauled by the iron horse across the Mississippi and on more prairies till I see you and Jewell and a cross-bred sheep dog. If you remind me I have a fine old El-a-noy song, quaint as a black walnut four post bed, and an Eskimo sex story as good as a Chaplin picture.

> Faithfully—
> Potato Face

249 | TO HARRIET MONROE

> [Chicago]
> April 29, 1926.

Dear Harriet—

I shall mail you in a day or two, or as soon as I put my hands on it, a poem by Carl Lamsen Carmer of the University of Alabama. When I read it in a group down there I thought it would look good in Poetry, told him so, and he said it had been through your mill. Of course, I know all, or at least the half of your difficulties in picking 'em. But this particular piece is far out of the ordinary, one that I would save to the last if sitting rabbinically on a prize award board, stroking my long invisible beard as to who on earth should have the medals, money, berries or what have we? So, I repeat, it would look good in Poetry.

> Faithfully yours—
> Carl

250 | TO ALFRED HARCOURT

> [Chicago]
> May 17, 1926.

Dear Alf—

Here are the latest corrections for the fourth printing. De Witt Clinton's father was born at Little Britain near Newburgh and the Paltz; I tried to slip that in but it wouldn't fit.

Please send back this page of corrections when you are through with it, because I didn't make a carbon, and sometime I want to make a list of all these changes. Barton in his description of how the rifle was loaded in Kentucky, doesn't tag me at all with that, because my account of how a rifle was loaded in them days, is, with abridgement, taken almost word for word from Audubon's autobiography; it's Audubon against Barton and we'll leave it to posterity as to which is sending an empty booming sound against the whiffletree.

I suppose Gus has told you how Bostwick conducted the slave auction of authors in St. Louis. Each shivering naked author was trotted out to show he had good teeth, his knee hinges worked, and he was worth buying. . . Gus had a mysterious chuckle as though he is enjoying the passes you are making at shaping up this early limited edition songbook. I am mystified too.

A committee from the Illinois Bankers' Assn said I could address 2,000 (count 'em) bankers at their state convention in Springfield June 17. I told 'em I would for two bits a banker, and haven't heard as yet and don't expect to. Would you call that standing pat?. . Haven't got a speaking date for six months; stood off six invites to give a commencement address.

Tell the good scout, Howard Clark, there may be two more corrections in a day or two, but I doubt it.

When you are ready to send Hastings [Harcourt] out here, there will be a clean bed and a pennant ball team spread of victuals. . . Luck to you and yours—

As always—

Carl

251 | TO NEGLEY D. COCHRAN

[Chicago]
May 18. [1926]

Dear N.D.—

Your letter about God came. If I mentioned God in my letter to you I believe I meant to use the word God as meaning N.D. Cochran plus everything in the universe that is non-N.D. Cochran. Your letter only explains N.D. Cochran.

I see an A.P. story about Scripps drawing his last breath and being thrown to the fishes. I read the Editor & Publisher story. And a thing takes hold of me and shakes me inside. It is a thing I knew as a boy often but as a grown-up only once in a great while. When it hits me it is a surprise. . . I suppose too in the case of Scripps, besides what I knew of him as a real man, there is romance and a grand gaunt laughter about a landsman who knows the turmoil and intricacy of the big furious cities through and through, telling good-by to his piles of gold before he is dead, saying he is taking to the high seas to "play dead" and writing that he shall be buried wheresoever on the wide salt waters the heartbeats of him come to a stop. There was a lot more too. I think you were too close to Scripps to get his grandest gestures. He had something that runs through old Irish lore. "The crying of water." And "Oh for the crying out loud.". .

The big fact for me about Woolworth is that when at last he had topped his ambition to have the biggest building in the world, he used to walk around it every morning, ride to the top and down, and again walk around it wondering what it was all about. While with Bill Wrigley the big fact is that he wanted his poor goddam name spelled on the tower-clock instead of the hour numbers. And with Scripps it is the playing dead on the high seas and a burial with gulls crying between sky and water.

You note that I scribbled myself through the Lincoln book. Well, who pounded it into my poor head for five years straight that there is no "uncolored" news?. . May your joints never creak; may there be Canadian ale whenever you call for it; may your memory and your forgettery work as you command them; may your daughters always believe you're the finest man in the big round world.

As always—

CS

252 | TO LINCOLN STEFFENS

[Chicago]
May 18, 1926.

Dear Lincoln Steffens—

Well, it must have been worth while to tussle through the writing of that Lincoln book if it gets past you. . . I read your John

Reed obituary three or four times while I was writing the Lincoln; for you caught Jack and all the fine tragic turmoil of him in that little sketch. It will be good to read your Moses book.

I suppose you'll be sure to read Mark Sullivan's history; and then you'll have the feeling the stress and the weave ought to be different; the very thorough index doesn't mention Standard Oil; Rockefeller is mentioned only once and that in connection with a hospital endowment; the U.S. Steel Corporation gets 13 lines in a 602-page book about the years 1900-1904. At least he could have been a little technical about steel; his fear of being non-ethical shunted him into being completely non-technical about steel. So goes history. . . A Swede down at Birmingham shows me how they are making steel without smoke; electric furnaces; workmen that look like tennis champions in white duck; another Swede at Ford's River Rouge plant shows me the same thing. Ford is calling for a universal five-day workweek, in the Sat. Eve. Post; while men work they can't consume; two Sundays a week means bigger markets. . . There are $85 radios that realize all that Edward Bellamy had in his Utopia about music on tap in the home. . .

I'll tell you more when you get over here. And if you don't make it in a year or so I'm liable to knock on your door and ask to sleep in the garage at the Casa. . . If there were as much reliable material available about Diogenes as there is about Lincoln I would do a Life of that old bird; he kidded culture and the culture hounds. And he had some of your elusive laughter.

Luck and health be for you and yours.

Faithfully—
Carl Sandburg

Steffens was writing muckraking articles while Sandburg was active in the Social Democratic party. In the 1920's Steffens was still searching for economic utopias. He and Sandburg both admired John Reed, an American radical and author of Ten Days That Shook the World, *the story of the Soviet revolution. Mark Sullivan's* Our Times *was a three-volume history of America. Edward Bellamy's utopia was described in* Looking Backward.

1926

Elmhurst [Illinois]
Aug. 23. [1926]

Dear Mrs. Buchbinder—

I am dropping the work of writing Notes for the songs to attend to what I have put off too long, a decent reply to your letter, a communication from one who has toiled at length and fought valiantly through the hot dog days of this summer, on harmonic costumes for a lot of doggone songs. . . Yes, Taps can and ought to go without chords or pianistic divertissement, or embellishment—or is it garnish?. . . With some it has been garnish. And a few you gave an investiture as important and solemn as the red robe and hat of Cardinal Bonzano.

The aftermath of your whirl of work looks good, seems to hold on in all its first values. I hope you sleep like a hired man on a farm, like a growing baby, like a lazy and independent mountaineer, like a sinner whose sins are few and deserving of grace and redemption. You know what I mean. Make it a real vacation. Let the magnets of the Old Earth slow down your head and bones. In the mood of Zek'l Weep, Zek'l Mo'n. After Fish Creek and the falling leaves will be time enough to think about whether you are one of those meant in "People come a-runnin' and de train done gone.". . Luck stars be yours—

Boll Weevil

Hazel Felman Buchbinder, wife of a Chicago doctor, wrote the music for some of the songs in The American Songbag. *The Buchbinders had a country home at Fish Creek, Wisconsin.*

254 | TO LOUIS AND JEAN UNTERMEYER

[St. Joseph, Missouri]
[Circa November, 1926]

Dear Louis and Jean:

Being where Jesse James lived and died—and where The Big Muddy performs a sickle shape around bluffs—and there is Fried Catfish on the menu—

and so to day—
Your
Carl

255 | TO EZRA POUND

[Chicago]
December 3, 1926

Dear Pound—

It was good to have a letter from you again, though I do not see that I have anything to get off my chest just now for such a publication that would not be as well launched 50 or 100 years from now. I still read "Lustra", "Provenca". And three of your prose works that I have. If I get to Paris next year I shall look you up and give you a cross-examination.

Faithfully yours—
Sandburg

In Rapallo, Ezra Pound planned a poetry-and-arts quarterly, because, he said, "time has again worked round to point where I ought again to try to cause a little liveliness, as I perhaps managed to do a decade ago, when we were all so much younger and wiser."

256 | TO L. W. PAYNE, JR.

[Chicago]
December 3, 1926.

Dear Old Scout—

You have my permission to use the lines you ask about to fill out the space.

I am surprised at the Conrad Aiken essay being included in your book. There are more logical, eloquent and pointed critics and analysts of Masters and myself. He designates me with no reservations as a "Socialist". For ten years I have been designated in Who's Who as an "Independent". He is inaccurate in this manner forty ways, and is the only young squirt that has ever called me "sadistic". So the information you supply young Texans through this essay is what in a court of law would be called false testimony.

With the exception of Aiken's essay I enjoyed your book thoroughly. It looks like one of the best anthologies. And I can see that an immense amount of reading supports your own extensive notes.

Faithfully yours—
Sandburg

257 | TO SARA TEASDALE

[Chicago]
December 16, 1926

Dear Sara Teasdale—

I have always thought the best poetry something close to the line of silence; it almost crosses over; you get this in "Dark of the Moon"; I put it along with Emily Dickinson; isolate, golden moths; you murmur briefly at times what the Potato Face Blind Man in the Rootabaga books talks of gabbily. Luck stars be over you.

Carl Sandburg

258 | TO PAULA SANDBURG

[The California Limited, en route to Galesburg, Illinois]
Thursday [Early January, 1927]

Dearest Paula—

And I think over and over of what a fine thing grew between
you and mama—and how she cherished it.

And I do a lot of figuring and dreaming about the coming
summer in the sand for us and Co.

Carl

*Sandburg wrote this coming back from Santa Fe, where he had
been notified by his brother Martin that their mother had died of
heart failure on December 30, 1926.*

259 | TO MRS. JACOB BUCHBINDER

[Elmhurst, Illinois?]
[Circa January, 1927]

Dear Hazel—

The chronicle in the day's log is that two songs are lost. We
know the hour they were here, Sunday 3.30 p.m., God's time. And
we know they are gone. And only one other thing we know; we
have searched every goddam corner into which they could have
crawled or fallen. It is what the Insurance Policies call An Act
of God. The two are, first, that fine music box stunt CUCKOO WALTZ,
and second, OLD BRASS WAGON. Do you happen to have copies? If
you could send them they would be copied and returned on day
of receipt. If you don't have copies please weep with all others
concerned. There is a malignant and dark Personal Devil hanging
around and operating.

Yours cursing—
Carl

You have heard of the Nantucket sea captain who used to tell his
crew, "All I want from you is silence and damned little of that"?
There is a Personal Devil.

1927

The American Songbag was a difficult job of bookmaking. A little later Sandburg wrote to Mrs. Buchbinder, "We're on the last pizzicatta pinnacles of the peaks."

260 | TO MITCHELL DAWSON

[Chicago]
Feb. 10, [1927]

Dear Mitchell:

Would you send about a dozen of the circulars and a dozen posters to Dr. Hugh E. Brown, 1110 Judson Ave., Evanston, Ill.? We're on there at Community Service club, in a church on Sunday afternoon, Feb. 27.

And would you send right away some 20 of the circulars and 10 posters to Isadora Bennett Reed, Municipal Theater, Columbia, South Carolina? And again about 10 of the circulars to Du Bose Heyward, 76 Church St., Charleston, S.C.?

And I will remember you in my will and have you draw it. . . I wonder if as a lawyer you know Rabelais' will, which read, "I have nothing; I owe much; I leave the remainder to the poor.". . . And that ain't no lie neither.

Yours southbound and earthbound,
Carl

Mitchell Dawson, friend and attorney, served as Sandburg's booking agent.

261 | TO JAMES STEVENS

[Elmhurst, Illinois?]
March 3, 1927.

Dear Jim:

I wish that I could have read your Bear story when I was in Oregon so that we could have talked about it. I know precisely the mood that generates this kind of a story and gets the darn thing on to paper. In a day or two I shall mail you one of my own stories on this order, which I have never offered to a publisher; it has kicked around my workshop, my caboose for six or seven years; it is too good to print, too intelligent; the spink bug and the huck are a little too far out of the three-dimension world for most people to get them. Singly, a story much as yours of the eggnog vines, bothers most people. A big book of fifty or sixty of them, however, would be an achievement. Herman Melville in Moby Dick, and Rabelais, got away with it, but they have their limited audience.

The writing mood of these is so different from the mood in which a man does his more factual work, that the brain operates in two shifts like a day and night gang . . . fantasy, I suppose, must always be laid to one side, and "tested and tasted" in many ways, for a long time, before a fellow can be sure what are the good lasting high-spots. All that a fellow can do is to write his head off when the mood comes and the next day, or a week or two later, pick it up and look at it with the gravity of a lunacy commission.

Faithfully yours,
Carl

James Stevens wrote novels about the Northwest. Paul Bunyan *was his first book.*

262 | TO VACHEL LINDSAY

[Elmhurst, Illinois?]
April 6, 1927.

Dear Vachel:

If beggars from Holland New York come my way with your "Handy Guide" in their hip pockets, I shall salute them, give them a cup of coffee apiece, and read them a Rootabaga story.

I meant to write to you months ago about your handling of the Lincoln book in your Saturday Evening Post article on poets. Of course, you helped write the book and I know that such hours as I have had with your mother and people of her prayers and dreams, helped write the book.

Just now, I am trying to finish up "The American Song Bag." It has mounted beyond all first plans for it. It is not so much my

book as that of a thousand other people who have made its 260
colonial, pioneer, railroad, work-gang, hobo, Irish, Negro, Mexican,
gutter, Gossamer songs, chants and ditties. . . . All luck to you—
Faithfully yours—
CS

*Vachel Lindsay had written to Sandburg about two people in
Holland, New York, "who seem to have so much our point of view
that I have urged them in my name to get acquainted and to
exchange thoughts and views." Lindsay once walked from Illinois
to New Mexico, exchanging his poems for handout meals and
shelter ("Rhymes to Be Traded for Bread"), and his book about
these experiences was* Adventures While Preaching the Gospel of
Beauty. *He and Sandburg first knew each other from the early days
of the Harriet Monroe* Poetry *circle.*

263 | TO HENRY JUSTIN SMITH

[Elmhurst, Illinois?]
April 25, 1927.

Dear Harry:
   On this notebook stuff, which I have not looked over since
dictating, I will leave it to you to change any verbs or adjectives you
choose, and to leave out such notes as the ones on Alfred Noyes and
Billy Sunday, if they haven't got the right stiletto and accuracy. I
will give President Coolidge your highest personal regards and for
your sake tell New York the truth about Chicago.
Carl

264 | TO MRS. EUGENE MEYER

[New York]
May 13, 1927.

Dear Mrs. Meyer:
   Could you find out for me, in the copyright division of the
Congressional Library, whether a song has ever been copyrighted,

probably titled, "Cabahges, Cabeans, and Carotts," and having these lines—

"Cabahges, cabeans, and carotts
Carotts, cabeans, and cabahges
Sweetest of flowers, I love you so;
Some people like rhododendrons
And some forget-me-nots,
But what I like best is the dish of ka-beef
With cabahges, cabeans, and carotts."

This is one of the best nonsense songs ever done the melody having quizzical charm. . . . . Our Songbag material mounted bigger than expected; I have cut a total of 338 songs down to 255 so that we will have a single big volume instead of a two-volume set.

Thank you for the other material which came so promptly. I may have another look-in on Washington before Memorial Day. Remember me to Eugene.

Faithfully,
Carl

Eugene Meyer, the editor and publisher of the Washington Post, *discovered that the song had been copyrighted on April 15, 1919.*

265 | TO THE EDITOR OF *THE NATION*

[Elmhurst, Illinois]
June 15, 1927.

Dear Sir:

My source of information as to Harriet Beecher Stowe doing shoemaking and tailoring for her family, was the biography of Mrs. Stowe by Martha Foote Crowe and conversations with Mrs. Crowe. It is difficult to enter into a controversy with a man living in the year 1927 who disputes allegations about his mother and her craftsmanship in the year 1847 when he was a babe in arms or un-born. Mr. Stowe believes he is a veracious man. He wishes accuracy of statement regarding his mother. Let him refresh his recollections and write a memoir of how his beloved and lovable mother kept house in Walnut Hills, Cincinnati, whether she called in dress-

makers to make her dresses, whether the family footwear was factory made or done by a journeyman shoemaker and what was the
monthly stipend of her husband, a professor of biblical exegesis in
a struggling western theological seminary.

"I was married to a man rich in Greek and Hebrew, Latin and
Arabic, and alas! in nothing else," she wrote to Mrs. Follen in
London (I am quoting from Constance Mayfield Rourke's "Trumpets of Jubilee"), "I had married into poverty and without a dowry
. . . my husband had only a large library of books and a great deal
of learning." On arrival of the Stowe family in Brunswick, Maine,
Mrs. Rourke informs the world in her just published book, "Mrs.
Stowe was obliged to begin the work of the pioneer all over again.
She papered the walls of her house, and painted and varnished the
floors and the woodwork, and laid carpets and made barrel-chairs
and recovered sofas and decorated them with gimp, and rehabili-
tated pillows and bolsters and bedspreads. . . In the midst of her
labors came a low-spirited letter from Professor Stowe, announcing
that he was sick in bed, inquiring what his wife would do in case
she was left a widow, as she almost certainly would be, warning
her that she would have a mere pittance to live on, and so must not
be extravagant. . . The following spring a clergyman from Harps-
well happened to be loitering near the wharf late one afternoon, and
saw the entire Stowe family seated on casks, apparently in silence.
Tired and worn, unkempt and even dilapidated, with holes as large
as silver dollars showing at the heels of her low shoes, Mrs. Stowe
made an oblivious center of the group."

With each increase of evidence we are led to believe that in her
material poverty, Harriet Beecher Stowe was a good deal of a
working-woman, having not merely mother wit but deft manual
cleverness. Her memory does not require the guardianship of a
ninety year old son who considers it important that she must not be
recorded as having made shoes, of a sort, for her family, and tailored,
in a way, for her husband.

Carl Sandburg

*The Lincoln biography brought letters about certain disputed points
all during Sandburg's life. Mrs. Stowe's son had written that his
mother did not do the things Sandburg said.*

266 | TO CHARLES S. DUNNING

[Three Oaks, Michigan]
August 20, 1927.

Dear Charlie:

I have been ordered to a pretty strict regime, a long lay off. I have a good machine, but the motor and propeller have been in the air too much and are ordered to ground work. If you come to Chicago for the fight, or for anything else, I will want to see you. If I should decide not to come into Chicago for the fight then I would want you to run out to where my family and I are hung up for this summer and fall near Three Oaks, Michigan. The route there you can learn from Miss Betty Peterman of the Chicago Daily News office who is sandwiched between Margaret Mann of the motion picture page and Jessie Ozias Donohue of the society columns. It is bracing to have your letter. Whether I can get to call on Miss Taylor will depend on the outcome of several of my errands in town; my doctors are as dirty and domineering as hers are. I have had more work, travel, fun and philosophy than the law allows and am taking a jail sentence. But if I can't leave the jail, I want you to come to it for a couple of days in September if you are making a Chicago trip.

Faithfully yours,
Carl

Charles S. Dunning, a Hollywood publicity man, had suggested that Sandburg talk to the actress Estelle Taylor. In the big fight of September 22, 1927, Gene Tunney outpointed Jack Dempsey in ten rounds. Betty Peterman (later Mrs. Michael Gole) was Sandburg's secretary.

267 | TO ALFRED HARCOURT

[Chicago]
September 23, 1927.

Dear Alfred:

I have sent a long letter to Howard [Clark] explaining how matters stand on the Songbag. I ought to have everything on that in your hands on October 1st. I have done some work on the condensation and should have that in your hands by the middle of October. Perhaps if necessary, I could send you half of it about October 7. I have been sleeping an average of nine hours a night for six weeks and broke training last night for the first time to see the Fight; I gained in weight; I cut out all meats, liquor, pastries; have handled an ax an hour a day and done puttering work of different kinds another hour and then have laid around lazy whenever I felt like it. Now I believe I can make the grade on the Songbag, and the condensation, on the date named. I hate to talk or write about health, as I have here, and would not do it except that we are embarked on these enterprises together. . . . My schedule with Feakins this year is short; "dates" are on alternate days. I will have a few days in New York in October, camp there till the condensation is finished and will reserve November as entirely a vacation month.   Yours as always.

Carlo

268 | TO HOWARD CLARK

[Chicago]
[Circa September 30, 1927]

Dear Howard—

I am wondering what to do about our book cover. The design we have now, on the dummy, as I stick along with it, is off key. It looks like a Ginn & Co. textbook on book-keeping cross-bred with an Appleton geography. The letters of "The" and the scrolls alongside are mainly what's wrong. Would there be such a thing, at this time, as throwing out this "The" and scrolls and putting a small "The" in the upper left, as per rough sketch enclosed? As we have been sticking along with the present design the impression has grown that it looks cheap, that it's a case of our trying for an effect that we don't get.

2. Could a light gray be substituted for tan as cover?

3. In binding, in size, in blue edging for pages, in heft and feel the dummy is perfect; it gives an immediate impression that it will stand wear, stand on pianos, stand punishment, stand throwing at cats or dogs. It is perfection till we open our eyes and look at it.

4. I know you have troubles of your own and that both of us have to watch our step on the insides of the book; on that alone we have enough to keep us out of mischief without trying to get artistic, esthetic and ticklish about the outside cover. At the same time, I am telling you how a hazy first impression has grown and deepened—there is strength, value, fiber, stuff (as distinguished from stuffing) inside the book that isn't done right by the cover. . . . And as I said to start with, I am wondering what can be done. My conscience hurts me about this.

Yours as always—
Carl

To Howard Clark, designer at Harcourt, Brace and Company, Sandburg had previously written, "You mention the book being a sort of mess of knots that needs unknotting. My guess is that it is a batch of sausages ground to a fine point that needs only a little seasoning and wrapping in packages."

269 | TO H. L. MENCKEN

[Chicago]
October 10, 1927.

Dear Hank:

Your spies were correct in telling you that the Grand Canyon poem is ageing in the wood, whether it is "high-toned." Sometimes I think this poem summarizes in a nutshell the gist and residuum of all that has been printed in the Mercury. And then again I think any Beatrice Fairfax with two ginrickeys could do better. . . . I have done a one sentence sketch of you in The American Songbag to which I point with pride. . . . Your Review of Reviews article is great workmanship, fine reportorial job.

Faithfully,
Carl

Mencken had written to Sandburg on August 6: "Spies in my employ tell me that you have written a high-toned poem on the Grand Canyon and are now ageing it in the wood." He wanted this poem ("Many Hats") for The American Mercury.

270 | TO H. L. MENCKEN

[Chicago]
Nov. 3, 1927.

Dear Hank:

An early copy of the Songbag will go to you. The detail work on it nearly killed me and for a good many weeks I am the laziest man in the United States. The Grand Canyon poem, titled "Many Hats," would take five pages of the Mercury. Many of your subscribers would clip this poem, cancel their subscriptions and read this once a month instead of the magazine. But I have other and shorter poems, more comical, which I hope to dig up from the rag bag some week this winter when there is a blizzard.

Faithfully,
Carl

271 | TO HENRY JUSTIN SMITH

[Chicago]
December 1, 1927.

Dear Harry:

Please for the love of humanity cut that picture with the notebook to one half the size it now is. Considering how short the notebook is, the picture is too big and as a feature it is over balanced.

Valentino or Lindy can stand this highlight public mugging twice a week but it won't do for Swedes like Fred Lundin and me.

Carl

272 | TO ALFRED HARCOURT

[Chicago]
December 23, 1927.

Dear Alfred:

I have had to turn down an official invitation to be the main speaker at the Lincoln dinner, February 13, of the National Republican Club of New York City. In doing so, I had to recall our common thought (It hit both of us about the same time) that the Lincoln book would make us "respectable."

However, I have accepted an invitation to deliver the Poem before the Phi Beta Kappa Chapter of Harvard University next June. They pay $100 and board you two days. Somehow, I have to laugh about it rather than take it solemnly. There is something Rootabaga about it. Please don't say anything about it; let any announcements come from Harvard. The only thing certain is that I will not read the Sacco-Vanzetti Poem now in manuscript. Yours patriotic as hell.

Carl

273 | TO THE EDITOR OF THE *CENTURY MAGAZINE*

[Chicago]
[Circa end of December, 1927]

To the Editor:—

Would you kindly correct the statement published a number of times that in the song-offering in my recital-concerts I employ a banjo?

The instrument used is one with less repercussion, and more intimations of silence, than a banjo.

Sometimes when the strings of it are thrummed one has to listen twice to find the chords and melody.

The box of the instrument is entirely of wood, with a cunning of construction having had centuries of study, rehearsal, and try-out by Italians, Spaniards, and the same Arabians who hunted up the Arabic numerals.

At music stores and pawn shops the instrument is called a guitar, a Guitar.

The banjo is meant for jigs, buck and wing dances, attack, surprise, riot and rout. The guitar is intended for serenades, croons, for retreat, retirement, fadeaway.

I thank you.

Carl Sandburg.

274 | TO GAMALIEL BRADFORD

[Chicago]
February 20, 1928.

Dear Gamaliel Bradford:

Your letter is worth having from forty angles. For a long time I have intended to write you greetings and consultations. Only three weeks ago, I wrote a little commentary, for my note-book corner in The Chicago Daily News, and quoted your verse about you yourself being a ghost: That verse had the elusive quality of Emily Dickinson. One line of yours somewhere has haunted me for years: "The inferno of the furnace of life." And your Lee, of course, is unforgettable.

I did the Lincoln book stubbornly, hewing to a design that was clear in my own mind, and considering the conditions, I have been amazed at the size of the audience the book has had. The "moon-light chapters," as I call them which sketch streams of American and world events that connect with the Lincoln fate, were much longer in the original; about thirty thousand words were cut from them because they would have thrown the design out of balance . . . I know precisely what you mean by your saying you yourself are a ghost. There were times when I was on the Lincoln book, that I felt as if in a trance, saw automobiles as horses and wagons, and saw cities of brick and stone dissolve into lumber cottages and shanties . . . I suppose as two biographers who have stood considerable wear and tear we can say to each other like two battered gypsy palmists, it's a great life if you don't weaken . . . May luck and health stay by you.

Faithfully yours,
Carl Sandburg

Gamaliel Bradford, a descendant of Governor William Bradford of Plymouth Colony, was a poet and the author of Lee the American *and other biographies.*

275 | TO ROBERT GRANT

[Chicago]
February 29, 1928.

Dear Mr. Grant:

For three years I have been working on a piece of verse called "Good Morning America" and chose this piece for the Phi Beta poem next June. I made a final draft of it this winter. While lunching with an old Chicago friend, William L. Chenery, editor of Collier's Weekly, I gave him a draft of it for his free and friendly comment. He passed it to the Woman's Home Companion editors who telegraphed me they wanted it for publication. I was surprised, even though my publisher Alfred Harcourt, regards it as the best piece of verse I have written. It will require at least two of the large pages of the Woman's Home Companion and I had believed that the space consideration alone would prohibit its publication. The editors mentioned above are the only ones who have seen the manuscript and I had no intention of offering it to any editors. I am sending you this information so that you may know what happened in an incident that came to me as a surprise. With greetings and all good wishes.

Faithfully,
Carl Sandburg

Judge Robert Grant was in charge of the Harvard ceremonies at which Sandburg had been invited to read "Good Morning, America" as the Phi Beta Kappa poem in June. Willa Roberts of the Woman's Home Companion had requested permission of Grant to publish the poem in the July issue, which actually came out in June, before the reading at Harvard. Judge Grant refused. Sandburg was anxious that there should be no misunderstanding about his role in this. The poem came out in the August issue instead.

276 | TO H. L. MENCKEN

[Chicago]
March 3, 1928.

Dear Hank:

I am leaving in a day or two for Arkansas and hope to mail you from there a batch of verses. The only stipulation if you use any of them is that you must use three (3). Somehow people are less aggravated by the time they have taken three of them.

Thank you for trying to increase the traffic on The American Songbag. I said at the beginning it would be a thankless job and my gratification about the book is merely that of a patriot who has seen duty and done it.

I am glad your eye did not light on the really big mistakes in the Songbag. "It's The Syme The Whole World Over" is a very sad song, too sad for common time; the hard eggs who gave me the tune read your paper and call me on the phone to say you are wrong. As to your own harmonization, I am having the manuscript looked up and shall publish the disputed versions in deadly parallel columns.

Sincerely yours,
Carl

277 | TO ALFRED HARCOURT

[Chicago]
May 1, 1928.

Dear Alfred:

The manuscript of Good Morning, America was put on the 20th Century today for you.

Perhaps you should know that there is extra pressure now because we must make the move from Elmhurst to Michigan next week. I am taking along all of my books, notes, manuscripts and this means not merely hours but days; a nine years accumulation has to be handled. . . . I got my speaking voice back two days ago and my singing voice, if you ain't particular, is back today. I have never had bronchitis before nor lost my voice so it was a little adventure among the cripples of the world.

Enclosed is the leading article of the American Magazine for this month with the paragraph about the Lincoln book. Will Payne in the Saturday Evening Post about four weeks ago had a similar endorsement. So I want to tackle the abridged edition and do a thorough job. And soon.

At regular intervals I have a moment of wonderment about Hastings and how the old boy is coming along with his beans and corn.

Yours as always
Carl

278 | TO HELEN KELLER

[Chicago]
June 5, 1928.

Dear Miss Keller:

Sometime ago when I was on a long vacation and receiving no mail I was asked to write to you on your birthday anniversary. I could not comply with that request then, deeply as I wished to.

However, in moving from one house to another and reorganizing desks, files and papers, I came across a letter written to you six years ago. I did not sign it—nor did I send it to you—just why I do not know—perhaps I felt the style of the letter was a little high flown. Anyhow, I do not feel now that it is high flown and send it to you with greetings and love.

Faithfully yours,
Carl Sandburg

[April 8, 1922]

Dear Helen Keller:

I saw and heard you last night at the Palace and enjoyed it a thousand ways. It was interesting to watch that audience minute by minute come along till they loved you big and far. For myself, the surprise was to find you something of a dancer, shifting in easy postures like a good blooded race horse. I thrilled along with the audience to your saying you hear applause with your feet registering to vibration of the stage boards. Possibly the finest thing about your performance is that those who hear and see you feel that zest for living, the zest you radiate, is more important than any formula about how to live life.

Carl Sandburg

279 | TO MARTIN SANDBURG

[Harbert, Michigan]
June 5, 1928.

Dear Mart:

Enclosed is a time table showing you the way to our place. Please send us a special delivery letter as to when you expect to come on. Telegrams are slower than air special delivery.

If I could know a week beforehand as to when you are coming then I would be sure to be on hand. I have not yet made the trip to Detroit that I was planning. And I would not like to be in Detroit when you are at Harbert. Bring Marty or Merrill along, if you can.

Also things are further mixed just now by the fact that I have been summoned for grand jury duty. Of course, I can insist that your business should be investigated and you called as a witness— which would be one free ride that we would have copped off from the great Burlington Railroad.

All good luck to you, Mart.

Carl

280 | TO HARRY HANSEN

[Chicago]
September 11, 1928.

Dear Harry:

At this hour of writing, neither wild horses nor wild women could drag from me a disclosure of the secret as to who I shall vote for in November, and above all, why. Only the fact that we are both Alpha Omegas and former racketeers in the same business in Chicago, is responsible for your innocent inquiry being answered.

Carl

Harry Hansen, an old Chicago friend, later literary critic of the New York World, *had asked, "In view of the general interest in the Presidential campaign among writers, please tell me, for purposes of publication, for whom you intend to vote and why."*

281 | TO SHERWOOD ANDERSON

[Chicago]
October 5, 1928.

Dear Sherwood:

You are one grand scout—and I am ashamed of myself that I have let so much time go by without sending you word of some kind. I don't see just how I could find the six or eight weeks for a trip to Sweden next spring. All that I am sure of is that sometime before next summer I am going to roll down into your town and hang around a couple of days . . . An uncle of Carl Rothstein is a neighbor of mine in the Michigan sandhills overlooking the old Lake. He has ordered me to sleep a lot and the last year I have slept more than in any two years of my life previously.

I dip into three books of your stories and A Story Teller's Story at regular intervals and they stand up and I am glad I know your voice and ways and that we have knocked around together. Please send me your paper; I will remit if the rates are not too high.

Faithfully yours,
Carl

1928

Sherwood Anderson was running two newspapers in Marion, Va., and passed along the idea from Rothstein, in Sweden, about having Swedish-American writers lecture there.

282 | TO LINCOLN STEFFENS

[Chicago]
October 10, 1928.

Dear Link:

The Carmelite is a bully paper for many reasons and I have read nearly every number all the way through the past two months. I shall pay my annual subscription when visiting Carmel sometime this winter. I enclose a number of notes from my Notebook; they are a few out of several thousand to be published in a book two or three years from now. These are as go-as-you-please as your valuable paper. You have the highest batting average of any paper I know of for honest-to-God bright sayings of children. I read all the baby talk you print.

Faithfully yours,
Carl

Lincoln Steffens printed this letter in The Carmelite, *in Carmel, California. In the same issue he said, in an article he had written about Sandburg entitled "When God Made Chicago": "The bone and the flesh that God took from Chicago and blew upon, He made into one that could only hear and see and feel and plainly report what God had made; for it was a reporter that God chose to be the lover and the prophet of Chicago."*

283 | TO SHERWOOD ANDERSON

[Harbert, Michigan]
October 11, 1928.

Dear Sherwood:

Send the paper to Harbert, Michigan. I am there with my family most of the year now. It is as lonely as your own hills. I am starting work on Abraham Lincoln: The War Years. You will have to tell me a little about why Virginia went into the war, why men fight, and what were some of the innermost thoughts of Robert E. Lee and Stonewall Jackson. You will be asked about these things when I get down there. You will not have to answer any more than if I asked you, how do seeds and eggs pass life on?

As ever
Carl

284 | TO WILLIAM ALLEN WHITE

[Chicago]
October 20, 1928.

Dear Bill White:

I shall be glad to add "Masks In A Pageant" to my little row of your books; and I shall read it first.

Beveridge's Lincoln is in an extended though not particularly essential way what we have gleaned hitherto from the Herndon and Weik books. Your friend Lloyd Lewis, calls the turn fairly well in the enclosed review. Beveridge should have done Douglas who was handsome, fluent and born under a star like Beveridge. He could have gotten inside of Douglas and given the breath of a man. He rattles the dry bones of Lincoln. I don't care to be quoted on this. It runs back into many things. As a young man, I admired Beveridge and studied him and sometime hope to write a sketch of him.

I am glad you like Good Morning, America. I feel about its pages as a Zebra does about his stripes; they are there for weal or woe, sink or swim, cross my heart.

You have been on the map during this campaign. Your "Battle Hum Of The Republic" is a real document.

Faithfully yours,
Carl Sandburg

285 | TO CHARLES DUNNING

[Harbert, Michigan]
January 4, 1929.

Dear Charlie:

Several times lately while eating tangerines I had the feeling of riding in a Studebaker 1922 model and you at the left philosophizing. [D. W.] Griffith called me on long distance from Los Angeles and offered $10,000 for me to spend a week with him going over the script. I thought it over and wired him the next day the arrangement would not be fair to him nor me nor the picture; that I would take on the job for thirty thousand dollars, one-third before starting, one-third at New Years and one-third at the completion of the picture. That was the last of it . . . The sweater hasn't come. If you still have it keep it as a remembrance. Our house is lousy with sweaters though none of the sweaters are lousy . . . I don't know when the next west coast tour will shape up but will let you know. That desert ride of ours is a highlight with me for a long time. Santa Barbara was almost like Boston, except for the Cactus Lady and her man, whom I find to be one of the big men in teaching the dumb to talk.

Faithfully,
Carl

286 | TO ALFRED HARCOURT

[Harbert, Michigan]
January 6, 1929.

Dear Alfred:

I have been toiling on Lincoln and have actually got his feet planted in Washington and hope this month to have him sworn in. Otherwise I would have sent you the Christmas letter that was written in my head several times and never got onto paper . . . Milton [Berg, a Michigan friend], of course, will always haunt us and hurt us and gladden us because he is what he is . . . I made a bunch of illustrations all by myself which I considered might run as an appendice to Potato Face, but I guess we better not experiment with them on this first edition. Steichen said they were good but mostly too sophisticated . . . From stories about and quotations from Red in the labor papers my guess is that there will be a powerful punch to his next novel and that it will be the best all around novel of the labor movement ever done . . .

All good luck to you and yours.

As always,
Carl

P.S. Steichen is making a photograph which he will send you for use as a frontispiece to the Potato Face book. It is the one the Pictorial Review used in launching the Lincoln serial. This suggestion came from Paula and Ed.

"Red" (Sinclair Lewis) planned to write a novel around the life of Eugene Debs, but he got sidetracked and lost interest.

287 | TO LEO SOWERBY

[Harbert, Michigan]
March 21, 1929.

Dear Leo:

Of course, you know there is a pleasant thrill for me about your doing a Symphonic Poem based on a passage from "Prairie." Naturally, you are free as the west wind or a sunrise on Lake Michigan in the matter of using the name "Prairie" and printing such lines as you please. From about the first of May and then on for six months or more I expect to be at Harbert, Michigan and shall pray that you come out some time, and we will have a day of it. I shall let you know as soon as I am back in May. Our piano is a big Conover which I believe you will like. Also I have new songs— and would like to show you a mammoth Civil War and Lincoln library which I am using in writing about Lincoln and the War Years.

Faithfully yours,
Carl

1929

Leo Sowerby, Chicago composer, had written scores for The American Songbag.

288 | TO THOMAS HORNSBY FERRIL

[Harbert, Michigan]
March 28, 1929.

Dear Tom Ferril:

I am still carrying with me the address of your daughter, to whom a Rootabaga book is to go when I am in New York next month. . . I have not lost faith in the hat coming back. . . Nor, above all, have I lost faith in the Lamon interview coming along. Please watch that. . . The Fort Laramie poem is tremendous. A man who can write like that has an immense life to handle. It is one of those poems that Shelley had in mind when he said that what gets on to paper is but a faint adumbration of what shook the writer when the high surge of it was on him. I congratulate you on being so alive and registering.

Faithfully yours,
Carl Sandburg

Sandburg had left his hat at Ferril's house. Ferril wrote him an amusing letter, saying that he would return the hat, though he couldn't figure out just how yet, since he was not a package wrapper. "Maybe I could just put stamps on the hat, or maybe some day I'll happen across some hatless pilgrim bound for Harbert."

289 | TO HELGA SANDBURG

[Atlanta, Georgia]
April 15, 1929

Dear Swipes—

My heart is glad to have your letter. And the news about turtles and crows makes me homesick. Love to your beautiful mother, your sweet sisters, and your angel faced self—

Daddy

290 | TO CLARK P. BISSETT

[Harbert, Michigan]
May 18, 1929

Dear Clark Bissett:

The books came, as I wired you. Half of them probably should be back in your hands by next January. On any cross country trip that you make this year or next I hope you will come to my place at Harbert, Michigan, overlooking Lake Michigan (we could see Chicago across the Lake if it were not for the curve of the earth). It would not be much of an interruption on your journey eastward from Chicago as we can motor you to the main line, Michigan Central, fast trains.

It may be a five or six year job that I am now on. Lincoln ran the war. That is, it is almost universally conceded that the South could have won a peace and achieved some form of independence had it not been for Lincoln and his ways of running the war. Therefore, the war and its personalities must have presentation. Nicolay and Hay saw this clearly but the idea ran away with them till their book was lopsided and its portraiture all out of proportion.

It is good to have a friend like you. Just the thought of it sometimes makes the grind and the heaviness go easier. All health and luck to you.

Faithfully yours,
Carl Sandburg

Clark P. Bissett, a collector of Lincolniana, was Professor of Law at the University of Washington, Seattle.

291 | TO EMANUEL HERTZ

[Harbert, Michigan]
May 18, 1929

Dear Mr. Hertz:

I am waiting for the consignment of books here with the same patience and the same endless scanning of the horizon familiar to the California '49ers watching for a mule team bringing them new tools. Passover Week this year will be to me unforgettable . . . yes, I shall send back books as soon as I am through with them. I am sure that one-half to three-fourths of them will be back on your shelves by next January. Of course, I regret disturbing the shelves, but you know my reasons, and I hope that in the end your time and thoughtfulness will prove worthwhile.

Faithfully yours,
Carl Sandburg

Emanuel Hertz, New York attorney and Lincoln collector, wrote and edited numerous Lincoln books.

292 | TO PAUL M. ANGLE

[Harbert, Michigan]
July 16, 1929.

Dear Paul:

Oliver [Barrett] sent me your manuscript. And I guess you are a good enough workman to know you are doing an important job with a beautiful thoroughness. I am about half way through so far. I would suggest a footing in connection with the Carlinville speech to the effect that while the text of the speech as written out by the reporter probably delivers a fairly accurate outline of the ideas presented by Lincoln, the use of the word "Nigger" was never indulged in by Lincoln unless he was quoting somebody, and to this extent only, and probably not more, the report is erroneous. I also have the feeling that some kind of acknowledgment to Oliver in the preface would be in order; it is more than convenient that we can have available as a counsellor and friend a fellow of his range of abilities.

Faithfully—
Carl

Paul M. Angle was secretary of the Lincoln Centennial Association in Springfield when his book New Letters and Papers of Lincoln *was published in 1930. He and Sandburg collaborated on* Mary Lincoln: Wife and Widow (*1932*).

293 | TO HENRY HORNER

[Chicago]
July 25, 1929

Dear Judge Horner:

I am mailing you a scrapbook of yours which I have gone through and made notes from.

Also I am sending you one of the few scarce and lonesome copies of a book called "Clover Leaves," which you will see looks like a book, tastes like a book, and to handle weighs like a book. This should be in your collection, and I can get along very well if I can have photostats of the pages indicated on attached sheet.

The horseshoes arrived and have been broken in. Perhaps some time in August we can have the biennial tournament.

Faithfully yours,
Carl Sandburg

P.S. Now the fashion and vogue is setting in to sculpt faces and phizzogs on noble mountains not deserving mutilation, why not have some profiles on the county building of faces and phizzogs already familiar to us from postage stamps and dollar bills and faithful rotogravure reproductions by the million? As I have told you, art is hell.

> *Judge Henry Horner, of the Cook County probate court, was a Lincoln collector who became governor of Illinois in 1932. The biennial tournament refers to the games between Horner, Barrett, Al Hannah, and Sandburg.*

294 | TO ALFRED HARCOURT

[Chicago]
September 7, 1929.

Dear Alfred:

On coming to town today for the first time in three weeks, I learned from Lloyd [Lewis] that he has a decision from you that a Pinkerton book is not for now. If I had rambled into your office at the time you were making your decision and you had asked me for my slant on it, I would have answered: Allen Pinkerton is the classical detective of America; he operated the biggest and weirdest secret service department the country has ever had in war time; he inaugurated industrial espionage and strikebreaking as a business; he wrote a dozen or more books telling how good he was, and though he was suave, flatulent, garrulous, he was often a cunning and cruel instrument used by predatory business. Nobody has touched him in a book. If I were to name five or six of the leading *wanted* biographies, one about Pinkerton would be named. Lloyd is lit up about it. Pinkerton is so devious, crooked and shadowy that he makes a foil for Sherman. A fact story about Pinkerton will be written one of these days which, as a biography, will be among the "perennials."

And you know I write this with affection, and with an understanding of many of the things which prompted you to your decision, and which neither of us have time for now. If you don't see this matter as I do now, you know I am a good soldier and you won't hear a whimper out of me.

Carl

P.S. Enclosed is a letter which came and a carbon of my reply.

Lloyd Lewis's biography, Sherman: Fighting Prophet, *was published by Harcourt, Brace and Company in 1932.*

295 | TO HELEN KELLER

[Harbert, Michigan]
October 10, 1929.

Dear Miss Keller:

Since your good letter came to my hands I have read not only that but also your book "Midstream." So it has been the biggest Helen Keller summer I have ever had. I have written three notes which are to run in my Notebook in The Chicago Daily News during the month of publication. These will be clipped and sent on to you, for whatever they are worth of your time.

I tried to read your letter out loud to my family and some friends at dinner one evening in my home. As I got into the last three paragraphs of your letter I knew all of a sudden that if I went on reading it I would be crying, and knowing this, I stopped reading and said, "I won't read the rest of the letter. You can read it for yourselves if you want to. All she says is that we are good friends because both of us are a little dumb and understand all living things that are dumb."

I have an impression that you are not acquainted with my Potato Face Blind Man. He is the leading character in two books, Rootabaga Stories and Rootabaga Pigeons, which I wrote for young people, meaning by young people those who are children and those grownups who keep something of the child heart. If you do not have these books I should love to send them to you, for there are pages which travel somewhat as my heart and mind would have if I had gone blind, which twice in my life came near happening. On some trip to New York I shall phone and ask whether I can come out and bring my guitar and songs. I am a vaudevillian too. Perhaps you know my panoramic, tumultuous, transcontinental "The American Songbag."

May luck stars be over you.

Faithfully yours,
Carl Sandburg

296 | TO FLOYD DELL

[Harbert, Michigan]
December 5, 1929.

Dear Floyd:

"Memoir Of A Proud Boy," the piece about Don MacGregor, is in my second book of verse titled Cornhuskers; Henry Holt and Co. Of course, you are welcome to use it. What I wrote was more of a ragged memorandum than a poem, perhaps, but for me there was something about this fair haired Scotch boy with a soft heart, beautiful dreams and rare courage of both instinct and mind. (You can quote that if you want to.) It is a long time since we took cat-naps on a table in the city hall in Chicago during the pressmen's strike. . . As a headline hunter why not give one evening to a story of Carl Person, Frank Comerford and yourself; that is no small story. . . I hope I will be listening in the night you tell of MacGregor. Your voice is good and the mike and you are doing good team work. With all good wishes.

Faithfully,
Carl

Don MacGregor was a newspaperman who had voiced his indignation over the treatment of the striking miners at Ludlow, Colorado. He had written to Sandburg before the famous Ludlow massacre on April 20, 1914 (when thirty-three people, including women and children, were shot or burned to death, and a hundred others wounded or badly burned), to say that if Cochran did not take him back on The Day Book, *he might go to Trinidad, Colorado, and work on the miners' paper there. He joined the strikers, and was later, ironically, "named by a grand jury as a murderer," as Sandburg put it, and had to skip to Mexico. Sandburg wrote more than one poem about him, but "Memoir of a Proud Boy" is the only one that was published. Floyd Dell had known MacGregor also, and wished to use this poem.*

297 | TO ANNE CARROLL MOORE

[Harbert, Michigan]
December 7, 1929.

Dear Miss Moore:

Someone sent me your comment on the Rootabaga Country of October 13. You have always been a shrewd and kindly commentator. If my next book, "Potato Face" is not a little better than the earlier one it is not your fault. Harcourt plans on publishing the book next year. It will have no illustrations. I had decided some time ago that there should before long be a reissue of Rootabaga stories, all of them, in a book without pictures. Some day when in

New York we will talk over this whole matter of illustrations. More often than not it is a vicious, stultifying business. The mind of a child is creatively occupied with making its own country, shaping something for itself in its own independent world; then it turns a page and sees something by Maxfield Parrish which topples the child's imaginative creation as blasphemously as a big ignorant foot kicking over a playhouse which a child had designed out of its own mind. This is an extreme view given to you offhand. I don't want to start a fight about it; I am a Quaker in this regard and don't see where fighting would do any good. However, I know you would reimpart—and some day we will talk it over in various phases.

God love you.

Carl Sandburg

Miss Moore had written an enthusiastic review of Rootabaga Stories *in New York* Herald Tribune Books.

298 | TO EZRA POUND

[Harbert, Michigan]
March 22, 1930

Dear Ezra:

I address you as Ezra not by way of getting fresh or familiar, but because nine times out of ten in conversation in this country you are designated as Ezra, and it is almost as though your surname is lost and only the Christian remains. I have been away from my mail or would have answered you sooner. I shall send you a photo for Variétés and two or three pieces from which you can pick for translation. I hope some time to get over and have with you the long deferred talk.

Faithfully yours,
Carl Sandburg

In reply to a request by Ezra Pound for a photograph for Variétés, *which he called "the livest magazine in Europe," Sandburg sent one of himself by Edward Steichen.*

1930

[Harbert, Michigan]
April 1, 1930.

Dear Joe:

You send along a letter that says many things which I know about the art of poetry and the science of criticism, which, however, I had not thought my way through as thoroughly as you have. That is, back of your fine friendly assurances to me personally there is the Book of Joe Beach on the question "What Is Art?". . . From one angle I am not bad off, at all. When at thirty-eight years of age I issued Chicago Poems, I didn't care about fame or distinction. Each book of mine has been issued in somewhat the same spirit as I give my songs at the end of a recital; if the whole audience walks out on me I am only doing what I would be doing if I were at home alone . . . I ordered sent to you a copy of Potato Face, the latest folly; it was mailed to you care of the University. Of course, Dagmar, the giver of priceless, ancient spoons, has a one half share in the book . . . If you drive this way along the east shore of Lake Michigan next summer, be sure to stop in and we will find a bunk for you overnight.

As ever,
Carlo

[Harbert, Michigan]
April 1, 1930.

Dear Brother Barrows:

When it comes to writing a letter to you I always know that at the end I will say to myself I have left the most of it unsaid. You have had skyriding dangers and have known borderlands of suffering which I have not. I can imagine I might write as bravely and gayly as you, with never a whimper, but I doubt it. I have enjoyed reading your story, "The Art Spirit." It is authentic and comes from you as something inevitable. . . Don't mind if editors send it back. Write more of them and send them on to editors. Often the editors don't know their own minds nor their public. Of course, this sounds trite yet it is so. Most of the best sellers of the past ten years were mediocre or rotten, while I could name five or six books which are practically unknown yet they will live beyond our generation. . . I am ordering sent to you a fool book of mine published this month which goes by no standards, as such. If you find time, tell me whether it celebrates some of the cheap things of life which you have found precious.

Faithfully yours,
Carl Sandburg

301 | TO FANNY BUTCHER

[Chicago]
June 23, 1930.

Dear Fanny:

Sometimes it is like a long stretch at Joliet to go on with this job of putting down the Lincoln of The War Years. I cannot say he was Here when he was There when a dozen witnesses or documents put him There in broad daylight. At moments I feel like the old gazabo [Thornton] Wilder had in San Luis Rey tracking down the lives, deeds and consciences of the people who fell off the bridge. This is an explanation and an alibi but there will yet be a song and story evening we have talked about. You will enlighten me on some drifts in the book world and among people who read. But I won't trouble you to tell me about Humanism, an invisible crusade of imperceptible crusaders stopping on phantom islands where each earns a living by taking in the other's washing, each keeping it a secret from the others that he ever does any work which would be democracy and therefore vulgar and noisy.

All good luck to you.

Faithfully,
Carl

302 | TO PAUL M. ANGLE

Harbert, [Michigan]
Dec. 31, 1930

Dear Paul—

That's a good shot. You blaze away at the theme the way it looks to you. And jot down any and all scraps of ideas, slants, facts. And if I don't get down to Springfield next week I surely will on my way to a Missouri date the last week in Jan. Then out of the scraggly mass of our joint material we'll carve a plan.

Keckley tells in her book, 231-6, gives what she says was Mrs. L's account to her of how they came to marry. If Mary Todd told the same in Springfield that was a factor. . . And by the way this Lizzie Keckley had something. For all the flourishes and put-on, just look at that frontispiece picture of her, read page 330 a couple of times, and you have to say she had one grand heart. Then too she must have had some of A. Lincoln's patience and understanding to be in the end the only woman Mary Lincoln ever trusted and to whom she wrote an apology (p 362) for bad behavior.

Hug Polly for me and give her singing mother my New Years wishes which also go to you—

Carl

The book was Behind the Scenes *by Elizabeth Hobbs Keckley.*

303 | TO OLE RÖLVAAG

[Chicago]
January 6, 1931.

Dear Ole Rölvaag:

Forgive a poor Swede for not answering your letter sooner. My home address is *Harbert, Michigan.* In case you lose that you can always reach me at The Chicago Daily News. It is hard to try to write you a letter because there is so much ground to be covered one way and another. Some time this year or next you will have to date me up for another platform evening at St. Olaf's; I can come without guarantees for whatever the receipts, minus the expenses may be. I have several songs I did not sing last time. We will try to plan it so that we could have a good get-together. While east I was pleased to hear of New Jersey high schools which have adopted Giants In The Earth and The Prairie Years as text books. On hearing of it I gave New Jersey a higher rating as a civilized state. I am struggling away at Lincoln of the War Years; it is a long time job dark with turmoil lighted up by occasional sublimities. I had a dandy hour's talk with Julia in New York last year when she was in the hospital; and we talked about you. I think we are a trio linked by silent prayers for each other. May your health hold on and luck stars be over you.

Faithfully,
Carl Sandburg

Ole Rölvaag, author of Giants in the Earth, *was secretary of the Norwegian-American Historical Association.*

304 | TO ALBERT BARROWS

[Harbert, Michigan]
January 25, 1931.

Brother Barrows:

Thank you for sending the Potato Face drawings. I have enjoyed them keenly. What to do about them I don't know. I am having no time for work with my nonsense tales now. Robert Andrews, who writes art comment under the signature of the Previewer, is delighted with the pictures and is doing a note about them for the paper. . . Yes, when "Late Train" is finished I shall like to see it. There are three or four little pieces from my next book of verse which I am going to send on to you as they belong in your kitbag. I have been tending to my teeth and my eyes lately. A ball players legs give out at thirty-five, and author's eyes a decade or two later. If you would like more statistics in this field consult your own set of them for all you will need. . . The town was honored that you stepped off and walked around—but the town doesn't know it, except for your toiling.

As ever,
Carl Sandburg

305 | TO WILLIAM TOWNSEND

[Harbert, Michigan]
March 12, 1931.

Brother Townsend:

A mighty good piece of writing—your review of the Masters' book—the best commentary I have seen thus far. Very curious, it seems to be one of those books that people like to read, forget, and not have around the house. Masters and I were close friends at the time he wrote The Spoon River Anthology. I could do a book on phases and origins of his latest work. The only decent thing for me to do now is say nothing. Lincoln of the War Years? It may be ready in four years, more likely five. I am hoping to get to Lexington some time this year. I will tell you then about your book Lincoln In His Wife's Home Town; I reread it early this winter; it is packed solid; as a writer you have learned your craft.

Faithfully yours,
Carl Sandburg

William Townsend was Kentucky's resident Lincoln authority. The Edgar Lee Masters book, Lincoln the Man, *was antagonistic to its subject.*

306 | TO JENS JENSEN

[Harbert, Michigan]
May 12, 1931.

Dear Jens Jensen:

I could find Edna Millay for you but I cannot locate Edna Ferber. These Ednas are an elusive lot . . . I shall yet drop in on you all of a sudden out at Ravinia and we will talk about old and new sagas.

Faithfully yours,
Carl Sandburg

Jensen shared Frank Lloyd Wright's friendship with Sandburg. He lived in Ravinia, Ill., and had sent an urgent request for Edna Ferber's address.

307 | TO OLE RÖLVAAG

[Harbert, Michigan]
August 6, 1931.

Dear Rölvaag:

Thank you for sending the clippings. The visit this summer was all too short but I feel that fate will be kind to us sometime in the next year. And if you come across a Typewriter Blessing or Fountain Pen Blessing, please let me know.

As ever,
Sandburg

The clippings, from the Chicago papers, reported Sandburg's recent automobile accident. Rölvaag had sent Sandburg "The Blessing of Automobiles" and "The Blessing of Oil-Stocks" in Latin. He said that he might need these, especially the first. "The Blessing of Automobiles," translated, read: "O God, our Lord, vouchsafe to hear our prayers, and bless this car with Thy right hand; bid Thy holy angels stand by it, to save and protect from every danger all those who travel in it; and, just as, through Thy levite Philip, Thou didst grant faith and grace to the Ethiopian who was sitting in his chariot and reading Thy sacred words, show likewise to Thy servants the way of salvation, that, helped by Thy grace and ever striving to do good works, they may, after all the vicissitudes of their life and journey here below, rejoice forever. Through Christ our Lord. Amen."

308 | TO MRS. VACHEL LINDSAY

[Harbert, Michigan]
November 13, 1931.

Dear Elizabeth:

My word does not go far with the Guggenheim people. Out of
six recommendations one of mine has gone over. I will go the limit
for Vachel . . . Those books are being gathered to be sent to you
. . . It was a good visit and we must have it again.

Faithfully yours,
Carl

*Sandburg recommended Vachel Lindsay for a Guggenheim fellow-
ship, but, less than a month later, the Springfield poet committed
suicide.*

309 | TO LOUIS ADAMIC

[Harbert, Michigan]
November 13, 1931.

Dear Adamic:

You can refer the Guggenheim Fellowship to me and I will
tell them I consider you outstanding among those worth the money.
Your book Dynamite is one that has run in my own head for years.
Within its scope and range I doubt whether a better book could be
done. There were a few inaccuracies but they were slight. If you
should chance to look through my first four books of free verse
you will find this same class violence a recurring theme.

Faithfully yours,
Carl Sandburg

Sandburg reread Louis Adamic's Dynamite, *a book about class
violence in America, a number of times.*

310 | TO WILLIAM ROSE BENÉT

[Harbert, Michigan]
December 2, 1931.

Dear Mr. Benét:

Talking with Mrs. Vachel Lindsay a few weeks ago I learned that neither she nor Vachel happened to see those paragraphs which you wrote about Vachel some months ago. Those were beautiful and forthright sentiments—a fine statement of the case for Lindsay. Please dig out that number, mark those paragraphs and send them on to Vachel Lindsay, Springfield, Illinois. I give you greetings and wish more power to you.

Faithfully,

Dec. 7—The above was finished too late for me to sign and send to you. . . While I was in Minnesota, Lindsay died. . . They printed my editorial on him just as I wrote it. . . You were one of his large visioned friends while he was alive—

Carl Sandburg

311 | TO GENE MARKEY

[Harbert, Michigan]
April 22, 1932.

Dear Gene:

It is a long time since we gathered at Schlogl's, and since we spoke greetings at Keith Preston's funeral. At regular intervals out of some college audience springs a young galoot with a book of your cartoons wherein he has some of the victims autographing your sketches. I am writing you now directly about a friend of mine of many years standing—Charles S. Dunning. I have probably exchanged more long letters with him than anybody else in recent years. He has a freegoing, independent mind; I don't know any critics in the various art fields who are more sure of what they know, who have wrought out a scheme of thought and viewpoint that stands by itself. Also, on my California visits, Charlie takes out his 1922 Dodge and we drive to Santa Barbara or Death Valley. I have always found him on the level, with no cheap tricks or forced plays. If he comes your way he is worth your time.

I shall probably look you up when in Hollywood next winter—if work on Lincoln of the War Years, a long job that I am about half way through, permits the time.

Faithfully yours,
Carl

Gene Markey, the Hollywood producer, had been part of the Chicago newspaper group at Schlogl's, the round-table restaurant.

312 | TO ARCHIBALD MAC LEISH

Harbert Michigan
22 June 32

Dear MacLeish—

Thank you for Fortune and a greeting. Your books are among my permanent treasures, invisible securities that the tax assessor passes up to list other belongings. May you have many strengths to get on with what you want to do next. Sometime I hope to drop in and go out for coffee.

Faithfully yours—
Carl Sandburg

Archibald MacLeish and Sandburg became literary and political allies. MacLeish was one of the original editors of Fortune. *At the same time that he sent an issue of the magazine, he forwarded a copy of his book* Conquistador, *which received a Pulitzer Prize.*

313 | TO NEGLEY D. COCHRAN

[Harbert, Michigan]
July 24, '32

Dear Neg—

This is only to say that your Scripps book haunts me, that I talked off parts of the book to Harcourt, that I felt I overtalked, said I would shut up about it, and then came right back with more. The scheme of the book works so that it packs more meaning than a reader feels on first reading; you have sifted out the man's implicative and pregnant utterances; it weaves into what isn't merely a Scripps bible for his newspaper organization; it is a testament for America by a great modern genius of democracy and science who was also a wizard in mass production. I doubt whether five or ten years from now I will revise my present judgement that the book belongs alongside Lincoln, Jefferson, Franklin, Thoreau, Emerson, Whitman. You were thoughtful so many ways from driving a car and cooking steak to opening beer bottles and talking like an honest Quaker that the day went like a long session in a saloon where I had my natural religion deepened.

As always,
Carl

314 | TO FREDERICK BABCOCK

29 July [1932] Harbert Michigan

Friend Babcock—

At present I am under certain strict instructions from my eye specialist and could not possibly undertake the reading of the proofs of the novel. I have so worn my eyes while working on Lincoln: the War Years that it is a serious question whether they last to finish the job which is only about half done, a 3-vol affair. I hate to make this explanation of a sorry condition and would not do it did I not know that your book will have a sincerity and forthrightness only too rare. Two months ago I quit the News, chiefly for the reason that the work there would mean an added year or two before my main work would be finished. I hope to look you up one of these days and hear the news of you.

Faithfully yours—
Carl Sandburg

Frederick Babcock, of the Chicago Tribune, *had written* Blood of the Lamb, *using the pseudonym "Matthew Mark," and sought Sandburg's comments on the novel.*

315 | TO HARRIET MONROE

[Harbert, Michigan]
[August 28, 1932]

Dear dear Harriet

Take any three (3) of these. They have not had the goings over they should have had and I send them with many dubious and lingering feelings. Pick THREE if there are that number worth print and let it go at that for now. Out of the whole mess of goddam patriots over the land you are one of five or six who could make me drop all else and go to this.

As ever
Carl

In Harriet Monroe's October, 1932, issue of Poetry, *nine Sandburg poems appeared.*

316 | TO ALFRED HARCOURT

Sioux City, Iowa
Oct 11, 1932

Dear Alf

After six months silence with the guitar am barnstorming again. Am hoping my letter to Howard [Clark] was clear, about my having done the last bit I could think of on the Mrs. L book and index queries could only be answered by [Paul] Angle. Enclosed is Angle signature on the new royalty clause. Have just finished a long gloom and bitterness chapter on L and am now going thru material of many years accumulation in one corner for the midway portrait chapter which probably starts the second half of the book. Those pieces of verse MD had are only part of a portfolio; this sixth book of verse will be slowly given its final form, with more brooding care and long handling than any of the previous five. That you can be lit up some by them counts with me for it's been a sort of long journey together for you and me on this series starting with Chicago Poems sixteen years ago and running on to what in 1937 or 1938—if we live—may be a volume called Wahwah. Janet goes to school again in fine trim this week. . . That Grimm author asks anonymity for some months yet. . . Please send me the T S Eliot essays, on account, and let me have Lloyd's [Lewis] Sherman soon as there are copies.

Corn is selling at 6¢ a bushel here but they laugh about it rather than cry and go on hoping like pioneers.

Yrs
Carl

Sandburg and Angle had just completed Mary Lincoln: Wife and Widow. *The poems were later published in* The People, Yes. *Janet Sandburg was severely injured in an automobile accident in September.*

317 | TO WAYNE GARD

Harbert Mich Oct 26, [1932]

Dear Wayne Gard

Certainly you are welcome to refer the Guggenheim F. to me. I can truthfully elaborate on an integrity I know you have, on a rare mind which, as I told the Conde Nast people, seems always to be widening its reach so that one may be sure your future is not behind you. I am sure you are the sort of fellow old Gugg. had a picture of when he created the foundation. . . Progress may be reported

on the Lincoln: War Years book but it's the long slogging kind of a
job that sometimes puts men under the grassroots before their time;
if I didn't have verse nonsense ping pong songs friends for detours
I too would check out. . . Either art or war is hell. . . Greetings
to Mrs Gard and luck and health to you.

Faithfully yours
Carl Sandburg

Wayne Gard first met Sandburg at Grinnell College, where he edited
The Tanager. *Later he joined* Vanity Fair, *in New York, before
going to work as a newspaperman in Texas.*

318 | TO OLIVER R. BARRETT

[Harbert, Michigan]
[November 14, 1932]

Dear Oliver

I almost feel like getting drunk about Henry being Gov of Ill.
And then comes the thought that for a man with his sense of justice
it will be a hell of a job and shorten his life. Any day or hour this
side of Nov 21 that he would like perfect seclusion and something
like rest tell him to run out here. Of course the same goes for you
always. One Nov 22 I am to be the distinguished tho I hope not
pifflicated guest of the Wisconsin Society of Mayflower Descendants
in Milwaukee. So I have been studying up a little on just how pure
the Puritans were. What will Tuesday's storm do to the country?
Doesn't Mel Traylor's statement about hit it off?

As ever
Carl

*Judge Henry Horner had just won the election as governor of
Illinois.*

319 | TO ALFRED HARCOURT

[Harbert, Michigan]
Tuesday [January 24, 1933]

Dear Alf

It was a good visit. We didn't get anywhere near to covering all the topics tho we did cover a lot of ground. Some things are still in the air, points I would have made, such as my decisive judgement that my own time would only be wasted in ever giving serious consideration to the Stockholm thing because 1. even more than Eugene O'Neill I have failed to "click" in Europe 2. too much of my language is a departure from the educated Englishman's speech, is too Americanese, and might seem almost nationalistic in its flaunting of the North American airs and syllables 3. there are a good many jibes at Stockholm and quite "fresh" they are 4. in both the poetry and the Rootabaga stories there is a batty and queer, if not crazy, approach, that has already bothered the sedate who give reasons. It was good to have your slant confirming my own that I should keep hands off in every way. My song was and is that of the Sonora dove down on the Mexican border: no hope no hope. You should have stayed the next two days and seen Florida weather; the midday hours would dispel your impression that a norther is visiting; I worked three hours sitting out on the deck yesterday afternoon.

As always
Carl

320 | TO ALFRED HARCOURT

[Harbert, Michigan]
Feb 7, [1933]

Dear Alf

Would you see that a copy of Mary Lincoln goes to Allan Nevins —and a copy of Potato Face to Archibald MacLeish at the Fortune editorial rooms? These on my account. I had planned after a good visit with you to see these fellows too. Nevins is letting me know of any Lincoln material he runs across, has made two nice finds at Columbia—and MacLeish is just now about the healthiest individual force in American poetry. . . When I get to where I can clearly see the end of this job, which I still love from the writing angle tho the drudgery is oppressive, there will be less need for miserliness as to time for friends and fun. Lloyd [Lewis] writes me his next big drive across the years will be on Jefferson; I've written him Jefferson is the only other President I can think of whose character and lights would nourish and keep a biographer going on a long work. Lloyd will grow on it and you will be thanked by republicans and democrats, patriots and freethinkers, redheaded men and fiddlers, vegetarians and philosophers, farmers and the civil liberties bunch.

As always
Carl

321 | TO ALICE CORBIN HENDERSON

Harbert Mich   March 17   33

Dear Alice

Next season I am making a Southwest and west coast trip, shall positively let you know beforehand months and months so you can, as you must, set up a bureau and book three or four programs at Feakins commissions; it ought to be some fun; and there will be the point that no guarantee is required, no goddam contracts to sign. Lincoln of the War Years travels slowly; probably will go three or four volumes; dont know whether Im half way or two thirds gone on on it; but the man grows on me all along, has symphonic values if I can catch and gather them; he was one ecco homo prize galoot tho I mustnt say it just like that for the reading public tho I will in poickry. Thats from Orpheus C. Kerr—poickry. Harcourt says a large sheaf I have now is the best poickry I have done but Im going to wait years before committing my sixth book of verse to the frozen assets of fixed and irremediable and immitigible printers ink. By now how you must know your red clay and the

Indians. We could talk for hours without getting it all told. Please remember me to th Gus Baumans both and each, also Lynn Riggs, to Willie and to each and every under your rooftree.

As ever
Carl

Gus Bauman was a Santa Fe newspaperman, a friend of Alice Corbin Henderson and of Haniel Long, the Western poet. Lynn Riggs was the author of Green Grow the Lilacs, *the book that inspired the musical* Oklahoma!.

322 | TO JOSEPH WARREN BEACH

[Harbert, Michigan]
March 31   33

Dear Joe

I happened to give my annual reading to that 1929 letter of yours giving me the lowdown on speed, curves, control, the whole man giving himself, and when I got thru I said I had me doubts whether any writer ever had more warm yet shrewd-spoken words from an understanding friend. If I had then been in the dumps and hesitating about going on that letter would have lifted me. In the present hour when I am spending occasional days in writing new verses and rewriting and revising old ones, shaping a book that I hope will stand alongside the others easily, it is good to go over your letter. Your pat remark on one winter visit, as to some new offerings, "Carl you're imitating yourself," is fastened in my left ear. . . When I wrote you this winter about reading your book on the 20th century novel, I had been reading the chapters on American novelists and had the impression later when writing to you that it was dealing with this country alone; now that I've read all the chapters I was more competent when drinking beer with R. M. Lovett last week to tell him how I enjoyed his review of it. . . The Lincoln of War Years progresses but the end is probably three years off; it is strange how he grows on me, how his great strength ran back to such thin tentacles, how his shadows and riddles are alive now. Incidentally and as between us Harcourt having read some

340,000 words that lead up to Gettysburg writes, "It's a great job, more so than any other that ever came under my fingers." Also as between us is a piece of maybe juvenilia that I wrote a couple of years before Elbert Hubbard printed it in The Fra; Judge Horner, now governor of Illinois, had 50 copies reprinted without asking me. Also of course this communication goes for the blessed Dagmar and wishing you both many grand hard realities and fine shimmering tokens.

As ever
Carlo

323 | TO WILLIAM LEISERSON

[Harbert, Michigan]
April 10, 1933.

Dear Bill:—

Would there be any chance of our putting on an evening on May 9 or May 10. These are the only dates available on an eastern trip I am making. I know all about everybody around Antioch being broke just like the New York depositors in the Bank of the United Snakes. More than half the idea is that I stop at Antioch to see old friends and to soak in more than I exude. Therefore you will hear no holler from me in case the intake at the door should merely equal that of one of my soap box meetings in Oshkosh which brought forty-two cents. So if either of those dates are feasible we will go to bat.

As ever,
Carl

324 | TO WILLIAM TOWNSEND

[Harbert, Michigan]
April 12   33

Dear Colonel

I am sure I could locate the Dr Henry reference in your letter but it might be a two or three day job. If I should attempt a cross-reference classification of my material I would be just about one-fourth longer getting anything done. Usually in slight matters I can give some sources where a point would *probably* be found while *always* in the *important* ones I can give it *approximately*. That the Lincolns bought rum at the Smith store on account is recorded on the Smith daybook. That a physician such as Henry under the circumstances would prescribe brandy is probable, but I wouldn't have mentioned Henry as prescribing brandy unless I saw some statement by someone in a degree familiar with the situation. If I run across that statement or if the source occurs to me I shall let you know immediately. . . The rum from the Smith store was generally supposed to be for medicinal purposes. I made notes in the old Smith store about ten years ago from those account books but I would have to dig a week or so perhaps to locate those notes. Angle could give the entries from those account books more completely than those I jotted down. . . The Shutes medical life of Lincoln which ran in the Journal of the American Medical Association last year should serve you. . . You should go strong on the newspaper advertisements of those days. Also use some photographs of exteriors and particularly interiors of those old time saloons; I have one dandy out of Chicago in 1860 which you could use. From your book should obtrude a few spittoons, feller! A brass rail a blowsy barkeep the Germans for lager the Irish fer the sarpint to be unchained. Walt Whitman writes the NY Times in '63 he just couldnt find any good lager in Washington and didnt believe it existed. . . Give us pocket histories of the liquor trade wholesale and retail, of the temperance and prohibition movements. . . It will be a good book and a real contribution like each of your other works, I know. . . Yes, I wont get tangled in the military bog; I know precisely what your warning means. But in the matter of political issues, mass psychology, economic currents, cultural backgrounds I cant do Lincoln isolated from his social roots; the proportions there are not easy to maintain; I sometimes wonder if I'll end up like that painter of that picture in the Capitol at Washington where the wind blows from five different cardinal points at the same moment. . . Lots of luck and health to you.

As ever—
Carl

1933

Dr. Anson G. Henry was Lincoln's physician in Springfield. Townsend had questioned Sandburg's source for the statement that Dr. Henry had "prescribed brandy in large quantities during Lincoln's illness following his estrangement from Mary Todd" in Mary Lincoln: Wife and Widow. *The medical life of Lincoln by Dr. Milton Henry Shutes was* Lincoln and the Doctors.

325 | TO WORTHINGTON C. FORD

[Harbert, Michigan]
April 22, 1933.

Dear Mr. Ford:—

Your letter about our Mary Lincoln book is a cum laude and to one who has collected many leather medals it is good to have such a decoration as you send. On the basis of more than finished workmanship at present I am slogging along on Abraham Lincoln: The War Years and have become acquainted with all of the elations and depressed moods of the mural painters who did the interior of the Vatican. Paul Angle and Oliver Barrett often mention you, with a lighting up of the face; to Angle you are one of the inspirations of his life. . . If you should be in this country some three years from now when I have a completed Lincoln manuscript you will find me asking you to give it a reading.

Faithfully yours,
Carl Sandburg

Worthington C. Ford, former head of the manuscript division at the Library of Congress, prepared the manuscript for Beveridge's biography of Lincoln.

326 | TO PAUL M. ANGLE

[Harbert, Michigan]
[Circa April, 1933]

Dear Paul

On the story that fits the little one you win. The earliest memories of my life are of several stunts somewhat like what you tell of him. I climbed a wagon and was starting to drive a team of horses at three years of age one Sunday afternoon and the farmer visiting our folks ran out of the house and got the horses by the bits just in time to stop my having some kind of a drive. He's the lad I had in mind when writing of "Googler and Gaggler" in Rootabaga Stories. They are hard to raise, Paul, but usually they are original, and sometimes solitary, and independent, when grown. I always bet on that kind as against the orderly and wellbehaved.

Yrs
Carl

327 | TO PAUL M. ANGLE

[Harbert, Michigan]
May 3 33

Dear Paul

Today I was a little surprised to find that a telegram of Lincoln on Oct 1, 1863 given on page 180 of "Lincoln in the Telegraph Office" by David Homer Bates is not in any of the collected letter volumes. Hertz told me that he had specifically had this book combed for such items. As I find such items from time to time I will let you know of them, as with the Noah Brooks in the Century which we spoke of, if you feel that sometime in the future you might want to do a definitive work or in case these might be wanted for publications you are editing or which may come out of the Press you are considering in Springfield. No one is better equipped than you for doing a definitive collection of Lincoln letters tho whether it is worth your time and labor is another matter. The extent of the overlapping, however, and the closeness of scrutiny that must be exercised to get at all of Lincoln's writings continues to surprise me. I have tried to repeat your own description of your boy's recklessness but cant quite make it. The gist of it seems to be like the story of the mule that crashed head on into a tree while the farmer trying to sell the mule explained, "He's a good mule but he's just plain stubborn sometimes."

Yrs
Carl

[Harbert, Michigan]
May 25, 1933.

Dear Julia:—

Please let me know at about what time you are coming to the Chicago Fair this summer. I am going to be away about two weeks during the summer and I am praying that I will not be away when you come north. You will have quiet, no callers unless you wish, no parties unless impromptu, and you will find the Dune country has something all its own as truly as Lang Syne. Also there will be deep love and a lot of understanding. I love the human spirit of you and I adore the sagacity and the fine intuitions that guide you. As the feller said of the whiskey with swamp root in it: it is good for whatever ails you and if nothing ails you it is good for that.

As always,
Carl

[Harbert, Michigan]
June 26   33

Dear Lloyd

Enclosed are notes on Grant and John Morgan material made while going thru files in the Newberry Lib.

You will do an immemorial Grant. (Its quite a chore for me to write out a name that several hundred times I have just let go at Gt; if its just "Gt" youll know its an old Swedish custom). Perhaps that may yet lead on into a Jefferson. You have no such intimacy with the basic mystery of Gt, whatever it may have been, as you naturally have with the deeper shadows of Sherman—and of Jefferson. Possible no honest chronicling biographer, with the requisite roving humptydumpty imaginative and speculative temperament, can be identified with Gt, as you were with Sherman. Yet at that you will do a Gt life that will stand up I believe beyond any other now or to come—and that partly because of the time values, living as the voices pass out that say, I saw him. . . For a great Gt biog I have merely a normal appetite. For a 2,3,4-vol Jefferson I have depths of hunger. . . So much of the Gt material and essential feel is already in your hands and eyes that you are already well begun on him. But the Jefferson work is worth a dream and a prayer.

Yrs

Carl

330 | TO THOMAS HORNSBY FERRIL

[Harbert, Michigan]
July 8, 1933.

Dear Tom:—

It is good to have a note from you like a twilight voice up an arroyo or the echo of a pony neigh up a canyon. As I look at it now I believe your next reincarnation will be a painthorse. Be sure to read MacLeish's two bit pamphlet of verse on the Rockefeller City frescoes, just published. Him and you and me has drunk the same pulque and eaten from the same enchiladas. Remember me to Helen and all under your roof. I shall drift in when least expected. If you come this way you can put your horses in our corrall.

Yrs.

Carl

Thomas Hornsby Ferril, editor of the Rocky Mountain Herald, *wrote poetry about the West.*

331 | TO ALFRED HARCOURT

[Harbert, Michigan]
August 7, 1933.

Dear Alfred:

This enclosure is mighty good nonsense. I have tried reading it aloud to children. Perhaps Ellen [Mrs. Harcourt] can try it out on her gang. Perhaps there is a book in it. This is the first one I have noticed but it seems to be one of a series in the Times. . . Two long chapters and one short one on Lincoln will go to you in a week or so. I seem actually to have gotten Abe out of sixty-three into sixty-four. In classifying the sixty-four material this week it seems impossible to tell whether I am one-third or one-fourth way through the job. . . Am sunk fathoms deep where some good poems just stepped out and wrote themselves. One titled "Moonlight and Maggots" has been accepted by Fortune. It will be the first poetry they have ever run and it seems to me the distinction of breaking in is almost equal to Maxwell Anderson's being first to arrive in The New Republic with "sonofabitch". Time has been available the last six weeks for golf and the swing is improving. . . It would be a treat to hear you talk of all the ins and outs of the NRA as it has come under your eyes and ears.

As always
Carl

332 | TO THE EDITOR OF *THE NEW REPUBLIC*

[Harbert, Michigan]
Aug. 26, 1933.

Sir:

As regards the allegation of your contributor, Michael Gold, that Archibald MacLeish's "Frescoes for Mr. Rockefeller's City" is Anti-Jewish and Hitlerish, may I add the point that on meeting Rabbi Gerson Levy, a Scotch Jew, I find that he does not agree with the judgement of Mr. Gold? Of course, Mr. Gold may say that it is a case of the Scotch strain in Rabbi Levy being prejudiced in favor of MacLeish, in which event I would point to the Chicago bookseller, Ben Abrahams, a Russian Jew who has sold many copies of Mr. Gold's book "Jews Without Money." Mr. Abrahams agrees with Rabbi Levy that MacLeish is a great poet and quite beyond any business of jewbaiting which Mr. Gold tries to read into MacLeish's latest offering. In this babel of tongues known as the United States of America it has become a genial custom for men

295

to give imitations of brogues and dialects and we may hope that the use of Yiddish fumbling with the American language, by a literary artist, is no more Anti-Jewish propaganda than an imitation of Harry Lauder is a way of saying to hell with the Scotch.

Carl Sandburg

333 | TO EDWARD LAROCQUE TINKER

[Harbert, Michigan]
Oct 6 33

Dear Tinker

As one who never ventures out in either hot or cold or indifferent weather without a pair of bones and a readiness to try wrists with whosoever is wooing lady luck and as one who has dug deep in caverns and tomes of the past arriving at the conclusion that many momentous actions or so hailed were merely so many passes with galloping ivories I am one of those who knows all that actuated you in this historical dissertation that should in all justice have won you a doctorate   yes you should have been crowned with a mortarboard and handed a sheekspin sheepskin on it   now collect the proverbs going therewith   beginning: the best throw of the dice is to throw 'em away   and proceeding to the folktale of Jesus and Saint Peter in a rat skeller on north clarkstreet chicago   JC threw six sixes high man to win   Peter clamored for another throw: None of your goddam miracles goes   here is hoping the luck of events the next years brings us together again either in New York or New Orleans   our long walks around NLeens with you stay among good memories

as ever
Carl Sandburg

Edward Larocque Tinker, an authority on old New Orleans, had sent Sandburg a bibliography of Franco-Louisiana newspapers and a document, "Palingenesis of Craps."

334 | TO ARCHIBALD MACLEISH

Aberdeen, South Dakota
Oct 6 33

Dear MacLeish

'Twas good to have your note about the New Republic letters.
I kept to one issue with Mike [Gold]. I had to hold in because I
have Mike's number from so many directions. I would like to have
had his answer as to whether that section of the Frescoes series dealing with the railroad builders would not have been accepted by any
of the trying-to-be-proletarian communist magazines if it had been
sent in under some other name than yours. It would have been hailed
and reprinted as a fine sorrow song over the exploited. . . Mike
has so often pointed to Upton Sinclair as one of the best instances
of the American writer who knows how to propagandize and now
Upton up and runs on the Democratic ticket for governor of California. . . This later issue between you and [Malcolm] Cowley is
dangerously like the darkey debate on whether the sun or the moon
gives more light; it would take a three day barbecue with each of
you spilling all the beans out of his head before you became clear to
your audience, to yourselves and each other so that resolutions expressing the sense of the meeting could be framed and passed unanimously. . . Hoping to see you this fall or winter when in New York

As always
Carl

335 | TO RAYMOND MOLEY

[Harbert, Michigan]
Oct 20 33

Dear Mr Moley

Your letter to me is mislaid and cannot be found in an attic
where I can put my hand on any one of a thousand meticulously
classified items about Lincoln and the National Recovery he was
at the head of. However I am very clear as to what your letter held

for I read it twice before it got away. . . There is some verse at hand which when it gets a final shaping-over will go to you. Aside from these occasional detours into verse all my time is going into A. Lincoln: the War Years which will be a three- or more probably a four-volume work. I see many striking parallels between Lincoln and Franklin Roosevelt in political method, in decision amid chaos, in reading trends, in development of policy so as to gather momentum, in resilience and acknowledgement of hazards—and much else. If your magazine lasts thru the Roosevelt term I may work out the parallel before the term is over, for you to print. . . Man, you have your job cut out for you; to really be saying something and yet also win circulation and an audience against the present magazine field. . . When in New York sometime this year I hope to see you and shall pass along any hunches. You are worth praying for and I send you all good wishes.

Faithfully yours
Carl Sandburg

Raymond Moley, one of the early New Dealers, founded Today, *a journal of political affairs, which later merged with* Newsweek.

336 | TO ROY BASLER

[Harbert, Michigan]
January 3, 1934

Dear Mr. Basler

Your book arrived and I have just finished reading the manuscript. One who travels through this piece of writing of yours gets an impression of Lincoln as a man along with an appraisal of the Lincoln legend as distinct from the man—and your approach and treatment is somewhat different from all similar attempts. The work has for me a distinct originality. The main criticism, I believe, will be that perhaps half or more than half the book is a presentation of material and view points already worked out by numerous writers on Lincoln so that the book as a whole does not sufficiently focus on your personal original contribution. I am taking the manuscript to my friend Oliver R. Barrett (see preface to Prairie Years) for him to read and comment on. The book has a peculiar honesty; I can see how its themes took possession of you and its writing was inevitable.

Faithfully yours,
Carl Sandburg

337 | TO JOHN LEWIS HERVEY

[Harbert, Michigan]
Jan 5 34

Dear John

Soon will go to your hands a large section of the Lincoln scroll and folio. Your eyes always catch some matters, minor or major, that ought to be caught. My own eyes are far spent and it is getting so that I can not use them as I would like to on the work; they are not so good as they once were; I am 57 this week. I feel that serious derelictions have been cut to a minimum on each of those chapters that have had your reading and comment. We belong to no Greek letter body but you have been a good frater to yours in faith—

Carl

> *John Lewis Hervey, the editor of* The Horse Review, *was an eccentric critic with a passion for poetry and a deep knowledge of literature and history. Sandburg had been sending him the manuscript of* The War Years *as he finished parts of it. Hervey had just read Chapter 34 and was putting down notes, which he called very minor criticisms.*

338 | TO ROY BASLER

Harbert, Michigan
Jan 15   33 [34]

Dear Mr Basler

Your original contribution, as I meant in referring to it, lay in two points: 1) a number of quotations hitherto not used in everything in the Fish and Oakleaf bibliographies 2) your meditations on Lincoln as interweaving myth and reality. This represents perhaps a third or fourth of the book. Of course it was more than ordinarily interesting to me as I have now reached typewritten sheet No. 1958 of Lincoln: the War Years and I have all along had to deal with problems touching the two above points of how much quotation should be inflicted on the reader, and of the curiously living Lincoln, in the very years while he was alive being at once reality and myth. It belongs in the record to say that a London Spectator writer said, "The thoughts of the man are too big for his mouth," and to try to get at what mysteries of democracy were in the mind of that Spectator man; but there can be no finality about the operation . . . It will be interesting to see what Mr Barrett will have to report on your script.

Faithfully yours
Carl Sandburg

339 | TO JOHN LEWIS HERVEY

[Harbert, Michigan]
Feb. 24   1934

Fellow Millionaire John

Much of the time that word millionaire is used satirically rather than earnestly and seriously. I have known a whole legion of vagabonds and bums in Chicago who lived and died richer than Bill Wrigley. And who would wish on himself the retreating chin of the quasi-imbecilic Phil Armour III or the pathetic frustrations of Marshall Field III?

And what I really started to say was that you decently and beautifully woke me up to the deficiencies of the Sumner sketch—and if you will maintain this candor it will mean a better book along with more work. What you did was to send me to a rereading of Sumner's Collected Works—so the whole sketch has to be recast. He had touches of the heroic. Yet there was a curious density, an obliviousness to what was going on in the minds of others, akin to that of Jeff Davis. Also there was a quality of glee over being right.

If the other side was as completely wrong as he made out he might have wept rather than vocalized.

Yr Obt Svt
Carl

It was a standing joke between Hervey and Sandburg that they were both possessors of millions—millions of clippings and millions of words. Hervey's critical letter on Sumner, which Sandburg said woke him up to the deficiencies of his Sumner sketch, so that he did it over, was signed "Your devoted Croesus."

340 | TO JOHN LEWIS HERVEY

[Harbert, Michigan]
March 5   34

Dear John—

You are a comrade in drudgery to send me those copyings from Longfellow on Sumner. It is a hard fate for me to have to write about Sumner. Among his own anti-slavery associates there was personal dislike of him. Riddle in his life of Wade, your father's old friend, wrote, "For Wade there was a suspicion of arrogance, a flavor of sham, in the grand assumption of the splendid Sumner. . . Most men at each interview with him had to tell him who and what they were." As I think about it I wonder why I have affection for Wade, Wendell Phillips, and Longfellow, and only aversion for Sumner as a false alarm and a stuffed shirt. He wanted to be a dangerous agitator and a perfect gentleman both at once and his critics were correct that you may be either a skunk or a white swan but not both. His method and counsels would have resulted at the start in the border states joining the seceders and putting over the Confederacy, leaving a weird and aborted area for slavery to flourish as the banyan tree, to languish here and effloresce there, a set of western-world Balkans to raise hell for an interminable period. Yet the same counsels came from Wade and Phillips. But they were artists. In a hundred ways they were artists where Sumner was a pedant. They were born for their roles while Sumner to begin with was bewildered and wrote Bigelow and confided in Longfellow he was not at home in politics. Where your notes have value is in making it clear that he must have had qualities not generally known for Longfellow to have loved him so unfailingly. The line "a man to whom all children come" hits me of course. He had a slow lumbering St-Bernard-dog ease that drew the little ones. They found in him either the reality or yearning to be what Longfellow saw: "a colossus holding his burning heart in his hand to light up the sea of life." However Longfellow was two-sided, at his best profound, musical, vivid. But he had his wooden side, the sheerly pedagogical and pedantic. And he and Sumner may have met on the basis of certain likenesses tho Longfellow wrote nothing at all that ran in spirit and was used for propaganda in key with Sumner's speeches. Longfellow was polite. Sumner was polite, rambunctious and cantankerous. He and Henry Ward Beecher are my hardest nuts to crack. They are spinach, haywire and skunk-cabbage—not skunks, understand. Sumner had a basic integrity lacking in Beecher. Phillips is one that I could write a book about and enjoy traveling with him. With Sumner perhaps the point is that he was made for martyrdom, for some scene as big and tragic as the one that John Brown faded out in. Yet what he had was a peculiar sort of respectable mcguffeys-reader success and acclaim. And now John if you will overlook the gab herein I may do better work tho God in this case has loaded the dice against me. Thanking you again—

Carl

The reference is to A. G. Riddle's Life of Benjamin F. Wade. *Hervey had written to Sandburg that he was sending him two sheets of notes on Sumner gathered from his own books. He added: "There are also some quite extensive notes on him gathered from the Longfellow journals. . . . I do not know that any of it will be of any assistance to you, except that I tried to dig out items that were revealing and help to show the man as he was when not on dress parade." Hervey did not agree with Sandburg about Charles Sumner, of whom he wrote: "His feet were of clay, but his heart was not of marble, neither was his brain of gutta-percha as nowadays the professors who have taken over the manufacture of history endeavor to make out."*

Harbert, [Michigan] March 5 34

Dear Alf

More than a week now I have been revising the sketch of Sumner. It now runs over 7,000 words. In its first draft it was unjust and had also made no use of the Longfellow letters and journals, Longfellow being his best friend. Ten days given to this piece of work had me groaning over the delay. Each day it was to be finished.

There is one phase of this job you should know about. THIS BOOK CAN NOT BE READ WITH ONE READING. I dont mean it is profound in writing or implicative in treatment. But I find that many events and scenes on successive readings take on new lights. And there are more than a few moments so vivid and stupendous that a single reading does not gather them to the mind. When I talked of this to Governor Horner he said, "You dont get *the slow motion* effect till you read it several times—is that it?" And I said Yes. . . You will understand that I mention this to you as an experience that other people will have. I would not have believed that during these revisions it would happen that on the sixth reading (of certain long chapters) within three months, I should say so often, "Now I am just beginning to get the men and the events in perspective and proportion." It has lamentations and beatitudes enough to make an American Bible, has enough political wisdom to guide this country thru several crises and depressions, has a garland of short stories and a gallery of interacting characters, a handbook and manual of defamation, several sagas of action. The point might be made that with proper selective treatment the book would be simple and understandable at one reading. Often I have made this point to myself. But I am not inventing the scenes and characters. They were and they are and they did in life what they do in the book and the stage is so immense and the action and speech so varied and swift that repeated performances for the reader are necessary for him to get it, to see and hear it. . . You know the most of what I am telling you but I am emphasizing here what has surprisingly and curiously happened to me. While the thing lay in its first draft I did not believe it a sequel to the Prairie

Years but out of the reshapings of the last year I know it is far more than that. Seldom do I feel like talking about it. I have hesitations about meeting you and talking about it. What is darkly great and subtly beautiful in it was made entirely by other men who are faded and gone. They lived the book before it could be written.

Carl

At the bottom of this letter addressed to Alfred Harcourt, Sandburg wrote a note to Catherine McCarthy, his editor, saying: "Dear Kitty—had this copied from a yellowing sheet. I would believe I didn't send it. Yrs. C. S." She received it on November 19, 1953.

342 | TO HENRY HORNER

[Harbert, Michigan]
April 11   1934

Dear Judge

It was good of you and Oliver to wigwag a wireless "rootabaga aloha" to me on the Island of Oahu where there is much hoomali-mali not to mention opakapaka. Of the only two copies of the biography of Lincoln in the Hawaiian language, known to be in the islands, one was presented to me, and later speaking as grantee to grantor I said the book would properly belong in your collection and would there end up. The grantor on hearing that you were as freehanded a man as himself said this would be very proper. It will be good to see you at the Barton dedicatory exercises on the 20th.

Yours as always
Carl

Sandburg was one of the speakers at the ceremonies April 20, 1934, when the University of Chicago announced the acquisition of the William E. Barton Library of Lincolniana.

343 | TO J. FRANK DOBIE

[Harbert, Michigan]
May 9 '34

Dear Dobie
You are of the salt of the earth. I was going to say but while thinking of you as made of the same plain red clay as the general run of Texans I had a flash that the Hand of the Potter felt experimental and threw in honey kindling phosphorus H2 SO4 ashes sheepguts horsenecks ironore coal radium songs thongs horizon-blue rainbows maps documents disguises chilibeans jumpingbeans muchelse saying: we will see what this piece of humus can stand and not go under. . . Thank you for those all and several items for the Dobie corner, for the Juan Oso and its inscription, for the horse-rider-wildcat photograph that would serve any sculptor. The visit with you was too short. If chance or errands bring you toward this corner of the country you will remember there is a room and a hide-out for you, here, any time. . . Several friends make the point that the random sketch you did for the Austin papers is a piece of good writing and permanent memoranda. I hope I can put a similar shine into a sketch I am to do for the American Dictionary of Biography of Philip Green Wright, a professor-teacher-mathematician-astron-omer-poet-friend. . . Revision of a 2,200-sheet manuscript is about two-thirds done; then after writing about 200,000 more words the job will be over. I hope some of its pages will have the tender and beautiful craziness of the highspots of Coronado's Children. And I wish Frank you may have time health and money for spending in mexican style for the american work ahead, for the human job in american art you have set out to carry farther. As always
Faithfully yours
Carl Sandburg

J. Frank Dobie was a historian, folklorist, and teacher at the University of Texas.

344 | TO ALAN LOMAX

[Harbert, Michigan]
Nov 3   34

Dear Alan

Our letters crossed either at St Louis or Texarkana and now we know less than ever having more facts   when Tagore was leaving London for America Yeats told him "Be sure to wear your night shirt" and Tagore did and Chicago and Los Angeles enjoyed the outfit and he went over big looking so Christlike and Ezekielish alongside the American cops   you need a nightshirt to book   your prospective customers want a nightshirt or a big name that has been pounded home to their ears by the kind of a campaign we could put on only we havent the time   they pay one grand per night for Schipa two grand for Will Rogers or Chaliapin five grand for MacCormack   and Rogers says to me "They will remember you long after Im forgotten" and apologizes for having read only the Lincoln book while his boy has read the p[o]ickry books too   it is malicious mischief for me to say I would rather hear you sing Po Lazus than anything Schipa or MacCormack have in their whole repertoire or that your father's performance in the present hour is more momentous to America than Rosa Ponselle or John Chas Thomas at two grand per   this is not complaint   I have no more pride to be wounded than the hotel lavatory man who hands out towel and soap at a dime per guest   I might even try to remind the lavatory man that Cromwell Washington Lincoln Lenin at the height of their labors confessed to the humility of a well-bludgeoned and cursedout government mule   as to business we first got mixed up thru my saying that if anything came your way without your bucking a line or assaulting ramparts to go to it   San Antonio Open Forum, S.M.U. at Dallas, booked me at $200; Redpaths from Kansas City booked three in Oklahoma at $300 each; Univ of So'n Calif Mar 3 1933 paid $300; of ten Redpath books for this winter all are for $200 except three that have special conditions attaching   no college school club or individual who sold tickets and made an event of it ever failed to make money on the show   Arden Club at th

Univ of Wis three times paid $200 and profited from 100 to 200 per cent if we do no business we shall at least not have brought our figures down below first estimates if we do any business we can leave compensation to an adjudicatory board of Frank Dobie and L. W. Payne and Ex-Gov Pat Neff at any rate I am sure you and I can never be American business men with straight faces there are a hundred facets of the matter burnished in a piece I have written called Success which I hope to send you a carbon of soon health and luck be yours

CS

John Lomax's son, Alan, was trying to earn a commission by getting Texas lecture dates for Sandburg. He had written asking if Sandburg would reduce his fee.

345 | TO LLOYD LEWIS

[Harbert, Michigan]
[November 19, 1934]

Dear Lloyd

A few weeks ago I got a thrill from your passing phrase, "am wholly New Deal", and now you send a letter gloriously amplifying that little text and burning up the paper with the same feelings and notions that have had me alive for many months. Last February I had an article in Today on the parallels of the New Deal and Emancipation policies. But to see you shooting so straight from that particular citadel is like meeting religion. When your "annual report" letter came along with its "am wholly New Deal" I was going to write you that I could vividly understand a couple of prospectors who had whored around a lot being parted for a long time and suddenly coming together were amazed that each had gone and got religion and believed in Christ and said prayers at table and bed-time. . . Partly what we see is a great actor living up to his audience and his audience collaborating, like those Illinois crowds who made the Lincoln-Douglas debates more than the two orators. . . Of course the New Deal is going to have hard going from several angles. In Russia they would have shot the fellow who deliberately did what the Nashes did in their below-specifications concrete on a PWA job. And yet we have both seen the word conscience come to mean more and it is not as liable now as it was for a man to be under suspicion if he speaks of honesty and integrity in public service. I suppose I mean that Ickes, Hopkins, Wallace look less like boobs and goody-goods than they did. . . Lately I have had a hell of a time throwing Cameron out of the Cabinet and rewriting my sketch of Davis, and other chores. When I see you one of these days before long I can pour out various miseries like one umbrella mender speaking his trade and craft jargon to another umbrella mender. Out of references from time to time my respect for your Sherman as a piece of workmanship grows.

As ever

Carl

Simon Cameron was Lincoln's first Secretary of War when, owing to his partiality in the letting of government contracts, Lincoln requested his resignation. He was later censured by the House of Representatives.

346 | TO ARCHIBALD MACLEISH

[Harbert, Michigan]
Jan 20   35

Dear Archie

The enclosed truncated epistle was done a month ago. When you get to this spot sometime and see how things program you will not be hardhearted about it. Incidentally I am almost invariably here unless away on a platform trip. And the W. Colston Leigh Bureau, Inc. NY, knows my dates even before I do, so that any time you might be heading this way, if you would call them they would let you know whether I am here. You are welcome to drop in any time. You may get a poem out of a biblical herd of goats here, nine does and three kids and more kids coming soon. They gaze profoundly into your eyes, fathom your innermost secrets, and then go on ruminating with their alfalfa as though your secrets are not worth their time. . . Your Pole Star piece has deeper lights and moving glow than any other you have done: if the test is to be how many times a reader like myself knows he will re-read it. My impression is that each of us has his best ten years of work ahead and I would say that applies much more strictly to you than to me. We spoke of sometime riding to Mammoth Cave and trying out the echoes and I hope we get to it this spring or summer. Shall be in NY late Feb and early March and drop in as usual, perhaps having by that time a decently revised copy of this long piece which has strangely effloresced and has such length and windings (it is a book by itself) that I would have doubts about it had I not lived so long with the authorities inside me who say I will not handle this particular theme any better until I flit hither and yon in reincarnated flesh and feathers. May you live to ate the hin that scratches over your grave.

As always
Carl

The long piece of poetry was The People, Yes, *published in 1936.*

347 | TO MALCOLM COWLEY

[Harbert, Michigan]
Jan 20 35

Dear Cowley

The last week in Feb and first week of March I will be ducking in and out of NY and maybe we can get together then for what I hope will not be on your part too merciless a once-over. These enclosures are by fellows of somewhat your own drollery though not viewpoint. Some of the paragraphs might be worth your time. Let me have them back when you are through with them. . . The delay in replying to you was partly that I seem to delay on all letters and the longer I live the more difficulty I find about answering letters, partly on account of time and partly because writing letters too is writing. Then, too, the past month I have been rewriting the longest piece of verse I have ever done, a ballad pamphlet harangue sonata and fugue titled "The People,

Yes," standing now somewhat over 100 typed sheets, an almanac, a scroll, a palimpsest, the last will and testament of Mr. John Public, John Doe, Richard Roe, and the autobiography of whoever it was the alfalfaland governor meant in saying, "The common people will do anything you say except stay hitched." . . . No, I didn't smash the guitar like you said, but went and bought a better one. When you have three daughters and no sons, and one of the daughters is a semi-invalid and another not entirely recovered from a head fractured in an automobile accident, you don't travel always as you might like to, and you try not to talk about it and I suppose I would not bring it in here if you had not written Tumbleweed and some other things with the tumbling and the weediness of life in them. Without the platform work, of which the guitar and songs are a part, I could not get by for a living while doing the sort of long-time books I am on. And at the same time I would argue that the movements of labor and of the people have too little of singing and when they do sing it is too often nice, polite, derivative, aimless, not knowing its own. You won't have to tell me the enclosed Bureau Circular is bushwah in trend. But the further fact is that nine out of ten engagements are at schools and colleges and the performance a long way from bushwah. You might be interested to go to Garfield, NJ, High School, Feb 25, or Brooklyn Institute of Arts and Sciences Feb 26 and see tryouts before quite different audiences from the last one where we met. Anyhow may you live to ate the hin that scratches over your grave.

Faithfully yours
Carl Sandburg

348 | TO JANET POST

[Harbert, Michigan]
Feb 2   35

Dear Janet Post

You may recall that in 1927 at Knox I laid stress on the three actors in the college campus drama of 1858: the two debaters and the People. Now for four months I have been writing and revising a long piece "The People, Yes" which Harcourt is to publish this summer. It is a saga that requires four hours to read aloud. It may do for reading, in part, at the dedication of the restored Old Main. . . Of course I hated to take this time away from Lincoln: The War Years which calls for at least two more years of time and work. . . Of course I want to see you and to give any slightest morsel of counsel or suggestion that I can. . . On Feb 7 at Monmouth College I start on a platform trip that takes me to Iowa, Kentucky, Ohio, Virginia, New York, ending about the middle of March: and it is mainly a breadwinning exploit. . . Somehow I hope to find an hour for talk with you about next year. If not before spring then certainly sometime before summer this should be. . . And as I look at it this letter could go on pages and pages, the bitter campaign this year, the bitterest since 1858 and 1860, the A.A.A. and the supreme court and the many peculiar straws in the wind in the corn belt, why so great a college president as [Alfred] Britt is quitting, and where does one Janet Post lean in these days, she who could stand with a forlorn hope in the old days, and so much else. . . . To thank you for the annual windfall of pecans is easy. . . To write an intelligent and adequate letter in these days is not in the cards.

Faithfully
Carl Sandburg

Mrs. Post was general chairman of the Knox College Centenary. Old Main on campus was a site of the Lincoln-Douglas debates in 1858.

349 | TO BRENDA UELAND

[Berea, Kentucky]
Feb 14   35

Dear Brenda

This is to say that two letters to you got started and never finished, that your letter was a smooth poem that should not have a reply that is more an acknowledgement than a true answer. And even this is not much beyond an acknowledgement—except to give the report that it was a hard driving winter on that long piece The People, Yes, which now stands 112 typed pages and is quite indeed something else again, a saga sonata fugue with deliberate haywire interludes and jigtime babblings. Harcourt is to publish it next summer. I shall try to send a carbon copy to you for your comment. When it arrives to your hands parts of it must stand with you as done with your voice echoing and lingering.

Carl

Brenda Ueland was an author and newspaper columnist for the Askow Amerikan, *a weekly in Minneapolis.*

350 | TO ALFRED HARCOURT

[Harbert, Michigan]
Feb. 28, 1935.

Dear Alfred
This is a very peculiar job we are on. Some of the personal portraits will go into our book as they stand now while, others, like those of Sumner and Stevens, will be in a state of revision till the second set of page proofs is kissed good-by with prayers for Quinn and Boden and the innate cussedness of inanimate things including jersey justice at Rahway. I have purposely been holding back over 400 pages of the revised text, additional to the 149 you have, intending that when this whole batch arrives in your office it will have had the advantage of all new material bearing on it that has come to my hands. While it has waited here many important changes and insertions have been made. Three historical works, six biographies, not to mention the great and well-done 4-volume Lee by Freeman, have come along. Also I have been sitting in with two friends, one literary and stylistic, the other legal and evidentiary, in temperament who have carefully read the revised text. The weighing and the winnowing has gone on to a point where I know that you and your office have had certain major anxieties and minor toils reduced to a minimum. The delay now is entirely on re-

visions in the 400-odd pages at hand. I know you well enough to know that in each case you would say I was doing the right thing to make the changes made. As it looks now it will be some time in April that I will have in your hands somewhat over 600 pages of the revised text. About three weeks of that time will be spent filling dates and lazying in Minnesota and Texas.

Weeks ago I began wondering—and I see by your letter you have been doing the same kind of wondering—whether a synopsis or set of headings could be devised for each chapter that might help editors and readers. Enclosed are two sheets of notations, one on the Gettysburg speech chapter, the other on the one preceding. I had decided they would not do, and it would be difficult to devise anything like it that would do, for publication in our book. I enclose these however as possibly having suggestions for your editor. Please return them to me as I am going to do one for each chapter before starting on the closing year. I shall not fail to see you in April, God willing. Your letter has a General Grant awareness and I have reported to you as completely as Sherman ever did to Grant.

As Always,
Carl

Oliver Barrett and John L. Hervey were the two friends who read the text.

351 | TO DR. ARTHUR W. FREESE

[Harbert, Michigan]
[Circa February, 1935]

Dear Jim

The expedition will go down in history as one of the most daring enterprises ever executed during the break of day across the three state lines of Ill Ind and Mich Paul Revere only took care of himself and his horse We took care of a roll call of three and a La Salle car that had already seen 79,000 miles Suppose Paul Revere had rode his horse 79,000 miles? You can't suppose it And was his horse ever in three states? And suppose he was No we did better than Paul Revere The James boys Frank and Jesse are the only night riders that can be brought in for comparison. Anyhow it was a large luminous evening These enclosures are from the ragbag of the latest job

As always
Carl

Dr. Arthur Freese was called Jim by his friends.

352 | TO LLOYD LEWIS

[Harbert, Michigan]
March 9, 1935

Dear Lloyd

Long before I reached the comradely finish of your Lee-Freeman review I said it was the keenest of the nine or ten reviews I have read of that work. In justice you could have handed Freeman much more on his workmanship and his rich depth of sentiment always under nice control. I cried with his last chapter as I did with yours on Sherman. Then on rereading and considering I felt nearly all of the old mystery of Lee was there for me. When I see Freeman sometime I shall tell him his grand book lacked a chapter on what Lee's men from their hells and golgothas did to him; what poverty, shabbiness, rain, mud, rats, vermin, the scurvy, endured in comradeship by that final remnant which stuck to the last, did to the aristocrat in Lee. Also I would like to know if so good a fighter did not enjoy fighting, and when he did what became of the christian gentleman? It is either paradox or mystery. Where Freeman wins is that he can answer that he put all the essential facts in his book, loved his man as a man, and the reader can make his own derivations. My mind keeps on turning to how a book like Freeman's Lee could be done about Mannerheim of Finland or Hindenburg of Germany and I turn often to Lee and his army having a certain flair of Sam Hall and his god-damn-your-eyes. Often there is a fearful taint and corruption that goes with success, acclaim and a too-good physical health. Frank James was about the same character as Jesse but the name of Jesse James is the one sort of impurpled. The moment Jeff Davis was put into a lousy jail his aura took on new shadings. What happened to Lee from Gettysburg on was a slow, titanic, merciless series of operations which brought him thoughts, writhings, outlooks he had never known before. What they did to him, whether he changed slightly or deeply, is the mystery. And part of the mystery maybe only the familiar one of the front line fighting man who comes back from the human slaughter-house and has nothing to say because he knows it can't be told. "How did you lose your leg, grandpa?" "A bear bit it off." . . . As you have noticed by this time I am trying to clear my mind by sending a fog toward yours. Hoping to see you soon.

As always,
Carl

Sandburg was commenting to Lloyd Lewis on Douglas Southall Freeman's biography of Robert E. Lee, a four-volume work (as Sandburg's The War Years *came to be) that won a Pulitzer Prize.*

353 | TO BRENDA UELAND

[Harbert, Michigan]
[Circa mid-March, 1935]

Dear Brenda

I hope your novel walked right straight into you and said "I defy you not to write me, you can't help yourself, it is a decree and you will have to get me written, good or bad this is your fate and you will begin to dry and blow away in the wind unless you give this now what you've got to give it". I have no misgivings. Writing is your trade. Or else you have a mind and personality so operating that when you sit down it is as when the elements send rain. The rain itself is no effort nor phenomenon when connected with all that went before it. "Writing is a trade." Maybe so. Also "the good boxer is a craftsman" but how would that account for Joe Louis? And, skipping several bars, I have been wondering what becomes of the old theory that the genial climates favor singing when it happens that the Scandinavian sopranos from ice and fog are not particularly suffering alongside the tropical warblers? And, skipping more bars, why should it be that you who are an indurated and deep-riven Norwegian might anywhere pass for an indubitable Spaniard, a child of figs and castanets instead of fjords and fish? Your three articles and the one short story are here. The two on art and conversation are handbooks and play with underhums of humor. Writing costs you though you write because you would rather write than dance or paint. What am I getting at? The rag-bag of the mind. In the key of Whitman "What is the grass? I guess it is the handkerchief of the Lord." Perhaps I was trying to say you have courage and awareness amid shadows. That piece "The People, Yes" grows with the faith of potatoes in June. It is now about double the length it was when you glimpsed it. I think Joe [Beach] was perfectly justified in demurrers to it. In the past I have unjustly flung unfinished things at him and he has been a friend with help and patience, the sort of counselor whose half-spoken asides have more value than his forthright decisions. Once over a sheaf of verse of mine, he said, "Carl, you're beginning to imitate yourself," and later I agreed with him perfectly. Or again I would refuse to surrender, retreated and consolidated my forces and reorganized, and acknowledged him as a good brigadier. Some spots in this latest piece were bad. They were miss shots. A lot of my work only gets done by many preliminary miss shots. And there are plenty of them in the finished work, the word "finished" meaning merely that I have given it every last measure of toil and devotion I could summon and for a better piece of work I shall have to wait until time has done something to me or I have entered another incarnation, so to speak. On one score in working on your novel you need have no worry. That is the technic of story-telling. The Viking is not a great story. But it is above mediocrity, is beautifully modern, and is a good straightaway handling of reader interest which was why the WHC [*Woman's Home Companion*] editors, who are no slouches, made it the lead fiction for that number. I am mentioning this I suppose because, except for my brief Rootabaga Stories, I have been denied the time for trying a hand at fiction as such. Our lives shape whimsically. Had I not got going on this Lincoln project which has stretched out unimaginably beyond what was first planned, I would probably have set up one of those little fiction shops that dot the hard highways the 'ard 'ighways of this land of Goshen. Just now I dont like it that because of this long piece of verse I am delayed on the Lincoln which demands at least two more years. But the case is as inevitable as the boy who said "I didnt sneeze, the sneeze sneezed me" and has no parallel with the farm-hand who saw the letters "P C" in a dream and found out after a while they didnt mean "Preach Christ" but "Plow Corn." One impelling drive is that there is not out of all the stretches of experiment in democracy any extended handling that begins to touch the reach and majesty of the theme. Of prose treatises and oratorical discussion there is much. Whitman pioneered and was too transcendental and I will have plenty of miss shots but some poet will get it sometime and it will be no worry to me for Lindbergh will have flown a plane over Chicago and scattered my ashes from west side over into lake Michigan harbor. And while going along on "The People, Yes" I have thought about how curiously it has been ordered that I should over and again put into a verse form (of a sort) what could also be employed in fiction or drama. The latter pay, when they get by, in dollars, a thousandfold over poetry but whenever it occurs to me to shape characters and action thru which the theme would be delivered I balk and hesitate and go back to the first scheme that came, the medium of free verse.

Carl

354 | TO FRANKLIN D. ROOSEVELT

[Harbert, Michigan]
March 29   35

Dear Mr. President:

All the time you keep growing—so it seems to some of us who read you from a distance. In wide human outlook—in utterance and in silence—in an austerity that deepens from year to year—

you seem as a Chief Magistrate almost too good to be true. The tests you have stood and passed thus far in this chaotic democracy of ours I would not in 1932 have believed possible. The forces so implacably against you have such resources that some of us expected long ago you would be sunk. The genius and the intestinal fortitude with which you have managed to navigate a series of storms go to form something touched with myth. The spiritual air and quality of this country now, the winds of doctrine, the intangibles that underlie art works and the cultural status, the mystic themes for which men are willing to fight and die—these are all under immense contribution from you.

Having written for ten years now on "Abraham Lincoln: the War Years", starting this year on the fourth and final volume, I have my eyes and ears in two eras and can not help drawing parallels. One runs to the effect that you are the best light of democracy that has occupied the White House since Lincoln. You have set in motion trends that to many are banners of dawn. This may be praise to your face but it is also a recording of a hope and a prayer that you go on as steadfast as you have in loyalty to the whole people, that in your difficult war with their exploiters your cunning may increase.

Your speeches like Lincoln's will stand the test of time. In going thru letters, diaries, speeches and newspaper files of the time of Lincoln's administration nothing stands out more strangely in this hour than that most of the utterance of that time now is touched with the pathetic or the ridiculous. Only a small remnant knew what was going on, had the clairvoyance to read what the deep underlying streams might shape across the future, with relation to decisions of the immediate moment. Your grand cascades of speech last fall are comparable only to your fine silences on the sit-down strike.

What many of us have come to see is that you had long preparation for what you are doing—and as with Lincoln there has been a response of the People to you: they have done something to you and made you what you could not have been without them, this interplay operating steadily in your growth. It is a terrific game you are up against—and many who can't find the time to send you a message are aware of it. When the enclosed article appeared in the Red Book last year I was surprised at the number of persons who saw parallels in your own turmoils and those Lincoln was immersed in. Anyhow may the cunning of your right hand increase. More power to you. And in this Easter time, Peace Be to You—

Carl Sandburg

The article Sandburg sent to President Franklin D. Roosevelt was called "Lincoln in the Shadows," which appeared in Redbook *in 1934.*

355 | TO EDWARD STEICHEN

Harbert, [Michigan] April 28   35

Dear Ed

Enclosed is a fair-to-middlin photographer's story. . . While I was east they bought a horse here. They found out a horse could be fed on what the goats don't care for. Then when I went west for a week they bought a couple of pigs. So there will be side-meat from a pork barrel for your bean soup next time you are here. And if you and Dana will bring your riding boots you can get on a nice horse that rares up unless you hold a tight rein. Its color, they wish you to know, is designated as buckskin tho its really more like olive-mist. One of the pigs is deep black poland-china while the other is bright brown with a big white belly-band, very wide, sort of as tho one of the war camouflage artists had designed him. . . Finished revisions and additions to The People, Yes and mailed it to Harcourt last week and am now reading what the hell I last wrote on the Lincoln last fall so that where I take up again the transition will be smooth as an eel swimming in oil. . . One of the added lunch-counter proverbs goes: There ain't no strong coffee, there's only weak people. . . Under this roof they have prayers for you and send you love always

Carl

356 | TO OLIVER R. BARRETT

[Harbert, Michigan]
April 29   35

Dear Oliver

The quote as of "April of '64" is from the Hodges letter April 4, 1864 and so can stand. The other one may be in error or lacking sequence which I am sure you can smooth out.

Howsoever: "Whitman never personally met Lincoln" is fairly accurate. They never shook hands. They never spoke conventional greetings. He did meet Hay and Hay got him a railroad ticket to go home and vote the Union ticket. But Whitman's repeated references "I saw the President today" or "I see the President almost daily" meant he was among the spectators, one of the crowd, who saw Lincoln in the streets. From this aloof viewpoint Whitman measured Lincoln as "a Hoosier Michael Angelo" and got Lincoln's stature more definitely than Sumner who was corporeally and vocally dealing with Lincoln so often.

You can easily add a sentence or phrase covering the point that one of the source items presents notes for a book intended probably as war memoranda. Perhaps too a sentence should be added somewhat like this: "A constantly increasing number of source items indicate there was far more reality than pretense in Whitman's assumption of a role of hospital visitor and friend of the physically wrecked soldier. His frequent characterization of himself, in his poetry, as 'a loafer', had its point. Nevertheless the evidence grows that he gave many days to the help and comfort of hospitalized men, doing this work in a unique and personal way."

I have gone through that catalog of the Bucke collection which you sent. I would hardly have expected there was so much material which has not been used in the Whitman books now written. Thank you for sending it; it will get back to you soon. Also I shall go thru all the photographs and bring in a bundle soon.

The manuscript of The People, Yes went to Harcourt last Saturday, for weal or woe. And now the attic is being reorganized for going ahead again on the Lincoln job, after a seven month detour that included visits to Tulsa, Oklahoma and Penn Yann, New York, Berea, Kentucky and Reading, Pa., not forgetting Spartanburg, South Carolina and a convent in Minnesota. . . They took on a couple of pigs here last time I was away. It was a horse the time before. So you'll find the country life out here any day you come out. Hoping to see you soon—

As always
Carl

357 | TO PAUL AND RHEA DE KRUIF

Harbert, [Michigan] April 29   35

Dear Paul and Rhea

The last book is your best which is saying you are momentously alive and growing. The east-Michigan-shore spots had a special appeal for us, of course. If you ever pass this way you will find much more of a biological exhibit. When I went away in February they decided a goat herd, hens, ducks, geese and rabbits were not enough, and took on a horse. When I left in April for ten days they took on two pigs. The horse can live on what the goats reject. And the pigs get by on leavings no others will touch, though like very ancient farmers we can not begin to get God's intention in curling the tails of the pigs. Get a couple of oink-oinks, Paul. Raise your own side-meat and embellish your bean soup next winter with what it takes. And stop in when you're riding by. After a detour for a long poem I am reorganizing the attic for starting again on the war Lincoln. You are so alive, I can see, that you are having one hell of a time making sure just which of several fields you should throw yourself into. As between two scribblers I'm telling you that if we live to a ripe old age we will pass out saying we didn't get our best books written: there wasn't time.

As always
Carl

1935

Paul de Kruif, the bacteriologist and writer who supplied Sinclair Lewis with technical material for Arrowsmith, *was a Michigan friend of the Sandburgs. The De Kruif book Sandburg referred to was* Men Against Death.

358 | TO OLIVER R. BARRETT

Harbert, [Michigan] May 9 35

Dear Oliver

Your long letter is good to have. I have had one simmering in me. The opposed viewpoints, I suppose, rest back on what for a better word is usually called temperament, having to do with the blood and bile. Jefferson, Hamilton, Washington, were three temperaments. One was 100 per cent for the French revolution, the second was totally opposed to it, the third was skeptical of it but would not denounce it. Or I think of Toombs and Stephens, whom I know better. Toombs was for secession, war, slavery, and Stephens bitterly opposed to secession, half-hearted about war, and a forecaster that slavery would die of its inherent contradictions. Yet somehow they negotiated a fine lifelong friendship, with candor, humor, and an understanding of what each had that was good for the other.

In this piece The People, Yes is no intention of stirring class hatred or violence. If I had a purpose to rouse and inflame the masses of people against the small fraction of the population who own control of the large industries, I would employ the methods of an agitator and frame appeals and shape issues and coin slogans. Only time will tell whether what I have put down has the element of true history and valid memoranda. "Democracy", "popular government", "the republican form of government", "republican rule", "vox populi", "we, the people," these are all word usages never yet adequately defined. True democracy is as difficult and as mystic in its operations as true religion or true art. One of my theses, in so far as I have any, in this piece, hovers around the point that the masses of people have gone wrong often in the past and will again in the future—but in the main their direction is right. With decades of passing years I have had a deepening melancholy about

322

the masters of finance and industry in America. How few and how rare are the ones who realize that the roots and sources of their holdings are in the people, the workers, the consumers, the customers, the traveling public! How seldom is there one like Julius Rosenwald who could say to Henry Horner under a special circumstance, "I'm ashamed to have so much money!" (In the probating of Mrs. Rosenwald's estate an attorney said to Rosenwald that an item of something like $100,000 could probably be contested and won but Rosenwald said, Let it go, I'm ashamed to have so much money.) The proverb does run among them, "The second million is always easier than the first"—and I have never seen greed, fear, brutality among the masses to surpass what may be seen among the rich. I happen to have a liking for one of the two American billionaires. I have a shelf of books about him and could offhandedly do a biography that would have more admirations and affections than regrets and demurrers. I disagree diametrically with some of his most emphatic viewpoints. But what do I find among other rich men as to feeling about this billionaire? He's a pretender with luck, he's a charlatan with a gift for publicity that will sell cars, he is lacking in standards and something of a stinker if not just a sonofabitch. And for why is this? First of all, it is partly a jealousy because he has a way of winning the affections of masses of people, becoming a sort of folk figure, and the point is registered that he doesn't really care about the people but is merely after selling cars; a commercial demagogue. Secondly, I have heard from big employers that when Ford declared for a minimum wage based on decent living standards he did it 1) for car selling publicity and 2) to attract to his plant the cream of the automotive labor world. That Ford might incidentally love humanity and this be at least a slight operating motive could not be considered. That Ford has never sold securities and brought woe to investors, including widows and orphans, for this he has some dark reason of his own. And to me it is melancholy-comic in gargoyle fashion that for more than a decade, at regular intervals, the SatEvePost sends Sam Crowther to interview Ford and once more the country gets the basic proposition on which permanent prosperity can thrive under the capitalistic competitive system, viz: Under a steadily increasing buying power of the masses of the people no collapse is possible: such buying power is to be had by the invariable expedient and rule: every cut in production cost must be (after certain items to protect future operating cost are taken care of) shared with the workers through higher wages and the consumers through lowered prices. Who chimes in with Ford on this? Hardly anybody among those who would count in saying it. The Brookings Institute is with him on it. So is the Fortune magazine. But the SatEvePost seems to scour the country and look in vain for other voices. Johnson of the shoe business and Owen D. Young of General Electric and a few odd ones here and there seem to be speaking and striving for goals beyond mere profit, for human records surpassing yesterday. But they are a feeble minority. Old Horace Lorimer has lost the vision and enthusiasms of the Bull Moose days when he could publish devastating articles such as Will Payne on The Cheat of Overcapitalization and David Graham Phillips on The Billionaires. Willie Hearst has turned 73: no diner in the presence may mention death: he is a convinced Nazi. Silas Strawn, Charley Dawes, Charlie Schwab, Andy Mellon—theirs is the predominant philosophy vocalized by the press of the country. They are entirely for the Past. The Future must be the same as the Past. They do not see first of all that History does not permit this. Science, inevitable changes, inventions, moods of the people, condition the future. It is whimsical, unreadable. You and I would probably not concur on whether the present depression has essential characteristics differing from previous depressions. The Governor of the Bank of England, Norman Montagu, in taking note that it is the first known WORLD depression, emphasizes that the picture is too complicated for any one mind to grasp. It would be interesting to try to write a modern version of the [Lincoln's] House Divided Speech and its main text, "If we could first know where we are and whither we are tending, we could better judge what to do and how to do it." I am with the people as against the exploiters of the people and if pinned down to a definition of exploiters I could answer, "All of those who completely disregard the Ford proposition on what should be done with the surplus from reduced production costs."

As the girl said to the bashful feller who said little and stayed late, "I hope I'm not keeping you up."

Some form of controlled capitalism, pressure for good or bad results on the large financial and industrial establishments, seems to be ahead. If I could see more signs of human awareness among those now controlling those establishments, if they were showing more signs of response to some of the deeper underlying human currents of the time, I could more serenely watch the floodtide of the times. Where I have written with irony I know it is a subdued irony. I belong to no political party and have not for 24 years. I belong to no organizations open or secret except the Veterans of Foreign Wars and the Authors League of America. I read both the outgivings of the US Chamber of Commerce and the diatribes of the Daily Worker. I could write a book out of my years as a reporter who daily made the rounds of the labor union offices and annually reported state and national Federation of Labor conventions: there would be as much of the heroic as of the drab and the vile in it. I could do another book on the newspaper life, some of the best fellows that walk the earth, along with scoundrels and prostitutes. I could mention two Chicago Tribune men, one an executive and the other a staff reporter, who are weary of daily issuing a propaganda pamphlet emanating from the temperament of Bertie McCormick, saying, "We'd like to get out a real newspaper." They have a sense of news as a somewhat definite commodity known to trained craftsmen; they would like to be craftsmen and not strumpets. This matter I should not have mentioned, perhaps, as it is an extreme instance in the fields of shaping public opinion, of the practice of free speech, of the making of propaganda, overlapping and interweaving with the general establishment of public education, schools, radio, drama.

When proofs of The People, Yes come along we might go over it together and you can point out where to you it is spotty or even rotten, to use egg terms. I have no more aimed this piece at any particular audience than I did my first books, and for those I was surprised at getting a publisher. It is as independent and freegoing a job as Potato Face, of which the first printing of 2,500 copies is not yet sold. It is a confession of faith and in one phase autobiographic. I have been wrong often in my life and have incarnated in me many kinds of fools and will die without having articulated all of them.

If you'll get Al to drive you out here in his new petite car I will knock off work and go into a battle of the mashies with you.

As always
Carl

P.S.—This enclosure was in an envelope ready for mailing to you when your letter arrived.

AND THIS LETTER SHOULD BE REGARDED AS SORT OF CONFIDENTIAL DON'T YOU THINK?

PSS. I shall have Harcourt send you a set of proofs. He knows you have been the best counselor and coadjutor on the Lincoln book past and present. . . Perhaps I shall be driven to the recourse of Harriet Beecher Stowe who had to write that awful (in the Old Testament sense of "awful") sequel *Key* to Uncle Tom's Cabin, tho I have lived closer to my materials and have therefore done a book not so simple and negative as hers. . . On your point as to expressions intended "to convey the thought that the laboring class are exploited by wealthy malefactors and should be made to feel hate and resentment against their employers": if Sam Adams, Tom Jefferson and Patrick Henry had kept silence on the exploitation of the American colonists by the imbecile British crown there would have been no American revolution and this country today would be an English dominion: if Garrison, Phillips, Lovejoy, the radicals, along with the moderates Seward and Lincoln had submitted to the rule that slavery should not be mentioned in polite society, the Southern exploiters of human chattels would have had their way: today the sinister and forbidden topic is something else and in the so-called best circles it is considered either bad taste or some sort of treason to mention plain and known facts and to ask where they may be leading us. The matter has now reached the irrational and ridiculous stage where you are déclassé lacking class if you mention an employer like Johnson of Endicott-Johnson who shares profits with his workmen and lives with them as a good neighbor, or if you mention that Ford has never cheated an investor by the overcapitalization device or if you merely raise the inquiry as to why there is not more discussion and widespread approval of Ford's theory that a more equitable distribution of profits resulting from lowered production costs, is a safeguard against the frequently recurring collapses of the capitalist structure. If in polite society I raise certain points that have come to me out of reporting dozens of strikes and interviewing hundreds of strikers, the atmosphere is immediately tense and a man knows he is touching the deep and sensitive issue around which the next historic crisis ranges. Merely to say, "I have found the general run of labor leaders having about the same mixture of honesty and crookedness as the general run of business and industrial leaders", is considered improper. The stress is supposed to be laid on the labor racketeers, on the few small-time rakeoffs of Con Shea or Tim Murphy, rather than the merciless twelve-hour workday which went on in the U.S. Steel Co. plants until the fantastic N.R.A. arrived. Nearly always a strike results not from outside agitators coming in and fomenting discontent and hate so much as conditions that have bred discontent and hate before the arrival of the outsiders. In the railroad, building trades, steel, textile and other fields this has almost invariably been the case. The majority of the strikes, as I gather from the newspaper files of Lincoln's time, were against the 12-hour workday with a demand for 10 hours. The fact is a sad one to chronicle: the shorter workday of the American workingman resulted not as a reasonable and human arrangement instigated by the employers but by reason of workingmen forming unions, pulling strikes and going in for the whole sorry program of violence and hate that runs with such warfare. I was on the ground at Gary, making one trip out there to strike headquarters with William Allen White, when the steel workers had "downed tools". It was a perfect case of the discontent and hate being already there, eager for revolt, before ever the union organizers arrived. Out of the enormous war profits of the Steel corporation had been no thought of sharing a part of it to the workers (many of whose kinsmen had gone to camps and battle-fronts) in wage increases or lowering the 12-hour work shift or of moderating a daily regime of labor so fierce in pace and dragout that only the exceptional can stand up to it when they reach the forties. It is a saying, "In the steel works old age comes at forty." One comment might be, "Well, what of it. The strike was lost and won nothing." The answer is in the labor world proverb, "No strike is ever lost." The first strikes against the 12-hour day were lost. A weak foozle of a street car strike which I saw from start to finish in Milwaukee in 1911, tying up traffic less than a day, brought immediate correction of a series of minor grievances concerning working conditions and better attention to wage schedules. In Pittsburgh a few years ago I went over a steel plant with a former superintendent who was a foreman inside the works during the Homestead strike. (For the moment I forget his name. His wife was along. In the gay '90's she was an American tennis champion. She said, "Making steel is like cooking marmalade; you put in the ore, bring it to a boil, let it jell, skim off the scraps, and there is your iron.") Amid the ins and outs of what resulted from the Homestead strike he said, "After a strike or when there is talk about organizing and striking, the men always get more consideration." Out near Honolulu the Missus and I drove around one of the largest plantations in the Islands, with a big sugar mill that was the last word in modern mass production; after the stalks have the cane juice pressed out of them they are ground to fine pulp which then is burned as fuel. The manager, Ernest Green, was to me a phenomenon in the way he really cares about his people, some 2,000 Filipinos and Japs. He and his directors recognize insecurity of employment, disregard as to unavoidable sickness and accidents, lack of genuine care about housing, hygiene, education, can play hell in the creation of the sort of unrest and writhing that has brought class hatred into too many corners of America. "Of course I have to do many things I don't like to do," said Ernest Green, and I answered, "I think I understand you, and from what I see of your special attention to the *human* factors in your plant I wish there were more of it on the Mainland."

The entire matter of "discontent" is involved. All progress comes from a certain measure of unrest. "I want discontented workmen," says Ford to Paul Kellogg who prints it. "It is the discontented workman who finds an easier way to do what he is doing.

This eventually cuts the production cost." . . . That life is whimsical, paradoxical, tragic, and plays tricks with us all, high and low, is one of the drifts of The People, Yes. It may or may not hold the sort of discontent that is health and light to the young. Across the next fifty years I believe the young of today are going to effect profound changes in the world we see. But what I am trying to say here would require a book. I can no more put my wide-ranging viewpoints in a few letter pages than you put the full essence of your life philosophy in your letter of yesterday.

Some of the reasoning in this private communication to Oliver R. Barrett, the Chicago attorney, was reflected in the prose-poem The People, Yes. *Barrett was a conservative; Sandburg's sympathies were with the progressives and radicals. They often disagreed, but this never interfered with their friendship and mutual esteem. Robert Toombs, of Georgia, had led the fight for secession. Alexander Stephens, who was from the same state, bitterly opposed it, but, when Georgia seceded, went along with it. Sandburg had a long shelf of books about Henry Ford. He used this argument often about the billionaire. David Graham Phillips and William Howard Payne were two of the early muckrakers. Al Hannah was a close friend of Oliver Barrett.*

359 | TO IDA M. TARBELL

[Harbert, Michigan]
May 19, 1935

Dear Ida Tarbell

Your note about the Gettysburg piece is worth having amid the work of going on and trying to complete Abraham Lincoln: The War Years. Thus far I have something like 700,000 words, leading up to August of '64 and shall probably require about 200,000 more words and three years to the finish. In order to feel the scale and proportion better for the final quarter I have spent the past year in revisions and rewritings. When I began on it in the fall of 1928 my estimate was that I would have it done by 1934 or 1935—and with your familiarity with the materials involved you know why it goes slow! And the past eight months I have had a detour into a long poem (very free verse!) titled THE PEOPLE, YES which I am sure holds some of your heartbeats about democracy and these times. I handle your Lincoln books regularly while working. And your Standard Oil (1st ed. 2 vols. $20. 1928) is on a front-room bookshelf downstairs. Perhaps every two years I reread that classic commentary: Commercial Machiavellianism. So you are never forgotten here and there are brightnesses you might not know of about this note of yours fluttering out of the day's mail yesterday.

Faithfully yours
Carl Sandburg

360 | TO ALFRED HARCOURT

Harbert, [Michigan] June 3   35

Dear Alfred

Proofs of 56 corrected galleys are being mailed to you today. The other and remaining ten will go to you within a few days. The added text, I believe you will say, is worth the time.

The news note point that it is in the Whitman tradition is not so apt. Its pedigree is woefully mixed rather by way of Piers Ploughman, Norse and Icelandic Sagas, the Bible, Villon, assorted modernists and the latest extras.

Editor Graeve of the Delineator picks a piece titled "Father and Son" which is one of the inserts up front in The People, Yes. I enclose his letter and shall write him that you are handling the matter of prices and everything so there will be no confusions. Tell him the text herein enclosed is the one I would prefer he should use; it has material changes in the closing lines.

The New Yorkers say the fragments sent them are "not up our street." Of course there might be parts in the entire piece they would like.

Gould is okay so far as I am concerned. His forerunner Schuler would have thrown it all out the first reading.

ITEM: There was a page of prefatory lines in the Mss of The People, Yes, which should have gone to the printer. It does not appear in the proofs I have. Is this to come in the page proofs?

Can you send me the latest Edmund Wilson book? The New Republic extracts show it has something—and the letters hollering about his lack of reverence are just what might be expected. . . About Sherwood Anderson I'll tell you when I see you; we had a winter visit. When I mentioned Ben Hecht as tho I still like Ben, Sherwood said, "He has a child's mind." When I spoke of William Allen White as nearing 70 and having run a good race, he said White was a tool of Mark Hanna. And so it went on. I felt sorry for his accumulated and pointless hates. He himself couldn't see a shade of the comic in his trying to instruct Schevil and me about our publisher.

Meantime we are having three responsible witnesses look on at our milkings of picked goats. They will attest that Felicia, Carlotta and Meggi yielded during three milkings in a 12-hour period an amount each of more than ten pounds. Three such performances every 30 days entitled the doe to Advanced Registry with the American Goat Raisers' Society.

As always
Carl

Sandburg meant the American Milk Goat Record Association.

361 | TO ALFRED HARCOURT

Harbert, [Michigan]
July 6, [1935]

Dear Alf
Would you tell Reid and Herzberg that I have been staying away from all radio work, that I have refused offers from the Lincoln Life Insurance Co., the A. & P. Stores, and others because it is something by itself and a ten minute broadcast is a days work?

On July 11 I am going to Springfield and help dedicate the

Vachel Lindsay Bridge. At first I thought I ought not to spare the time, and then I got to thinking about Vachel and how two of his best poems are on Lincoln and Altgeld ("Sleep Softly, Eagle Forgotten") and with the sixth letter and the third long distance phone call I admitted it was my duty to be there.

If you suppose also it is not my duty to read about all of Black Reconstruction you are mistaken. Why do these books keep coming along, each of them stealing a day, two days, of time? [William E.] Du Bois has done a big document that will stand in its field for a long time as an essential. But he doesn't know what Wendell Phillips had in mind in telling a young agitator, "If you call the dead George Washington an unmitigated scoundrel of a slaveholder what have you got left for the living Frank Pierce?"

Yours in the depths
Carl

362 | TO ARCHIBALD MACLEISH

Harbert, [Michigan] Aug 10 35

Dear Archie

Yes neither of us could find anything but hard uphill work in doing a NY Times book review that met the standard requirements. And many a day this summer I knew you were slogging along and calling on all your reserves. For you had Japan in your blood and bones. And you threw added and fleeting gleams into the simplest statements of fact—so I knew you had in your system a book that for personal emanations would stand alongside of Me and My Shadow which is always my nickname for The Hamlet of A. McL. I knew it would cost you more than it did me to do The Chicago Race Riots because Japan is so much bigger than the Black Belt of Chicago tho the population density is about the same. I will understand if you forswear all writing till the leaves are gone and the snow flies again. When I finished the American Songbag some 18 months after the Prairie Years, I had to learn to sleep again, I had to learn to have no shame over ten to twelve hours a day in bed, and no shame over being lazy. Your Japan piece written you have all the license there is to be lazy. You are too good a human stick to be worth the fate of a Detroit man I met who on being first aware in the morning that he is awake, says, "Conscious again goddam it!"

As ever
Carl

363 | TO LLOYD LEWIS

Harbert, [Michigan] Sept 8, [1935]

Dear Lloyd

I thought I had laid away Fighting Prophet for keeps during this job. But yesterday I had to go back to it, using the incident of Sherman handing Johnston that assassination-news telegram before giving it to his army. Those pages along there are beautifully thoughtful in getting inside Sherman. They will stand and it is a tenderly lighted story. I could not resist using one of your surmises, the sentence running:

"In the surrender terms they were to sign, Sherman's motive, according to his keenest interpreter, probably ranged around a thought: 'Lincoln is dead. I will make his kind of a peace.'"

As ever
Carl

364 | TO BRUCE BLIVEN

[Harbert, Michigan]
Sept 12 35

Dear Bruce Bliven

Returning from a longer than usual trip I find your letter. I shall vote in November for Roosevelt—and for a long time have had no hesitations or reservations on the point that he is a momentous historic character more thoroughly aware of what he is doing and where he is going than most of the commentators. SEC, TVA, NLRB and much else deserve continuation. Against the claim that for the first time class hate has been preached from the White House may be set the counterclaim that for the first time in American history a President has openly approved in principle and as a practice collective bargaining between the Owners and the Workers of industry. As a political independent, at present attached to no party, a nonpartisan observer, I have been surprised at the record of substantial accomplishments in working measures, at the pettiness of the corruptions in contrast with the immense moneys spent, at the human spirit of the Administration which has permitted such sway to Ickes, Wallace, Tugwell, Perkins, Hopkins. What the underlying and dominant economic streams of the time are shaping now and are to dictate in the future, only historians decades hence can tell. In the present national chaos and international entanglements, considering the amount of combustibles lying loose every way for Sunday, I'll take Roosevelt.

Faithfully yours

Carl Sandburg

P.S.—You can hold this confidential—or print it or use it any way you choose. For your own information perhaps I should say I have done no shadow boxing and that for three years anyone who has asked me if I was for Roosevelt has had the answer that thus far I was amazed that a President could get away with what he was putting across and that I would stay with him until he changed his direction. In an article in Moley's Today Feb. of '34 I drew a parallel between Lincoln's Emancipation Proclamation and the NRA 7a clause. Neither had proper authority in law. Neither could be enforced. But the announcement alone had far reaching results, beyond calculation, best estimated by the wrath of those opposed. Early last year the New York Daily News ran an interview in which I gave something of the same view. I mention these points so you may know I have not been in any bomb-proof shelter. My work, of course, writing The People, Yes and going on toward finishing the 4-vol Abraham Lincoln: th War Years, has kept me from several activities I would like to go in for. May I thank you for the Newton Arvin article? There was to it a peculiarly generous tone and measured regard, with the stress on intentions, which I have to value.

Bruce Bliven edited The New Republic.

365 | TO LEWIS GANNETT

Harbert, Mich. Sept 21   35

Dear Mr Gannett

Among the more neglected books of this decade is "Some Folks Won't Work" by Clinch Calkins. It mingles abysmal statistics and case reports with a profound and beautiful genius of contemplation.

Two biographies have deserved better than they got. Allan Nevins' "Fremont" is entirely statement of fact but has for me the values of a Balzac novel with the added satisfaction that life and not Balzac is performing on the stage. The same goes for Walter Davenport's "Boise Penrose." One learns of Pennsylvania and Washington, D.C. Mr. Davenport admits it would have been a grander biography if Penrose had written letters available to the biographer instead of running up telephone bills of $12,000 a year.

"Fiddler's Green" by Albert Wetjen is the best assemblage of the myths and fantasies that pass among men of the sea. Parts of it should be in school readers. It is rich with imagination and folly.

Leading all crime classics should be Jack Black's "You Can't Win." I would rather have my copy than all the offhand outpourings of E. Phillips Oppenheim. It has some dandy stories incidental to picturing an underworld with penetration and savvy. "Oh room rent! what crimes are committed in thy name!"

Yours

Carl Sandburg

Lewis Gannett was the book critic of the New York Herald Tribune.

Harbert Mich Sept 26   35

Dear George

As the January California schedule looks now it will be short shrift for us and maybe not much more than a passing hello like when going to Hawaii. Or if I am as worn as in March of '33 I won't seek out anyone in Frisco. Anyhow I can tell now of reading a few evenings ago some of the pieces of Marie de L Welch written several years back and the contrast of them with her writings of th past two years. I see new holds and a curious growth going on. She has a surer strength now than ever, and works with controlled effects and spare lines as though she had sought far and deliberated long over what she is reciting. They could be read aloud to the music of certain 16th century violin pieces that are likewise spare and sometimes muted. If I should sometime get around to writing about modern poets I would name instances and inquire why some of these are not in the school-books. When I occasionally name the five most significant original poets who have the highlights of today and glimmerings of tomorrow in them, I name her as one of the five. She has the compressions of Emily Dickinson, a quality of the lonely onlooker in Gaucho songs, and of the informed modern not overwhelmed by the facts—and at her best she achieves music that for me has its parallel in the quieter passages of Sibelius. You might tell her when that first long poem of hers ran in Pacific Weekly I wrote a fan letter to her but like so many letters I write in my head it didn't get onto paper. Your feel and direction is the same as hers, as I know out of books you have talked of to me and never written, and around which I could do a story that wouldnt be a short short. And what I am glad of is that you have an ear for sin, folly, science, and the living fact bastions of deep song. Nevertheless—since correcting page proofs of The People, Yes in June I have not read the book till last night. It has a curious craziness. Maybe I was a little crazy to publish it. Maybe you are a little crazy to say it gets by with you. On many a page the workmanship is slovenly: I would like now to go back and revise; this as the lawyers say being inadmissible. Also for those birds who have twittered so far so good but the theme lacks final cohesion for want of a constructive program, I would superimpose an appendix with the horns of municipal ownership contrapuntal to the woodwinds of collective bargaining, the entire orchestra in the finale giving three cheers for the C.I.O. However I have this summer finished three long chapters that bring Lincoln thru the lowest gloom of th war to the election of November '64: this as workmanship I can defend: it sets forth a record based on documents, transcripts, letters, diaries, all admissible: where there may be poetry it is sneaked in and spoonfed to the reader. I have had to do research jobs where long ago you might have believed the ground had been competently covered in special treatises. There isn't one half decent narrative of the course of conscription and Lincoln's relation to it. No one has done the economic backgrounds of the war in the massive and diverse treatment they require. As a wit and personality Thad Stevens had all the nice shine of Charles Lamb or J. McNeil Whistler but no one has written it. As an earlier and heavier edition of Glenn Frank there was Salmon Portland Chase; no ironist with a sense of values has touched off Chase. And suddenly without warnings I get flung from this trail into what was once termed "essays in the art of poesy." Or I depart into a four or five-dimensional realm of nonsense where justice prevails because each absurdity cancels another, and only children (the more lawless and unruly) and half-wits (the more luminous ones) know the answers and get fun out of it. Poetry can be laughed off by anybody who doesn't respond to its music or mockery or experience. Their allegation "It doesn't mean a thing to me" proves the case that for them it is not poetry and that for all in fellowship or attunement with them it is not poetry. . . This is one of the times when overwork has me down to feeling like a fumbling shadow. I shall slowly pull out of it as I have done before. And if we don't get to a real talk this winter it will be later. It is quite in the cards that you and I have our best ten years of work just ahead of us. Please remember if you are ever making the trip cross country again that the latch is out for you here. The Missus remembers when you were joined with "Frank P. Walsh and his troupe of trained nuisances." We grow all the vegetables we use and a herd of nine goats supplies our milk, butter and cheese. Felicia and Meggi by yielding a daily average of more than ten pounds three months this summer have made Advanced Registry with the American Goat Raisers' Society. We do practically all the work ourselves, an Indiana Quaker maid being included in "we." The eldest daughter is an invalid, the second is still below normal from being struck and run over by a careless motorist, the youngest is as good as God ever bestowed on a house; she is as nice as anything in a Russian ballet when she rides her horse out into Lake Michigan for a swim together. It is an odd corner of the world, a slow sickle of beach curving twenty-two miles to the headland where at night we see the pier lights of Benton Harbor—and in winter the splinters of the Northern Lights. Across the lake to the west we see the half-circle moving white spike of the Lindbergh beacon in Chicago. The lake performs. The lake runs a gamut of all moods. Nothing ever told of in the New York Times or the Encyclopaedia Britannica but the apparition of it will be shaped for you by this Lake Michigan. Anyhow the welcome sign is out for you and yours, and fresh milk from the gentle and allwise Felicia ready and waiting, if you should ever be this way.

Faithfully yours
Carl

George P. West, associate editor of the San Francisco News, *was an old labor friend of Sandburg's who had done publicity for President Wilson's campaign in 1916. His wife was the poet Marie de L. Welch. Janet still suffered from recurring headaches and sometimes sharp pains in the head, as a result of the accident.*

367 | TO MARTIN SANDBURG

[Harbert, Michigan]
Oct 5 35

Dear Mart

Often I wonder how you are. We have not got so many years ahead but what we ought to be visiting oftener. What with neuritis this summer maybe I understand your rheumatism better. Sort of expected you would roll in sometime this summer and see your nieces and lazy around some in this country. I have Minnesota dates the last week of October and shall try to stop off at Gt [Galesburg] a day and have a look at you. At a little golf picnic with G E Q Johnson we talked about you. Some Swede neighbors here are starting for Stockholm next week. When I get this gigantic book off my hands maybe we will do some touring. See you soon.

Carl

Gt in railroad parlance stood for Galesburg terminal.

368 | TO ALFRED HARCOURT

Harbert, [Michigan] Nov 27   35

Dear Alfred

I think you will have a large intelligent horselaugh if sometime you compare this final draft of that poem with the first one sent you. It's peculiar how it effloresces; I would be afraid of it if it were not so definitely pentup and inevitable. Frank Lloyd Wright was at a neighbor house (designed by a son of his, Jack Lloyd Wright) and we had a long talk. The first time I've seen him in seven years. His group of young associates at his Wisconsin place Taliesen (he cant call it a school) are working on an evening of marionette production of Rootabaga stories. That last visit was the best of all. Tell Ellen her many thoughtfulnesses linger with me.

Yrs
Carl

PS At regular intervals I get queried when am I going to do an autobiography. Any attempt at it is long years away. And "The People, Yes" may carry about all that would be essential in that usually foolish undertaking that persons style The Story of My Life. . . Two of our does have been taken this week to a big white horned and pronged buck who is affirmative in his attitude toward life. The barn has its walls up and the roof going on today.

369 | TO JOSEPH WARREN BEACH

[Harbert, Michigan]
April 29, 1936

Dear Joe

Of course I understand perfectly that slip of the line o' type man. "Mr. Song-Bug's Sand-Bag" is one version, "Mr. Sand-Bag the Song-Bug" another, of the twists that fellows not in their cups have put on it. . . The People, Yes has undergone an immense efflorescence and much toil and change since you saw it and I believe you will find the main deep drift somewhat different. . . When I have more poems I will bring them around for your once-over, which has never failed to be a proceeding wholesome for my work. Love to you and Dagmar.

Carl

370 | TO ALFRED HARCOURT

[Harbert, Michigan]
June 10 36

Dear Alf

The proofs entire were sent by express last Monday June 8 and are probably in your hands by now. The many inserts had to be made. Those who will say it looks as tho I shovelled in every thing I had might be interested to see that about an equal mass of rejected material failed of the shovel and there was some sort of rudimentary sense of discrimination operating.

I note in Edmund Wilson's book where he is bothered about Lincoln: the Prairie Years and its readers who reject the Herndon Lincoln. Twenty years ago he was bothered by Chicago Poems and wrote a Vanity Fair article on its monstrous lack of form. Still and all I go on reading Wilson just as I go on reading Ben Stollberg tho both of them constantly warn their publics that I have nothing on the ball and my writings should be eschewed being too mushy to chew. A year or two ago when you cleaned the files and passed along the reviews of the Mary Lincoln book, I read some two or three years after it was printed, Stollberg's estimate and appraisal of me. Until then I had no notion he puts me on his index expurgatorius of trash writers.

The enclosures show the doe Felicia who is sure to make the grade for Advanced Registry, also two oink-oinks who will be our sausage and salt pork next winter, and Helga with the flock of kids.

When the page proofs arrive they will get few or no inserts, few changes, and will be here probably only two days.

As ever

Carl

371 | TO ARCHIBALD MACLEISH

[Harbert, Michigan]
June 30 36

Dear Archie

As I reread today a letter and memo from George E Q Johnson (former federal judge, and US Dist Atty who prosecuted and convicted Al Capone) I thought it had some quirks to it that were up your alley. I am enclosing it. Take your time with it, if it interests you, before returning it. The underlying instinct weaves thru some of the present upheaval. If the lawyer in yuh ain't interested try the poet.

Also you should receive in the mails a peculiar poem-photograph showing what can be done in Connecticut muck when the muck is decently coaxed. That is, you should take the picture on its own as something andrew marvel would have looked at twice. It is not propaganda aimed at steering you into the American Delphinium Society.

Today I saw my 17-year-old girl ride her horse out into Lake Michigan and the two of them have a swim together. Day before yesterday my farmer-publisher showed me that "beans always grow contra clockwise", which was new to me. And a few evenings previous I travelled from the Waldorf Circular Bar thru Luchow's to a smoke-filled Committee-on-Literature room with a man of music having a rare capacity for toil and solitude. So just now I have decided to go on living. That was an unforgettable evening, packed with enough said and unsaid to keep me going a good while. May your high sensitivity always have a reciprocal of intestinal fortitude.

Yrs
Carl

Archibald MacLeish told David C. Mearns, of the Library of Congress, that this was "my most precious letter from Carl," adding that he kept it in his copy of The People, Yes. *Edward Steichen, who was breeding delphiniums in Connecticut, had photographed Sandburg with the plant he had named after him.*

372 | TO BENJAMIN CARDOZO

[Harbert, Michigan]
June 30   36

Dear Mr. Cardozo

It is good to have your three books standing alongside each other, and the one first published having an inscription worth treasuring. In an envelope between two of the volumes are clippings from the New York Times of two of your decisions. Six feet away from this booknook the full strength of the 50- and 60-miles-an-hour gales of Lake Michigan roars along sometimes. In the course of the years they will blow the house away. And perhaps your books too. But in many windproof houses elsewhere your writings will stand the test of time and erosion with a fine steel strength.

Harcourt's are to send you in August "The People, Yes" which has some of the chaos and turmoil of our time and of all time in it. Parts of it are superb: the creations of free imagination operating among the people. The rest of it may or may not be a songswept footnote to the stride of democracy in our era. Anyhow I send it to you with salutations and affection.

Faithfully yours,
Carl Sandburg

1936

Some of Associate Justice of the Supreme Court Benjamin Cardozo's books on the Sandburg shelf were The Growth of the Law, The Paradoxes of Legal Science, *and* Law and Literature.

373 | TO HENRY R. LUCE

[Harbert, Michigan]
July 3   36

Dear Harry
  If we had had the lunch, and I had not finished my New York business and headed home for work waiting here, I would have told you that this forthcoming book of mine has in part the answers to some of the points you asked me about in a letter early last year. This book arose partly out of the monstrous efforts at debauching the public mind which have gone on with increased intensity the past three years. I salute you on having had no hand in it. In a time of marvelous chaos your gang has fairly well earned its stereotyped and streamlined announcement "the ablest historians of our time." But too many have luxuriated in the power of their rostrums, petted their passions, wreaked their whims. They think the people lap it up and everything is as it always was. Their conception of the public, the circulation, the audience, does not run with mine as I have presented it in The People, Yes. They can't monkey with the public mind as they do without consequences. To bewilder a public with lies, half lies, texts torn from contexts, and then have that public sober and well-ordered in its processes, is not in the cards. I would like to have heard you talk about the paradox and whimsicality of Fortune, dubbed "the magazine of the plutes", being the first periodical to report comprehensively on the munitions makers, on Berghoff, on other topics not brought up in polite society, so that it has earned a curious reputation as a current historian, as no personal baggage of any peacock or poobah—held in an affection by a large following that reads copies they can't afford to buy. With your expanding power insidiously corrosive forces will try to reach you. They are subtly intricate and work while you sleep. They have

343

a technic of ganging up to get the results they want. You may have to study what Old Man Scripps had in mind in saying, "I don't want to mix with the rich—they corrupt me!". . . And the rest of it maybe and of course much of "the rest of it" tho not all you will get in the book which, as I said before, would be a better book if I could rewrite it fifty years from now, will keep till we eventually have the deferred luncheon. Is it so?

Faithfully yours
Carl Sandburg

374 | TO GEORGE P. WEST

Harbert Mich   Aug 13 35
[Misdated for 1936]

Dear George

It is good to have your letter for the book ranges around so many things we have had long talks about and left in the air; and here and there are pieces that came directly from you, such as the Brandeis-Hughes line, the quote from Older, and others. MacLeish, by the way, was finely helpful. At a time when my reading sensitivity on the thing was blunted, he read the script three times, once out loud, and made three specific suggestions, two of which I saw should be worked out. Your point that you are glad I "poured it all in" and let it go without waiting a year or two for shaping it into more approved form—this comes nice now when I am jaded and making a comeback. Your Marie knows my intentions down to fine fractions: we listen to what the Quakers call "the dayspring of the heart" and then hope to christ the music and the murmurous fall of the syllables will follow. . . And now Steffens goes; and we would have loved years more of him. . . Hoping to see you next winter

As always
Carl

The book referred to was The People, Yes. *The Brandeis-Hughes line is: "Who was the twentieth century lawyer who said of another*

lawyer, 'He has one of the most enlightened minds of the eighteenth century'? and why did fate later put them on the Supreme Court bench?" Lincoln Steffens died on August 9, 1936.

375 | TO PAUL DE KRUIF

[Harbert, Michigan]
Nov 26   36

Dear Paul

Thanks were given today that you and Rhea are alive and are what you are. Your note about The People, Yes is heart warming. The book may be a help across turmoils to get worse before they get better. It was the best memorandum I could file for the present stress.

I saw Alf at his office three days after he had returned from Baltimore. His face was drawn and the marks of pain were there as I had never seen them: he said his nerves were "jumpy" and the sound of a phone bell would lift him from his seat. Ten days later however he looked like his old self: I was amazed at the recovery that was there in the exterior, in the appearance, whatever may be the course of events underneath. I was out at Riverside overnight and the air had a finality of loveliness: Alf always had rich streaks of sentiment underlying his ductile hardness: and these now are deeper than ever: those spinal anesthetics and other administerings were an adventure in suffering such as I have never known and can speak of only softly and distantly. . . His affection for you and thanks to you would come up in his talk every once in a while. . . . . I've tried to figure out a trip up to see you but can't quite make it in the near future. Should you be passing this way the little gang here would enjoy your faces and among other things you would get a kick out of seeing one of the best managed goat herds in this terrain.

As always
Carl

1936

[Harbert, Michigan]
Dec 5   36

Dear Robin Lampson

Thank you for that kindly letter in October. You did a fullsized book and a mansized job in LAUGHTER OUT OF THE GROUND. It is a story that was worth your writing, with its interspersals of authentic poetry. To me it seems so preponderantly a novel that your argument for casting it into the form of a poem with cadences indicated by your linebreaks is not sufficiently valid, or lacks appeal for those who would rather have their novels "straight".

I could point to many instances, such as Elizabeth Roberts' "The Time of Man", or my "Ab. Lincoln: The Prairie Years", of cadenced narrative where the reader gets the cadence without it being indicated by the linebreaks. I am quite sure The People, Yes would have gone to a larger audience had it been cast in a form indicating it had no relation to poetry. The existing prejudices and quirks regarding poetry, the aversion to it in wide circles, has a basis of a certain sort that is justifiable. Part of it connects with the contradictions, quarrels, pallors, pretenses, sicklinesses, snobberies, temperaments, isolations, poverties, of the poets themselves—while the critics in the main inhabit a pathetic lost world. Finally you must understand that there are neglected worthy books in plenty. My shelf of them across the past ten years is a long one: books of intrinsic merit, permanent high values for me: and they didnt get to first base: books in several fields that reached a meager audience while trash for later rubbish bins won best seller peaks. LAUGHTER OUT OF THE GROUND is a solid and worthy performance: my guess is that it will reach slowly a wider audience. Perhaps I will see you when giving my program at Berkeley sometime in January—and go farther on this.

Faithfully yours
Carl Sandburg

1937

Harbert, [Michigan] Dec 30 36

Dear Mart

I hope you go ahead with any plans that listen good to your own head and heart. And if I can help in any way whatever you have only to tell me how and when. On Feb 15 you may have heard I am dated to speak on Founders Day at Knox College—and I hope we can have another good visit then—and that you will watch your sleep and your rest so that in these later years of ours you can keep some of the magnificent vitality you have always had—

Carl

[Harbert, Michigan]
[Circa early 1937]

Dear Gregg Sinclair:

When in Honolulu one afternoon I spent two hours with a Japanese physician, Dr. Tomizo Katsunuma, in taking down his spoken translation from a book in Japanese, the autobiography of a Japanese translator who accompanied Townsend Harris, minister to Japan, on the return of Harris from Tokyo to Washington, at which time this translator had a brief interview with Lincoln. Dr. Katsunuma said that he would send me a copy of this book. I wish you or one of your students could see him and get the title of the book and order a copy, with bill, sent to me. In my Abraham Lincoln: the War Years I am using some of the material from the spoken translation but I should like to have a copy of the book for my library and for possible use of other portions of it. We are sorry your schedules did not permit you to pause a day or two with us while you were crossing America but we will hope for another time.

Faithfully yours
Carl Sandburg

379 | TO FRANK LLOYD WRIGHT

[Harbert, Michigan]
[Circa early 1937]

Dear Frank:

The news that you are out of the worst of it and making a comeback is good to hear, is blessed to hear considering what is in progress under the roofs of the Taliesen Fellowship. Having seen not one face that looked as though it would blackball me I am assuming that I have a foot in the door on a membership. Also I overheard more than half the passwords, having an ear for passwords and high signs. . . With his good letter Masselink sends along those poems of yours which I saw for the first time in your theater building. They have your personal sheen and corpuscles. . . Hoping to stay longer some next time, and that you will be on your feet then—

As ever,
Carl

380 | TO OLIVER R. BARRETT

[Harbert, Michigan]
Feb 22   37

Dear Oliver

Would you tell Bill Kittredge that I am more than half deaf in the right ear and must hold all speaking dates to a minimum but that next season we can try to work out something with the Caxton Club?

One thing I am noticing interferes constantly with headway on the Lincoln book. The mail is heavier than ever and I seem to spend of necessity twice as much time as ten years ago on it. Never have I had so high a proportion of letters from persons who are in economic distress and whose appeal is that the only way out seems to write something and sell it and what they would like to know is how can this be done.

Now hoping to be in next week and exchange the news.

As always

Carl

William Kittredge was the publisher of the Holiday Press. Sand-burg's Lincoln and Whitman Miscellany *was printed by him in 1938.*

381 | TO VIRGIL MARKHAM

[Harbeth, Pennsylvania]
[Circa March, 1937]

My dear Virgil Markham:

Your kind and beautifully thoughtful letter comes to my hands on return from an extended trip. It would give me pleasure to be present at the dinner to your father April 23, but I am under unusual difficulties. Because of a certain status in the work on my 4-volume Abraham Lincoln: the War Years I told the bureau to give me a heavy season this year as I would like a very light season next year when I would be in a stride of work in which I hope to go thru with the completion of a writing job that has now run ten years. Therefore April has been crowded with dates in such a way that even if the date of April 23 were to be cancelled the travel connections would be almost impossible. I might say "possible" instead of "impossible" if it were not that during February I had a hard three week siege with bronchial pneumonia and am under physician's orders to keep clear of the sort of railroad jumps which shorten sleeps, a factor in lowering my resistance and bringing on pneumonia, and no time for outdoor oxygen. I am at Harbeth, Pa. under the auspices of the Harbeth Community Library. Your points have urgency. It may indeed be the last opportunity to do honor to your heroic father. In lieu of personal attendance I would try to send you a message that would convey some of my appreciation of

349

a stalwart figure. Let me know whether you wish this and what the arrangements are, addressing me at Georgia State Woman's College, Valdosta, Ga.

Faithfully yrs
Carl Sandburg

Virgil Markham, son of the poet Edwin Markham, was a teacher and novelist. Sandburg had sent this message to Edwin Markham: "The years have borne down on you while you have been a witness of passing generations. There are lights of hope now somewhat surer than those you wrote of in 'The Man With The Hoe.' Your own light has never flickered down. Others have faded and gone out but you have been steadfast. There are friends and onlookers aware of this. They have only deep affection and high salutations for you in the course to which you have been so true."

382 | TO FRANK MURPHY

[Harbert, Michigan]
March 29, [1937]

Dear Governor Murphy

In these few months past, some of us feel, you have conducted yourself with the austerity and spare utterance of a true Chief Magistrate in a democracy.

The enclosed from the Grand Rapids Press of March 26 gives a fragment of a parallel which I drew between your involvements and those of President Lincoln, laying special stress on how Lincoln would have been bogged and sunk if he had tried to follow the published counsels of either Bennett and the New York Herald or Greeley and the New York Tribune, the two most powerful and widely circulated journals of the time. In Lansing a few years back I went thru the Civil War files of the Detroit Free Press, then venomously opposed to Lincoln and all his works as "illegal and unconstitutional", a "tyrant", a "usurper", an "imbecile", "this foul-mouthed teller of smutty stories", and so on ad lib. It might not be worth mentioning now did not the Free Press daily run its little streamer: "on guard for a century."

You should understand that I can not help drawing these parallels, as I have my feet in two eras, now beginning work on the fourth and final volume of a 4-volume book to be titled "Abraham Lincoln: the War Years", a sequel to the two-volume work titled "Abraham Lincoln: the Prairie Years." Also as an oldtime reporter who covered labor for Milwaukee and Chicago newspapers I know something of the inevitable historic foreground that has ushered in the C.I.O. Anyhow more power to you—and at this Easter time Peace Be to You—

Carl Sandburg

The enclosed clipping from the Grand Rapids paper reported Sandburg, in a talk before the Grand Rapids Teachers' Club at the South High School, praising Michigan Governor Murphy's sympathetic handling of strike negotiations. He had said: "Had he acted otherwise the dead would have been counted in hundreds and the wounded in thousands. History will vindicate his course as one of reason and justice. Few today understand the deep underlying streams in human life that are making history, just as few understood in Lincoln's day. Then, too, Lincoln had to ignore the clamor of gratuitous advisors."

383 | TO MRS. CHARLES J. BEDNAR

Harbert Mich May 28 37

Dear Mrs Bednar

When you come along this way sometime with "Chuck" and the little one, I may be able to show you my reasons, the alibi, for not sending you manuscript for exhibition. In what digging I have done I have not found a piece or a group that would be worth anybody's momentary gaze. If my methods were anything like what people might expect, or could give them a pleasant surprise it might be worth while. Then too there is a kind of monkeywork by a living author in connection with his manuscripts and his foottracks and what he deems his "career" that has no result except to hinder him in getting his best work done. What impressed Mr. J. Addison most of all when he visited Westminster Abbey was that there was "many a monument without a poet and many a poet without a monument." Under "Lombard" in the index to A Lincoln: the Prairie Years you will find an account of Lincoln just before going to Washington in '61 giving Delahay the Lombard College banner presented at Galesburg. "Friday" was Howard Lauer. The Brass Facet was Me Myself & Co. Your other queries I will try to answer when in Galesburg next. And please believe me I have my own memorabilia difficulties in connection with what might be worth saying into a mike for a large multitude June 15. Meantime good luck on the work you are doing with a fine bravery.

Yrs

Carl Sandburg

Juanita (Kelly) Bednar, Lombard 1929, was in charge of the Lombard memorabilia exhibit at the Knox College centenary, June 1937. Mark W. Delahay was the long-time friend of Lincoln, who appointed him judge of the U.S. District Court of Kansas in 1863.

384 | TO ALICE CORBIN HENDERSON

Harbert Mich Sept 1   37

Dear Alice

Hast not yet hadst a look at BROTHERS OF LIGHT but am hoping.

You have been—I can tell by quirks of your letter—adventuring in politics and executive labors—to an extent that you will more readily gather the pages that may yet come to you about Lincoln and his Cabinet. I have now brought him to Nov of '64, 3 vols done and one to go. They usually die about the second vol.

You were missed greatly at the memorial meeting for Harriet. When I see you again I'll give you the main points of my talk, wherein I believe you were one of those for whom I was speaking. Hoping it will not be too long before the next foregathering—

As always

Carl

Harriet Monroe, editor of Poetry, *died on September 26, 1936.*

385 | TO ALFRED HARCOURT

[Harbert, Michigan]
Sept 1 37

Dear Alfred

That bulletin from Johns Hopkins was good to read and I enjoy this latest one that you shot an 84 a few days ago.

The summer has gone too swiftly for me, spending June days at a Chicago Civic Opera House protest meeting over the East Chicago police slayings of strikers, at a Spanish Loyalist medical aid meeting, at a Knox College Centenary, the first two for the sake of self-respect, the last for loyalties not to be thrust aside. A few poems, among them some of the best I've ever done, could not be put off, had to be put down. And yesterday I placed the final touches, insertions and reshapings, on two long chapters (a book of 60,000 words by themselves) bringing Lincoln to the election day of Nov 8 1864. By stubborn ingenuity that laughter section once mentioned to you managed to get included. So I am on the ragged edge and as soon as I have handled some mail long waiting I am going to hike away from this attic.

The Chase book sounds good, is much wanted. Part of it is there in "Primer Lesson" in "Slabs of the Sunburnt West"—also in this piece Miss [Catherine] McCarthy inquires about. Tell her it ran in the Ladies Home Journal. What do we do here? Can you handle it?

Will you show Ellen this enclosed picture and ask her if it isn't as good as a Bach fugue?

As ever
Carl

The protest meeting was for strikers killed in the "Memorial Day massacre" at the Republic Steel Plant in South Chicago, May 30, 1937.

386 | TO HENRY R. LUCE

[Harbert, Michigan]
Sept 4 37

Dear Harry

Why in all your items and stories about personalities and publications do you never have any about the most authentic humorist of the American labor movement and one of its most picturesque figures? I refer to the inimitable and translucent Oscar Ameringer and his weekly The American Guardian of Oklahoma City. His 40,000 to 50,000 circulation goes to at least a quarter million readers and to a large fraction of the farmer-labor movement he has become an outstanding and rather priceless tradition. If I did not believe that you as publisher and editor are more than ordinarily scrupulous about what is newsworthy and currently historical, I would not bother to mention to you that Ameringer is newsworthy and historical and when I find more time for the immediate American scene Ameringer will figure in it. This week I am subscribing to TIME and LIFE for the next two years. With all your faults, some of which I know better than you, and with all your handicaps, more of which you know better than I can possibly know, you are holding pretty nicely to so difficult a course. So many who now pretend to transact a merchandising of news are so peculiarly personal and egregious about it that they have become incidental causes of the progressions of an unrest they fear. The publisher tribe in the main is smug and most often ludicrously unaware of its smugness. Your Williamstown address of Sept 2 is exceptional, quickening, self-searching, sharpshooting. I should much like to read the entire address, if you can send me a copy to keep or to read and return to you. Health and many strengths be yours—

As always
Carl

387 | TO LLOYD LEWIS

[Harbert, Michigan]
Sept 7 37

Dear Lloyd

Don't get my signals mixed. I know you've got a certain happiness in what you are doing. I understand you are not writhing under any yokes. But I can not be entirely free from a measure of writhing about two things. One is that a writer I consider great, picturesque, vital and versatile, should be detached from doing in history and biography what can not be so well done by others while he fills a job that it would be no great loss if someone else did. The second is that if you are to be held to the newspaper field it is a loss that you can't be covering grand chaotic stories where you would write your real heart out and have your stories clipped and reread by thankful readers. That is all. When I'm restless about you it is around those two points.

Yrs
Carl

Lloyd Lewis was drama critic of the Chicago Daily News *from 1930 to 1945, and sports editor from 1936 to 1943.*

388 | TO FRANK MURPHY

[Harbert, Michigan]
Oct 2 37

Dear Governor Murphy

You came to your one great crisis and met it as though you had trained all your life for it. Many you know not of pray for your health and your inner grace and strength—that they may keep.

The above was written as dated shortly after your good letter came, and not long afterward I went down and out from overwork. . . Meeting my old friend Paul De Kruif at an evening party with our publisher Alfred Harcourt a while ago, you would have been interested in the way both of us lighted up about your record on human rights and started a line of talk as tho Michigan is up front with a torch and the complete antithesis of Ontario's Hepburn and Jersey City's Hague. Either of these encumberers of the earth, holding your seat a year ago, would have made a shambles and exulted over it. What was impressive to me, and still is, was the care, precision and brevity of your utterance from one crisis to another: you were on a spot much like Lincoln and handled the crises with the same approach. The words joined with the executive acts make sense and justice and hold good today. Sometime this spring or summer I hope to have a talk with you. If nothing else it might help me put an added shine on some spots of my 4-vol Lincoln of th War Years which, if I have health, will be finished this year.

Incidentally, if you should be riding over your state in this section sometime the family here would be glad, would have joy, out of spreading a dinner for you and then showing you one of the best goat herds in the USA. (Your official milk testers come once a month, stay with us a day, and milk the goats and compare their figures with ours. Our Cloverleaf Carlotta on a ten month test ending in January made the grade for the highest milk production of any living Toggenburg registered in this country.) Also at the De Kruifs' near Holland you would find friends who understand. De Kruif has moved toward the left, has risked his nice connections with the Curtis magazines and felt the chills of misunderstanding, because he has not followed the usual course and become a ready yes-man of interests who would like to use him.

I have tough going in handling some of the opposition to Lincoln. Some of them fought clean, had fine minds, sturdy integrity considering how impossible perfect integrity is in politics. They got involved in procedures of violence and came to overstress what could be permanently accomplished by methods of force. Their judgement and vision, running counter to that of Lincoln, was as sincere as his, though lacking his sense of realities, his guesses which time proved to be correct. Maybe we shall talk sometime about this and the mystery of justice.

These enclosures are just for fun. Sometime we may put on The Higher Vaudeville in your executive mansion. Meantime health and grace be yours—

Carl Sandburg

389 | TO JULIA PETERKIN

Harbert Mich
Jan 13 38

Dear Julia

The ills and toils here that have delayed answer are not worth mentioning alongside of your short note of desolation. There was a pallor and a wistful calm about him on the last visit—it haunted me. And I was haunted too by your talk, the wide range of it, the shelves of unwritten books you hold and how they have come to you because you are first of all a great hearted woman. Your range of love and hate is something vast and when I think about you I often go back to the Chinese saying, "The heart of man was made to be broken." You have compassed so much. Jesus, what these last few years have brought you that is beyond the range or ken of most folk, either city or country. What I know is that your heart is terribly strong. I can not think of anyone more sensitive to suffering, more keen at registering to big or little tragedy as it passes, who at the same time has deep strong roots that will survive, that in the end will actually use the grief for growth. Always, for me, you keep growing, you are deeper and darker and surer than the last time I saw you. Just now I can't write it all, nor ever will, but my hand is in yours now, in depths of faith and friendship—and when heavy work now on hand is over sometime within the year I hope for another of the unforgettable visits with you—

As ever
Carl

1938

[Harbert, Michigan]
Jan 14 38

Dear Miss Lord

It was good to have your New Year's card about our journey-ings ahead this year. It is an adventure. You will make some de-cisions on your own—and I am glad they are in your hands—while I am wondering what the hell my preface will look like when I get around to it. After writing Governor Pierpont and Pierrepont I am finally able to get it correctly as Pierpoint. Shellabarger, the congressman, I am finally definite about. Likewise Preetorius. News-papers, ships and books, the capitalization of Negro, the type and spacing for documents and letters, is left mainly to you. Some chapters I was tempted to have recopied and decided against it because recopying means more errors, at least a few, a certain mini-mum, to again go over. Several incidents repeated (not as many as I had expected) I have deleted. You may catch one or two and in that case have full license to delete whichever is your choice. All chapters bringing the narrative to Jan 1 of '65 will be mailed to you next week—and the final chapters within a week after that, and possibly sooner. I shall try to get on to NY for a final conference with you before the manuscript goes to the printers. May 1938 be kind to you.

Faithfully yours
Carl Sandburg

Isabel Ely Lord did the copy editing of The War Years.

[Harbert, Michigan]
Feb 1 38

Dear Paul

A few days ago I wrote Alf that if my health should hold out the next seven or eight months as it has the past two we would have a finished manuscript of th war years Lincoln and could publish next year. Just now I am somewhat punchdrunk from a concentrated drive that has brought the story on into 1865. You will understand it is only something like this that could have kept me for so long from not answering your grand blizzard letter.

Your drift toward the left, as some would call it, is not a thing happening to you in politics, but is something humanly mystic and emotional and based on intuition: it connects directly with the best and most deeply moving writing you have done, with finalities in your blood for which you would fight and in a crisis be willing to die. Anyhow some tangled passion about humanity, a motive not there in the exploiters and Tories, is part of the reason why more color and song and abrupt eloquence gets into your later writings.

While you are dealing with scientists and experimenters who are handling realities that, like the wild geese and the recurring seasons and the insistent growths of fingernails, will be with us across all the future wars and revolutions, I have some realistic trial-and-error fellows under the same roof. Enclosed is a picture of Cloverleaf Carlotta whose 2,610.0 pounds of milk the past ten months classes her as the largest milk producer of living Toggenburg goats of advanced registry. Paula and Helga and everybody here was amazed that their care and coaxing of her should put her tops. A deceased doe at the New Mexico state agricultural college is the only one having equalled this east shore of Lake Michigan record.

Friday we go in to a consulate luncheon where the Swedish minister decorates me with the Order of the North Star sent from Stockholm by King Gustaf. Considering what I've written about the upper and ruling classes as such I can stand this if the King of Sweden can. No conditions attach. They know I am a Social Democrat, a laborite. . . Feb 8 I start for Texas and the west coast to be gone three weeks. Come along here anytime, you two, whether I'm here or not. Sometime this spring or summer I'm liable to pile two or three days' work into the car and drive up and board with you.

As ever
Carl

1938

92 | TO FRANKLIN D. ROOSEVELT

[Harbert, Michigan]
March 9   38

Dear Mr. President

The matter is only of the slightest importance. I hope by chance you did not see an interview with me which the Denver Post ran in which I was quoted as saying you are "slipping." What I did say was more like the enclosed quotes about you the next day in the Grand Junction Sentinel. No man is going to handle your job across the next ten years (if it is written in the fates that the job shall continue to exist!) without being hawked at from many sides. My respect for Emil Ludwig ran higher on seeing the work he did with you. When I finish my six-volume Lincoln, possibly this year, I may try my hand at a sketch of you. Meantime you may expect me some day at the White House door with a guitar, for an evening of songs and of stories from the hinterlands which may rest you on one hell of a job. You are on a spot where more personal passion, love, and malice concentrate than anywhere else in the U.S.A.

Faithfully yours
Carl Sandburg

In the Grand Junction Sentinel, Sandburg was quoted as saying, "As for Roosevelt, a half-hour with him at the White House last year left a lasting impression of 'a great actor . . . with something more than just acting to it.'" President Roosevelt wrote back, "I am grateful to you for your thoughtful note of March ninth and appreciate the fine sense of justice which prompted you to write as you did. It was a delight to hear from you."

393 | TO GEORGE P. WEST

[Harbert, Michigan]
March 28   38

Dear George

These enclosures are out of the week in which the Wanted Child was written. Send them back when you and Marie have read them: the only other copy went to the "plant breeding clown." Further shipments of these random experiments will not continue till next year. I would not go so far as this if you did not have a face with much the same brooding abstract melancholy as AL [Lincoln] who was Will Shakespeare's Hamlet carried many equations farther with a plus sign for infinity.

Yrs
Carl

"A Wanted Child Is Born" was an unpublished poem. The "plant breeding clown" referred to Edward Steichen.

394 | TO ROBERT FROST

[Harbert, Michigan]
March 28, 1938

Dear Robert

Sorrow here too. Always she was infinitely gracious to me in a way I can never forget. Your grief is deep and beyond any others knowing. Now it is past any of the sharp griefs you have sung.

As ever,
Carl

Robert Frost's wife, Elinor, died March 21, 1938, in Florida, where Frost had been lecturing.

395 | TO LILLA PERRY

[Harbert, Michigan]
April 15   38

Dear Lilla

Enclosed are two of those letters, from those bright ones we both met on the day FDR closed all banks. I had a notion to keep Mary Lou's letter against sometime when the blues were bad. The Gordon Ray Young I shall keep: tell him we shall yet have that visit and the bond that we both once were box car bums still holds.

Tell Mr Metzgar in Smoke and Steel is a Hokusai poem: also that I accept with thanks the Japanese name he puts on me and shall learn how to say and write it. Am sunk here on the Lincoln job with high hopes of finishing it, with no skimping, by next winter. Norman is sheer genius: of that I am more than ever convinced: we shall stand by and pray: it is a rare mind he has: my admiration for it is the keener because he works in regions where I am footless and he has wings. I am not yet over all the vivid impressions of that last visit, the rotunda, your house, the Paramount lot, and so forth etcetera. Blessings on all under your gracious roof—

As always
Carl

Gordon Ray Young had sent some Lincoln material to Sandburg to use with The War Years. *The hokusai poem referred to is "His Own Face Hidden." Judson D. Metzgar, a collector of Japanese prints, and a hokusai enthusiast, met Sandburg through Mrs. Perry, and had written to him in February addressing him as "Dear Katsushika." Metzgar was also a friend of Witter Bynner and Arthur Davison Ficke, whom he knew at the time of the Spectra hoax. Mrs. Perry's son Norman was interested in mathematics.*

396 | TO LLOYD LEWIS

[Harbert, Michigan]
April 22 38

Dear Lloyd

It would be great to have a session with you and Burgess when I get in next midweek. Then too I hope to sit down with you and go over these Lincoln chapters and perhaps work out a few spots where there might be a chance of lessening the monotony. You are calling for a Beethoven treatment of a theme now having too much of Sibelius bleakness and Bach repetition. Maybe it can be done. If it isn't done soon it wont be done at all. It was a hell of a war, so often stupid, monotonous, stale, flat, stinking, hypocritical, heroic, plodding, gorgeous, hayfoot strawfoot, bang bang, the nigger the nigger, freedom, crap, gangrene, peanut politics, pus, grand slogans and lousy catchwords, every phase having its facts and stories, with motives overlapping and intertangled beyond any interpretations that wont stand further clarification and interpretation. Well, Mr. Sibelius Bach will talk it over with Mr. Beethoven and some good will come of it.

As ever
Carlo

397 | TO OLIVER R. BARRETT

[Harbert, Michigan]
April 23 38

Dear Oliver

For the moment I cant lay my hands on that letter to Jas Gordon Bennett, saying Lincoln would appoint him Minister to France, and the matter was to be "shut pan." I used parts of the text of that in a chapter in late 1864. Now I am in '65 and need to be sure of the name of the writer of that letter to Bennett. My belief is it was Bartlett. On this belief I am assuming that Lincoln's telegram of Jan 23 '65 to W. O. Bartlett, Esq. NY: "Please come and see me at once", was probably in reference to th French mission. If I am correct about the name dont bother to answer this. But if the writer was another than a Bartlett please steer me away from such an error. . . . I remember your interest in that odd word "shut pan" and we agreed we had not met it elsewhere ever. Since then I have found one other instance of Lincoln using that Ky [Kentucky] colloquialism. As I recall now it is in the Hay Diary.

As always
Carl

Sandburg was correct about the telegram.

398 | TO ALFRED HARCOURT

[Harbert, Michigan]
June 2 38

Dear Alf

The job travels faster than I had expected. I am now thru with Lee's surrender and th jubilation of April 10. Remains Ap 11, 12,

13, 14—then the blackout and funeral. It looks as tho the first main rough draft will be done by July 4. Weaves, inserts, revisions should be done by Oct 1. If present health holds out your editors will have th script before Jan 1. Have tried for a statement such as you mentioned, on what the work comprises, and the status of the Robert T. Lincoln papers in Washington. Couldnt get going on the former—and somehow have an impression that it is a very restricted circle that gives any thought to the R.T.L. papers in the Lib of Cong. Except for your mention of them as possibly having important material, or a belief existing to that effect, I have not heard them spoken of except by way of idle curiosity or as indifferent source material. They have no slightest flash that will compare with what our friend Hertz the Emmanuel dug up and presented in "The Hidden Lincoln" whereby hangs an unpleasant story too long to tell here. . . You know I think of you oftener than I write. The mail is piled high and for weeks now I have answered only telegrams or the second letter asking what about the first. How goes it with you? With every old affection here

Carl

399 | TO JOHN HERVEY

[Harbert, Michigan]
June 18 38

Dear John

Two of your three points are adopted and revisions made accordingly. About the Hall of Valhalla we will hold a session. I hope to be in sometime next week and go over with you what you have thus far read. It is good to have these comments drawn from your wells of lore and horse sense. Parts of the book have required the strictest sobriety. In this finish the buildings reel and chandeliers dance and the moon is tipsy. Wherefore you must help me walk not too straight a line yet one not too tipsily crooked. Seeing you soon

As ever
Carl

John Hervey had finished reading the last chapter of The War
Years, *and had offered some minor points of criticism. First, he
suggested that if the words "dooryard lilacs" were used in the
opening phrase, it would be termed by nigglers an echo of Whitman. Second, he pointed out that the brown thrush sang from
brush and thickets, not from trees. He also suggested that some
word other than "technic" should be used, because it was a me-
chanical term. As to the Hall of Valhalla, he wrote: "I think the
verbal (or, rather, oral) beauty would be helped by using some
other word for* Hall, *as it is followed so closely by* Valhalla; *which
on that account takes something away from the value of the latter
word in force, while also making something of a clash in sound."*

400 | TO ALFRED HARCOURT

Harbert, [Michigan] June 30, [1938]

Dear Alfred

Have finished now on the last day and the last night. Dr. Leale
has smoothed the drawn face, put coins over the eyes, laid a white
sheet over the body and face, stepped out of the door of the house
to find cold rain falling on his bare head, remembering he left his
hat in his theater seat. He looks at his detachable cuffs bloodsoaked
and decides he will keep them as long as he lives. The 2-page piece
here is to go narrow column italics opening the last day chapter.
The piece on dust is now planned to end the book. Return these. . . .
I am frazzled and punchdrunk but can see the Aftermath chapter
finished by mid-July. . . . The facts are assembled as never before,
never so completely, on the Last Day, yet I believe they shape with
something of the value of a Chekov short story: the Russians will
say this is up their alley. Probably be seeing you this summer.

As ever
Carl

*Dr. Leale was one of the physicians who attended Lincoln when he
was assassinated.*

1938

[Harbert, Michigan]
Thursday [August, 1938]

Dearest

Too much that has to be done, too wide a swing down around to Springfield, so many chores and particularly the one of preparing for the next Tuesday meeting. A ten minute talk with New York yesterday and they insist on five minutes of guitar and song. Blessings on you. Maybe next year you'll let pass so that others can have a shot at the ribbons. And maybe you wont. Whatever you do will be the best for the goat industry. Our prayers for all good luck on the home drive—

Carl

[Harbert, Michigan]
August 20 38

Dear George and Marie

Weeks ago I should have sent word that it was so good to have your letters and it is blessed to have such understanding—or forgiving and shriving friends. The Lincoln book has gone on now into its last chapter—though revisions and inserts of materials found since earlier chapters were written mean much heavy drudgery yet. The hope is to have the manuscript—somewhat over 1,200,000 words in the publishers hands next January and publication next year. Maybe I will get to your house for two or three days while revising or proofreading. The memorandum I did last winter while in California for the book of Steffens' letters is in the vein and color of you two fellows. I wish some reporter had caught what was said at Mills College about to this effect, in a random and casual discussion of Golden Gate poets: "Marie de Welch has probably written a deeper love for the land and people of California than any of them." Anyhow and ennyhoo kiss Marquita for me and keep a corner in your hearts for your remembering and struggling

Carl

PS Elation on these premises on taking 11 Toggenburgs to the Ill. State Fair (2d only to Calif. in goat exhibits at state fairs) and winning several blue ribbons and the Governor's Trophy for the Best Eight Head. The Missus and the daughter Helga have worked hard four years now gathering and breeding and tending what has become a beautiful herd from many angles.

Mariquita West, the daughter of George and Marie, inspired two Sandburg poems, "A Wanted Child Is Born" (unpublished) and "Portrait of a Child in California Settling Down for an Afternoon Nap" (which appeared in Wind Song).

403 | TO LLOYD LEWIS

Harbert, [Michigan] Aug 20 38

Dear Lloyd

It is mighty good to have your letter and I get your drift in every last phrase. Boy, I have studied about that "rise to symphonic proportions" but the fear is on me that if I put down a record of the events and involved issues and motives, as they stand out to my vision and feeling, it will still be too muddy and chaotic, a bloody and murky huggermugger, to have as definite and measurable symphonic value as I would like. If I had not faithfully plodded thru every last piece of material I could lay my hands on that concerns the essential record I would feel guilty. The final six chapters, dealing with March and April '65, have deliberate crescendo and diminuendo effects in the very facts themselves—with possibly running thru the shades and accents of statement the color and music values wanted—but of such a thing no artist can say a word: he can merely be sure that he himself has given all he's got. In the toil and the weariness of the finish it is fine to have a lavish and rich hearted letter such as yours.

As of old
Carlo

404 | TO FRANKLIN D. ROOSEVELT

[Harbert, Michigan]
[August 24, 1938]

Dear Mr. President

Somewhat over two years ago I wrote to you that all the time you keep growing. This still holds. I am with Governor Frank Murphy that it may be necessary to draft you for a third term.

As ever
Carl Sandburg

405 | TO ROY BASLER

Harbert Mich Aug 24 38

Dear Roy Basler

You are thoughtful to send me those poems of yours. I have read them twice and shall read them again. They have something of that sure touch which ran thru your book on "The Lincoln Legend." That book grows on me with time and it is not infrequently that I meet other readers of it who have the same feeling. Out of the ton or two of materials I have groped thru and sifted since I first read that manuscript when you sent it to me, it has changed hardly at all for me as an important, calm, valid commentary. And the North American Review essay is both quickening and comforting to me, quickening because it presents a few subtle phases that had not occurred to me, and comforting because across the 1,200,000 words I have now written I return again and again to the strange vivid spokesman. Don't fail to note the Douglas Freeman reference in his "R E Lee" to the "ponderables" of Lincoln as a factor in the war: it is in key with your own approach . . . Now that Jefferson is going on the new nickel when is someone going to do a commentary on him as pointed and luminous as yours on Lincoln? . . . Great good luck to you. If you should ever come this way by my doorway I would lay off anything at hand for a long talk with you.

Sincerely yours
Carl Sandburg

PS—The final chapter of AL: the War Years is now in the writing and the hope is to make all revisions and have the script in the publisher's hands by Jan and publication probably in Sept of 1939. Am mailing you two articles which indicate some trends in the flow of the book.

406 | TO ALFRED HARCOURT

Harbert [Michigan] Aug 28 38

Dear Alfred

Wilkes Booth could not be polished off as summarily as I believed. I am about half thru the final chapter, having done a more extended miniature biography of our American Judas than any other biographer has ever attempted. Remains now the obsequies and the world's greatest funeral. Also remains about a bushel of notes and fragments classified as "Weave", some of which must be inserted. . . Have been delayed on the main job perhaps two weeks since last April by writing and revising the enclosed long piece which is either a poem or a pamphlet or both. . . How goes your health? How moves the summer for you?. . . Paula and Helga took eleven goats to the Ill State Fair, won the Governor's Trophy for the Best Eight Head, one blue ribbon, four seconds, one third, one fourth. This week they are showing at the Ohio State Fair. They have done some keen phenomenal work in assembling and breeding this herd in so few years. . . And again how moves the summer for you?

As ever

Carl

407 | TO FRANK MURPHY

Harbert Michigan Sept 10 38

Dear Governor Murphy

This is only to say that you are always in mind here. The pressure of finishing the Lincoln book—probably this fall—has me hoarding time. Otherwise I would have sought you and asked what could be done in the fall campaign. I belong to no party but all who know me are well aware that I am a New Dealer, that I agree with you it may be necessary to draft Roosevelt for a third term, that I rate you in any one of a number of contingencies as presidential timber, that I argue you were in the Lincolnian tradition in your handling of the sit-down strike crises. If there should be anything specifically that I could do during this fall campaign you should let me know. I have not had time to skirmish around and really get at what is doing, tho I do know Toy is lining up some pretty clean workers and Fitzgerald is striking dirty bargains with gamblers— and your Detroit speech Sept 5 had some straightspoken doctrine that fits you like the feathers on a duck.

Yrs
Carl Sandburg

408 | TO FRANKLIN D. ROOSEVELT

Harbert, Mich. Sept. 21, 38.

Dear Mr. President

Shortly after Lincoln's assassination, you may be interested to know, one J. W. Phelps wrote to Senator Charles Sumner that in his opinion it was Lincoln's carelessness about his personal guards that resulted in the assassin's success. That point is minor. But in connection with it Phelps wrote of Lincoln:

> "His goodness, benevolence, and magnanimity were as much out of place at the head of a people so truculently cunning as we are, as would be a human head upon a snake's body."

Of course, as a verbal cartoon and metaphor it was not true and correct, but for grand vehemence in the American style, it has something surpassing Gen. William Tecumseh Sherman five weeks later: "Washington is as corrupt as Hell, made so by the looseness and extravagance of the war. I will avoid it as a pest house."

So you see there have been other vehement times in this country.

Yours as always
Carl Sandburg

1938

The President replied, "To paraphrase the Old Testament we might say: There were giants (of invective) on the earth in those days."

[Harbert, Michigan]
Sept. 21 38

Dear Douglas Freeman

You don't have to be modest—yet it is inconceivable that you could be anything but humble—after that long adventure in writing that book. And if I had not done considerable collateral reading I could not be so sure of the portrait you achieve. And with but few reservations I accept your portrait. And those reservations are in a realm where no one can prove anything. Lee was not a Union man— and he was. Lincoln didn't love the South—and he did. The paradoxes are terrific. . . Much of that war runs into the imponderable and the inarticulate. . . From the way you delineate Lee as an executive I would judge you handle men on your staff much as my old chief Henry Justin Smith on the Chicago Daily News. So sometime you may expect I shall try to avail myself of your invitation to see some of the shrines around Richmond under your guidance. I am now doing the last chapter of the only American biography equalling yours in length (though not footnoted with the fine fidelity that goes with yours) so perhaps we should meet as the only two biographers in the Western Hemisphere who have written a million-word-portrait. . . . I have given that final anecdote of your book to a score or more of audiences: always it is impressive—because R. E. Lee said it: it "goes over" because of what that name connotes North and South. . . You will be interested in various adventures of your book which I have seen.

Yours with more than esteem
Carl Sandburg

This got mislaid last fall and now being found perhaps should go on to you.

Harbert, [Michigan] Sept 22   38

Dear Alfred

They are all ready to see you when you can come. You have enough of real farmer streak to you so you will be interested in what Paula and Helga are doing here. They are sharks at genetics. Paula among the goats and kids is like her brother amid the delphiniums. It is genetics and much else.

And we should be having a long talk again. Sometimes I look at this damned vast manuscript and it seems just a memorandum I made for my own use in connection with a long adventure of reading, study and thought aimed at reaching into what actually went on in one terrific crisis—with occasional interpolations of meditations, sometimes musical, having to do with any and all human times. There are for instance a thousand vivid parallels for the present hour in Czechoslovakia, the Sudetenland, Europe in general. . . . There are spots not easy going for the reader. But the war was often monotonous and intricate—and for the poor reader who won't go along with me on that it will be just too bad for that reader. He will just have to let the book alone and stay ignorant: there are moments when I don't give a dam whether he turns the page—which isn't saying I haven't tried to be lucid and cogent and making use of all gags and "good theater" available. . . It will be good to see you in this attic again.

Yrs
Carl

[Harbert, Michigan]
Sept 24   38

Dear Lloyd

On a careful rereading of your letter of last month I get its drift more definitely. And since that letter I have come to the end of the first main rough draft. And the finish is symphonic: life made it so. But there are periods and passages of that war which must be touched on and they are involved or cheap or monotonous yet they belong: added years of writing and thought and craft could not make them any less involved, cheap, monotonous. And as I am traveling along now on revisions nothing at all can be done with some of these passages. This does not mean that I am not re-writing hundreds of sentences, scores of paragraphs, nor that I don't give myself a big horselaugh over things I once wrote that now must be wrecked and reorganized. And away and farther back where you and I might differ it would be basically maybe some personal preference, you taking the Beethoven and Berlioz end and me plopping for Bach and Sibelius. I can only go to the dumb primitive iterations and repetitions of the two latter for some of the passages that must stand: and maybe this is a cheap defense and I am a culprit, lack knowhow. Also there is a matter of timing we shall talk about: you can live with manuscripts and materials till they have an unfair domination with bad results. . . Always health and great luck to you—hoping to see you soon—

Carl

412 | TO ADDA GEORGE

[Harbert, Michigan]
March 15, 1939

Dear Adda George:

Your letter came when I was away on a long Eastern trip or I would have answered sooner. Sometime when in Galesburg I hope to have a good visit with you and we can decide then what lines it might be worthwhile to have written out for framing in the old building where for one year I rang the bell.

There have been a good many years of my life when I was sure I did not ring the bell. One year at Lombard I did have the satisfaction of knowing I rang the bell! . . . The spirit of your letter is deeply appreciated.

Faithfully yours,
Carl Sandburg

1939

Mrs. Adda George later became the moving spirit behind the restoration of the Carl Sandburg Birthplace, at 331 East Third Street, in Galesburg, Illinois.

413 | TO HELGA SANDBURG

[Harbert, Michigan]
Sunday night Oct 15   39

Dearest Swipes

The letters from you are lovely to have and each one is passed around and sometimes it is like the light of your face and voice are in the room. Running thru a bale of old belongings today I came across a book of dandy French comic drawings with a good deal of french text interspersed, the which will be sent along to you soon. Also will go along a study of french poets which may have some pages that interest you. All reports as to Jon are good. Jon is coming strong, in color and grace and disposition. I have taken him walking now every day lately. When he comes down or goes up a stairs his legs and paws fumble and he WADDLES and W A G G L E S and can't hide the fact that he's just a pup. I am glad you picked Jon. Martha was saying today it looks as tho Jon is going to rate as the best dog we have ever had. The time when I am most homesick for you to be here is when I look at the horses   the hosses   the fellows that know your language like nobody else that talks to them. Take care of yourself take keer uv yussef—and maybe about a month from now we can send you the 4-vol Lincoln just to show you that it did get done. Take care of yourself   take keer uv yussef.   Loads of love   colossal cargoes of affection   Swipes   you divvil dovel deevil baby kiddo keeddo   hows about a teeny weeny kiss?   good-a-bye   and dont take anything that's nailed down around the state capitol   much luv
Dad

Helga was a student at Michigan State College, at East Lansing. Jon was her new dog, a great Dane. Martha Moorman was the housekeeper.

[Harbert, Michigan]
Tuesday [October 17, 1939]

well it seems that about the same time I was writing to you about the horses you were writing to me about them and our letters passed each other about half way somewhere

the poem you send is the registration of a mood and a deep feeling it reminds me of certain chinese poems (as translated) which I will show you sometime it is intensely personal and you can't be sure about an intensely personal piece of that kind until you have had it by you for a year or two go ahead and feel free to let yourself go at any time like that in response to a deep feeling or a mood

homesick is a queer word as we use it sometimes when what we really mean is that we would like to be in two places at the same time and so we are trying to live more of life than can be lived in one place at a certain time several times this week I have felt sorry for myself and then changed to laughing at myself because I would like to stay home and go to east lansing next week when the orders are that I must go to Chicago on a dozen errands and on october 27 be in New York to receive a medal of the Roosevelt Memorial Association

I would like next week to be in four places at once 1) here at home 2) there at east lansing with you 3) in chicago 4) in new york so you would like to ride a horse recite french study english and do several other things all at once just like your mother and uncle ed they can never be in enough places at one time to get done and see and hear the things moving them and calling them many bushels of love much luv

Daddy

Helga had written her father on October 15, and their letters crossed.

415 | TO RALPH INGERSOLL

[Harbert, Michigan]
Nov 20   39

Dear Mr. Ingersoll

The rush was too heavy in New York for me to get in touch with you. I have read your outline for the newspaper and feel it the ablest constructive criticism that has been made of the modern newspaper. If you keep it adless, on principle, and show that the thing can be done, that will be something incalculable and colossal. I worked four years on Scripps' Day Book in Chicago and know some of the difficulties, involvements, dangers, as well as grand possibilities in such a paper. On some visit to New York this winter I hope we connect for a session. I haven't much to pass on to you but some of it may be very serviceable—and as I gather your drift now you are worth the time.

Sincerely
Carl Sandburg

Ralph Ingersoll was planning PM, *the adless New York daily, which recalled to Sandburg his own work on the adless newspaper* The Day Book.

416 | TO HELGA SANDBURG

[Harbert, Michigan]
[Fall, 1939]

Darling Swipes

it was so good to see and hear you yesterday   to feel a fine sincerity you have about your studies and what you are now doing and to know that you keep growing in mind and spirit   and to remember the little incident you told of Nancy [Helga's horse] and you

if you should get high excellent markings in chemistry and lose your infinitely fine feeling about Nancy that would be not so easy to look at you and Nancy are a kind of poem to me and your voice has music for me so take care of yourself and build slow but sure

   and keep on with that beautiful faith you have in your mother who is very rare and worth treasuring I sign here wid lub and wiv luv and with love

Daddy

417 | TO WALTER MILLIS

[Harbert, Michigan]
Nov 20 39

Dear Walter Millis
   At Olivet College Nov 13 they made a stenographic report of an informal, impromptu talk I made and the record arriving today says: "A book that is going to stand as a sort of classic in American history is Walter Millis' 'The Marshall Spirit.' It is the only book that has a good, straightforward, compact, reliable account of that imperialistic war in which this country indulged in 1898." The press of other matters long ago prevented my sending you a note about what a valuable book it is. I am hoping to reread it sometime and do a commentary based on your book and on the events and phantoms in my mind as a private in Co. C, 6th Ill. Vols. landing at Guanica, Porto Rico in July of '98. Whether or not I get to this piece of writing I hope we meet over something like beer and wiener schnitzel in New York and have a long talk about realities and shadows.

Sincerely yours
Carl Sandburg

P.S. "Marshall" for "martial" above is true phonography, recording the sound of the syllables and many reporters have gone farther and done worse.

1939

[Harbert, Michigan]
November 27, 1939

Dear Bill White:

It is good to have your note about the Lincoln book. I like to think of it being out there in your house where the Lincoln tradition has had such rare loyalty. By a number of signs (Lloyd Lewis and I were talking about it) some of us know that you are lately doing some of the best work of your life. Often you have a Lincoln manner of saying terrible things so gently that the reader goes back to make sure. That holds for the New York Times Thanksgiving piece. . . . There is much to talk over with you sometime when I drop off at Emporia. My shelf of your books is fairly complete, lacking perhaps a few baccalaureate addresses and a container that would assemble a number of articles. . . To you and Mrs. White, whom Vic Murdock smoothly refers to as "Sally", affectionate good wishes—

Faithfully yours,
Carl Sandburg

[Harbert, Michigan]
Dec 3 39

Dear Mr. Frankfurter

Below are the verse lines which you mentioned should be forwarded to you. It was very good, at long last, to see in reality that you have neither the cloven hooves of a demon nor the immeasurable wings of an immaculate angel—and that you proved enough of a contrast, for instance, to the immitigable Key Pittman for me to hope to see you again.

Sincerely
Carl Sandburg

1939

We live in company houses.
The company runs the schools.
We're workin' for the company
'Cording to the company's rules.
We all drink company water.
We all burn company light.
And the company's preachers teach us
What the company thinks is right.

Key Pittman was chairman of the Senate Committee on Foreign Relations.

420 | TO ALLAN NEVINS

[Harbert, Michigan]
Dec 16   39

Dear Allan Nevins
You were more than kind and you were something beyond obedient to lavish impulses in that sweeping review of the War Years. You wrote as an old friend but also as an ancient Anglo-Saxon bill-of-rights man who gathered with me the immensity of Lincoln as a spokesman. And then away back you were a Camp Point prairie boy, harboring now in your blood some of the instincts of that basic loyalist legion that never forsook Lincoln. You could have easily assessed a hundred serious minor errors against the book but instead you gave a vast approval to the major and driving passion that swept through it. So by the way you write you deepen my own deep faith in the country and our people—and you are firstly a man and secondarily a historian—and the matter is as involved as the play of Hamlet or the Gettysburg speech—and I give you salutation as between friends and two Illinois prairie boys.

Faithfully yours
Carl Sandburg

421 | TO THOMAS MANN

[Harbert, Michigan]
Dec 26 39

Dear Mr. Mann

If the use of my name can in any way be of use to an association
of writers exiled from the Germany of the present and the immediate past, you are more than welcome to it in your German American
Writers group. Should any regime similar to the one prevailing in
Germany now by any fate attain the power in this country I do not
doubt my choice would have to be that of death or exile—wherefore I am not lacking in emotions of kinship with your members
even though I have not known the thorns and the bitter drink
some of you have had to take.

Sincerely yours
Carl Sandburg

422 | TO EDWARD STEICHEN

[Harbert, Michigan]
Dec 28 39

Dear Ed

Of these enclosures one is by an old friend of yours [Alfred
Stieglitz]. I had been drifting away from him but with this he pulls
me toward him again. I dont know why I feel good over these two
old birds performing like this. I am sure they are more right than
Chamberlain, Churchill, and Daladier. . . . And one little thing I
am sure of about the whole goddam chaotic huggermugger—they
wont straighten out that map of Europe and they wont have a basis for
permanent peace, one or two generations of peace, until there has
been a long war and misery and destruction lasting many years—and
even at that the end may be compromises with no finality, no assurances. . . . Well whatever it was I started to say we will carry it on
sometime in January when I hope to see your good face again

Yrs
Carl

1940

[Harbert, Michigan]
[Circa 1940]

Dear Robert Hunter:

Of course I remember you. Two of your books are still on my library shelves, and I have clips of forty of your 1908 feuilletons. Steichen has lost his copy of your SOCIALISTS AT WORK, bemoaned to me that it was the only record he had of some of his photographs of that period. So I am going to send him my copy and trust to an old-book dealer to find one for me. What days those were! In what a smoke mist now we look back at them! The Missus here, whom you may recall is Steichen's sister, joins in all good wishes to you. Thank you for so lovely a letter as you send. And I shall hope that we meet sometime for a visit and talk.

Sincerely yours,
Carl Sandburg

Robert Hunter was a wealthy Socialist who had contributed articles to the Chicago Daily Socialist Review *in 1910.*

[Harbert, Michigan]
[Circa 1940]

Dear Stewart:

After the Doctor of Laws at Rollins College in February came the Diploma at Lincoln Memorial and Doctor of Letters at New York University, Lafayette, Wesleyan, Yale, Harvard. The NYU citation was printed in the NY Times for June 6. The one at Harvard read: "Poet and reporter seeking the rhythms of America, lately Washington correspondent of the Lincoln Administration, resulting in an epic that fortifies the national faith." For further data I would have to make an afternoon's search and then perhaps find nothing much. I wrote my Lincoln book with the hope it might find general readers over the whole country—and no particular group. Therefore when the academies and seats of learning wished to definitely recognize it as worthy service I was pleased to meet them more than half way, at Harvard telling them at the alumni dinner, "When your invitation came last winter I said to myself, as I did twelve years ago when asked to read a Phi Beta Kappa poem: 'Harvard has more of a reputation to lose than I have, so I'll go.' "

As always,
Carl

Stewart McClelland was president of Lincoln Memorial University in Harrogate, Tennessee, from 1932 to 1947. Sandburg received the Diploma of Honor from LMU June 2, 1940.

425 | TO RICHARD S. WEST, JR.

[Harbert, Michigan]
[Circa 1940]

Dear Mr. West:

Thank you for so kindly and thoughtful—and concretely helpful—a letter. Forthwith your recommendation is adopted. I was guided by Mr. [Frederick] Meserve, who is hardly ever incorrect in data. This is the first instance of such mistaken identity in my book—and there are mitigating circumstances. The true D.D. Porter's photograph presents the very sober, able and serious officer while the one used in my book seemed to convey a definite glint of the mirthful and prankish D.D., even though it is a brother and not D.D. From week to week in the years I worked on my book I checked carefully (as I believed) on the NY Times and Herald-Tribune book review supplements on all current issues of biography and history. There must have been a few weeks when I was slack about this—or I would not have been content to omit reading a fresh and recent work on David Dixon Porter. I had affection for him. I am sure Lincoln at times found relaxation in the gayeties and follies of D.D. I am still interested in Porter—and in biography as such—and have ordered your book. That your letter is not lacking in authentic mirth is one good sign for D.D. would require understanding of man, the laughing animal. When at a later time I shall list the errors which have been corrected in THE WAR YEARS—and they are fewer, major and minor, than I had expected—I shall give you my salutations on this one. Your metaphor is correct that the nurses brought home to the lady "the wrong baby". I find I have not even a slight satisfaction in rejoining that the right baby was a full and legitimate brother of the wrong one. Even though they had the same mother it is no way to do. I suppose I ramble on about this matter because of the lighted fellowship of your letter and because we have had a common experience of trying to write the best book we knew how, each about a man who knew danger and throve on laughter.

Faithfully yours,
Carl Sandburg

426 | TO ALEXANDER KING

Executed at Paw Paw Patch and
Chikaming Goat Farm [Harbert, Michigan]
6 January 1940 Anno Domini

LETTER AND CERTIFICATE

Dear Alexander King:

On hearing the circumstances relating to your exclusion from the Farragut Club by the lone blackball of Oliver Herford, I immediately summoned the Supreme Council of the organization which I founded and have maintained for the past decade, viz and namely: The North American Paw Paw Growers Association of which I am President—and wherein, upon my so designating an emergency to exist, I may solely and individually serve as the Supreme Council. The hereinbefore named Supreme Council has taken action upon your case with the result that you are definitely elected a member of the General Executive Board of the North American Paw Paw Growers Association. Inasmuch as one of the constituent conditions of the Association requires that membership of the General Board must at all times outnumber that of the rank and file, you will thereby understand that this is the most notable instance in the

Western Hemisphere of the rank and file of the organization not being thwarted and frustrated by the will of a minority. As you participate in future sessions we trust you will regard the dignity and authority of your new position with commensurate importance. With unspeakable salutations and the elaborately wrought sign manual of the indigenous paw paw which is yet to come into its own, I relieve you of the shadow of the horsetile Farragut Club and welcome you to the horsepitality of a bonded Association whose footprints are certain to echo down the corridors of time and life and fortune.

(signed): Carl Sandburg

Alexander King, artist and writer, who helped Sandburg find a Signal Corps photograph for The War Years, *had been blackballed from the Farragut Club, which Sandburg had been invited to join by Oliver Herford. Frank Crowninshield, however, explained that the only member of the Farragut Club was Herford.*

427 | TO WILLIAM TOWNSEND

[Harbert, Michigan]
Jan 8 40

Dear Bill

The enclosed sheet can be cut and tipped in your Vol I—and when sometime I am again in Lexington, as I shall be if I live, I can criss-cross the other volumes howsoever you wish. You will report to me then of your progress on Cash Clay's portrait. You may hunt out that Chicago-saloon-with-proud-brass-spittoons photograph which I hope to return to Oliver Barrett. And if the weather is right we will walk past that statue of J Morgan on a horse transsexed by the sculptor. Soberly and strictly, those long talks we had at various periods were a help perhaps beyond what you realize and I shall always be grateful that time and your inclinations gave us those sessions.

As ever
Carl

1940

[Harbert, Michigan]
Jan 11   40

Darlin Swipes

the encyclopedia is going to you right off   they are getting
ready to pack it and see that it is in your hands soon since you seem
to be of a mind it should be there SOON if not SOONER   dont try to
read it thru

but if you should try to then start at Z with Zebra and Zizzy
and work backward till you come to Adam and Asia   your letters
you should know are often read more than once and not for hidden
meanings but for the breath and the heartbeats they carry

yrs
Daddy

[Harbert, Michigan]
Jan 20   40

Dear Emil

Your letter arrived and I have read it slowly twice and enjoyed
the breath of it and the lights of your face when you wrote it. If I
should live on into the seventies I would hope to have this fine
human light that you carry. . . Not having your address when The
War Years was published, and being hard driven with many details, I did not get to send you a set. But next week in New York I
shall see that one goes to you. Several chapters at recurring intervals
you will find charming. And I am one of the few men on earth
who knows why. These chapters deal with a frenzy and desperation
that wore Old Abe as they wore Mayor Seidel: they deal with Office
Seekers, the Uses of Patronage—and I am sure I described them
better than otherwise had I not been your secretary in the outer
office as they swarmed in. I treasure your letter as do the Missus and
the girls, all sending you affectionate good wishes—

Carl

1940

Emil Seidel, the early Socialist mayor of Milwaukee, had received a wire from Sandburg on his seventy-fifth birthday, and had written to him, "Comrade: As the years pile up and perspectives lengthen, one begins to see the wonderful patterns life weaves into the social fabric. No one is too small to count. Altogether, it makes the picture of human progress."

430 | TO HELGA SANDBURG

[Harbert, Michigan]
[February, 1940]

Dearest Swipes

here it is wednesday night and mother has just gone for the train that takes her to massachussetts and uncle ed and leaves this place quite lonesome with its most important cog gone but she will be back in four or five days having had a much needed vacation to prepare her for the wild and tumultuous february at the chikaming barns how goes it? how about you? margaret comes along while I am writing this and both of us sends you idle loving thoughts along with our belief that you go on growing in inner grace all the time

Dad

431 | TO HELGA SANDBURG

[Harbert, Michigan]
March 7 40

Darling Swipes

It seems a month tho it was only about a week ago I last saw your gleaming face in the bus window heading for East Mary Mayo. The new lot of kids had their first run out in the sun today. Jake said they hesitated and he had to shove them out the little door: then they did much fancy leaping. This enclosure will show you that some people think Picasso is just a loose nut. I know some of these people: they are sincere and earnest and well meaning and they do truly believe that much of the modern movement in art is away from sanity. However some quite sober and admittedly sane critics have made the point that art originates with EXCESS. And most of those who plead for SANITY in art are afraid of the excess, the near madness, of the creative human spirit. Well, you get enough of this maybe. Or maybe we will talk about it for hours sometime soon.

Not yet has The NY TIMES shown up around these here premises and if you dont see that it begins coming there will be drastic measures, a blitzkrieg and maledictions visited on you. Take care of yourself.

Here always love
Daddy

432 | TO KARL DETZER

[Harbert, Michigan]
April 8   40

Brother Detzer

Harcourt writes you have done a fine "study" which as a little book may go to many schools and colleges. As between two Wolverines and two a lot else, I knew from the first you wouldnt do me wrong. And as I told you, if I am keenly aware I would have one hell of a time doing an autobiography, then too I know vividly what difficulties you had to overcome in a short piece. We should be meeting again sometime as members of some mystic order that aint got a name yet. Maybe it will come if and when the war ends in our lifetimes.

Yours
Carl Sandburg

Karl Detzer, an editor of The Reader's Digest, *wrote an article that grew into a brief 1941 biography.*

433 | TO HENRY HORNER

[Harbert, Michigan]
May 5 40

Dear Henry

It is good to have your letter. Old friends of ours to whom I showed it, enjoyed it. You have had hard trials. You have had subtle malice poured on you. And there are old friends who love you the more deeply because amid heavy ordeals you have kept your patience and humor. I shall let any and all of my petty affairs go by the board in order to be present at the ceremonial of presenting your library to the State. I have found several more items which belong and believe I shall eventually send on every last one. Just now I am hard driven by many chores that have followed in the wake of the WAR YEARS publication. You probably know very well that I never expected such a lavish reception as the book has met. From the first you were so kindly. Do you remember when you used to knock down that collapsible desk into a bed and spread sheets and fix pillow cases and then get sandwiches and beer for a vagabond writer in that library room of yours on Madison Park? The Missus here and the rather lovely daughters join me in affectionate good wishes.

Faithfully yours
Carl

Announcement of the donation of the Horner collection of Lincolniana to the State of Illinois was made on April 24, 1940. The formal dedication at the Illinois State Historical Library was on February 12, 1941. Sandburg was one of the speakers.

434 | TO ALFRED HARCOURT

[Harbert, Michigan]
Aug 20 40

Dear Alfred

Your good letter came just as I was starting for a roundup of Spanish War comrades at Galesburg, the only real reunion as to numbers and spirit that we have had in thirty years and probably the last we shall ever hold. Most of them are the real stuff and having had little fear of death or hardship will take old age and decrepitude without whimpering. After the July 12 date at Iowa U I began the first real vacation—not a date ahead—and to hell with letters and telegrams trying to use my time and keep me from doing what I want to do—which isn't definitely resolved at all yet— and may be months getting resolved—during which months I am going to see closeup many various layers of humanity in various locales. Shall hope to be seeing you in September—

As always
Carl

435 | TO CHARLES A. BEARD

[Harbert, Michigan]
Aug 24   40

Dear Mr. Beard

Long ago, months ago, I should have written to thank you for the way you wrote about my Lincoln war years book. On its publication I read your Rise of American Civilization carefully, tearing out pages 1-122 of Vol II and rereading them perhaps five times while writing The War Years, often having that sheaf of pages in my traveling bag. You and Mary Beard had no other reader who so thoroughly dug thru those pages. So your approval of my work when it came was one of the endorsements I was glad to have.

Faithfully yours,
Carl Sandburg

436 | TO ALFRED HARCOURT

[Harbert, Michigan]
Nov. 9, 1940

Dear Alfred:

Had to leave sooner than intended because of ground I wanted to cover that kept haunting me. Visited New Masses office, lunched

with five of the staff, visited Amalgamated Clothing Workers headquarters, arriving at Bill Leiserson's in Washington that Saturday
night 8 o'clock and we talked till 2 in the morning, having an
hour with FDR Sunday afternoon, three days of talks with old
friends in all camps, plane to Pittsburg and talks with CIO men,
then immersal in the Chicago turmoils. Will tell you of interesting
aftermath of broadcast when I see you. Have resigned from Council
for Democracy directors board, tho shall cooperate with them. Shall
have more than the chrysalis of an idea to lay before you when
next arriving. Certainly would like to hear Grace's concert the 17th
but if I can not make it I will be along by the first week in December. Enclosed is script of broadcast: if Kitty [McCarthy] will make
five or six copies I would use them. A flock of telegraph and mail
requests have come, from old friends, for a copy. The freegoing
independent voters set up a rather nice record to look at in Michigan, Illinois, Wisconsin. Shall be seeing you—and may heaven and
luck stars be with you—

Carl

437 | TO FRANKLIN D. ROOSEVELT

[Harbert, Michigan]
Nov. 9 40

Dear Mr. President

Enclosed is the script of the speech that closed the 1940 campaign.

The quotes in it are damned keen, vivid and human.

You might read these quotes sometime in a dark hour when
you are under compulsion to make a decision, not between right
and wrong, but when your course must be for the lesser of two
wrongs.

As always
Carl Sandburg

*After making comparisons to Lincoln's second term in this speech,
Sandburg said, "And for some of us, that goes, in the main, in the
present hour of national fate, for Franklin Delano Roosevelt."*

1940

[Harbert, Michigan]
December 2, 1940

Dear Frank:

Emerson arriving at the gate of heaven had from St. Peter the reluctant invitation: "You can come in and look around, Ralph Waldo, but I doubt whether it will meet with your approval." File this.

It was good to have your letter mentioning that maybe we should go on with our anthology of callers at the gate of heaven. I have laid by several items that can go in—and I hope to be in Austin sometime this winter or spring when perhaps we can make inventory. A few from the portal to hell should be included. Hitler now, Ben Butler earlier, possibly Benedict Arnold and Judas Iscariot in their time, arriving at the ticket-window to hades, heard the Head Demon called for and what Beelzebub had to say to each was: "Go away and start a little hell of your own." Also add gate of heaven items: Eight Nazi aviators showed up. St. Pete looked at a memo and said, "Two of you can come in. The Berlin D.N.B. (official Nazi news bureau) reported only two of you killed today. Other six will have to go below."

Affectionate regards as always,
Carl

[Harbert, Michigan]
December 2, 1940

Dear Sinclair:

The quote you refer to about the wooden shoe going up and the polished boot coming down the stairway of time first came to my attention in some essay or story of Jack London's. Since then, which was quite likely thirty years ago, I have met several variants of it. Where Jack London got it he did not indicate though I recall distinctly he used it as a quotation without giving his source. From there on it becomes a Ph.D. dissertation and research so far as I am concerned. You probably saw the Jack London version back there shortly after The Jungle.

Blessings on you and health and luck—

Sandburg

Upton Sinclair sought the source of: "The stairway of time ever echoes with the wooden shoe going up and the polished boot coming down."

440 | TO FRANKLIN D. ROOSEVELT

[Harbert, Michigan]
Dec 7   40

Dear Mr. President

Quite a flock of letters came to me after that November 4 broadcast—and a few letters and two telegrams curse me as a betrayer—but most of them carry a deep love for you—a love joined with faith and trust. In these hours of ordeal you command loyalties that no one else could. I am glad you are cunning—as Lincoln and Jackson were cunning. I am glad you have had suffering and exquisite pain such as few men have known. I am glad you have had preparations for the awful role you now fill. Two little notes before me refer to "the Greatheart in the White House." And I have met several who voted against you who are saying they feel safer that you are known and proved in such degree that they are glad you are still at the helm. With all good wishes—and deep prayers—

Carl Sandburg

P.S.—Please take no time to send any reply to this.

President Roosevelt had written to him, "I have not had a chance since the election to tell you really and truly how much that broadcast of yours closing the 1940 campaign meant to me."

1940

[Harbert, Michigan]
[Circa December 14, 1940]

Dear Mr. Wanger:

Bill Benton has sent me a copy of your letter to him of Dec 5, about your interest in making a picture about John C. Fremont, and my possibly helping. And I am now writing you regarding certain points so that you may have them direct, for whatever the results may be eventually. There are producers with whom I would not work "for all the oil in Texas"—and they are a majority—and you are in the meager minority. For 20 years I have lived rather actively with Fremont. When in my Chicago Daily News Note Book some 11 years ago I reviewed Nevins' life of Fremont, I wrote that it was one of the most dramatic lives America had ever seen, having the compass of a great novel, the facts surpassing fiction in elevations and downfalls, in vivid crises where at times dramatists couldn't invent better lines to come from the mouths, in the terrific backgrounds where the heroized John C. and his Jessie moved as in a dream and didn't sense the realities, going from nothing to international fame, ten millions in gold and land, high military authority, then by grades to a New York hall bedroom, finally looking back on it all from the utter silences of Arizona as territorial governor. The perfect monogamist—crazy over horses—immersed in money with no money sense—vain of his writings though he couldn't write—money honest and circled by swindlers as chosen aids—playing pool with Henry Ward Beecher while they belabored the prize dunce A. Lincoln—a vacuum where God had meant to put a sense of humor but went away and forgot about it.

One reason I am willing to consider working on a Fremont picture, aside from its personal appeal, is that during the time we worked on it, we could talk over the field of a Lincoln picture. I think I know why the Rockett film, the Griffith, the Sherwood-Massey failed to go over. It might be that I could lay before you a number of Lincoln scenes that would have their point for the crises that lie ahead the next few years. We would have no understanding at all that there is to be a Lincoln picture. Yet it might be that with a few long discussions, covering a thousand possible angles, we would arrive at a Lincoln story that would become a classic. My own approach to a Lincoln book has always been slow and tentative. Perhaps I mean that you and I could make some reconnaissance flights—afterward deciding whether to attack.

On Fremont I would not want to write the script. As adviser and consultant, with script writers and director, I might be worthwhile. During 1920-27 I reviewed for the Chicago Daily News five new releases each week, made several visits to Hollywood, count Chaplin a fellow dreamer. Griffith wanted me to do the script for his Lincoln picture but I saw it was to be too hurried an affair and said No.

Please wire me, on receiving this, as to whether a script has begun, when it is to be finished, when you begin shooting, so that I may be governed in any time commitments I make across this spring and summer. With salutations and all good wishes,

Sincerely yours,
Carl Sandburg

> *Sandburg did not join producer Walter Wanger for a Fremont film, but did go to Hollywood in the early 1960's as a consultant to George Stevens on a life of Christ.*

442 | TO DOROTHY PARKER

[Harbert, Michigan]
December 13, 1940.

Dear Dorothy Parker:

I tried to get you by phone today, finding that your organization seemed to have no number. I wanted to make sure that my telegram had reached you saying I could not help joining you and Helen Keller in sponsoring your work for Spanish refugees. The check enclosed I would like to make larger.

Though in FIGHTING WORDS you scorn some of your earlier work, we still have your books around the house and the boys and girls read them and enjoy them.

Sincerely yours,
Carl Sandburg

1941

[New York]
February 7, 1941

Dear Norman:

Have just seen your letters and script blueprinting TPY. I am not exactly stunned, but I am deeply and pleasantly surprised that you should throw in as you do. It looks swell to me—and I know Earl gets up earlier to work and is more restless in his sleep on account of the way you throw on the switches. It is just what was needed. Nowhere else in the country could we have found any one who could step in and hit here as you do. In that sense, the event has a touch of miracle—the happening of what you want to happen.

Signing off as you do to Earl,

Love,
Carl Sandburg

P.S. If you have copies of what you have sent to Earl that are not in use, I would like to go over them more slowly and carefully than I have today. I would return them to you at any date you indicate.

Playwright Norman Corwin and composer Earl Robinson created a one-act opera based on TPY—The People, Yes—that was broadcast over the CBS radio network on May 18, 1941, starring Burl Ives and Everett Sloane.

444 | TO CATHERINE MC CARTHY

[Harbert, Michigan]
Feb 19   41

Dear Catherine

Suppose you ask the Columbia people for a transcript copied from my Feb 12 broadcast. I made changes in the script up to the finish. They should give this accommodation as I travelled to Springfield and did the assignment without fee, for the ceremonial, refusing pay broadcasts for the day. . . Last Saturday afternoon and evening with the Life photographer Bernard Hoffman, who did that previous series: he says they plan a 3-page story. Monday six hours with Karl Detzer of Readers Digest for an article. Today three hours with a camera man and writer from Friends of which Chevrolet dealers put out a million copies a month. This now approaches overfeeding the country and me. And for some months at least arrangements of this kind are going to be hard to get. There is other work. Miss Oswald and Jerry Marks are beautifully lit up about that song: they made points this week about one more addition which I have sent on: I would not be surprised to see it go to town: certainly in the name of God the country wants the kind of a song we are trying to make this: it does have some of the best essence of the War Years. I liked your sentence: "It was good to have you around." Sounding a little like the sweet laughing St. Bernard dog Helga and her Joe are planning to get. Probably coming on soon to do a song album for Decca. All my recordings previous to The Pr. Ys album were not deliberate and well considered as this one is to be. That's the news. Share this with AH [Alfred Harcourt]. And blessings on you—

Carl

Catherine McCarthy, at Harcourt, co-ordinated the many demands on Sandburg's time that came to his publisher.

445 | TO ARCHIBALD MACLEISH

[Harbert, Michigan]
Feb 23   41

Dear Archie

Since we are both poets—and MAJOR poets at that—and only Posterity can dispute it—and we will be pickled and bleached so pretty before ever Posterity gets in its say-so as to whether we are MAJOR OR MINOR—I am sending you dese dose and dem, viz and namely, 38 definitions of poetry hot off the pan—or rather aged in charred oak casks for several years. I am going to charge some magazine ten dollars a definition for them. Or I may tell an agent he must get twenty dollars per definition. Or I may refuse to print them and continue to proudly publish them orally before audiences who say I am as good as Houdini defying them to bring on hand-cuffs I cant get out of. I shall be as independent as the mischievous anonymous sonofagun who invented the British Ambassador and the Spanish Minister's Wife into a nifty compromise wherein A LAD-DER was inevitable, inexorable—and who better to bring the ladder than the sauntering Seward and the laughing Lincoln? What a honey of perfectly apocryphal aneckdote! It encourages me to go on with my short story about Judas Iscariot, rigging up a dummy to look like himself in the Garden of Gethsemane, then hiking to Damascus and becoming a paperhanger till the affair blew over, then with the 30 pieces going into utilities and cosmetics and cleaning up.

Anyhow the two of us being MAJOR poets (and what misbe-gotten officiators with weights and measures can prove otherwise?) anyhow keep these around the desk a week or two and I will be along. As the war gets going and the fog deeper you better follow me in MORE PRIVATE CLOWNING whatsoever we may be doing publicly. Look to your laughter, Archie. You have rich gifts of it and it will help you in the loads you are carrying—

Carlo

Archibald MacLeish was appointed Librarian of Congress in 1939 and held the post until 1944, when he became Assistant Secretary of State.

446 | TO ARCHIBALD MACLEISH

[Washington, D.C.?]
March 6, 1941

Dear Mr. MacLeish:

Herewith is the memorandum on the Herndon-Weik Collection: I examined a part of it yesterday, read carefully the list of items it holds. Before actually handling these curious old documents, I had a mild preference that they should be located here in Washington under the one government roof appropriate to them. However, as I went through these documents, I found moving in me all of the deepest motives that were swaying me when I wrote *Abraham Lincoln: The Prairie Years*. A feeling deepened in me that there were only two libraries in America where it would be distinctly and absolutely appropriate for this collection to be lodged—either the Illinois State Historical Library in Springfield, Illinois, the old home town of Lincoln, or in the Library of Congress in Washington, his last home town, the locale wherein his labors and sayings made him a world figure whose familiar silhouette will be alive among generations remote to us.

If I had the responsibility of advising as to whether this collection is worth this or that price, I would have to be frank that sentiment, having to do with the inexplicable things for which men are willing to die, a motivation where money was a very minor matter, would be operating. There are times when money is a ridiculous aside and one recalls the sergeant of historic distinction at the high tide of the battle crying to his men in common, "Come on, come on, you sons-o-bitches; do you want to live forever?"

Lincoln was the pivotal figure in the national ordeal and agony from which came the living and amalgamated Union of States which today faces the world with a solidarity beyond price. As such—and as the one American figure cherished by the human family the earth over as the foremost incarnation or patriot saint of democracy—he will be continuously, endlessly, across the future, a subject for the use of materials of more and more biographies, special studies of certain phases of his personality—and perhaps more important yet the work of the writers having creative imagination, who, with the modern devices of screen and radio, reach audiences running into tens of millions of people. Too much stress cannot be laid on the importance of the creative writer of integrity having access to all possible primary source materials on Lincoln. This, and other considerations, made me feel that if, possibly, the price asked for this collection should be somewhat high, I would favor the payment of a price perhaps from the sheer money standpoint inequitable. There is such a thing as a nuisance value, I understand, also there is its opposite, I believe, termed *assurance value*. I would be willing to pay more than a strictly cold appraisal value for these source documents merely for the assurance against the danger, and I would say the genuine shame, that might follow from these passing into private hands. They belong so strictly to the American people, to the true statesmen and creative artists of future generations, that one cannot contemplate purchase of them by the Library of Congress without looking at this *assurance value*.

While presenting the foregoing factors, I have been well aware of an analysis on market reports based on sales of Lincoln documents, and I state frankly that it is a far more convincing presentation than I believed could have been made. In closing, I would stress the point that sentiment, curious and sometimes inarticulate promptings in the heart and mind, operate dominantly in the area where human manuscripts are bought and sold. This Herndon-Weik Collection covers the youth and the formative period of Abraham Lincoln—with primary source documents—as nothing else on that period. It represents the life work of a man who was Lincoln's law partner and office associate for sixteen years, and author of what many writers, including men of vast labors in the Lincoln field, such as Paul M. Angle and Albert J. Beveridge, consider the greatest biography written by men of Lincoln's own generation. The only other biography written from personal knowledge of Lincoln, which is sometimes rated higher than Herndon's, is the massive Nicolay-Hay tome. I could dwell further on how sentiment must join with arithmetic in trying to solve the price problem in this instance.

When I was writing *The Prairie Years,* and when like The Reverend Dr. William E. Barton, I could not gain access to these papers, I felt it appalling and somewhat preposterous that they should be in private hands. Today, I favor them going immediately into the public domain, even if there should be some degree of extortion practiced somewhere in the transaction. Closing with salutations to you of the Library of Congress for the kind of interest you are showing in the accession of basic Lincolniana, I remain

Sincerely yours,
Carl Sandburg

The Library of Congress purchased the collection in 1941 from G. A. Baker & Co. of New York, who had acquired it from the son of Jesse Weik.

1941

447 | TO JUNE PROVINE

[Harbert, Michigan]
[Circa March, 1941]

Dear June:

Ain't writing no biog of anybody and not planning to do [Henry] Horner. That arose probably out of my going to make the main speech at the exercises formally dedicating Horner's Lincoln Library to the State of Illinois on Feb. 12. For me the highspot of that speech was telling about how several times when I worked till 2 and 3 o'clock in the morning at the Madison Park apartment of the then Probate Judge Henry Horner, he would humorously and democratically go through a ritual of making a big grand desk collapse into a bed. The judge would then find sheets and spread them for me as dutifully as any chambermaid, ending with both of us putting the pillows into cases. Then he would leave me to sleep amid four walls holding just about all the known and available books and brochures about Abraham Lincoln. Though in case I wanted a cheese sandwich with a little beer he would offer to bring that. Also I referred to the time and care he gave to his Lincoln Library, how some of his friends referred to them as his "Bachelor's children." If this has a story you are welcome to it. Shall yet be seeing you this 1941.

As always,
Carl

June Provine, a columnist for the Chicago Tribune, *had asked Sandburg, not long after Governor Horner's death on October 6, 1940, if he were going to write a biography of him.*

[Harbert, Michigan]
March 12   41

Dear Irving

Back from a trip I find your good letter, and separately those editorial pages—and that roto. Were I running for something in PD territory that roto would be a fast start. To me it was rather deeply moving that the PD, which has standards, and you fellers Dilliard and Fitzpatrick, who are damned rigorous and arrogant and independent, should make news of me and publicity for me. I am still and yet enough of a hobo so that if I am outside of jails and eating three decent meals a day, and the family provided for, I dont require news treatment nor ask publicity. So it gets back to fellowship and personal humors and fun of a sort. In 1922 when I first arrived in San Francisco, Fremont Older had a reporter and photographer meet me at the train and put me on the front page—because he was really a hobo at heart and read Frisco as a hobo town in the main. I can cheer for democracy when I see you and Fitzpatrick operating. We may not agree on administrative details but the heart impulses run parallel.

Do you suppose you can send me three or four more of that roto page? And if I send Witman a copy of The People, Yes, do you think he would send on prints of those four photographs? This is not important—but I might be able to use them. At least my daughters would.

And I am still hoping to drop off at St. Louis and have a field day with you fellows.

Faithfully yours
Carl

At the St. Louis Post-Dispatch—*"PD territory"—Sandburg's good friends included its editor, Irving Dilliard, and the great cartoonist Daniel R. Fitzpatrick.*

[Harbert, Michigan]
March 13   41

Dear Archie

A note from Frederick H Meserve reminds me of a neglected memo I did not get to your ear. You have somewhere on the Lib of Cong walls, or did have in '39, a photograph of the Second Inaugural of Lincoln, in clarity the best I had ever seen. Roberts had an excellent copy of it made for me and it is used opp page 85 Vol IV. Meserve wishes you to make a good copy and send to him. You should know Meserve. A plain business man, in wholesale wool and cotton for the textiles trade, no pretenses, but THE ONE man on Lincoln photographs—as well as an immense collection of other Americana photographs 1850-1890—30,000 stage subjects. I am to have one or two sessions with him before doing an introduction to a book he is doing which will be near the last word on Lincoln's life as told through photographs. Please remind me when I am along again that you are to have your fellows get me thoroughly informed on what you are lacking in original prints of Lincoln. Meserve may have the negatives for printing you some of these. Also, for years you had the only known stereoscopic photograph of Lincoln. Then I located one more, and just today have received a third one. This with other angles we can discuss with a view perhaps of having at the Lib of Cong, for all visitors to enjoy, a little gallery holding every known photograph of Lincoln, with brief data as to where and when made. This will constitute a rational commentary on the cat-vomit miscellany of Lincoln illustrative material which abounds and exudes at too many points of the compass. Dont bother to acknowledge this. Enroute to a Va. state college in about ten days shall be seeing you.

Yrs
Carl

P.S. Mr. [Joseph] Auslander should know his telegram to me was received and read on my arrival home and I have noted with interest and care that the series of programs is "dedicated to theme

THE POET IN A DEMOCRACY." And I now incline still more to believe that the Lorraine evening will not be merely extraordinary and compelling as performance but will touch some of the deepest shadowy gongs among the meanings of democracy. If I can find the time I am going to write in longhand on special rag MR. LONG-FELLOW AND HIS BOY, to go to the President on the day we give it vocal publication with music.

450 | TO NORMAN CORWIN

Harbert Mich
[March 24, 1941]

Dear Norman

Your ears should have burned a little this March 24 there being talk about you in these parts. Ye maestro Erll Robinson on The Wolverine fast train eases out of his berth at Niles whereas I have always been on my feet 40 min. earlier at Kalamazoo and he must be a more high class bum than me because he got them to stop the train at a tank town named after the eminent James Buchanan, one of our presidents, which I have never been able to do, so I guess he sang Ballad for Amurrikuns and told engineer and brake-men about The Lonesome Train, and called off all those stations on the NYCentral main line without looking at a time-table. Now The Lonesome Train never touched Buchanan but it did flag down at the next stop Michigan City which was his proper destination. But Erll was dreaming out a cantata where the Volga would flow into the Mississippi and the Mississippi in brotherly reciprocation flowing into the Volga and all water is H2O. But persiflage aside and with no fear of being puns drunk like Jake Buchbinder to-night said I was, the Missus drove to Buchanan and picked up our best songster since S. Foster and they got along swell she always seeing a fine wholesome demon in him even when his political course was the nuts. So I write all this because you are in on it with your love and understanding and we got a right to some di-vine fellowship if we can get it on the fly while the holocaust roars toward ends no man knows. It was one of the great all-time radio shows last Tuesday night and when Simon & Schuster have published & Decca recorded & Warners screened and it grows up and goes to town we will be saying we knew it when it was in its swaddling clothes and had a bib for its burps. Take care of yourself.

As always
Carl

POSTSCRIPT FOR YE SCRIPTSMITH: "That banjo, didnt it come in good? not too much just enough of it?" asks Erll at the front-room luncheon of plain proletarian baked beans with a classy divertissement of goat's milk, and he goes on how it's an old timer with five strings and all Manhattan and the Atlantic seaboard didnt have any one could play it and you had to send to Alabama for a melodious galoot who knew how. Comes out then Erll has been on the lookout for such a banjo and no luck. So yrs truly reaches over, tipping back in his chair, into a corner behind two guitars and a Filipino 3-string fiddle and produces a banjo tt yrs truly has had going on 30 yrs, not playing it for 20 yrs because a guitar had priority. So he hands this identical banjo to Erll with a brief and pointed speech: "You are the one man in the USA to have this and I give it to you quoting the Cossack proverb: He owns the wild horse who can ride him." So we wrap it in a burlap bag, nickel plated with a tight drum, long narrow fretboard, a honey. Nobody else could have taken it away like that. It was like a good deacon giving away an adopted child, that had always been well behaved, to another good deacon who pledged to bring it up well behaved and godly. We are returning you now to our studios and the next voice you hear will be next voice you hear will be next voice you hear will be—goddam that transcription!

451 | TO EUGENE MEYER

[Harbert, Michigan]
April 30   41

Dear Eugene

One enclosure herewith is part of a piece I shall probably give the syndicate for May 10. This and more will form part of my talk introducing Marian Lorraine. After the intermission I make another short talk, with readings of the same trend from The People, Yes and two unpublished free verse pieces, one on Night Over Europe. I have theories and ideas about propaganda that may work out and may not. In this May 8 evening I am adventuring, taking a chance, just as I will in writing soundtrack narration for government films. If I find that I get the fishy eye too often, as to my suggestions for breaking apathy and winning loyalty, for joining up all the fair and decent methods and practices possible in winning the masses, I shall probably settle down on the farm here and hold myself to the written and printed word. Incidentally I hope you saw Ben Hecht's Testament of a Reporter in PM. That ought to be widely reprinted. That he and Gene Fowler and other hardboiled fellers that never before believed passionately in any human causes are out now thundering vehemently has its meaning.

The other enclosure—PLEASE RETURN IT—is a foreword they asked me to do for a book of the addresses made at the Horner funeral. I miss him and with others I am still sentimental about him as I am about you who are alive and may it be long.

As always
Carlo

At the Library of Congress, a program of American poetry was given, with Sandburg, Archibald MacLeish, and Marian Lorraine. The Sandburg poems "Mr. Lincoln and His Gloves" and "Mr. Longfellow and His Boy" had been set to music for Marian Lorraine by Gerald Marks.

452 | TO ARCHIBALD MACLEISH

[Harbert, Michigan]
May 21   41

Dear Archie
Every day your advice keeps coming back to me, the admonition "Keep your shoes shined." So, every day I wash my neck.

Possibly I am owing you a rare book, certainly a tall seidel of dark ale at least, on Colliers getting that poem thru your decision as to where the manuscript should go. Be seeing you first week of June or anyhow around June 10 when I hike to Chapel Hill for commencement address. Meantime I know you are going on heavy chores—and I think it is nice a good wind blew you to where the coco is under the rococo—

As always
Carlo

MacLeish replied in part: "That's wonderful news about your neck. I can see the shine of your shoes from here. It looks like a huge prairie fire reflecting up over the Alleghenys."

453 | TO CATHERINE MCCARTHY

[Harbert, Michigan]
June 28, 1941

Dear Catherine:

Among several statements of mistaken color in the Detzer piece is one sweeping and unreserved that Detzer would have modified if we had had more time to work on it. This statement goes, "To him a strikebreaker is always a scab." Detzer, with more time, would here have written something like, "To him a strikebreaker is always a scab—unless it is a jurisdictional strike where the fool issue is whether carpenters or sheet metal workers shall install metal trim—or unless it is a strike called by racketeer labor leaders for extortion in which case he is a laughing neutral—or unless it is a strike called by racketeer labor leaders for the purposes of extortion in which case he favors the employer and whatever faction in the union favors arrest, trial and conviction of the betrayers of labor—or unless it is a strike in a national defense industry where the instigators of the strike have evident objectives beyond such issues as wages, hours and union recognition." That is all. I could go much farther but that is all. The labor movement and industry in general is, since the days I was a labor reporter, on so vastly different a basis, that I wouldn't like to see a Harcourt Brace book in the hands of college and high school students, putting me on the side of any and all racketeers who call strikes for the payoff. That is all. Suppose you take this up with Isabel Ely Lord and either add to the sentence or delete it.

A general trend in the Detzer piece indicates that my interest in the socialist and labor movements was entirely rooted in sympathy for labor and the masses. That was only part of it. I sensed these movements, even when a boy, as having terrific potential power, that they would be worth knowing close-up. For the writing of the Lincoln I knew the Abolitionists better for having known the I.W.W. I knew Garrison better for having known Debs. Do the best you can, Kitty. This is 50-50 for HB and me. You and Isabel can quote any way you like from the above. Or just delete the one sentence that puts me out on a limb as never having learned anything out of all I have seen and heard since I wrote Chicago Poems, though even then I wrote hundreds of stories about strikes called by labor fakers.

May be seeing you when going to or from Washington in July.

As always,

C.S.

P.S. Enclosed is Detzer letter which please return. Also a University of Kentucky letter where I suppose we tell him to go ahead with our blessing. Photograph on way.

Karl Detzer's Carl Sandburg: A Study in Personality and Background *was published by Harcourt, Brace and Company in 1941.*

454 | TO LOUIS UNTERMEYER

[Harbert, Michigan]
[June 28, 1941]

Dear Louie

Out of Good Morning America suppose you consider the pieces titled Cheap Blue, We Have Gone Through Great Rooms Together, and Maybe. And in The People, Yes the passages numbered 9, 12,

41—and as one piece the passage starting on page 114 with the line "The sea has fish for every man" to end with the line on page 117 ending "the grey rain of May." Also one piece starting at the top of page 200 and ending with the line 'to behemoths and constellations" on page 201. Then from the close of the book whatever you like out of pages 283 to end of 286, making sure to use at least the last half of the last page. Consider, weigh, edit, relax with a couple of puns, then bow thy head in labor again. I am betting it will be one good book. You come to it with the wide preparation and training. Meantime I will write the soundtrack for "Bombers for Britain", a litry form I have not yet tried my pitching arm on. When I promised to do it I did not know and only God was sure that it would turn out to be close cooperation with the Moscow party line. Aint she some war now? My love to you and Esther.

Carl

455 | TO HELGA SANDBURG

[Harbert, Michigan]
Friday afternoon
[December 5, 1941]

Dear Swipes

This is just to say I never met a finer poem than you were yesterday. The next best poem I met yesterday was the little feller who didn't look at me through the glass. But he did yawn twice and I am going to ask him later whether he yawned to show me he knows how to yawn or whether he just didn't know he was yawning. When his legs were uncovered for me I noticed they were fine legs and he was trying to tell me something by signals with his toes. Anyhow you know his language better than anybody else and I will be asking you about it. We are all saying prayers of thanks and your voice and face say them deep.

Daddy

Helga's son, John, was born at midnight on December 3, 1941.

1942

[Harbert, Michigan]
[December 8, 1941]

Dear Jake

Deep thanks to you. It is good to know there is such a blend of sagacity, humor and good fellowship as yours. As soon as the grandson arrives at a vocabulary of 100 words I shall tell him about you. I was going to append "As always" here but last night made that a little more so—

Carl

In Sandburg's opinion, Dr. Buchbinder, who performed a Caesarian operation because of a complicated delivery, had saved Helga's life as well as her son's.

457 | TO DON RUSSELL

[Harbert, Michigan]
[Circa January, 1942]

Dear Don:

Months ago you wrote to me keenly about how Dr. Shutes notified you of finding a double demise of one [Paul Joseph] Revere in the War Years. All other demises in the book were single. Yet the double one is there glaringly and guiltily, all the worse to look at because it stands alone. If there had been one triple with which to compare it then it would look less unsufferable. The patience of your "I suppose there is not much we can do about it at this late date" belongs in the kitbag of a military expert. Some of your notes about elements of strategy and tactics I have clipped for second reading. Good going to you—

Sincerely yours,
Carl

Don Russell, of the Chicago Daily News, *had called Sandburg's attention to a mistake found by Dr. Milton H. Shutes, of Oakland, Calif., a doctor of medicine and Lincoln scholar, in* The War Years.

458 | TO GEORGE P. WEST

[Harbert, Michigan]
March 12, 1942

Dear George:

I gave your memorandum to MacLeish and spoke of you. It was amid several interruptions and I wouldn't be sure I made any definite impression. He is hard pressed. There are no precedents to guide him. If I could have gotten into a full discussion with him I would probably have told him that your own tie-up with him could very well be like my own. I send him my own hunches and have laid before him several ideas that others wanted to get to him.

The tensions in Washington are different from 1918, tighter, every phase and angle of this war felt as more complicated and portentous. I have kept free from any official tie-ups except a few weeks when I helped on a bomber film.

You and Marie are in my thoughts often and I wish we were nearer neighbors. That newspaper column, I should have told you, was not my idea. They came to me insisting I had no business keeping silent in this time. And that you should feel my work is somewhat effective does count. I am entirely humble about it.

By the way you should and must do your personal portrait of Older. Write it. The interest I know I would have in it I know is shared by others. And Heney, [Frank P.] Walsh, [Tom] Mooney, [George] Sterling—I don't mean an autobiography—but I do mean some of those portraits that would go into a story of your life.

Take care of yourself. Your mind now, I felt on that last visit, is keener and surer about what it has learned in the journey than any time I have known you. You have trained your eyes to spot how, when and where democracy works—and why it can't and won't work under certain conditions. Maybe you should write about that. The future world may be needing such pages, even though in this chaotic present they don't seem so immediate.

Kiss the two little ones for me. And maybe we'll be meeting this year.

Faithfully yours,
Carl

1942

[Harbert, Michigan]
March 17, 1942

Dear Chris:

Your Lincoln's Birthday letter has your breath, laughter and hope in it. Since I have three or four times narrowly missed seeing you in recent years, it was good to have this greeting—and to get your lighted registration to that little note of Lincoln to Governor Curtin. Once Lincoln gently admonished an oversure visitor with asking, "Do you suppose there is any one mind anywhere that has a grasp of this stupendous war?" If that was stupendous, what of this one? . . . Maybe I should refer you to an odd little book, a Decca album of six sides, twelve-inch, recording from THE PEOPLE, YES. Hear it as an oddity and a venture. . . And why do I think of you as not diminishing in strength and love of life?

Faithfully yours,
Carl

[Harbert, Michigan]
[Fall, 1942]

Dear Swipes

Every one of your letters I read first for the facts and the fun— and then a second time to see how the red inside heart of you is ticking. I feel mighty good about how you are now and where you are and the way things are going. To love the good old earth and to make a little piece of it behave under your hands, that is to have riches if along with it you have health and strength. Jiminy, those is nice photographs of Joe Carl: he is giving a good account of himself. And the one showing you with a laugh from every last rib of you, that for me is a song. Love to your Joe, to your Joe Carl, and to your blessed self—

Daddy

461 | TO PAULA SANDBURG

[New York]
June 18, 1943

Dearest Paula

It has been like old times here what with finishing and starting books in sweltering summer. Have now gone far with [Frederick] Meserve on our book The Photographs of Abraham Lincoln. We expect to let the printer have it in Sept. and publication Xmas. This weekend out at Bill Benton's finishing page proofs of *Home Front Memo* (Collier's is taking The Two Maggots fable.) H F Memo probably comes out this August. Will have all sorts of odd news for you out of radio and movie lands. May be June 23 before I can break away from here. I miss the house, the air, the trees, the goats, and my loved ones and you most of all—love and blessings—

Carl

462 | TO BRENDA UELAND

[Harbert, Michigan]
June 20, [1943]

Dear Brenda

It is good to have that column coming along from day to day   so many of them have your full authentic voice and eyes   and now and then such a flashing rich abrupt poem   and I wonder who else could intone such finality in a closing "You bet" instead of a "verily verily I say unto you"   dont give a flickering moment of worry or anxiety about what I will hand them in Hollywood it will be as stubborn and norsk a book as I have ever done breaking some of the ground to begin with was not easy but I have a framework and content now as far as I have gone that travels in key and tone with my other works   possibly a wider and farther reach   we cant tell about such a thing till years have

passed and the work has had the attrition of use   I may get a chance
to run up your way   though the work pressure will be rather keen
this side of going to Hollywood in August   the fall months will
not be so heavy   I want it to be a book on the order of my others
each done with the wish that someone else had done such a book
for me to read when a youth and carry on from there instead of
starting where I do   blessings on you   no days go by I dont have
thoughts of you and the big life sweeps of which you are a registering and radiating center

Carl

463 | TO ARCHIBALD MACLEISH

[Harbert, Michigan]
July 2, 1943

Dear Archie:

The book got done and should be along in your hands before
the end of August. You and Steichen are the most definite stand-
outs in it. I could write you as John Hay did to Robert Lincoln
when he and Nicolay had finished their ten volumes, saying in
effect, "We hope we have not injured your father's fame." Perhaps
I will let it go with a note to Ada and Peter saying I doubt whether
you could win a zoot suit for libeling your labels when you have
no labels.

A preface dedication goes to Stevie Benét. When I saw him last
December I told him that he and you and I were a sort of movement but each of us being sort of on the anarchist side we had
no interest in organizing and proceeding as a movement.

The book is mulligatawny. It has everything but the kitchen
stove. I was going to leave out a couple of mean Lindbergh pieces.
Then I put 'em in again because he is the best 1941 exhibit of the
respectable American Nazi mind and spirit.

Take care of yourself. When I get a chance to duck down and
see you I shall avail myself of a house where I can lurk behind
the front windows and draw a squirrel rifle bead on what is near
to being Public Enemy No. 1. My second grandchild arrived this

week, so I am feeling affirmative about the firmaments of life. Excuse letter so long. Long time no see. Hope soon look see your good face.

Yours,
Carlo

Home Front Memo was dedicated "To the life, works and memory of Stephen Vincent Benét, who knew the distinction between pure art and propaganda in the written or spoken word." The second grandchild was Helga's daughter, Karlen Paula, born June 28, 1943. Ada MacLeish was the poet's wife; Peter, his son.

464 | TO JESSE RICKS

[Harbert, Michigan]
July 14   43

Dear Jess

It is a long time since we sat up till four o'clock in the morning playing checkers and dominoes, being in agreement next day that we had brothel haziness of mind and would thereafter better watch our sleep. Now last week comes to me a little figment of a pigment designated as a granddaughter, looking like Rhoda when I last saw Rhoda. When she yawns the whole face yawns and there are tremors at the toes sort of saying they too are joining on the yawn.

Oliver shows me some of your letters. I always set store by that old saying "I want money so as to buy the time to enjoy the things money can't buy." Now you are taking time to poke around in the mystic pavilions and odd shanties of that wide ranging mind of yours. In one corner of this attic I've laid away materials on Diogenes. If I ever write about him I'll submit it to you for you have become very Diogenesian. And having so mentioned this I recall your reduction of Thoreau into a first-rate phony and maybe you would do the same with the old Grick. The only item on birds I have for you is that often when I work on an outdoor deck here, hummingbirds flutter stationary before trumpet-vine blossoms, sending their long bills into the tube of the flower, enjoying these meals only three or four feet from my chair. It sounds trite and of course is only a commonplace action of getting a living for them. But it always stops me in whatever I am doing and always has a little of miracle about it. May you have good going. Affectionate regard to all under your roof—

Carl

Jesse Ricks was a Chicago businessman and a friend of Sandburg. Rhoda was Ricks's granddaughter.

465 | TO JULIA PETERKIN

Harbert, Mich. July 14 43

Dear Julia

For fourteen weeks I have been in New York and Washington, mostly finishing a book to be published in Sept along with some odd jobs on the war effort besides completing some albums Decca is to issue when manufacturing material is available. Twice I ducked home for six day periods, neither time getting at more than half my mail. So your treasure of a greeting-poem-letter of April didnt get read till July. And it is definitely one of those not meant in my very common explanation "I dont answer letters." My thoughts never cease recurring to you. Fanny B. told me of tragedy that came to you. And what I thought mostly was that there were no words and no angle of philosophy that you didnt already have at hand—but I would have liked to sit in silence or to walk in fog or mist with you. I remember your good friend whose mind failed saying "Why did I do it?" and repeating it. I remember when a magnolia garden suddenly flashed before our eyes and your saying, "We mustnt close our eyes—when we open them it might not be there." I remember some of the loveliest speech and questionings I have ever heard come from you in plain quiet talk, spoken meditation. I would have seen more of you but the finishing of that Lincoln book meant hard hoarding of time. Then came the war and I threw in with what I had, as you will see in this book Home Front Memo holding pamphlets, broadcasts, newspaper pieces, poems of these last three wild years. I shall be seeing you. Forgive my delay. So soon as time comes a little easier with me I want talk again or the sharing of silence. As always—

Carl

466 | TO THOMAS HORNSBY FERRIL

[Harbert, Michigan]
[Circa late 1943]

Dear Tom:

The matter of what unnamed major poets got hit below the belt maybe in Home Front Memo we can leave to future discussion. There was a two-year crisis when those poets were so completely silent that their extent of silence and its nature and backgrounds make a debatable and controversial subject about which the issues and history of this time range. What you do know, I am sure, is that you have spoken and written, made yourself clear. Some of those paragraphs, where for moments you abandon all whim and fooling are beautifully keen. . . Perhaps you should know that I have not had time to make my case clear as a political independent, and as a writer a free lance. I have kept out of literary politics as well as partisan politics.

Carl

Home Front Memo *contains several comments about wartime words, including these: "Men of ideas vanish first when freedom vanishes . . . a writer's silence on living issues can in itself constitute a propaganda of conduct leading toward the deterioration or death of freedom."*

1944

[Harbert, Michigan]
[Circa early 1944]

Dear Archie

You and I are never down till we are out and never flabbergasted till we are kaflooberated. I think of the suave and imperious pink-whiskered United States Senator James Hamilton Lewis when the brusque and abrupt roughneck Sheriff of Cook County, John Thoman, from Back o' the Yards, refused to await entry into Senator Lewis' office and busted out to the secretary, "You tell that dude sonofabitch I got work to do and we're going to hang a man in the morning and he can look fer me to be walkin' right through the door and I don't take no from any bastard like him." By now, what with this uproar of a bawling and authoritative voice, Senator Lewis himself, immaculate and near bespangled in apparel and accessories, had opened the door and stood there calm and unconcerned as any irreproachable lily of the fields that toileth not nor spins. And as at the door he gave an iridescently manicured hand to the horny mitt of his adamant visitor, his dulcet voice spoke the brief admonition face to face, "Don't beshit me, John, don't beshit me." This was the same day that earlier he had at the Sherman Hotel barber shop showered a plain and humble manicure girl with vast and obvious compliments to the point where she at last had to interrupt his bestowal of bold and cunning praises with, "You can go on, Senator, if you like, but it's no use. I've been kidded by experts before." And what I'm thinking Archie is that we dont hate nobody nowhere unless it might be that soprano bitch in Alexandria who across the street from your house where the shadow of Robert E. Lee lingers howls like a stuck pig for the ears of good people who have done a day's work and seek nothing more than the feathery foam flights of sleep God gives to his own children providing no goddam practicing sopranos are around the premises. . . Overlook and forgive all lapses herein. Write poems when they come knocking. Stick to your mocking and ingenious wheelbarrow ballet dance that has Ada and me in stitches. And health shine from your countenance ever. So be it.

Yrs
Carlo

468 | TO ARCHIBALD MACLEISH

[Harbert, Michigan]
September 14, 1944

Dear Archie:

If by any chance there are mimeographed copies of the texts of these broadcasts they will be prized and used by the undersigned young theological student who was formerly associated with you in the liquor traffic before it became legalized.

As always,
Carl

Also, kind sir, if can do, slip me this Bill Rogers speech.

469 | TO KENNETH DODSON

[Harbert, Michigan]
October 30, 1944.

Dear Lieutenant Dodson:

A Los Angeles friend, the wife of a Naval officer, let me have four typed pages which have been copied from letters of yours. I found them extraordinarily vivid, the larger part of them unforgettable. I found myself using parts of them in a novel I am doing which, after publication in book form, Metro-Goldwyn-Mayer will make into a screen play. I would like your permission to quote somewhere between 200 to 300 words. I would go over anything so used with Navy men to make sure that in matters of identity and information there would be nothing used improperly. To say that I would expect to pay for the use of such material is to grope around for words trying to say something that can't be said. Such words as yours are beyond price, but since this is a commercial enterprise, I would not care to profit by use of your material without paying for it. I would expect to give you salutations up front in a preface, along with a statement of my opinion that the body of your letters should have some sort of permanent form where they are accessible. Out of what you write arises something like a definition of the terribly indefinable word "Patriot."

I shall write to Mrs. Dodson at the Seattle address given to me by your sister, Miss Ellen Dodson in Los Angeles, and shall send to her my six-volume set, ABRAHAM LINCOLN: THE PRAIRIE YEARS and THE WAR YEARS, along with copies of THE PEOPLE, YES, HOME FRONT MEMO, and (for the "Pipsqueak") ROOTABAGA STORIES. The sending of these books is just a sort of salutation to you as a fighting Navy man and a rare personality. If there should be any reasons why you should hesitate about having these quotations from your letters used, I shall understand. However, you should know that it has been good to meet you through these letters of yours and to know that there are Americans in the South Pacific with your range, sensitivity, vision, and hope.

Faithfully yours,
Carl Sandburg

So began a firm friendship with Kenneth Dodson, executive officer of a Navy attack transport, whose letters in the epilogue of Remembrance Rock *were signed by a fictional "Kenneth MacDougall." Dodson later said: "Were it not for the repeated and sustained encouragement received from Carl Sandburg, it is very doubtful that I would have kept trying during the five years of struggle in writing and finding a publisher for my first book,* Away All Boats.*"*

470 | TO KENNETH DODSON

[Harbert, Michigan]
Jan 27   1945

Dear Lieut. Dodson:

Your letter addressed to me at Harbert came a week ago and every day I was going to answer it and there was guilt on my soul when today there came your letter of January 14 sent to New York. So I am dictating this to a daughter who is the mother of my two pipsqueak grandchildren and we will get it into the Harbert postoffice for the last departing mail this evening, Saturday, there being no other mail till next Monday. One thing about your letters, as a fellow reads them, is that he gets no impression one way or the other about your being a writer. He is with you where you are and getting the feel of what it is that moves you. And you have unusual faculties of observation and of keen sensitive registration to what you see. I heard Steichen (notched up from Commander to Captain since I wrote you last) once saying, "You get a great photograph when life is performing and you are there with the camera." Of course that does not apply to all times and occasions but it has its parallel in your letters. I hope and trust that all your journals and letters can go into a fireproof vault, to be edited and published at some future time under conditions suitable to you. At least once a week, on an average, the last two or three years I have refused to write a preface or introduction to this or that book. But I would make you the pledge that if and when you get back to Puget Sound for a stay I would work with you on shaping up a book. I have come to know and love great source documents. And out of your writings, with no eye to publication, something has been created that will last. There will be generations beyond ours who will respond to certain spots in your letters with moist eyes as I saw them in Los Angeles last fall and here in my home this winter. Next week I shall be mailing you a copy of a poem the Sat. Eve. Post is running early February and you will see, I believe, that I am trying to get something said that is rather beyond saying and I am not sure but you come nearer getting it said in your letters from scenes of sacrifice. Your faith in America is like a good poem: it is mostly mystery with but little meaning but that little is terrific and beyond destruction. It is good to know you and I shall be bothering your blessed ears with more letters and you shall not be forgotten in prayers here.

Faithfully yours
Carl Sandburg

1945

[Harbert, Michigan]
February 21, 1945

Dear Eugene:

It was a nice ride we had for three years or more. You were a good sport. I shall hope to see you when in Washington again. My feeling is definite that every year the Post grows in human quality and in reader interest. Sometimes I wonder whether your editorial writers ever ride on the street-cars or buses or whether they go in the chain stores with their wives occasionally and whether they go to ball games and whether they listen to sailor and soldier slang. They go to their goddam dictionaries so often that they lose their Man in the Street. What I mean is that you can afford one 8 or 10 line editorial a day in monosyllabics and it won't hurt you none on circulation. This is not saying you don't have some fellow on your staff who gets me with his keen writing and moving wisdom. He probably did that wonderful front page prayer on Inauguration Day. The Sunday editorial section I salute—solid, timely, nicely provocative, never cheap.

Tell Agnes it is good to have her book and that I follow her reports. Deep good wishes to you always—

Faithfully yours,
Carl

Eugene Meyer had run Sandburg's column in the Washington Post *during three wartime years.*

472 | TO KENNETH HOLDEN

[Harbert, Michigan]
May 19, 1945

Dear Ken:

Did you hear about the Nazi in Magdeburg who crept into a bomb-washed store where once in the heil-hitler days they sold picture frames and the poor goddam Nazi licked off a mouthful of gold leaf from one of the frames? Two MPs watched him shiver in his guts and crumple up and die and one of the MPs said, "Suicide" and the other MP, "How could a little gold leaf like that kill a guy?" and the first one, "It wasn't so much the gold leaf as he was smitten with a sense of inner gilt."

And you may be sure I hope and trust we go on being a couple of sons of puns.

As ever:
Carl

Kenneth Holden was a member of the Lafayette Escadrille in World War I, and a fellow punner.

473 | TO KENNETH HOLDEN

[Harbert, Michigan]
May 26   45

Dear Ken:

King Arthur and his knights you have heard of, a good king he was and his knights bold and having what it takes, you might say. And one of the knights was short. They had to pile three Webster's Unabridged dictionaries on a chair for him when he sat at the table with other knights. Instead of a horse he rode a dog. One evening when it was snow and sleet and it grew darker and the winds howled, the midget knight on his dog got lost in the storm. They rassled their way through tall timber and mean underbrush and came suddenly to a house with candlelights gleaming from every window. The midget knight got off his dog, knocked on the door, and said to the lord of the manor:

"Wouldst thou be so kind as to yield to a knight the hospitality of thy manor?"

The lord of the manor took a look at the midget and a look at the dog with a hanging tongue and all tuckered out, completely petered, you might say. Then the lord of the manor laughed till his innards shook and busted out:

"Come in, shortboy, you and your dog, I couldn't think of throwing a knight out on a dog like this."

And at the supper table the midget had to reach up and stretch more than he was used to, because the lord of the manor had only two Webster's Unabridged dictionaries and the midget had got into the habit of three under him.

The dog saw this, lay by the fire and saw it. He was a talking dog and talked about what he saw. But what he said can't be told because this is not one of those cheap detestable darnfool talking dog stories.

I send you this, Ken, because we are both odd fellows, prominent citizens, and acquainted with ducksoup.

yours
Carl

474 | TO VOLDEMAR VETLUGUIN

[Harbert, Michigan]
[June 20, 1945]

Dear Mr. Vetluguin:

The title I favor now is

AMERICAN SCROLL: STORM AND DREAM

Am now working on that final chapter of the American Revolution sequence besides many chores involved in packing my manuscripts, notes, and books for our moving to North Carolina, where at Hendersonville we have bought the 235 acre place that was the summer home of C. G. Memminger, Secretary of the Treasury in the Cabinet of the Confederate States of American government. Three pieces of writing that I promised to do some 2 years ago I am trying to finish now: (1) a sketch of Oliver R. Barrett and his collection of Lincoln manuscripts: he is an old-time friend and helper, now 72 years of age, and I can't put it off any longer (2) an introduction to a book of Lincoln's writings and speeches by Roy P. Basler: the book won't get published unless I do this intro and how and why Basler is extraordinarily deserving I will tell you later (3) a 3,500 word commentary on Lincoln's style as speaker and writer and its progressions, this for a cyclopedia of American literature edited by Robert Spiller of Swarthmore. These, besides the chapter, I believe I will have done by Nov. 20, with perhaps by then an outline of the Civil War sequence for discussion with you and the Rev. Vetluguin and Professor [Sidney] Franklin.

Sincerely yours,
Carl Sandburg

The final title was Remembrance Rock.

475 | TO ALLAN NEVINS

[Harbert, Michigan]
June 25, 1945

Dear Allan:

Enclosed you may use as you like. I may decide to give it to some newspaper as a review.

Did you ever see the panegyric I wrote on the Commager-Nevins Pocket Hist. USA in my syndicated newspaper column of a year or so ago? In viewpoint and feeling what you did on F.D.R. and the New Deal years, I went right along with you and swore if it wasn't history it was great righteous preaching. Once in New York I phoned for you and you were in London. Another time I think they said you were in Burma, India. Good going to you,

Sincerely yours,
Carl

476 | TO HARRY S TRUMAN

[Harbert, Michigan]
September 15, 1945

Dear Mr. President:

Your deeply moving letter about those Lincoln volumes has been framed and put on a wall in our house because near twenty years in the house was given to those books and your words are a sort of attestation that the work has a living use.

From your public acts and speeches, beginning with those remarkable reports of the Truman Committee up to some of these latest hair-trigger decisions, along with private anecdotes given me by your and my old friend Russ Stewart, I have come to know you as I have known Lincoln and FDR, from a distance and in the perspective that the People sense a friend in office and high power. And I believe if Lincoln and FDR from the shadowland could be watching you now they would say something like, "He is of our fellowship, one of us, trying to keep close to the people in what they want done and keeping just a little ahead of them all the time." You are making your own style and shaping a tradition personal to you. I can reconcile your piety, prayer, profanity, piano playing and persiflage and it's all of a weave and makes for sanity and sagacity, from my seat in the bleachers. Your sense of timing, your solemnity and brevity, your devotion to duty and capacity for toil, your peculiar grasp of events in moments having no precedent to guide you—it all adds up to something distinctive and superb in our history. You are deep in many hearts and they speak prayers for you. May health and the good faith stay by you ever.

Faithfully yours,
Carl Sandburg

P.S. When in 1897 I was 19 and you were 13, I worked as a railroad section hand at Bean Lake, Missouri, not so far from where you were a 13 year old kid at Independence, Missouri which I knew then as merely the home town of Jesse James. How tempus shore do fugit!

President Harry S Truman thanked Sandburg for the six Lincoln volumes in a letter written Aug. 14, 1945, saying "not in my day will there be produced another study of the great Civil War President which will supersede them."

477 | TO ROGER BARRETT

[Kenilworth, Illinois]
[October 6, 1945]

Dear Roger

The news of you keeps coming to me regularly thru your folks—all your folks except Victoria—she won't talk. For your information, Victoria has atomic tendencies. She carries neutrons, cyclotrons, and has enough uranium under one thumbnail to blow Chicago to cinders and flinders.—We been talking about you, boy, sort of proud of you. And herewith affectionate regard—as always—

Carl Sandburg

Kenilworth Oct 6 1945 and I'm sleeping in your old room and looking at the west wall crib of Vicky with dolls, bears, a tiny wagon & what not. You have decided to keep her, it is reported, & I think you're wise.

> *Roger Barrett was the son of the great Lincoln collector Oliver Barrett; Victoria was his baby daughter.*

478 | TO BRENDA UELAND

[Harbert, Michigan]
[Circa Fall, 1945]

Dear Brenda

You may not know I am of that select company which not merely reads Brenda Ueland but RE-reads. And not merely rereads but collects. Except for four mos of the column (when I was drunk with a job I am doing and not sobered up yet) I have clipped about 3 out of 4 of the columns. And I have about the same proportion of your mag. articles and stories, besides having your books. So much of durable value in them. I am a good reader. What I keep and reread has what will be kept and reread and written about. When I shall get around to the piece I am to do about you I dont know but the day will come. She has peculiar sanity, queer and real valor, and paradoxical blends of pride and humility, about the time you have her spotted as a mystic and a transcendentalist she is out amidst a jam of plain folks giving you the horselaugh. She is ancient Aztec, modern minneapolis—and loves water, weather, moods of changing lights in the sky, rain, snow, jokes, and any speech that jets out irresistibly and has the kinetic flow of something worth telling and remembering after told. "Me" I read again in a series of breakfasts. Sweet company. The mother and father, Julie, Gaby, come alive so darkly and tenderly. Having seen and known Gaby I rode along with you in every lavish caress and cry of praise you gave her: and it would be convincing had I not known Gaby. And the house—what a house—having known its rooms and outlooks as I have—the house sort of breathed and shook in my reading "Me." Now I am half way thru a third reading "If You Want to Write." It has your questing and your laughter. It is the best treatise on what is termed creative writing that I can name.

Should it be that you have slack and lingering moments when you feel useless, completely useless, that is okay and you neednt be afraid of its pressing you down: it is a wonderfully small container they hand us at the crematory when we duly acknowledge receipt of the total known ash and cinders of a rare vital human person. Maybe I am leading up to saying I am sure you have a congregation of at least several hundred to whom you preach and they listen and they cherish your miniatures and they get from you the breath of a living companion and helper. You range around in the tremendous themes of all time and can shift to cameos of Bill Robinson and nice fool phone conversations. You are not a transient in writing and the proverb Nothing is so dead as yesterday's newspaper, wont go for you. My book goes winding, zigzagging, careening, and will be a strange affair and like each of my other books will be a book that I wish I could have had to read years ago. Luck stars be over you.

As ever

Carl

The enclosed kitkats happen to be at hand.—On account of *time* have had to quit the column but will go to it again later.—You have done some keen political pieces Brenda writing as tho no one else had ever touched the theme you were handling.

479 | TO DOUGLAS SOUTHALL FREEMAN

[Harbert, Michigan]
November 5, 1945

Dear Douglas Freeman:

Having recently read various biographies of Washington and several hundred pages of Washington letters and addresses, I find myself often thinking of you, as I understand you are working on a biography of the man. Not until lately did I begin to get bursts of light rather than gleams of what made him the superb figure he was. I pray now and shall continue to pray that your health and marvelous capacity for heavy labor shall go on. For I know that if you live you will do the book that is wanted about Washington. It is a commentary on I know not what that so long a time had gone by without an adequate work about him. You come to it with the preparations and backgrounds. I meet others saying the same. You should know there are others thoughtful and prayerful about you.

Faithfully yours,
Carl Sandburg

480 | TO EUGENE MEYER

Harbert, Michigan
November 10, 1945

Dear Eugene:

You should know I was not anywhere in the neighborhood when the luncheon on your 70th birthday was put on. I would have been there to see you, to see your face and hear your voice having attained three score and ten. If I had made a speech at the luncheon I would have said, for one thing, that it is good to look at a friend who probably has grown in mental reach and spiritual quality and the virtues of St. Francis as much in his 7th decade as in any other previous decade. The number of unburied dead who are still ambulant and vocal about the premises of our National household is sometimes melancholy and again comic. Pax tecum—and many more years

Carl

481 | TO HELEN PAGE AND GALE WILHELM

Harbert, [Michigan] Nov 19 45

Dear Helen and Gale

A sweetness and grace about having your note today it leaving Oakdale Thurs 5PM and here for my Mon breakfast carrying the shine of your countenances and the tones of your voices and clock-tick moments of silence we have had telling me you are as the carnival spielers cry Alive! Alive! which comes nice since I have so often thought of you across months past when I didnt write th letters that ran thru my head on account of being drunk with a book in the writing one letter would have been about last summer reading over Chico letters and re-reading all th GWilhelm books which are now aboard a box car of 42,000 pds cargo somewhere between here and Hendersonville NC the novel runs now above 300,000 words and will go upward of 400,000 when finished it is really 4 books that could have been published separately and serially and I have meant to ask you fellers whether a novel that is cyclic must be sickly and believing you would sing out it isnt necessarily so hoping to bring parts of it to Oakdale this winter whether I go to the new North Carolina home (the house built in 1836) before going to MGM and Culver City isnt sure as yet the Missus and daughter Janet and a nephew Eric drove away this morning in a rain with a station wagon and a trailer holding 16 blue ribbon Nubian does and daughters Margaret and Helga with the two grandchildren we are keeping house amid the ruins till a VAN comes sometime before Dec what to pick and choose for my work at hand hasnt been easy your presences have been here in this attic always and they will be in the 3d-floor room down there look-ing toward the Great Smokies forty miles away and the Blue Ridge summits fifty miles off thank you for your breath of blessing that came this morning

Carl

Gale Wilhelm, novelist, and Helen Page, a friend, lived in Oakdale, California. Miss Page was a great-granddaughter of Stephen A. Douglas.

482 | TO MARY SANDBURG JOHNSON

[Harbert, Michigan]
[December, 1945]

Dear Mary

Moving is a terrific business   heavy accumulations of note and manuscripts   so much of it unfinished and irreplaceable   and of course it aint the work—it's all the time the goddam decisions that wear a fellow down   having filled a big Box-Car that left last week now we are getting ready for a VAN   one telegram from the Great Smokies says the trailer of goats arrived safe and a second telegram that a truckload came thru alive and well   and I dont know now whether I go from here to the Smokies or here to New York or here to the West Coast   it was good to see your work corner and the sunslants there   speak a silent prayer for Book III and the Epilogue in this world of smoke and fog and atomic mystery   and I pray for your health and luck

Carl

483 | TO LLOYD LEWIS

[Flat Rock, North Carolina]
[End of December, 1945]

Dear Lloyd

Your Sunday column is what I long ago wanted and knew was there. The [Robert] Hutchins panegyric is about the only one I havent fallen for and heavy. This latest one on humor in the White House is a honey—and with others eventually should make a book that I would like to have handy. I think I shall get a clip of it to the President with word that it has no slightest tincture of malice and is counsel and prayer from your deepest heart.

Take care of yourself. You have a mind and heart now living richly out of long turmoils and accumulations.

Carl

1946

How can the author of THE PEOPLE, YES be a colonel or a poobah? The health of the Missus, the ancient desire of Helga for a farm and horses, the plight of barn-fed goats who want pasture, these sent us to N.C. I told 'em I'd go any place they picked and it was just an accident that the Memminger place was there at a price near silly.

484 | TO LLOYD LEWIS

[Flat Rock, North Carolina]
[Circa January, 1946]

Dear Lloyd

Kiplinger says we're riding into good times that will last till definitely 1948 at least. So, don't set 1948 as any absolute deadline for your Grant. I could have done a smooth fast piece of work, 75,000 to 100,000 words for MGM, that they would have taken but the book runs 200,000 and will run above 350,000 when finished next year, God willing. And it will be a book as I want it and they dont interfere. . . Do a column on AN AMERICAN DILEMMA (Harpers 1942) by a doggone Swede named Gunnar Myrdal, 2 heavy vols. The old lovable Quaker streak in you will answer to it and you won't be worse off about the Negroes and whites of Grant's time. . . Grant I keep seeing in two great crescendos (1) his genius in the war (2) and his fadeout, the writing of the book against heavy odds and then after his death the response to the book: how his heart would have warmed to the way that book has travelled. Talk with old bookstore men about it: they sell it, buy it, sell it again: he wouldn't have believed that under the grassroots he would live on in that curious massive self-portrait. Alongside it the equestrian statues are a negligible amount of horseshit, excuse pliz. . . Stop over here at Flat Rock NC whenever you should get this way and bigosh I am yet going to get to that vacant spot in your house where FLW [Frank Lloyd Wright] wouldn't let you put the grand old heirloom clock. . . Such good news about the next book. It will have some of your best pieces that I have missed. Do you remember when we agreed that if we had a little less intelligence, of a sort, we

431

would have made a vaudeville team good as McIntyre & Heath or Moss & Hart in How High Is Up? . . . When certain aimless people now ask 'What are you writing?' I tell 'em, 'The Biography of an imaginary bacteriologist and the title is FUN WITH FUNGUS.' Affection to Katherine and Nancy.

Yrs as always
Carl

Lloyd Lewis lived in a house designed by FLW—Frank Lloyd Wright—a mutual friend. His next book, It Takes All Kinds, *was published in 1947.*

485 | TO THOMAS HORNSBY FERRIL

Flat Rock NC 4/1/[1946]

Dear Tom

When last I saw you at the [Edward] Davison party I guess we both had the same virus. The next night I went to bed and stayed on my back six days getting well acquainted with Terramycin. I give thanks to Terramycin which struggled with the virus and cast it out of me. (Been reading New Testament. In Chapter XI, John, verse 39, I find, "Lord, by this time he stinketh." Why hasnt that been quoted more often??) I go on rereading your best paragraphs. I bespeak the Lord to not let your inner grace dwindle.

Yrs
Carl

486 | TO MARY HASTINGS BRADLEY

[Flat Rock, North Carolina]
June 18, 1946

Dear Mary Bradley:

You should know that when your letter came months ago its timing was good. It was a case of my not knowing how I needed it till after I had read it. Needing it again today I read it again.

That remarkable genealogy is good to have. It is companionable. The job here goes weaving on and I hope to show you more sequences of it this fall. I have the kind of admiration for your themes and your craftsmanship—so that all points you make, positive or negative, sink in and have consideration and use. When in Chicago again, probably this summer, shall seek you out.

Faithfully and with deep thanks,
and affectionate good wishes—
Carl Sandburg

487 | TO MARY HASTINGS BRADLEY

[Flat Rock, North Carolina]
[Circa Fall, 1946]

Dear Mary Bradley

It was good you could take time to look over Book II and see that it has an organic current running along from Book I. Before long shall be sending Book III to Oliver and you, the Epilog sometime this summer. . . Your quotes from Henry VIII and Anne B keep lingering with me, seem to have tragic-poem quality. . . I told Gene MacDonald that you can talk off a portrait sketch of Inez "unusual, real, rather lovely and fascinating the way Mary tells it." I'm all for taking my guitar and going with you and Herbert to dinner at Gene's—this with hope and prayer that Herbert has made a nice recovery. . . Again you should know you were a friend in time of need, health and a mainstay when I had moments of groping on this long tough and involved job. It made a difference that I had read those two short magazine novels of yours and could put a certain trust in your eye as to workmanship, both style and content. That trust deepened on going thru Five Minute Girl, African lore, and the memory of one keen radio talk on African colonies. You have had rich living—with more ahead. With depths of admiration and affection—

Carl

Flat Rock [North Carolina] Oct 1 [1946]

Dear Paul

When you play Santa Klaus you make a real business of it: at Xmas I will say I had some of it in Sept. Those finely bound volumes about your and my Chicago will be keepsakes—and the kids will long treasure their signed books wherein their grampaw has keen attestation from a loyal friend. The news of your work is interesting: I would lay bets on the book you are on. Your arthritis reminds me my fingers dont do so good on the guitar as they used to. The news of Vesta and the young ones is good to have. You've had luck with those young ones. I'll tell you about my three daughters when I see you, all three having distinctive personalities and each making a pretty good life of it. The two grandchildren are amazing and intricate in loveliness, almost too good to be true, and a fellow wondering what time will bring. . . No one has done the book you mentioned to me one time that could have the title, "Others In the Cast." We have all got parts of it in our scrivenings. But the fellowship or lack of it in all the many interweavings of Browning, Lamon, Judd, Swett, Trumbull, Horace White, Joe Medill, Douglas, Davis, Fell, "those who knew him when"—maybe it would be too big and rambling an affair. . . We will talk about our ghosts but rather than go along till daylight we'd better begin on the bottle at noon and go on summoning ghosts till a little past midnight. . . You've done a bangup smackdab job on that Historical Society job: I think by contrast of my forlorn friend Miss McElvaine. . . Somewhere this winter be seeing you.

Ever yours
Carl

1946

[Flat Rock, North Carolina]
[November 1, 1946]

Dear Ken

Just this week finished the long haul over the hump of Book Three which leaves only the Epilog and which means that now there must be the decision as to when it is best for a west coast conference to be held. When that is held I head your way. During a sickness and during delays and hindrances on my work I have had letters of yours in sight, have wondered about you and your two loved ones, have re-read certain lines of yours and found them as at first deeply moving, with an outgiving as in ancient psalms, though telling of moments in our terribly modern ways of war.

Faithfully yrs
Carl

Lieutenant Commander Kenneth Dodson was recuperating in the Naval Hospital in Seattle.

[Flat Rock, North Carolina]
December 12, 1946

Dear Quincy:

It was deeply moving to have your October letter and to read through the paper you read in Galesburg. I will always be sentimental about your father and I hope the day will come when I can do the portrait of him that I want to do. He was so truly The Teacher and for me in the best and oldest sense of that word. Before I write it I want one or two long sessions with you. He would take a pride, I am sure, could he know of what solid and requisite work you are doing.

About printing the letters you included in your paper I have my hesitations. I have held off twice when fellows came to me about doing a biography and I cant say exactly why it is that I would rather see those letters printed in full at some later time, years from now, preferably when I am under the grass-roots. The selections you made from the published juvenilia, with your comment, carry the paper well enough, I would say.

Give your mother my love and tell her that those Sunday evenings when she served chocolate and nabisco wafers it was to a set of youth who remember. I read and opened discussion one evening with George Ade's Fables in Slang and another evening on Whiting's novel No 5 John Street. Also tell her it was not till last winter that I got to a thorough reading of the Elizur Wright biography. Reading it makes one understand better your father's versatility, wide ranging genius. It is good straightaway writing, delivers a fascinating portrait, and I can see it is going to rate as one of the indispensable items in two fields, the abolitionist movement and American life insurance.

Your letter and the paper you read sent my memory flooding back to those days of quiet years when we couldn't read the forces breeding the terrific storms that you and I have been witness to. May your good work, in that tremendously complicated realm of international relations, go on. When in Chicago again, perhaps this winter, I shall try to be seeing you.

Yours,
Carl Sandburg

Professor Quincy Wright, an eminent authority on international law at the University of Chicago, was the son of Sandburg's friend Professor Philip Green Wright. Quincy had helped to set the type on Sandburg's first book which was printed in the Wright home in Galesburg. George Ade's Fables in Slang *was a long-time favorite with Sandburg. Philip Green Wright had written a biography of his great-grandfather Elizur Wright.*

1946

Flat Roc NC Dec 28   46

Dear Ben

Let it ride, as is. I can only find these pages you send to be rather deeply moving. And part of it is that I see a healthy unrest and an endless questing in you about what the unfathomable Lincoln means along with his enigmatic indecipherable America. I know I will find the book fascinating reading. You seem to ride no hobbies nor personal predilections. Its as tho you had lived long with your findings and contemplations and judgements and could write no otherwise if you took longer. As between friends I see your growing in what Pete Cartwright would term "inner grace." With Ida Tarbell there was the factor that I saw those first articles of hers in McClures as they came out, later following her in the Standard Oil series, and other formidable stuff of current history: it was a deep and genuine admiration I had for that tall keen gracious woman. Hoping to do a certain sketch and study of her sometime. Shall seek you out when in Springfield sometime next year and have two beers apiece or boilermaker and helper as between two Seekers.

Yrs
Carl

PS: Two Seekers of what? Well, maybe of that hectic mystic imponderable The American Dream and how it will ride thru The Atomic Age!

Benjamin P. Thomas, executive secretary of the Abraham Lincoln Association in Springfield, Ill., 1932–1936, was working on Portrait for Posterity: Lincoln and His Biographers, *published in 1947.*

492 | TO ARCHIBALD MACLEISH

[Flat Rock, North Carolina]
February 7, 1947

Dear Archie,

The days go by. The months flit. I go to New York and you are in Paris. I get back home and you are in New York. You have done some good poems and hard work for UNESCO. I have laid an egg in the shape of another long chaotic book. We should talk these things over. We should drink from commodious beer glasses. Ada and I dare you to do your wheel barrow dance on East 70th street. I go to New York this March or next June and where are you?

Yrs,
Carl

493 | TO BEN HIBBS

[Flat Rock, North Carolina]
February 13, 1947

Dear Ben Hibbs

If it happens that another world war is staved off for a generation or two it will be a result of the kind of awareness Edgar Snow is showing in this first article. It has the broad-gauge quality of Ben Franklin. In printing it you are in the best tradition of the early George Horace Lorimer. You will have a variety of forces clamoring at you. Some of those forces would like the war now, right off. I could name them and go into the evidence. Wherefore I welcome and give salutations to those not caught in our everyday floodstreams of passion demanding vent. I could go on. What I started out to say was that I am sure others join in a feeling that the future will vindicate you.

Yrs
Carl Sandburg

Edgar Snow had written "Why We Don't Understand Russia" in The Saturday Evening Post, *edited by Ben Hibbs, of February 15, 1947.*

494 | TO OLIVER R. BARRETT

[Flat Rock, North Carolina]
[Circa winter, 1947]

Dear Oliver

Thank you for the letter about the manuscript. I am hardworn and it comes along as cheer and mainstay—as before in pinches of circumstance you have been a help and standby. I am finishing revisions of The Epilog this week and should soon have it in your hands. Will you see that the blessed Mary Bradley gets a look at Book 3? All your suggestions shall have attention. Thanks for the letter about a title. I have done both well and poorly when it comes to titles and will probably study about it till they are closing the forms at press time. Expecting to reach Chicago late June or early July, and ready to take another whirl at the text about the collection, also one or two jiggers of bourbon while enjoying the lake view and our usual discussions of the State of the Union. Remember me to the folks, emphatically including that precious token Victoria. My own grandchildren are almost too lovely to be true. Be seeing you—

Carl

495 | TO J. B. CECIL

[Flat Rock, North Carolina]
17 March 1947

Dear Mr. Cecil:

From the time I was eight years of age until I was twenty I saw hundreds of base-ball and football games on the southeast corner of the Knox campus. In the earlier years when I lacked the two-bits admission, I watched games through a fence knot-hole or from a tree branch across the street. In those boyhood days I probably never idolized any national figures more than I did Speedy Gonterman and above all that remarkable all-round athlete, pitcher, fullback, track man, Nelson Willard. One winter when my job was on a milk wagon I spent one evening a week in the Knox gym, as a guard being pitted against Louis Arnold and I believe Arnold and I are agreed that in those four years of bumping each other there was never a foul called on either of us and we had a respect for each other's code of sportsmanship. On various occasions on the old campus and in its buildings I hear John Finley, Otto Harbach, Chauncey Depew, Frank Sisson, Bob Ingersoll (in a big tent at the southwest corner of the campus, an anti-free silver speech 1896). When Fridtjof Nansen arrived for a Knox lecture course number, I was at the depot and saw the Polar explorer in blowing snow get into a hack for a hotel, after which I went home lacking the fifty cents admission to the Auditorium. . .

And now excuse pliz I ain't going to write no autobiography. My salutations to Knox for what I have seen it do for the youth of America.

Sincerely yours,
Carl Sandburg

This letter was written to J. B. Cecil, at Knox College, which had absorbed Sandburg's alma mater, Lombard College.

496 | TO MARJORIE ARNETTE BRAYE

[Flat Rock, North Carolina]
[March 20, 1947]

Well the days have gone by as the days will and the evenings marched on into nights and mornings and no day seeing you having gone unremembered nor ever written off as a loss nor ever thought of unless with a thankfulness somewhat beyond a mention of thanks—and the several moments when you took with a mute look of acceptance a volley of chaste Addisonian speech and archaic polysyllabics and made a quiet recovery with "Y e s like you said" and the snow pelted the windows and the streets filled with snow and the night club neons bade the customers come in for more of what

they had already fled from and with the dawn and the hangover
would still be trying to evade avoid and vamoose from "yeslikeyousaid" those were grand storm days shaping over the goddam said
and lovely Epilog where will be spots in print for your eyes and
you saying "There's a hurdle where I helped 'em get over" or
"Here I put a little fingerprint and it was fun" so now each of the
1480 typed pages of 973,000 words has gone to the printer and each
of the more or less 150 chapters has had a smooth and precise title
written for it leaving only a little preface with acknowledgements
to be done along with the doggone galley proofs and the fuddy-
duddy page proofs to be read and criss-crossed one by one like the
leaves of autumn falling to be blown they know not whither.

I like your strengths and awareness and your blue pools of
quaker quietude and your gamut of color flashes and much not
tabulated in the dictionaries nor caught in the rabinowitz slogan
"everything for horses" nor among the names of ponies in to-
morrow's racing form.

Books arriving to your hands from hereaways you are to keep
unless you hear a holler otherwise like I will hold to dockaments
you send unless you stipulate to the contrary wid or widout stipples.
Take notice you should look into Saturday Review of Literature for
March 20 and a piece about Ike and Me 95 per cent accurate.

Have told the publishers our book has enough storm and dark
turmoil so that whatever action is on next fall and winter the book
will be at home. There have been hours before when we hung to the
rim of the moon with greased fingers. Send along letters. Put in
news or thoughts and contemplations or light and airy foamfeathers
of vagrant fancy "yeslikeyousaid".

Don't throw away the wickerbasket. Sometime I'll tell Ernie
Byfield of your and Bill's heroic days there in January. Very keen
editor at · Harcourt-Brace one Bob Giroux a commander on the
carrier Essex we did well on deletions inserts changes and when he
says he's looked at it long and we should ought to cut out that second
commercial on double-wonder-cream I says that's what Marjorie said
and the same dictum of taste and feeling bigosh out it goes for I aint
got the kind of vanity that would keep it in the script. I am jaded.

It was the kind of long haul a feller didnt know he'd been on till the finish came and you were health and help at a mean turn of the road.

                                                                    CS

Marjorie Arnette Braye and her husband, Dr. William Braye, were close friends who lived in Washington. She had objected to the second "commercial" in Remembrance Rock. *His editor, Robert Giroux, agreed, and it was eliminated.*

497 | TO BRENDA UELAND

[Flat Rock, North Carolina]
[Circa May, 1947]

Brenda dear girl

Your letter was almost too good to be true, with its "God its been a long time." Yet long ago I used the word "permanent" about you and me. My trip west now looks more like late June or early July. I couldnt begin to tell you about the book, this long novel, so strangely inevitable in its growth and progressions. Prolog (our time) Book I (Plymouth Colony and Roger Williams time) Book II (Lexington-Valley Forge time) Book III (Lincoln time) Epilog (our time). Each of the books is about 120,000 words. It has had revisions and changes and next week I put it on ice and about Sept will take it up saying What the hell have we here? The tentative title, confidentially, Remembrance Rock: an American Timesweep. I may bring along a separate unit for your Papagos eyes, the Indian woman at Tucson I told you of who could make herself vanish into past and future realms. I never miss a column. I have clipped more than half to keep, prizing some like personal letters holding your eyes and voice. Yours have been tumultuous years since I saw you, Norway, prize fights, politics, lighted ideas, a starglimmer of a grandchild, a rather rich processional your life, from my seat. . . So much to talk of when we meet and we are also good at silences, the creative hush of either the Quakers or Scandinavians. Thank you for writing and luck stars be over your fine Spanish-Norsk head—

                                                                    Carl

498 | TO JUNIUS B. WOOD

[Flat Rock, North Carolina]
[Circa June, 1947]

Dear Junius:

If I had answered your letter right off the bat when it came, and had poured into it all the ins and outs that occur to me, it would have been a book. As between 2 rare birds who reported in extenso on the Chicago Black Belt, and their findings but slightly improved in big thick books that came later—and as the inheritor of your battered CDN desk—and as 1 who remembers you went and did factual reporting rather than think pieces—to Russia as 1 whose nostalgia about the old Wells Street ramshackle matches your own—I have to answer you. It would be a sin and the guilt lay on me should I put your letter in a box marked ANSWER ANY TIME which credits me with good intentions though the letters never get answered. We must meet up 1 of these days and talk about old times and the State of the Globe. I like the note of health and humor in your letter. Maybe I will see you about July 26 when we creep into the R. T. Lincoln crypt. Shall give you a ring then and it could be we will interview each other, off the record. Always good wishes—

Yours,
Carl

499 | TO LLOYD LEWIS

[Flat Rock, North Carolina]
[Circa June, 1947]

Dear Lloyd

Should it be that I left those definitions of poetry with you maybe you would send them on to me. . . More important, take a ride thru THE NEON WILDERNESS by Nelson Algren and give him a phone call and do a column. He's worth your knowing and writing about. What he has that too many of the hardboiled school haven't is reverence and compassion along with a style, color and cadence, speech tones out of the abyss. . . Reading GEORGE ADE by Fred Kelly I found myself saying at times, "What the hell that's Lloyd, the furtive and authentic Hoosier horse nicker." Ade wears well for me. So will Algren, I know it. He's modest, didn't get a fair greeting on his NEVER COME MORNING, now out of print. . . It was good to see you. I felt sort of timeless with you. Could be we have our best work yet ahead of us.

As always
Carl

500 | TO KENNETH DODSON

[Flat Rock, North Carolina]
June 6   1947

Dear Kenneth:

On this anniversary of D-Day I have finished reading about a dozen of your letters. I find them now as at first deeply moving. Some paragraphs go so far beyond mere national patriotism. I am revising and rewriting The Epilog and must use among other things that incident of the little Japanese gardener in Yokohama and "love me love my plants." Your letters have given me a lift to go on in the final shapings of this long book that curiously and inevitably has gone so much longer than originally planned. It may be that I shall have presented, across a timesweep running back to England in 1608, parts of an American testament. Perhaps the gist of it is in your sentence on the U.S.S. Pierce January 14, 1945: "Nothing seems sure and there is little to hang on to but faith." The time of my west coast trip now depends on when a hardworn editor returns from a vacation. Before I start for the conference at MGM I will mail to you, in confidence, the entire manuscript of the book. Then when I head north to your place you can give me your slants at the thing and I hope to have a few days with your letters along with talk about this "game of words" called writing. We'll dig up a guitar and I'll run off my repertory or rip-and-tear for you and Letha and Dickie. I had intended on the same trip to have a look-in on Evans Carlson: now he's gone and we're here and you should know there has been no time I've been on this book that I havent prayed I could be faithful to the best gleams of you and Carlson. Perhaps I told you of Steichen on the Lexington. A disabled plane hit the flight deck with its engine slewing off to kill two men and cripple five others, its whirling propellor knocking off Steichen's cap! So when we meet I call him The Phantom. And I'll call you the same. My thoughts go to you often and prayers that you have many years among your loved ones with your authentic "kinship of the earth and growing things."

As always
Carl

501 | TO KENNETH DODSON

[Flat Rock, North Carolina]
June 14   47

Dear Kennie

Have been living rather close to you for a week or more. There are passages in those letters of yours ranging from shrewd and witty to the keen and lovely and on into an august human dignity. I knew you had a rangey personality but I didn't realize till the readings of the past week how rangey. I think you will see, when manuscript arrives to you, that there has been no sloven use of your letters, that there has been sober care and an anxiety about America somewhat like your own. There is such a timely importance, in my viewpoint, bound up in some of your utterances that I have gone back in The Epilog and made a place for them. You are the further confirmation of what a great (according to your lights and mine) character, a retired justice of the U.S. Supreme Court says in a radio speech in The Prolog. . . I have been lax about writing you and am hoping across the silence that all goes well with you and yours.

As always
Carl

502 | TO DAVID C. MEARNS

[Flat Rock, North Carolina]
June 27, 1947

Dear Dave:

In re yours of May 14, his name was H. E. Barker—he owned and ran Barker's Art Store in Springfield, Illinois, died in Los Angeles about 1941. His store had a line of old and new Lincoln books and he became an authority on the books Lincoln was known to have read. He was the only person I ever heard say that Robert Lincoln sought the letters of his mother for the purpose of destroying them. As I recollect, Barker said that the arrangement continued for some years and then was discontinued by Robert Lincoln. Barker was a well contained person whom I would rate as credible. He was making no special point and he mentioned the matter in connection with a letter or two of Mrs. Lincoln that he had on sale and the fact that Robert Lincoln had by purchase and destruction diminished the number of available letters of Mrs. Lincoln. I send you this memo for your personal files and for your use as you require and with the understanding my name is not to be connected with it until my demise is complete and any and all disputants of my veracity are welcome to piss on my grave and see what it will get 'em.

Yours—
Carl

Sandburg wrote "Pvt and Confidential" on this letter to the distinguished historian and director of the reference department at the Library of Congress.

503 | TO FRANK LLOYD WRIGHT

[Flat Rock, North Carolina]
[June 28, 1947]

Dear Frank:

Your letter of years ago (Nov 25, 1935) about the Rootabaga Stories came to my hands today for a slow reading once and then again. I was pleased when it first came but today it left me with a film over the eyes. I remembered many things, the gay first visit to Taliesin with Lloyd Lewis, the second visit when you went down with pneumonia but there had been time for you to take me thru that little theatre where your students had put on plays from the Rootabaga Stories, then that winter night at the [Ken] Holdens when you dropped in to hear a reading of The People, Yes in manuscript. . . Anyhow we are standing this Rootabaga letter of yours on a mantel for a while and making copies of it so that text can't be lost. It is more than an Award of Merit. You termed it a little posy for my hat-band which it was for that hour though now it is more like a small bronze luckpiece to be kept hidden and taken out when the heart is heavy and dark for a lightsheen it carries. I hope—and have a premonition that way—our ways will cross sometime this coming year. Lloyd Lewis and I in his house last winter, in a long talk about you, agreed it wouldn't quite do for your epitaph but it had something, what the fellow on your place said to the inquiring truck driver: HE'S THE BIGGEST GODDAM ARCHITECK OF 'EM ALL. I suppose I'm extra sentimental about this old letter of yours because of the loveliness and rare lights of a grandson (5) and a granddaughter (4) who shake the house with their promises. . . Prayers for your health and luck stars be over you and Olga and yours.

As always,
Carl

Frank Lloyd Wright had written, "I read your fairy tales every night before I go to bed. They fill a long-felt want—Poetry."

504 | TO JAMES G. RANDALL

[Flat Rock, North Carolina]
[September, 1947]

Dear Jim—

I added a sentence or two to our article to include the Douglas letter Cutts carried to Lincoln. Thank you for sending on further findings. I go along with your surmise that Lincoln read a reprimand & kept the record of it—and then went into conversation and perhaps further admonition.

I miss doing post-graduate Lincoln work with you and Mrs. Randall.

Whatever happens with the Chi. Times squib, we may yet throw in on a little book wrapping the Cutts affair in one well-rounded package titled What I Am to Say to You, to begin and end with the reprimand. I would have the main outline ready & write it in four or five days at Urbana or Chicago & you checking, adding, modifying—sometime this winter, depending on our other work.

Yours
Carl

When this letter was written to James G. Randall, the distinguished Lincoln scholar, they were collaborating on an article for the Chicago Sun-Times about Lincoln's reprimand of Captain James Madison Cutts. Cutts was the brother of Senator Douglas's second wife. He was appointed a captain by Lincoln, then found guilty of insubordination against General A. E. Burnside as well as of a minor charge of Peeping Tomism. Lincoln wrote him a fatherly letter ("What I am to say to you . . ."), and Cutts went on to gallantry in action.

505 | TO ADDA GEORGE

[Flat Rock, North Carolina]
[Circa December, 1947]

Dear Adda George—

The memo sheet noted in entirety. You go branching out into new methods and resources in an amazing way. There are enterprises that would seize on you if they should know what you have on the ball as an organizer. I shall keep the first week of Jan 1948 clear of dates and possibly go to Gt. two or three days that week. The novel runs above 400,000 words, flutters darkly around the Knox County area of 1840-1865 for a few chapters. It will not go to the printer till about a year from now. And as the picture goes

3-hours or more, it will not be finished till sometime in 1949, if then, as Sidney Franklin takes his time to get what he wants. That typewriter was used in Chicago for some Rootabaga Stories and for about a fourth of The Prairie Years: it has interest mainly as a No. 15 Remington: the carriage had to be lifted to see what you had written. . . I am still not at ease about a non-posthumous B-P: it would require an ego and assurance I don't have. Yet a man must meet more than halfway the clean and fine regard of certain old and tried friends. I shall write this more in extenso sometime perhaps and with tribute to your extraordinary sincerity and thoughtfulness. As always—with affectionate good wishes

Carl Sandburg

Adda George was gathering mementos—including the No. 15 Remington—for the B-P (Sandburg's birthplace) in Galesburg.

506 | TO MARJORIE ARNETTE BRAYE

[Flat Rock, North Carolina]
[Circa December, 1947]

Dear Marj—

You in copying must decide where a sentence ends and thus where a period belongs. You can often decide that where you skip from sentences in one paragraph to another it is left to you whether they follow along in a continuity that makes sense.

In a quoted passage wherever there are omissions of phrases or sentences indicated by my pencil brackets, there you put in the famous, even notorious, "three dots of elision" like these . . . or these . . . always these . . . or the reviewers or critics will give us hell, even tho Sibelius asks, "Was there ever a statue to a critic?"

I have tried to be careful about inserts marked by the little red caret or arrowhead ∧ and to make such inserts plain as the nasal beak of Cyrano de Bergerac.

It is a butchery business we are on. You will need at times to be as remorseless as a headsman lopping off the skypiece of an important king.

Of course, there is the good old phone and you can call collect any time you have a real problem. I will be praying here in Flat Rock while you pray in Baltimore. In both places God is on the watch.

Buppong.

Marjorie Braye was copying Remembrance Rock.

507 | TO FANNY BUTCHER

[Chicago]
December 17, 1947

Dear Fanny Butcher:

As between tried and long time friends—and forgetting for a brief moment prices, wages, inflation, atomic and bacterial hazards —as I look at it from this biblical milepost, I recall the Chinese proverb, "At 70 man is a candle in the wind," and consider it is time for melodic pause in the playing of Harmonica Humdrums—

As always,
Carl Sandburg

508 | TO EDWARD AND NATALIE DAVISON

[Flat Rock, North Carolina]
March 20, 1948

Dear Ted and Natalie:

Been putting to bed a book. A Russian (white) critic at MGM says it may be a novel, a dramatic epic poem or "a new fawrm". Runs to a book of some 1000 pages. Manuscript 1480 pages, 673,000 words. Just finished writing 152 chapter titles. Preface yet to write and the mess of galley and page proofs. Confer remarkable photograph made in your backyard at Boulder as to proper position [for] reading proofs. The foregoing appendenda relates to my alibi for indecent delay in replying to decent and lovable friends. Have cut all lecture dates this coming season but shall hope that next fall or winter we could fix up a meeting. It's a hair-trigger time to be living in. My love to all four of you. You and your house always had blessings for me and we must not lose touch.

As always—

Carl

Edward (Ted) Davison was dean of Washington and Jefferson College, Pennsylvania.

509 | TO ALFRED HARCOURT

[Flat Rock, North Carolina]
May 17 48

Dear Alf

Your letter comes as a high song. It does give with a music restful to my bones at this time. I wouldnt have believed that the book would start out with themes and on a scale that dictated a structure and length not in mind at the beginning. I threw all I had into it and I know out of past experience that I cant now make any adequate judgement of it, cant get the measure of it till a later time. So when your old familiar handwriting beats it out that the book was worth the time and struggle, you take the edge off the punch-drunk feeling, you dust off some of the weariness. Helga has made a copy of your letter for Kitty McCarthy who has through-out been a honey of a helper. Shall hope to have a good summer day with you and Ellen—loving regard to you both—

Carl

510 | TO ALLAN NEVINS

[Flat Rock, North Carolina]
May 18 48

Dear Allan:

This is a case where silence can not possibly bring later regrets. I can never forget the way Beard slugged it out with Hearst years

451

back. Nor can I forget that he has been a friend of great help to me in the same way that you and Jim Randall and Paul Angle have been. There are the instances, among friends and kinfolk, where a fellow can respect a viewpoint with which he differs radically and basically. (Toombs and Little Aleck!) Beard once wrote me of a Quaker ancestor of his who was "read out of meeting." Let it ride, for now, Allan.

For months I have meant to let you know that Ordeal of the Nation [*The Ordeal of the Union*] arrived, that I have read thus far perhaps only a fourth of it and am saving it for slow reading later this year, that I find it having a grace of style or some quality I dont find a word for just now. I dont mean you write more "purple patches" than formerly yet it could be that the stream of it lies deeper in you with more color than anything you have written hitherto. I hope sometime again we can have a dinner and walk two miles to a subway station.

As always
Carl

511 | TO HOLLY BARRETT

Kenilworth, Illinois, USA
November Eight 1948

Dear Holly

Here now it is your first birthday and a year you have had of this phantasmagoria they call life. Another year and you will be two years of age and that will be the last time you double your age in one year. And seventy-four years from now you will be the same age in years as your grandfather ORB is now though he will not be here then nor will the little bird who is writing this by dipping his feet in ink & then walking across the paper. Go to it Holly and learn all you can and then unlearn what you can't use. I will close saying I love you & that is no arkymalarky.

Carl Sandburg

[Flat Rock, North Carolina]
11/30/48

Dear Fanny

Thank you for affirmations and eloquence. As I look back, what happened, I'm sure, is something like this: after being long possessed by it, I wrote a novel of theme and structure such as I wished someone else had written for me to read 40 or 50 years ago so I could have gone on from there. The theme is costly, tangled in dream and death. Tom Wolfe and Ross Lockridge died in their thirties, Stevie Benét at 45. Sometimes I wonder how and why I am ambulant & in my right mind, enjoying certain fool songs more than ever.—I don't forget a few bright fellowships, such as ours, running thru fair weather and foul, across two world wars.—Be seeing you and [Richard D.] Bokum this winter.—

As always,
Carl

[Flat Rock, North Carolina]
Dec 28 1948

Dear Tom:

I'm agin it. The idea isn't sound that you should be leashed to a series of fixed and frozen lecture subjects. For something that will transfix and instruct the listening student body, you should be given the old open range with no barbed wire. Foerster [E. M. Forster] had it in that dandy series "Aspects of the Novel" which rambles as random as "I Hate Thursday" and holds the reader and achieves a work of learning. What you have of importance about the various single figures you name could get told, with assurance and no forced notes in the telling, under the general subject without any of the compress bands used by the Egyptians for their mummies. Readers and Authors—or—Changing Trends in Poetry and Fiction—or—

Between You and Me, Who Reads a Book?—or—What Is It Authors Do To Readers?—or—What Authors Are Worth the Paper They Write On?—or—Living Books and Dead Authors—or—In Modern Literature, What Gives, I Ask You, Sir, What Gives? In any of these Tom could tie his hat to a saddle and ride and it would make a book to keep and cherish. Which Way Home in Modern Book Wilderness?—or—The Personal Element in Reading: One Man's Lettuce Author's Poison Ivy—or—How to Get Lost in Books and Reading—or—Fads, Foibles and Faiths Among the Modern Books—or—Green Lights and Red Amid the Literary Intersections —or—Much Ado About Books—or—You Can't Read with Only Your Eyes—which, Tom, is enough of an offhand list. What I stress is that if you are hogtied to a list of single figures it won't call out from you the best freegoing play of your mind and personality. The students would respond to such a series. All of which is submitted with ancient loving regard.

Carl

Thomas Hornsby Ferril had written a series of essays for his book I Hate Thursday.

514 | TO ALFRED HARCOURT

[Flat Rock, North Carolina]
Jan 6, 1949

Dear Alfred

Today on my 71st milestone I read again your letter coming out of a valley of shadows. I haven't had those grim adventures. I shudder—and then I'm infinitely thankful your old brains and aura seem now to be operative & lighted better than ever in your days and years. I shall hope to be seeing you when west in March. My love to you and the good Ellen. She knows I want to answer her shining October letter & will get to it. And as it says in Smoke & Steel, published 29 years ago, on the last page, 'The peace of great loves be for you. . . The peace of great phantoms be for you'

As always
Carl

PS   In the Mary McBride broadcast I told of your coming to our Mich. home when I had some 1100 typed sheets of the War Years done & saying to you, I didn't know whether I was a half or third way thru & your writing me from N.Y. a typewritten letter with a handwritten postscript: "Jesus! what a book!"—and Mary and the NBC announcer said they wouldn't have been surprised if we were cut off exactly there after that 'Jesus.' I read fm Rem Rock pp. 298-9 part of a speech of Remember & they said we were lucky not to be cut off at "More belongs to marriage than four bare legs in a bed." That Winwold prayer pp 890-891 is being widely re-printed.—After the present freeze that Calif. sun will be kind & genial & I count on your natural calm and tenacity.

515 | TO ALLAN NEVINS

[Flat Rock, North Carolina]
February 3, 1949

Dear Allan:

Your letter about Remembrance Rock was too fine and circum-ambient for an easy offhand reply. When I was in New York your phone number didn't answer the first time we tried and the second time you were on your way to Washington for a week—or we would have had the long delayed walk. I was alone four days at the Tom Maloney (U.S. Camera publisher) apartment at 5th Ave-nue and 102nd Street on the top 17th floor where I could see roofs of Columbia and we could have met halfway in a six minute walk apiece. I was shaping up the first rough draft of a book to be titled The Lincoln Collection of Oliver R. Barrett. At Harcourt-Brace they are pleased that it is a work for general readers. I wouldn't have undertaken it if it were not that Barrett has been friend and coun-selor across twenty-five years and I am beholden to him in a thousand ways as a beneficent influence. He has lived close to pri-mary sources in history and literature, steeped in Lincolniana and Americana, a trial lawyer with a hawk's eye for the involutions of evidence. We expect to have manuscript finished early in March in which case the publishers say they can issue it next fall.

Now about your letter from one Corn Belt Boy to Another. Harcourt-Brace want to print it in a booklet to be titled Remembrance Rock—Whither? I have written a short piece to go up front, a number of reviews will be printed in whole or part, along with several remarkable letters that we feel have curious and striking quality, that can stand as literature. Yours is a rather marvelous letter, in unity, flow and color, as between a Macomb-Galesburg axis, 2 cornfeds who have grown across the years, and had their influence on each other as inexorable drives sent them on from book to book. And as you wrote it with no thought of publication, you have merely to indicate your wish that it be not printed and that wish, with no explanation, will be respected. Your case is different from mine, when Ray Ginger of Cleveland, Ohio asked to print three letters of mine in a biography of Debs to come. I hesitated and then said Yes. But in that instance Debs is dead and near sainthood while you and I are living and neither of us in sight of canonization. Your "no, better not print", would have complete respect and understanding. It is enough that you could let yourself go and take time for so rich an outpouring. I showed it to Lloyd Lewis and the new Illinois governor Adlai Stevenson and they were lit up about it. I have roots and clinging vines holding me to Illinois. They pressed me to go October 27 to make the speech of dedication at the lake front memorial to Henry Horner. Then Stevenson, through Lloyd Lewis, pressed me to go to the inaugural at Springfield January 10 and speak or read after the new governor's address, this breaking all precedents. These were assignments of a kind I dont hanker after—I turn down ten for every one I fill—but the pull of old Illinois roots, memories, friends, sent me on.

Remembrance Rock got a peculiar press. About a fourth rated it The Great American novel, an epic and a testament. Another fourth rated it huge, muddled, overdone, and some the worst novel that had ever come to their hands, the evidence plain in most of these that they hadn't read the book. Then there were the in-betweens, sloven, self important. It has ranged from second to sixth in the best-seller score-board—and will be kicking up controversy for some time to come. My own appraisal of the book, which I will definitely trust, can not come till some years from now after I have been sunk in other work, and then give the story a long slow reading. My plans for the year include attention to the Nevins corner where years ago I read perhaps only a third of the Rockefeller, none of the Cleveland, and by now about half of the Ordeal. Fremont, Hewitt, Fish, Hone, Whitlock, I have got my head around and have used. That short history of the U.S. you did with Commager, that one I have bought in the pocket edition and given to a dozen various persons, some not liking your version of the New Deal. In the Ordeal I see you surpassing yourself, working toward one of the great landmarks in American history, in reach, range, style, going beyond the earlier work. Further deponent will say when this March or April we have that long postponed walk around Gotham.

Faithfully yours
Carl

Allan Nevins had written about Remembrance Rock *that "It is not strictly a novel, but rather a chronicle; and it is an impressive and enduring book. It does not create any one or two or three vital characters as the great novelists do; but it does recreate the multitudinous characters of America in a series of epochs."*

516 | TO OLIVER R. BARRETT

[Flat Rock, North Carolina]
February 25, 1949

Dear Oliver—

I beg to report that I have been working like an old time government mule on our book. Tomorrow if the pace keeps up I expect to put in the mail for you, insured, a manuscript of all but a closing chapter on which I will work while travelling, I hope. The manuscript is in folders and I would ask that you make no changes from one folder to another of any sheets until I come on and we work together on them. Where I have given the text of a letter or document I hope you can check and make any needed corrections. Where a photostat is indicated in the text please try and have that photostat next before or after the sheet where it is indicated to be placed. Of course we will go over these together, marking for the printers what portion is to be reproduced if it is not to be given entire. I believe if you can have the Mss. in that shape when I come along we may be able to lick it into final shape to be sent on to Harcourt-Brace for the demoniac and hawk-eyed Isabel Ely Lord to plough through it and employ her skilled and unmistakable directions to the Quinn Boden printers at Rahway, New Jersey who understand her signs and signals. I can see her coming from Episcopal services and joyously hurling herself into this mess as an assignment from God. I have had copies made of the full text of all letters and documents that I have here so that when I come along you will not have those minor tasks taking your time. There are places, as in the Cold War chapter where I have indicated a letter or document is to be inserted—and if you can have those indicated texts ready and copied when I arrive we may have the finished job ready for the printer before I leave Chicago on the evening of March 8. I am at Temple University, Philadelphia the evening of March 3 and expect to get a midnight blue-plate special that will have me in Chicago the morning of March 4 which I notice is Friday so we will have the weekend two days of March 7-8. Of course, all the time I say prayers and work any conjurations I can about your health. In closing up this piece of work we must be grave and reverend seigneurs acting with due deliberation and a high scorn of hustle and bustle. If as things shape up we don't have the job ready to go to the publishers on March 7 or 8 then I will return from Oklahoma about March 14 and we will go on with the work. If Harcourt-Brace can get the manuscript by the third week in March they are sure they can have it for "fall publication". Incidentally, I feel like saying that the only thing in the book you are unauthorized to delete is the Auld Lang Syne incident between you and Gunther. It is a beautiful luminous memorable little story. Blessings on you and love to you and yours.

Faithfully yours,
Carl

Lincoln Collector: The Story of Oliver R. Barrett's Great Private Collection *was published by Harcourt, Brace and Company in 1949.*

1949

[Flat Rock, North Carolina]
April 14 49

Dear Kennie

The week of the temblors and our prayers go it didnt shake your house. . . Hard going it has been for me. For I took on an uncompleted job last summer and fall and only last week did the final chores shaping up an Ms to go to the printer, much checking of letters and documents, 32 pages of half tones, many facsimiles of papers. It was partly that I saw a certain book that ought to be done and partly that I owed it to my old friend and co-worker Oliver R Barrett. He says it is the first time a book as such has been done about a collector. Probably to be titled A LINCOLN COLLECTOR. His is the largest and most important privately owned Lincoln collection.

Now I'm letting the dust settle and trying to ease a right hip that acts up. Of course you are unforgotten and unforgettable. I still plan on a west coast trip to see you and to see my sister, two years older than I, in Los Angeles. Bob Giroux told me of seeing you and mentioned something of your taking counsel of professors and supposed authorities on creative writing etc. etc. I doubt whether any of them can help you. Your genius at times is that of a prophet, a preacher, a spokesman, a wayshewer, a sailor, a commander, a mariner, a strong man with a great heart never lacking hopes and visions. The people you have met and known, the ports and streets you have seen, the memories of gardens and battles, the books and sermons you have read and heard that you still keep pondering on—I dont see how any counselor could go much farther than saying: You have been places and touched people. You are a man of a thousand stories. Find a framework. Then write it. Then overwrite it and cut it down. Let no day pass without writing it. When the going is good with you, your sentences march and hammer and sing low and what is called style is there in a simple perfection. Some of those paragraphs in the Epilog of Rem Rock I will keep rereading as long as I live. You have only to go to your memories and to the wellsprings of your own heart for what is termed material. You have an eye for the vivid and can render it sparely. You can make telling phrases and compress great teaching in a few sentences. Most of whatever you now need to be taught will have to come out of your own loving and toilsome practice. Some who have achieved masterpieces have said, "That was practice and if I live longer I can do better." Of course there is technique, structure, etc. etc. But what of the excellent novelists who have said, "My characters run away from me and become other than I first imagined them." I have known newspaper staffs where a saying ran, "The way to be a Star Reporter is to break all the rules." I heard Steinbeck say regarding Of Mice and Men, "I began with an equation and after that the story wrote itself." Paganini had a formula: toil, solitude, prayer. Steichen after World War I put in a year making a thousand photographs of a cup and saucer. Maugham crosses up Forster on how to write a novel and both heave Walter Scott into the ashcan. Shakespere wrote a certain amount of trash—because his theater had to have a new play next Tuesday. Enough of this—for this time. Ramble thru a couple of books I'm sending you but dont go scholastic. God love you—and Letha—and the pipsqueak. The west coast trip is a MUST with me and I'll be seeing you. "All the best."

Carl

518 | TO MRS. LLOYD LEWIS

[Flat Rock, North Carolina]
April 22   49

Dear Kathryn

It was lovely to talk with you tonight, to hear your voice come clear, to hear you tell about the services tomorrow morning under the trees by the river—so perfectly what Lloyd would have wanted. And your voice brave, sweet, dark but not breaking, it had something he would have wanted, exactly that music and tone from his longtime chum. . . As I look back it seems a rich and crowded lifetime he had, with you sharing and helping. He never had anything but lavish praise for you. You are part of his best books that will keep his memory green long after you and I are gone. I cry over his going but it isnt a bitter crying. He liked that line in Rem Rock: "To every man, be he who he may, comes a last happiness and a last day.". . When the trees are leafed out and the earth is giving with early summer laughter I'll hope to be seeing you and we can talk of rich days that have been and of a lad who is a shining memory.

yours in all faiths
Carl

Lloyd Lewis died of a heart attack on April 21, 1949.

519 | TO ADLAI E. STEVENSON

[Flat Rock, North Carolina]
May 4, 1949

Dear Adlai:

It's hard to lose Lloyd. Your loss is great. His affection for you and his admiration of you ran away deep. He could talk on and on about you, keen and warm. His feeling about you ran akin to what he had for FDR. Just to have had him for that kind of a friend and co-worker held something rich. And that is about all that mitigates your real loss in this hour. He knew the best heart of both you and me away deep. Sometime we can talk about a fine memory. All the best to you amid toils and tumults.

Yours
Carl

520 | TO JUNE PROVINE

[Flat Rock, North Carolina]
May 21, 1949

Dear June:

Thank you for the Knox Lincoln letter which belongs in the archives and thank you for remembering. A Stockholm publisher is putting out this year a Swedish translation of the Rootabaga Stories. Helene Champlain of the Waldorf-Astoria Bookshop says Remembrance Rock has now gone from their shop to sixteen different foreign countries. The book will be at home in any corner of the world where they have peace, revolution or war. I'm not yet ungimleted out of the book and won't have a judgement of it that I trust until several years from now. Why I get going on these jobs that run so much longer than originally planned I haven't yet figured out. Tell Neil I say you have a finely modeled head whether seen front view or profile. About our old office chum, Lloyd, not a word now. It is a deep grief. I'm going to write a piece for the Henry Justin Smith book. On a near wall I have a row of your Note Books —they wear well.

Yours
Carl

521 | TO FANNY BUTCHER

[Flat Rock, North Carolina]
May 22   49

Dear Fanny

We were a trio. It was thru Lloyd I first met you that summer evening, maybe 1916. Over the years he and I unfailingly exchanged the news about you. Now your piece in the Trib is just what he would have wanted, so rich hearted, the contemplative retrospective facts there, with an aura throughout and sudden little rainbows of correct understanding flowing into recessional praise, the right requiem for his Chicago and Midwest to hear. Now our bonds must be darker and deeper. Shall be seeking you this summer.

As ever
Carl

522 | TO OLIVE CARRUTHERS

Flat Rock, [North Carolina]
May 24, [1949]

Dear Olive

The Coggeshall diary item is handy-dandy and if or when you're going along with the Kate Chase story that should be woven in for atmosphere of the hour. I've been trying to find out what there is in accumulations of manuscript I have been excavating while also making a sane landing from the long flight of Rem Rock. Shall hope to be seeing you when in Chi probably sometime June. The work with ORB [Oliver R. Barrett] on galley proofs will not be as exacting as finishing that Ms wh runs to 125,000 words. Lloyd Lewis going isnt easy to take. He's the only fellow I ever sang duo with and we both called it nice. Be seeing you—all the best—many deep good wishes—

Carl

523 | TO MARJORIE ARNETTE BRAYE

Flat Rock, [North Carolina]
Aug 22 49

Dear Marge

In Chi I hear about you and Bill as tho it is as definite as some Domesday Book pronouncement that youse two are diagonalizing across USA to Miami. If it isnt that the moving work or illness account for the lack of messages, one or two, then I am in the doghouse. However when the book comes along to you this Nov you may see that it was a heavy set of chores. Never again am I going in for one of these documentary jobs where you check and double-check till the walls come falling. As always the thoughts have been constant and endless of you. Now comes an odd thing. You may remember my telling you that I wrote you a fairly good letter, with a pencil, outdoors, and didnt manage to get it typed. The aforesaid letter in pencil is enclosed as Exhibit A. The rendition goes as follows, body of letter written in July '48 and PS in Aug '48:

"So now you're back where you were. So now you're still of the same height weight complexion, same weave of the angelic and demoniac, same quarrelsome disposition, same habit of never looking in the dictionary so when an intelligent inquiry comes to you from an educated yentleman you ever employ a recourse of plopping courteous and child-eyed, a brimming reply like an answer dipped from the Presbyterian catechism: "YES, LIKE YOU SAID."—What did you learn from 2 thousand miles of the USA and Canada? That the earth is the footstool of the Lord. Yet you already heard that from two negroes one with a guitar and the other with a washboard on a summer Sunday afternoon on Maxwell St. Why should the Lord want a footstool? And if the earth keeps turning on the bottoms of His feet why dont the Lord get hotfoot? That's what comes of having an anthropomorphous God. I like mine with no feet, no footstool, or else feet so big if He put 'em in the Pacific Ocean a tidal wave would wash Los Angeles and Hollywood over into the Grand Canyon of Arizona beyond salvage and good riddance bad rubbish. A nice card from Bill, it carried his smile.

P.S. Above written in July, this being written August. Meantime reports from you, heart warming reports about the guitar. Reading the Guitar Review, wh is going forward to you (and wh you must return after reading it twice) will help make you unafraid of toil, solitude, prayer, practice and practice. I think you have the fingers, the patient strengths, the sensitivity of spirit, required to become a better than ordinary guitar player.—Your grave face and a gay one, jut forth on the ground floor front room wall. As always,"

So there you have it. . . Now make with a letter giving the high and low spots of the news. I would guess if you're going to be stationed at Miami we will see each other oftener. When you were in Wash DC I tried for a stopover there—no soap. . . Lloyd Lewis dies and too early. The sorrow in my heart will run long. . . Family news all to the good here. When in Chi next time I'll see ya for sure. . . Fine bulletins from Bruddah Dodson and his work. . . Finished galley proofs 3 wks ago, today heading to NY for page proofs, hundreds of line cuts to be overseen as fitted with txt. . . Your face, voice, jokes, admonitions grave and gay, linger ever. . . To you and Bill all the best—

Carl

524 | TO THOMAS L. STOKES

[Flat Rock, North Carolina]
December 26, 1949

Dear Tom Stokes,

What happened ran something like this. Arriving 4:40 PM after phoning you I phone Dave Mearns at the Library of Congress, wishing to see what the Library looks like, not having been there since July 1947 when the Lincoln papers were opened, at which time I wrote 12 newspaper columns, a third of it with lead pencil. Mearns says they are having tea and cocktails at a party for Robert Frost who is recording some of his poems for posterity. Not having seen Frost in 12 years, and we being old friends, I go over and take a hand in a many sided discussion of the Bollingen award to Ezra Pound. Leaving there I head for dinner at Leiserson's and Bill and I, not having seen each other in three years, talk til 1 AM. You should hear him sometime on the difference, physically and mentally, between airlines presidents and railroad presidents he has met in the course of Bill's mediating and arbitrating—the pay scales for pilots—and the oddity of railroad engineers paying twice as much for life insurance as passenger plane pilots. Next afternoon comes along their neighbor Millicent Todd Bingham, author of Ancestral Brocade about Emily Dickinson. Mrs. Bingham's grandmother was a Dickinson family close friend and is working on renditions and decipherings of many manuscript scraps of Emily Dickinson. As that picaresque Amherst wraith of a girl and woman has always fascinated and instructed me, and as once on a moonlit night I walked with Robert Frost past the Amherst home, I was a little spellbound at Mrs. Bingham's answers to my questions and her questions put to me. She will probably write the last word on the rumored love affair of Emily. Then to the Library of Congress where I made a preliminary survey of a book of 1,000 folk songs that Duncan Emrich, head of the folk song division, has done in collaboration with one Ruth Crawford Seeger, a Chicago gal who for years was a sort of added informal unadopted daughter at our house. Publishers say to

465

print the book would mean a retail price of $17.50, prohibitive. So they would like me to range over it and join them in making a book that can be sold. I am studying about it and will probably throw in with them. Then I recorded three fool songs: a Swedish folk ditty in the original with my translation, "It's All the Same Where You Go When You Die," "A Newspaper Man Meets Such Interesting People," and an irreverent ditty that Eugene Field gave the White-chapel Club (newspaper men) of Chicago. One recording of these Duncan Emrich assured me would go to you. In the whirl of these circumstances I forgot about the goddam WHITE tie. I had no intention of being a white crow in a flock of blacks. I just clean forgot. Also I should mention that in New York at my publishers we have been having furious conferences over a book that originates at their suggestion and not mine, a volume of Complete Poems to be issued September of 1950. What of magazine and periodical publication should go in, what of new pieces are worth going in, a group dealing with the present hour—and a Preface, Lord help us—riding to Washington I couldn't help making notes for the Preface. Some 800 odd poems or psalms—or contemplations—for which I must give the world an alibi or thumb my nose at the world and refuse, in so many words, to testify. I thank you for a good time at the Gridiron. Every American should see the Grand Canyon of Arizona, the Chicago Loop, one national party convention, and the Gridiron. I hope your copy of LINCOLN COLLECTOR has arrived. The 2,400 copies of the limited edition are all gone and a trade edition is to be published for February. Don't fail to read pages 243-247. It is one of the great all-time newspaper performances. Regularly, fellow, I read your column and value it as current history. You ramble along sometimes like Tom Corwin writing Lincoln, "I have gazed on this scene till I can view it calmly." A New York News man down here last summer told about one of their staff men being called back to New York to work and saying of New York, "It isn't a way of life—it's a rat race!" Well, some of us can see Washington too as something of a rat race. Excuse long letter. Next time I write you shorter. Holiday greetings to all under your roof.

Affectionately yours,
Carl Sandburg

1950

Columnist Thomas L. Stokes had invited Sandburg to a Gridiron dinner in Washington, and while there he was captured by many friends. This is one of the first mentions of Complete Poems. *The great newspaper performance he referred to was in the April 17, 1865, issue of the New York* Herald *under the head, "The Great Crime—Abraham Lincoln's Place in History."*

525 | TO EDWARD R. MURROW

Flat Rock, North Carolina
January 4, 1950

Dear Ed Murrow

Thank you for that New Year's Day broadcast of you and your staff. It had sanity, love of mankind and a sense of history, set forth a marvelous flow of human forces working inexorably toward unknown ends. If there should be a script of it please send me one to read and ponder. Your boys reminded me of Lincoln's line, "I shall do nothing in malice for what I deal with is too vast for malice."

Your well-willer
CS

Edward R. Murrow was linked to Carl Sandburg by North Carolina —and by a devotion to freedom. Sandburg regularly listened to the New Year's Day broadcasts of CBS foreign correspondents assembled under Chairman Murrow.

526 | TO THOMAS HORNSBY FERRIL

Flat Rock N.C. Jan 8 50

Dear Tom

Passed my 73d milestone yesterday. And I've been thinking about you and us. The piece you wrote about Complete Pms had a peculiar adequacy—out of long understanding and fellowship. The Complete Pms book came about oddly. I would never have thought of such a volume being published. This because something like a fifth or more of the material is "dated", belongs to periods, and must be read with an awareness of time shifts. So many of these, if not previously published, I wouldnt consider publishing now without many changes and revisions, if at all. Yet when Gene Reynal and Bob Giroux at Harcourt's plopped the idea before me as a "must" I went along with them and we printed the whole kit and caboodle of past books. I expected disfavor or short shrift in most of the reviews and was surprised at what came. There is a percentage of drivel or over-writing, sometimes "spewing" or again "running off the mouth" as you phrased it. But I had to let that percentage ride, with the alibi, "I wrote it like that then and read proof on it and saw it into print and now I stands mute."

It may be that time, circumstance and the world storm never-theless will let me get around to a poetry anthology I have had in mind for years. I am not at it now but hope some day to do it. It will be different from anything hitherto attempted, from my gleanings of fifty years. It would include the work of some fellows I have known, with sketches of them, intensely and indubitably drenched with the American scene—Ferril, Edwin Ford Piper, H. L. Davis, Bob Brown and others. Giovannitti might go in for a noble bitter psalm about New York. What goes in would be what I have lived with as a reader, not the collective judgement of any group or clique dictating. There are some marvelously fine and strong pieces of Americana not widely known as they should be. I would be so con-trary as to include those lines in Rem Rock pp 276-7. . . Maybe you take this as confidential till I get going on it when I shall detour to Denver and try your judgement on certain pieces.

It is curious how your stuff stands up week after week in the RMHerald. I find that I lay by about three numbers out of four, those first two pages. So many of them are like a nice straightaway personal letter from a widely aware friend who knows the score or says nobody knows it and the game ought to be called on account of darkness. Take care of yourself and go on, as you have been going, with no fears of your meditations. As always

Yrs
Carl

A few days before, Sandburg had written to Ferril, "I can't write you how the Thomas Hornsby Ferril Award of the Nobel Prize— from Denver instead of Stockholm—hit me."

527 | TO HARRY E. PRATT

[Flat Rock, North Carolina]
Jan 31 50

Dear Harry Pratt

Shall be in Detroit Feb 7 on the Denby Lecture Series—and again in Detroit Feb 15 at Highland Park Junior College at 9:45-11:15 A.M. The Denby is 8 P.M. If it should be convenient for you we could talk about your corrections on The Prairie Years. Of course I would like to make some payment for your painstaking labor backed by your extensive specialized research. . . We have each travelled long winding paths in the same field since so long ago we talked those hours when I was your overnight guest at Blackburn [College]. . . I don't know your work or hours at Muskegon. Between Feb 3 and Feb 13 letters will reach me at the office of Oliver R. Barrett, People's Gas Bldg., Chicago. I have duplicates and spares of various Lincoln items which I could send you: let me know what you most miss. Something tangible is due you for your enterprise and skill in corrections on the Barrett book, nearly all of which were made. . .

All the best to you—

Sincerely yours
Carl Sandburg

Harry E. Pratt, an important Lincoln scholar, became State Historian of the Illinois State Historical Library in the fall of 1950.

528 | TO DOUGLAS SOUTHALL FREEMAN

[Flat Rock, North Carolina]
March 12, 1950

Dear Douglas,

When in Richmond on March 25 my hope is that you will be in town and we can squeeze an hour in somewhere. It is not often that 4-volume biographers foregather.

Yrs,
Carl

529 | TO CATHERINE MCCARTHY

[Flat Rock, North Carolina]
April 14, [1950]

Dear Catherine

Nice news you send of Arthur Godfrey and of the lovable quizzical mad Irishman Dick Nugent whose word "köttebulle" means meatballs. He can do Swedish meatballs prime and we have a standing invitation to his place on 37th near Third ave for lunch. Captain Mooney of a roving detective squad can be present with enough advance notice, also Batch [C. D. Batchelor, New York *Daily News* cartoonist].

After the recent diabolical accuracy requisite to the job, I have been sunk in pools of nonsense and fantasy, asking: Were boxes made before bags or bags before boxes? The question is historical and important, as likewise, Why do boxes have corners and bags none? Or, why does a bag sag and a box not?

Enclosure from an HB [Harcourt, Brace] book may be considered to go alongside FLWright letter on new Rootabaga jacket. Reference to modern architects will sure interest FLW, who aint guilty, as charged.

Take care of yourself. You have so often been for me what FDR said of Lehman, "my good right arm." When chance offers, any time, run down to Connemara and loaf and ride a most peaceable and kindly sorrel horse named Storm.

Yrs
C.S.

530 | TO GREGORY D'ALESSIO

[Flat Rock, North Carolina]
April 29, 1950

Dear Gregory,

Enclosed, under federal insurance is the long delayed lesson in chords from Brother Segovia. You are to learn this lesson and pass it on to me. It was at the Buchbinder apartment in Chicago that I first met Segovia and failed to amaze him with my virtuosity. He had never met anyone so deeply loving of the guitar and nevertheless so faithless in his love. Then 13 years pass and Hazel Buchbinder nails him in Havana and he comes through with the much needed lesson.

Yrs,
Carl

Gregory d'Alessio, New York artist, was editor of The Guitar Review. *Segovia actually sent Sandburg chords to learn.*

531 | TO BRUCE WEIRICK

[Flat Rock, North Carolina]
May 2, 1950

Dear Bruce:

When I worked till five o'clock one morning and before going to sleep saw daylight flooding the bedroom, I said for you to hear, "Well, I haven't had this since the sacramental mornings in Urbana.". . . Heartwarming to see those letters you and Jim Randall wrote to Sister Esther. . . . About a degree in June I could carry one more if it came from the cornbelt of my native state of Illinois, to which commonwealth I can truly say, "Of thee I have sung.". . . The preface to Complete Poems got slashed considerable, with certain fresh additions that I believe are in line with what you indicated—one very curious page of autobiography at the end. . . . Good going to you, my nighthawk brother. Luck stars be over you.

As ever
Carl

P.S. Enclosed is data on Edward Steichen. In 1940 Wesleyan (Conn.) gave him a Masters degree but so far America's greatest photographer, a plant breeder extraordinary, hero of distinguished record in two wars, so far he hasn't a Doctorate from a great university. I think the event would have dignity, humor and gayety, if this great pioneer in photographic Art could be handed his honorific

471

parchment along with his biographer. He has been a Teacher in the truest sense of that word. He has taken time and care, giving the best of himself to scores of young photographers who later came thru as both craftsmen and artists. His influence on me has been immense and incalculable.

Professor Bruce Weirick, of the University of Illinois, had first written about Sandburg in 1924 in From Whitman to Sandburg, *calling him a "humanitarian revolutionist."*

532 | TO ARCHIBALD MACLEISH

[Flat Rock, North Carolina]
May 12 50

Dear Archie

So-o-o good to have your letter. . . About the GreyFund we'll make it next year, barring any and all Acts of God. . . I wrangled with a Preface that went 6,000 words and I cut it to 1,500. Lloyd Lewis' CAPTAIN GRANT came in galleys and my conscience wouldn't let me do other than read it and write an advance piece. My old friend and co-laborer Barrett died and I got up from four days of intestinal flu to write my little panegyric.

I can name several inescapable chores that came along taking one to three days apiece. I am the man who was on that train out of St. Louis—the fifth time he was kicked off he dusted himself and said, "I'm going to Cincinnati if my pants hold out.". . Hope to be seeing you May 25 amongst the immortals wearing immortelles. . . Font of titles in enclosure will be changed to larger and non-italic. The piece naming you is maybe a tract rather than a poem. And if John Bunyan or John Ball wrote tracts why shouldn't I? What is the Dec of Ind but a tract? Or the Four Freedoms?

Erewhiles I hope to put one arm around you and the other for Ada—

Carl

1950

[Flat Rock, North Carolina]
Dec. 10 50

Dear dear Sister

Days go by after the news and I go saying "What the hell is there to write?" The wonder is that both of us are still around above the grass-roots. I made the trip to see you last year knowing as the Irishman put it "Any minute may be your next!" Charlene sends a lovely letter about, for one thing, your sense of humor being nicely with you. To say "We will hope and pray for the best" doesn't mean much as between oldtimers like you and me. But I count on the vitality and savvy I believe you have to bring you thru and that it may be we'll have one more visit next year. You've been good for me, a fine helper in those young days. If I ever get around to an autobiography you'll have a sweet portrait. Believe there is warm old love here and there are no days go by you are not remembered with thankfulness. Sounds like our Mother. She liked that word "thankfulness." She'd have us thankful for each other.

Bulletin: Carmel writes me that our cousin Lily Holmes, blind, bedfast and cheerful, managed one Sept day to get out of bed and break one of those pipestem legs of hers. It is almost a laugh, Lily joining in. As has been said "Life is a dangerous thing and the chances are against our coming out of it alive." Jesus, am I cheerful! Just heard about a Kansas woman with a Swedish father. She made a trip to Sweden and came back saying, "I'm glad I went. I used to think my father was queer but now I have learned he was just Swedish."

Carl

[Flat Rock, North Carolina]
[Circa 1951]

Dear Don:

I find [this] among some notes.

Henry George 1876 when considered by the University of California for the Chair of Political Economy to which he was not appointed:

A monkey with a microscope, a mule packing a library, are fit emblems of the men—and unfortunately there are plenty—who pass through the whole educational machinery and come out but learned fools.

You have probably seen it. We could be a verbal Herblock, that monkey and mule. Also find a note:

Asheville bus station dirty boy grinning to newsboy and hollering: BUS STATION MURDER, MAN KILLED A RAT IN THE MEN'S ROOM.

Twas a sweet visit Saturday night, sort of like kinfolk looked in on us.

Yrs,
Carl

Don Shoemaker was editor of the Asheville Citizen. *He wrote an editorial greeting when Sandburg moved to North Carolina. They became fast friends, visiting at least once a week. Henry George was Shoemaker's great-uncle.*

[Flat Rock, North Carolina]
January 13, 1951.

Dear Al,

Your letter came. Your fine remembrances came. Will be along in February and it will be good to see you. Perhaps as long as I live I shall occasionally remember your answering a 'phone call early in the morning with neither a "hello" nor as in Mexico "Bueno" nor as in England "Are you there?" but you, sort of as though you were anticipating one world of free men: "SPEAK FREELY!"

Yrs
Carl

536 | TO ALFRED HARCOURT

[Flat Rock, North Carolina]
March 28, 1951

Dear Alf,

It is good to have your two last letters which I have been reading over again. A tumult of memories came over me—you winding in and out of them—on the news of Red Lewis passing. There flitted too the whimsical flash of my once saying, "Steffens is a kind of Jesus, isn't he?" And you instanter, "Yes, a sawed-off Jesus." Whatever is ahead we have had some great days.

Yrs,
Carlos

537 | TO THOMAS HORNSBY FERRIL

Flat Rock NC   May 22   51

Dear Tom

There was lure about going to Aspen—fellowship with you and Syd Harris—visiting the birthplace of Goethe—you once wrote so casually and incidentally that Goethe was born in Aspen that inasmuch as I dont know for sure where he was born I sometimes have a suspicion that some woman fled Germany, gave birth to a little one at Aspen and later lo and behold it turned out to be Goethe who wrote a book about how foolish it was to be born and scores of German youths committed suicide after reading it and when I tried to read it to see whether I would feel like committing suicide I couldnt get interested so here I am alive and in circulation writing to the author of Westering and Trial By Fire with such cherished pieces as Let Your Mind Wander Over America, Elegy Written in a Country Churchyard, The Grandsons, No Mark, Fable, and others that ought to be in anthologies and text books, that wear well and are timeless for me. . . Suddenly came across a photograph of your father and your daughter at a campfire, something sweet about it. . . Dont know how it will happen but somewhere across the next year I'll have a cross country trip with no set dates and I'll be sliding into Denver and seeing you and Helen and maybe the author of The Care and Feeding of Husbands and we'll talk about our daughters. . . I get it from many points I should do an autobiog. That's an assignment to go ahead and forget the present colossal world drama and every day write "I, I, I" and "Me, Me, Me," while singing that ditty of the 1880's "Listen to My Tale of Woe." Going to ponder on it, ponder on a lot of imponderables. . . Take care of yourself, Tom. You grow shrewder, keener, and yet more compassionate, all the time. The good Lord willing we'll be meeting like a couple of indurated alumni.

Yrs
Carl

Why do I nearly always read it as Trial by Fire & need a second look to see it is Trial by Time?

538 | TO ALLAN NEVINS

[Flat Rock, North Carolina]
June 12 1951

Dear Allan:

Having finished ORDEAL and THE EMERGENCE I have now come through the ROCKEFELLER. This last a tough assignment for the co-author of POCKET HISTORY OF THE USA. It is a great book—sweep and immensity. I might have shaded some statements but I wouldn't fling pebbles at a mountain. Now I'm going to get the Cleveland, go through it and then quit living with Nevins for a while. The Epilogue in ROCKEFELLER is vastly implicative and haunting, has your tone of voice. What a rounded and spacious life you are living! May your rugged body and mind go on with these heavy tasks.

Yrs
Carl

P.S. On page 527, Rockefeller Vol II, is the word "sprincipal". What oddities can escape printer and proofreader! Forty years ago I wrote "snob" and it came out "snot".

539 | TO ALAN JENKINS

[Flat Rock, North Carolina]
July 27 1951

Dear Alan:

The only suggestion I would have is the use of the word Socialist without definition. I have been a dozen varieties of Socialist in my time. Most of the time I have been what might be termed a Bernstein Revisionist—or Social Democrat—or a manner of Fabian. At the time I knew Wright we were as much Anarchist or Syndicalist in our leanings as we were Socialist. This was the time of some writer reasoning, "Jesus was an Anarchist. All good men are Anarchists. I am an Anarchist." . . . Have been overworking and after tending to some affairs in New York next week I will have to return home instead of heading to Chicago and Galesburg as I had hoped. I'd like to think of your getting here again this summer. Anyhow I hope we'll be meeting this fall.

Yrs
Carl

Dr. Alan Jenkins's manuscript was called "Carl Sandburg's Mentor and First Publisher," and was printed in the Illinois Historical Society Journal, *Winter, 1952.*

540 | TO LILLA PERRY

[Flat Rock, North Carolina]
Dec 7 51

Dear Lilla

They were great and memorable sessions we had. I came to know you and Alice in wider human ranges. Stayed a whole week with [Kenneth] Dodson, read the Ms of his book except for two unfinished chapters: he has woven into it the fine lights and sacred colors of his great personality: I will go the limit for him.

This enclosure is a shot at something, an experimental piece and confidential as between you and Alice and me. Trudy or Gesso is a haunting phenomenon. Maybe Sappho had as zigzag a life as hers. Her fragments hit me hard as the best of Sappho's.

A Chicago physician friend, when we had stayed late at his office, talking and drinking, took me for the 3-hour drive to our Michigan place. We arrived between daybreak and sunrise, the sky in the east talking all the colors there are. And he said with a smile, "There is something forgiving about the Dawn."

Yrs
Carl

541 | TO ALAN JENKINS

[Flat Rock, North Carolina]
Dec 17 51

Dear Alan

They were good visits. We covered a lot of ground. I am still haunted by some of the impressions. Didnt see a horse in all those days in that onetime superbly horsey town. . . We are lacking one thing in the Al Hawkinson case. Do you think you could find time or have someone look in the files of the Reg-Mail 1928 for what was reported of the testimony at the trial? I wd be pleased to pay someone fr such work. . . You might like this quote from Malraux: "Modern art is by no means easy to define; a fish is badly placed for judging what the aquarium looks like from the outside."

Yrs
Carl

"How do those people get in that box?"!!

While doing research for his autobiography, Always the Young Strangers, *Sandburg stayed with Dr. Jenkins. The P.S. refers to a comment, told to Sandburg by Jenkins, made by a local man who*

*was mentally ill and puzzled by the images inside a television set.
The Hawkinson case referred to a man in Galesburg who had returned home to find his wife in bed with another man, slashed both
their throats, and was convicted of manslaughter. The crime of
passion was described without names in the book, from news details
in the Galesburg* Register-Mail *files.*

542 | TO NATHAN LEOPOLD

[Flat Rock, North Carolina]
January 8 1952

Dear Nathan Leopold:

Your letter is good to have. It carries a certain brightness. I wish
I had your facility with languages. I still hope to get to a visit with
you sometime this year and we can try our Swedish in conversation.
I certainly am willing to write another letter, hoping it to be somewhat convincing and persuasive, when you come up for parole. I
know about Mike's loyalty and value him for it.

Sincerely yours
Carl Sandburg

*Sandburg had written to the Illinois State and Pardon Board for
a pardon for Nathan Leopold and, from Joliet Prison, Leopold
wrote to Sandburg that he was studying languages and was able to
read Swedish. Mike was his brother, Foreman Leopold. When
Leopold was later freed, Sandburg was among the first persons he
called.*

543 | TO MARY HASTINGS BRADLEY

[Flat Rock, North Carolina]
Feb 19   52

Dear Mary

With apologies could go explanations—being run down and
having a tough schedule. You will ever be in mind when I am
Chicago way. Today and yesterday Oliver's collection is under the

auctioneer's hammer & it is nobody's fault, no one to blame, but I am not easy about it being scattered & never will be. Across 30 years I became part of its corporeal entity. . . I shall yet hope on for a session of your always luminous talk. Ever affectionate regard—

Yrs
Carl

544 | TO HERB BLOCK

[Flat Rock, North Carolina]
March 18 1952

Dear Herb,

If you can send along the original of the smaller clip enclosed it will have tender care. The larger one has been constantly hanging from a library shelf now nearly five years. If you can't send the original of it please return this time-worn venerable clip. When I see you in April or May we'll talk about books or recordings of mine you might like. It was good to visit with you and to come away feeling that good and keen as you are you will move into greater work.

Yrs,
Carl

545 | TO ADLAI E. STEVENSON

Burlington, Vermont
April 25, 1952

Dear Adlai:

I have been carrying around the speeches made at the Harriman dinner. Your speech has paragraphs and sentences that I have read several times—profound thinking, subtle feeling, exactitude of phrasing—great utterance for this hour and for many tomorrows. Lloyd would have been elated over it. I gave part of it in a broadcast at WCAX and may have reached some Baffin Bay fisherman. Some weeks ago Lloyd's Katherine played the recording of your speech at the memorial dinner. Until I heard the record-ing, I had believed I was probably closer to Lloyd than anyone else. Now I am inclined to let you have it. . .

In the events now whirling about your head may the outcome be somewhat as you wish. It is a hell of a commentary on some-thing or other that you are the only one of the string of candidates being mentioned who seems aware that the next president, if he is in some degree sensitive, will live in a Golgotha.

Affectionately yours,

Carl

In Stevenson's reply, he said in part: "When Sandburg carries around Stevenson's speeches, it's news!—or perhaps it is sinister evidence of a pitiful deterioration in Sandburg's literary tastes. . . . I am so glad that you share my bewilderment that anyone should want to be President."

546 | TO THE EDITORS, HARPER & BROTHERS

[Flat Rock, North Carolina]
May 20 1952

Editors,

You may use this blurb for Ferril's NEW AND SELECTED POEMS with the understanding that it is to be run as a whole and no changes nor deletions made. I have sworn to write no more blurbs but in the case of Ferril I go by the Spanish proverb "Oaths are but wind." Also I have known horses-asses who monkey-doodled with my copy wherefore I make it explicit that there are to be no changes nor deletions. I could name cases as to the monkey-doodlers but there isn't time. Of course, you can lift any parts of the blurb you choose for use in ads though you are to make no textual changes. I hope you see I am as anxious as Harper & Brothers to sell Ferril and get him the widest possible audience. I have lived with his poems many years and have tried to write about him with the exactitude of an affidavit to be solemnly sworn and deposed. Him and me is brudders.

Yours,

Carl Sandburg

Reading Thomas Hornsby Ferril you will find him often pure crystal. Or again he may haunt you with horizon blurs in yellow dust and green mist. On the edge of losing him you find yourself walking hand in hand with him.

If I had to put Tom Ferril in a single classification, I would say, "He belongs among the Great Companions." He has much to tell us and sing us because he is young as any sorrel or amber colt in his poems—and he is old as the scraggiest antediluvian of the Rocky Mountains.

He is a Yes-sayer to life because so much of what he has seen and heard said Yes to him. Hills and canyons, yucca and cotton-woods, the old ox-wagons and the new plane propeller, barns and pack-rats, blue-stemmed grass and peaks with snowy beards, strong bad men and clean bold dreamers, these and three or four civili-zations past and present—they have all said Yes to Ferril. And his psalms and gnomics chant it.

He titles one section "American Testament." And why not? Enough men have toiled and died for the American Dream to be sacred and testamentary. This new book of Ferril's belongs on any shelf of modern poetry pretending to be complete. His book will have its "trial by time" and stand as one of our classics. He is poet, wit, historian, man of books and human affairs, and so defi-nitely one of the Great Companions.

547 | TO ARCHIBALD MACLEISH

[Flat Rock, North Carolina]
May 23 1952

Dear Archie:

Your letter is good to have. It sings and cavorts, carries a sea-breeze smell. Of course, an annual letter ought to be good, like a report to trustees. Also I see your poeticals in The Atlantic—and the old craft is there—somewhat like the best of your lovable early pieces. I will miss your solemn face if you are not there at the Academy May 28 when they award me bullion good at any USA mint or pawnshop. I suppose you have heard rumors that there is corruption in federal, state and municipal governments and The Republic is in peril and that you have accepted these reports as not being entirely ungrounded. And I hope you will consider with due gravity my forecast that the July conventions will be a wild night on the moors with plenty of combustibles and it will not be dark enough in Chicago to pick out any familiar stars in the overhead. At present I survey the complex scene with calm and persiflage.

I can tell the author of the poem "Eleven" that I have been giving my early years a wrap-up under the title "Always the Young Strangers" which Harcourts publish next January 6 when I am lifting my light feet over the 75th milestone. May I say in closing that you are good for me and I go on reading your psalms and gnomics and I believe we can in fellowship contemplate our labors and say that what is wrong with the country is none of our doing? My love to Ada. My word to you: Go on singing and dreaming.

As always
Carl

548 | TO RALPH MCGILL

[Flat Rock, North Carolina]
June 25 1952

Dear Ralph McGill:

Come along here anytime and I will knock off from what I am doing to see you and talk with you. I think you represent civilization. Away back I had a course in college based on one book Guizot's History of Civilization. One thing burned deep in my mind out of that course. Guizot wrote that the essential characteristic of civilization is "diversity of opinion." A photograph of you in a rocking chair has been on the front mantel ever since it came and will be there when you arrive.

Yrs,
Carl

Flat Rock N.C. Sept. 30, [1952]

Dear George

How goes it by the domicile flophouse named Royalton where I have often sojourned with pleasure and where you, if you live and stay on, will become a still more indurated philosopher?

The Angoff anthology is a good book. I have read 3 fourths way thru it but that tells nothing because I have read certain pieces 3 or 4 times. Sometimes before getting up in the morning to do my exercises I read you on exercise. Steichen is all your way as to exercise. Both of you are fine specimens for no exercise at all but Barney Baruch and Wm Cullen Bryant in their eighties liked starting the day with dumbbells. It is similar to art: you do what you do and nothing can be done about it. I've been thinking about you and this is merely sending affectionate regards and informing you that your days and works have not been useless and that there are others like myself who like a fine quality of companionship in your scrivenings. Give a salute to 44th Street for me. Be seeing you about Nov 20.

Ever yours
Carl

Sandburg knew George Jean Nathan through H. L. Mencken and the American Mercury. *When Sandburg stayed at a hotel in New York, it was usually the Royalton, where Nathan lived. Charles Angoff edited* The World of George Jean Nathan.

550 | TO PAULA STEICHEN

[Flat Rock, North Carolina]
Oct 14 52

Dear Snick

Your letter in your own sweet handwriting came and it is a good letter to have and I thank you for shaping the words on paper with a pen for me to read your thoughts and how things are going with you. Gramma and Marn and Janet have read it and what we all say is that you know how to write a good letter and anybody who can write so her voice and her face get into the letter she writes she should not hesitate nor be slow about it any time she feels like writing.

Your everloving
Buppong

Snick was Sandburg's name for his granddaughter Karlen Paula. After their mother's divorce from their father, Joseph Thomann, Paula and her brother took their grandmother's maiden name, Steichen. Sandburg wrote several poems for her, including "Foxgloves" and "First Sonata to Karlen Paula," which appeared in Honey and Salt.

551 | TO JOHN STEICHEN

[Flat Rock, North Carolina]
[October 14, 1952]

Dear John

You write a letter different from your sister. You write a letter that sounds like you and she writes a letter that sounds like her. One of you is one person and the other is another person and each of you has a mysterious personality by itself and that is the way it should be and that is why you are good for each other. I like it, John, that you are always asking questions, so I enclose here a bunch of questions and they are good to think about. I hope to be seeing you before the first snow comes flying.

Your everloving
Buppong

552 | TO PAULA STEICHEN

[Flat Rock, North Carolina]
[October 1952]

Dear Snick:

As you well know there is a widespread custom of one person saying to another, "Oh, shut up!" And the answer coming swiftly and immediately, "Oh, shut up yourself!" Now I find in Shakespeare's time it was done differently. Instead of "Oh, shut up!" it was "CHARM YOUR TONGUE!" to which came the response, "I WILL BE LIBERAL AS THE AIR IN MY SPEECH!" Now I have seen you often having not merely perfect but exquisite manners and I call your attention to the foregoing technique in behavior for whatever it may be worth to you and your studious lovable carrot-haired brother for whatever it may be worth to you and to him. Tall elegant bushels of love to the both of you. I think of you as my Mexican Zinnia. Others may have Mexicale Rose but you came in Zinnia time and I see three of them before me now, thoughtful in a quiet dreaminess. So I say Pax Vobiscum and

Yours Forever
Buppong

553 | TO ADLAI E. STEVENSON

[Flat Rock, North Carolina]
[November 5, 1952]

Dear Adlai

It was all worth the time and toil. Yours is a high name now and for a long time. You are cherished and remembered in multitudes of deep prayers. Love to you and Elizabeth [Stevenson's sister].

Yrs.
Carl

1952

[Flat Rock, North Carolina]
Nov 20 52

Dear Sis Mary and Mimi

Tell Char and Eric it is going the rounds that when a couple
had their first baby they began its name with the first letter of
the alphabet, a boy named Alan. The next baby, a boy, had his
name begin with the second letter of the alphabet, he was Bruce.
It was ten years till another child came, a fine girl baby they were
proud of, but the mother said, "I'll be damned if I'm going to go
thru the whole alphabet—we're going to name her ZARA!" Which
they did and lived happily ever after.

Char sent along a wonderful letter, a budget of news that made
you-all come very alive. The book she referred to shall be tended
to. . . At publishers they say they sent you proofs of the book. You
can read it like your brother is talking to you hour on hour. It will
be mighty fine to see you come January. . . Love to you and to
your dear ones. My prayers all the time for the December event.

Yours
Carl

[Flat Rock, North Carolina]
[Circa December, 1952]

Dear Ed and Dana

Nearest I have come so far to a poem on The Family of Man
is this enclosure. Kitty has insisted I make a hand written copy
to be reproduced on the program at the Chicago dinner. It is so
damned simple and childish that I expect some people to say it
runs over into the silly. . . Got Strange Lands and Friendly people, read it and last May wrote Justice Douglas that he had a rare
reportorial style for a jurist and that you read aloud the final pages

and I likewise read aloud those pages. Now comes a letter from him saying that on this summer's trip to Indonesia, Burma, Formosa, he carried this letter with him and didnt get to answer it till he was back in Wash, DC, which shows what comes of your reading aloud what interests you. . . Now Paula has reversed her decision not to go to Chicago for the Jan 6 dinner. She says, "If you can take it, I can—and you will never have another 75th birthday and I might have regrets if I didn't go.". . . But hell I only started writing this to send you the poem and let you know that I know it will be taken as very wise and nearly silly. . . Paula is in good trim, never so wise and lovely as now. Janet and Marn send smiles. All under this roof say to you two, "I love you, I luv yah, I luff you like big flowers bustin wit luff." May Santa climb down the big Um-pawaug chimney and kiss you while you sleep and leave you a good smell from his whiskers.

Carl

556 | TO CHESTER WRIGHT

[Flat Rock, North Carolina]
Dec 21   52

Dear Chet

Good to have your Xmas card tho I have had it in mind I'm owing you a letter. You perhaps heard of Frank Wolfe passing a few weeks ago. He had a good and deep place in my heart al-ways—the same which I wdnt say of E Julius. About six mos before he slid out he sent me a lot of back numbers of his The Free-man where in rambling around I read that I was a pathetic sap and you were some kind of a snake. As I knew how you were friend and helper to him in pinches I felt sorry for E J. . . Are you ever going to write some of your memories of Gompers? It stays with me how he once said to you, "Dont be a Man Hunter." He grows on me. How he could recite that poem with the recurring line, "Make me a man child, Lord!" You were close to him and if any yen comes to write about him you should give way to it. . . Along starting next April I'm going to be here nearly all the time and if you should be thisaway it will be good to see you. Would you believe its 37 years since you ran that Billy Sunday poem in The Call and you wired me of some town where the police stopped its sale? . . . Ever luck stars over you and June—

Yrs
Carl

Chester Wright, labor editor and later secretary to Samuel Gompers, was a voice and friend out of the Wisconsin Socialist past. E. Haldeman-Julius published the famous five-cent Little Blue Books.

557 | TO MARY HASTINGS BRADLEY

Flat Rock N C   Dec 23   52

Dear Mary

I can at least answer your last letter (last June) to the extent of saying I must not hold off from writing you that I have read your Alice's notes for a book she was doing. She can write, she CAN. I dont go along with her terrific interpretation of the face of Thad Stevens. If she hadnt given the portrait a name I would take it as a profound contemplation. Yet some who knew him in life and scorned and feared him would say she has done him to perfection. I went thru enough source materials about him to have written a full biog of him. Alice's written impression is one that I will read again more than once. You can have a quiet pride in her style and imagination. I think ol' Oliver would have been saying much the same. What a mother or father must do in such a case is to pray and pray that the daughter KEEPS her flame. I will pray with you.

Yrs
Carl

558 | TO CATHERINE MCCARTHY

[Flat Rock, North Carolina]
[Circa 1953]

Dear Kitty:

You may have heard me more than once saying that nearly every one of my books has been written with the thought: "I would like it to be a book of a kind that I could have met earlier in life." In doing this 1-volume Lincoln I would like it to be the kind of a book I could have met 40 or 50 years ago. For anything like a full measure of understanding Lincoln, who in the end is as baffling and completely inexplicable as Shakespeare, a skimpy volume as a concession and a gratuity to hustlers and timesavers who must have their capsules, wont do. Some of them are like the fellow who pasted the Lord's prayer at the foot of the bed and on getting up in the morning waves his hand toward it with, "Lord, there's my sentiments." If there isn't an audience for a somewhat truly adequate 1-volume life of Lincoln, that would be sorry to think about. We have the chance, however, and the materials at hand, to shape out the book that might become widely known as an indispensable classic 1-volume biography of Lincoln. But it cant be done as an accommodation for those readers who can be satisfied with a cramped and cryptic summation. . . 'Twas nice and bright talking with you over the phone this day.

As ever
CS

559 | TO KENNETH DODSON

Flat Rock NC 4/2, [1953]

Dear Kennie

You must know, I am sure, how pleased I have been about the big news, the good news. I would have written you weeks ago but I have been whirled about and buffeted in many ways and events that can never happen again, not to mention a six day siege of flu and minor ailments that demanded time and attention. I had been set for a west coast trip but the dates had to be cancelled or I would have had a visit with you and yours. I can't work the hours I used to, nor handle mail and write letters in proportion, as I used to, but you should know it is on my conscience when I delay a letter like this as long a time as I have. I should mention perhaps that if I were you I would go along in patience and accommodation with the Little-Brown people. What you don't get said or shaped up in this first book, and that you might have anxiety or sensitivity about, you CAN get said and shaped up in later writings. You can tell Little Brown that I will go the limit in any kind of a blurb or review, that I read the manuscript at your house slowly and with care, that on publication I would rate it one of the greatest sea books ever done, giving wonderful personality to a ship that had rare and strange adventures, bringing into fine focus vivid human characters on the ship. Or perhaps you will write me the latest status of the book and I will write Little Brown that I know the book well enough to go the limit for it. It is a world of shifts and ups and downs, this book world. I am trying to UNwrite the 6-vol Lincoln into 1-vol. At Harcourts they thought it would be nice to have it for publication next Dec and for 6 weeks I went on aiming at that target. Now I have had to tell them the job can not be decently done till a year from now. New material has come along since the writing of The Prairie Years 28 years ago, the which must be included. It will run perhaps 500,000 words and must have scale and proportion, working by the Paganini formula: toil, solitude and prayer. . . My love to Letha, to Dick and Jeanie. God bless—and the peace of great phantoms be for you.

As ever
Carl

Marjorie and Bill Braye send love. We speak of you often. You saw Marj in a valley of desolation from which she has come forth triumphant. They mention you, across the continent, as Good Neighbors.

Kenneth Dodson's Away All Boats *was published in 1954, to much acclaim.*

560 | TO DR. ARTHUR W. FREESE

Flat Rock NC   4/2, [1953]

Dear Jim

The box arrived. Everything came. I still think of those five days as half a vacation cruise and the other half filled with good work hours. You suddenly blossomed out as a copy editor—or a bracket cop lifting an authoritative hand and cryin out, "Where the hell's your bracket here? You can't pass here without a bracket!" Where a bracket was missing your eye for anatomy saw it like a bone was lacking or a tendon needing tending. So I dont know whether to credit you as a scholar or an anatomist or maybe the case is covered in two guests at 1260: "Who is in Room 1008?" "Oh, a couple of bracketeers and you better keep shy of 'em.". . . Four days ago I decided that too much incessant hard word wd be required to get the right kind of a book ready for publication by Nov or Dec. I so phoned Kitty McCarthy and she said her mind had run likewise. Next day she phoned that at the office they were agreed that fall of 1954 would be a better time for a real finished and polished One-Vol Life of Mister Linkern Hisself. So tension is eased all round. . . The medications seem to be working benefits, the discomforts lessening. I'd like to go on with 2 more bottles of LUSYN and several more of the small packets of PLANCELLO, if you can send these. . . Will be seeing you around June 6 when I'd like you to go to the Swedish anniversary after smorgasbord at the Swedish Club, maybe Al [Dreier] joining and possibly the three of us making a wild dash up into Wisconsin.

As ever yours
Carl

561 | TO MAX EASTMAN

Flat Rock N.C. 4/5, [1953]

Dear Max

I read your Freeman review twice and said, "Max and me is brudders yet." I recalled the Negro who said, "Duh sins uh commission is duh sins yuh did and duh sins uh omission is duh sins yuh wanted to commit and didn't." I may yet live to do a certain book of memories and portraits wherein I would hope the writing about you would be as fascinating reading, as fair in judgements and surmises, as grave and decent in fellowship, as this review of yours. I look at your row of books on a shelf and it is a formidable accounting you give of years not misspent. We should be having a session of good and forthright talk somewhere across the next year.

Yrs
Carl

Max Eastman helped to found and edit The Masses, *to which Sandburg contributed a number of poems. Reviewing* Always the Young Strangers *in* The Freeman, *April 6, 1953, Eastman called it "really the history and demography of a Midwestern settlement, a sort of 'Middletown' with love instead of sociology setting up the card catalogue."*

562 | TO ALAN JENKINS

[New York]
April 23, 1953

Dear Alan:

Don't you remember my telling you at least once and perhaps twice that I don't care to have a biography written about me while I am living? I think I named two of the fellows who proposed to do the story of my life in a book. One of the two was a good and tried friend, but I had to tell him nothing doing. If I am having difficulties about what sort of a book I should write about my life, to follow ALWAYS THE YOUNG STRANGERS, what would be the difficulties of a biographer? The matter is complicated, involved. At times I seriously consider writing other books and letting further autobiographical books have silence. A well-done biography by you would wear you down like no other task in all your life. You may know that it doesn't come easy for me to write to you such a letter as this.

Yours,
Carl

563 | TO PAULA STEICHEN

[Flat Rock, North Carolina]
[Circa September, 1953]

My dear Snick

You have on occasion a vehement, picturesque and eloquent flow of speech. I suspect that Shakespeare must have known some young lady somewhat like yourself who as a rebuff to one who had spoken a vile slander, let fly the three words:

"Filth, thou liest!"

I send this to you as merely the impression of a moment and a small oddity that might interest you and to say again pax vobiscum and may the good Lord guide your footsteps in righteous paths and may you often, if not ever, do what your deepest clean heart tells you to do.

Buppong

564 | TO ALFRED HARCOURT

Flat Rock [North Carolina] 9 24 53

Dear Alf

Very good to have your letter and to have Kitty's news and to give you my regrets that we wont see the world series together this fall. . . Working on rewrites and revisions needed in the

Prairie Years I have thot a thousand times of the bulging leather pouch of Mss brot to 383 and your wise decision not to rush publication and how galley proofs went with me from coast to coast and 1926 we had a toboggan ride. Since then some fine worthy intensive research has been done in the Prai Yrs field and corrections and minor changes have to be made and a major revision of the Ann Rutledge story. In the War Yrs area practically nothing new has come in those thirty years. Had dizzy spells in July, talked it over with doctors who said 6 to 8 hrs work day too much, so have slowed down to 3 or 4 a day, and it goes nicely. Paula is a wonder in all ways as a helpmeet. She is steadily reducing the herd but so long as she stays ambulant she will be breeding goats as her brother does delphiniums: it is a genius with her and the goat industry idolizes her for her knowledge and lighted enthusiasms. Janet says, "I love this place and hope we never move from it": she enjoys her chores with goats, chickens, the garden and buttermaking. Margaret has become widely read, a scholar who often surprises me with her erudition, knows the Bible and Shakespere better than I do. TV is a blessing for us all: that Ed Murrow report from Berlin was a marvel. If I live I hope to do a piece on the advantages of The Book over TV, radio, movies. With the Book you can skip the stupid, you can linger and go back and make completely your own what is for your mind and spirit, you can make your choice of what you believe you need for this hour and moment, you have controls, you don't have to sit and take it, you can carry it to where you use it, you own and manage the cultural process operating—and much furthermore. Why shouldn't a writer of books speak so to a good and grand book publisher? . . . Ever take care of yourself. Love to you and Ellen and to Hake and all under his roof.

As always
Carl

1954

[Flat Rock, North Carolina]
[Circa 1954]

Dear Adlai:

This Nast cartoon is up your alley. . . Hope to send you a 1-vol Lincoln next fall. . . A score of letters to you have run thru my head that never got onto paper. You're doing good, regularly surpassing yourself.

Ever yours,
Carl

Kestenbaum says Clarence Randall made the remark, "I am left of center," K then asking, "Where is center?"

> *The Nast cartoon showed Henry Clay saying "I would rather be right than be President." In reply Stevenson wrote: "While I don't feel exactly like Henry Clay, I have always approved his sentiments on the presidency."*

566 | TO BENJAMIN P. THOMAS

[Flat Rock, North Carolina]
Jan 12 54

Dear Ben

As the days go by and I think of you every day slugging away at your book while I slug away at mine, I can salute you as one old-time tailor sitting cross-legged and stitching salutes another sitting likewise. The more I work at this trade the more silly seems to me the frequency of the pronouncement that this or that book "is to endure", is already "a classic" or "of permanent value" or even destined "to be immortal." Of man's half million or so of years on this planet he has had the alphabet maybe 5,000 years, printing 300 years, the mass production of books less than 100 years. Across the next thousand years what the hell will last—or the next 100,000 years? Who can predict what will be the cultural media to come? The Book still stands as against TV, radio, movies; you have choice; you can pick what you want or need for the hour; you can skip the stupid or irrelevant; you can go back and linger on what you prefer. . . I'll go further on this if or when I see you when I am, as I hope and expect, in Springfield along the middle of Feb. I'll also tell you on what points your Lincoln book wears well for me and for others who go back to favorite spots in it. I am hoping that your Stanton will be about twice as long as your Lincoln—or longer yet. I am sure you have already traversed some areas of Stanton that will be new and fascinating reading. I suppose you have seen Autograph Collectors Journal for Oct of 1948. If you dont have it I can send it along. . . In the past year I have read every entry of your Day-by-Day, every line of the New Salem, and many remnants such as "The Pres Reads His Mail." I want to reminisce with you about Oakleaf, Beveridge, Barton, Barrett, Miss Osborn, Mrs. Palmer Weber, the Hon Geo A Lawrence, John Haugen, Denton Offutt. I came to Gov Ford's History this year with deepened admiration for him. I had to laugh at Beveridge's elaborate, meticulous footnotes with seldom a pause for appraisal of the goddam witness. Maybe I am getting garrulous with you because you have been in this room so much of this past year. So be it. And God love you.

Carl

567 | TO GERALD W. JOHNSON

Flat Rock NC 7 30 54

Dear Brother Johnson

Your letter comes along—a short chapter in a modern Book of Lamentations. I go along with every line of it. The man not having his moods of lamentation in these days is not alive and registering to the scenes around him. There was a Union brigadier in the spring of 1864 who, in his recoil from the tangled mass of blunders and corruption he saw as a daily reality, wrote to his wife, "May God save my country—if there is a God—and if I have a country!" Among other things Lincoln had been trying to get a conscription act, universal selective service, no buying of substitutes by the well-to-do, but Congress said No, young Jim Blaine of Maine in the House leading the fight against such a draft. A million good volunteers had stepped out at Lincoln's calls for troops and the volunteering breed was nearly run out; he wrote a cool, grim paper about this but decided not to give it to the country. One caller said he noticed a mistiness in Lincoln's eyes when he mentioned "the American volunteer soldier." There was a certain grand remnant of the people that stayed with him thru the darkest days. There seems to have been such a remnant in nearly every real crisis the country has had. I can't begin here on the Oppenheimer crisis. I believe the Alsop boys have been pretty straight shooters on it: it's a sorry indictment they draw. Sometimes in the national and international whirl of events these days I wonder if there is a smell to the political weather that I have known before: I get to wondering if I will see the Third World War. I have had enough good years so that I could take it personally and vanish without a murmur. But my lamentation would be that of the Union brigadier of '64. . . Will be sending you my 1-vol Lincoln soon. Where it doesn't have solace it does give companionship. In the refresher course I took in shaping up this book he kept growing on me. . . And you keep growing on me, you so sensitively alive to this colossal human drama that shifts in multiple mirrors every day. It will be good to have another visit this fall.

Ever yours
Carl Sandburg

Gerald W. Johnson, of Baltimore, was aroused by the treatment of J. Robert Oppenheimer, the growing menace of demagoguery in the country, and the antiliberal inertia in Washington.

568 | TO KENNETH DODSON

Flat Rock NC 7 30 54

Dear Ken

You are riding high now. And what I know is that nobody else but you knows how well the riding high has its dangers and you know how to meet them. . . Marjorie copied for me two of the letters you wrote to her when she was deep in the dark. They hold precious wisdom you gathered at cost. . . I expect never again to have such a curious eight days as last winter: three days for a slow reading of AWAY ALL BOATS: five days wrangling and writing that review: and I should add two days for getting it placed in the LA Times and the Chicago Trib. It was luck that the NY Her-Trib couldn't use it on acct of its dedication and that we could get it into two of the most powerful sales-pulling media in the country. Lacking "boy-and-girl" slant, lacking stress on violence and yet rendering appalling violence, having heroism without any heroizing, it has gone to an audience I'd like to hear more about; your readers must include much of that saving remnant that has been on hand when this country was in a real crisis. There is much to write but we will have to leave it for our talks sometime. . . Plans are for Murrow to make two TV half-hour films and Columbia a large album of recordings this August here. Oct 7 I'm in Chicago for a publishing day luncheon and Oct 10 at Palos Park, Ill. for dedication of a new consolidated Carl Sandburg High School; what to say I dont know but I will worm out of it somehow. In a pinch I can say I have nothing to say and its all there in the 22 books: go read 'em, you little rascals! . . . Watch your time and your sleep—on tour and in Hollywood. You're a writer. Let 'em steal as little as possible of your writing time. . . Love to Letha, Dick, Jeanie and yourself.

As ever and ever
Carl

569 | TO BEN HECHT

[Flat Rock, North Carolina]
September 1, 1954

Dear Ben,

I have by now moved my eyes across the six hundred thirty three pages, even fussing around a little in the index, of your book. I read twice the paragraph about my voice and put a marker there for use when I wheeze through the dentures like Douglas MacArthur of the present. Those two pages on the players, the actors and actresses, made a lovely armful of roses. Vivid and lovely is the portrait of Rose; I knew her girlish brightness in the local room when she first came within your vision; it is just as well that you omit mention of handing me sweet and gay singing letters of Rose to you for me to keep in my desk; Marie in her book publicly reproached me for being the secret custodian of this evidence. Those were not easy portraits of Sherwood and of Mencken; I found myself reading certain sentences two or three times for their keen penetration. I would like to have had more than a brief mention of Sam Hoffenstein; I enjoyed the Lydia picture and I go on re-reading Hoffenstein's poems . . . a lovable hurly-burly of a book that stands as a good companion along side A Book of Miracles. Love to all under your roof.

Carl

> *In Ben Hecht's* A Child of the Century, *he wrote of his old Chicago* Daily News *colleague, "To this day I remember it [Sandburg's] as the finest voice I ever heard, reading or talking."*

570 | TO J. FRANK DOBIE

[Flat Rock, North Carolina]
September 7, 1954

Dear Dobie:

Herewith are more for our anthology. Somewhere along the next two or three years maybe we will get together and shape up an anthology which we know very well will not save the country. Going the rounds now is one about Eisenhower arriving at the Gate of Hell and Satan saying, "You don't belong here, you belong UP." A few hours later Ike was back at the Gate saying to Satan, "WHICH WAY IS UP?" This, of course, is unfair, inimical, diabolical propaganda but it keeps going round and round. . . Your good face and voice linger with me.

Yrs
CS

571 | TO ADLAI E. STEVENSON

[Flat Rock, North Carolina]
September 7, 1954

Dear Adlai:

I am amazed at how you meet great and difficult moments and make them your own. The perfection of your timing for the past two years borders on the marvelous. You have had immense vitality and spent it lavishly. I am not much of a praying man but I do pray constantly that luck stars may be over you. I pray too that the confusions and turmoils may never be like those of April, 1864, when a Union brigadier wrote his wife, "may God save my country—if there is a God—and if I have a country.". . . Don't spend a fraction of time answering this note. . . From all under our roof love and blessings to you—

Carl

572 | TO HERB BLOCK

[Flat Rock, North Carolina]
September 16, 1954

Dear Herb Block:

Well, you go on hitting the ball, catching flies with one hand high in the air. I rate you above Willie Mays. This enclosure I have had thirty years and send on for you to have the next thirty years. I think maybe I wouldn't send it on at all if 'tweren't for the picture ending the series. . . My 1-Vol. Lincoln is ordered sent to you. It reports performances in Washington even more confusing and chaotic than at the present time. . . Will drop in one of these days and we will reminisce about the Chicago River and the limpidity and clarity of its waters moving under the Madison Street Bridge.

Ever yours,
CS

573 | TO MARK VAN DOREN

[Flat Rock, North Carolina]
November 16, 1954

Dear Mark:

A nice piece of writing you did on my Lincoln book. . . Last August I meant to write you that one afternoon I read your Walt Whitman sketch in the Dictionary of American Biography, a keen and sweet story and appraisal. I thought I would like to see it in a book along with Bob Ingersoll thunderous eulogy-lecture and the Whitman poems, too little known, of Edwin Arlington Robinson and Stephen Benet. . . My love to your Scandinavian wife who has an I.W.W. streak matching my own.

Ever yours,
Carl

574 | TO ERNEST AND MARY HEMINGWAY

[Flat Rock, North Carolina]
Dec. 8, 1954

Dear Mr. Ernest and Miss Mary:

Your letter came with your joined fingerprints and is one to hold close to the heart and to keep for two rare grandchildren. I would have written sooner only I had ailments whereas you two have taken wounds in the rain. When you wrote about it in Look you played some hard torments in low dulcet with no high diapason.

One result of your warm-hearted and record-breaking comment is that you have sent Hemingway readers to Sandburg and Sandburg readers to Hemingway. Enclosed clipping came from Lilla Perry of Los Angeles whose husband was 30 years public librarian there. The NO Times-Picayune printed a letter from a bird saying we're both lousy, Harnett Kane replying whynhell he didn't name his candidates. In some quarters you are reckoned as supremely big hearted, Carl Haverlin, President of Broadcast Music,

Inc, writing me, "I got quite a kick out of Hemingway's giving you the Nobel prize. If he hadn't been so broke I guess he would have refused it in your behalf." While Al Dreier of the Chi Trib, Western Mgr Genl Advertising, writes that somewhere in years to come will be people asking, "Did Sandburg ever get the Nobel prize?" the answer being, "Sure, it was awarded to him in 1954 by Ernest Hemingway."

I know enough of Swedish humor to believe that some member of the Academy said something like, "Hemingway is a Smalander," referring to the legend of the Lord seeing a Smalander in a bloody fight with the Devil and ordering an angel to go down and stop the fight. The angel came back saying he couldn't stop the fight and so cut off the heads of both of them. The Lord said, "Go down and put their heads back as they were." Which the angel did. But he put the head of the Devil back on the Smalander which is the reason why today every Smalander has a little of the Devil in him. Like that I had it from my Swedish mother 66 years ago soon after I got "dry behind the ears."

Mary, at the Royalton where George Jean Nathan has lived 44 years, he tells me of visiting Hemingway in Cuba. I ask, "how did you find him?" and the most fastidious and convivial critic in America says, "He's a wonderful companion!" And I thought of you in a flash . . . when some books arrive to your four hands I want Mary to hold Always the Young Strangers a half-a minute against the healed ribs. . . And that will do for now—with prayers that the healing goes well and fast and the old working strengths come back in full flow and stride.

Ever yours,
Carl

575 | TO ERNEST HEMINGWAY

[Flat Rock, North Carolina]
[Circa 1954]

Dear Ernest:

Your works and voice go farther than you have a way of knowing they do. That slim book "A Lincoln Preface" sent to you—some day I hope to do Hemingway in that length and he won't say it's "tinhorn" biography. . . . We think often of you both here and hold fast to hopes that you are both moving into oldtime form. . . Never bother to answer anything from me. The variety of pressures on you are terrific, I know well. What I send is out of knowing I am beholden to you.

Ever yrs,
Carl

Should you be interested in having one of our pure bred registered Nubian or Toggenburg kids we would gladly send one as some kind of a token—buck or doe—you say the word.

576 | TO EDWARD R. MURROW

[Flat Rock, North Carolina]
January 5, 1955

Dear Ed:

It was like traveling with fine and keen companions last Sunday when you had your Liberty Boys around the table. The pleasant but definite little riffle between Schoenbrun and Hottelet was pretty and like history. And what faces! There must have been some good folks saying, "Till now I have only seen overseas correspondents in the movies and I wasn't sure what they looked like. Now I know they look decent and thoughtful and they are good actors but no actors could talk so intelligent right off the cuff." Mobile faces, marked individual voices, what a ball team, Casey Stengel! Thank you for putting them on the phone for a lone Tar Heel down here. Ever yours—

Carl

Please send me script of your newscast Jan. 3 where you have both of Ezra Benson's shoulders pinned to the mat. You had him reductio ad absurdum.

577 | TO EDWARD R. MURROW

[Flat Rock, North Carolina]
March 11, 1955

Dear Ed:

You may have noticed the Newsweek statement that you "electronically canonized" me. I have looked it up and this means that you are a living Pope and I am a desiccated dusty cadaver dead and gone now for a long time. . . Lately you maintain your status as one of the best of the Liberty Boys.

Ever yours,
Carl

Murrow had sent with his note of March 7 a newspaper photo of Sandburg that had been captioned "President Eisenhower." Murrow's note ended, "It is not every press agent who can do this sort of thing, and I still hope to get you listed as the Pope."

578 | TO HERB BLOCK

[Flat Rock, North Carolina]
[Circa 1955]

Dear Herblock—

So long a time since our college days on the Chicago River & Drainage Canal.

There has been with me and many others an ever-deepening admiration and love of your drawing and ideas. Shall be seeing you next summer in Washington, D.C.

Carl.

579 | TO CATHERINE MCCARTHY

[Flat Rock, North Carolina]
[April 1, 1955]

Dear Kitty

The poem will stay unfinished for some weeks yet. Enclosures are from my subterranean cavern of skulls, memoranda, miscellany, monkeybusiness. Very tentatively I wonder about EVER THE WINDS OF CHANCE to follow ALWAYS THE YOUNG STRANGERS. I also think of PILGRIM'S PACKSACK—and more will come. And the blessed idea comes, "Hell, we dont have to think up a title till we get the doggone book written." Many miles to go and much skullpractice.

Ever yours
CS

580 | TO GEORGE C. MCCONNAUGHEY

[Flat Rock, North Carolina]
April 30, 1955

Dear Mr. McConnaughey:

It has become one of the national jokes that television as now conducted, while it presents a certain minimum of material that is priceless, decent, meritorious, never the less presents its viewers with a high maximum of trash and performances monotonously repeating the color and character of many previous shows. I write to your Commission as one of the many viewers in this country who would gladly welcome Subscription Television. I would like to think that we citizens who are supposed to be freemen in a free country could be free to exercise choice as to what we see on the TV screen, particularly when we choose to pay for what we choose to see.

Sincerely yours,
Carl Sandburg

George C. McConnaughey was chairman of the Federal Communications Commission.

[Flat Rock, North Carolina]
May 20, 1955

Dear Ed:

Often in my life, you should know, I have done foolish things with no bitterness about them. But when there is a color of treachery and betrayal in a foolish action of mine, I am in no health about it. When I wrote the F. C. C. a letter I was foolish enough (and why I can't fathom) to think it would be one more of many reposing in their files. My cue, if only out of loyalty to you, was silence. But a mood was on me about TV, from the only three stations we can receive here, and their steady deterioration from low standards to begin with. For a short time we did get Person-To-Person, Eric Sevareid, Chronoscope, Doug Edwards, to name a few that we like and want, but these are out, not shown, for a year and a half. In substitution has come a series of local shows or "features" with local advertising. I can name only three features of each week that we never fail to see: See-It-Now, You Bet Your Life, Ford Omnibus, if and when. . . Of course, I know that TV toll can lead to plenty of experiments and disasters. Meantime we feel helpless here about the many excellent things on a marvellous medium that we can't get.

Also meantime, in the toll controversy my cue is complete silence though in the commencement address at the University of North Carolina June 6 I shall make more than passing reference to you. Also meantime, I expect on occasion to do foolish things with a low minimum of bitter aftermath.

Carl

Murrow responded, "We both know there is a vast chasm between Corporate and personal loyalty. I would be incapable of regarding anything you said or wrote about television or radio as being in any way derogatory to myself."

582 | TO DON AND LYAL SHOEMAKER

[Flat Rock, North Carolina]
December 19, 1955

Dear Don and Lyal:

Sometime when the little witch is extra rampageous you might ask her, "Why do they put shoes on a dead man?" Then you wait a week or two and inform her, "Because he can't put them on himself." This, you can tell her, is a guaranteed antique and outdates the earliest mummies of Egypt.

We shall be looking for you on New Year's Day. Come along as early as you can. Hearts here beat in unison with yours.

Carl

PS—Have read [John] Gunther's Inside Africa: the book will do no harm indeed indeed.

583 | TO DON SHOEMAKER

[Flat Rock, North Carolina]
March 27, 1956

Dear Don:

Also Dear Lyal and my ownest own Dear Ebizaleth. It will be good to see you, Don, whensoever your head and feet guide you hitherward. Sometime this year I am going to fly to Atlanta and see Ralph and then to Nashville to see you fellers. Now that you have a farm I want to see how you farm it. I'd like a couple of fried eggs fresh from the hens. I'd like to see where the damn Yankees destroyed an entire Rebel army. Tell Charles S. Johnson I'd like a good long talk with him and that sometime I would like to meet his student body with one of my programs and that if anybody asks me what Brother Johnson and I are Alumni of it is The Chicago Race Riots and "the score" thereof. Tell Ebizaleth I have five stories that come to an end so sudden it takes your breath away and I have another very special story that goes on and on and never ends and I will tell her the five short stories into her right ear and the long story that never ends into her left ear. You needn't tell her that love is a many splendored thing; she has heard that highly embellished nonsense and will meet it, alas alas, so long as she lives. Kiss her for me on the big toe of her right foot.

Always and ever,
Carl

584 | TO FRANCIS BROWN

[Flat Rock, North Carolina]
April 6, 1956

Dear Francis Brown:

Thank you for sending me a photostat of those two pieces in the little Dartmouth magazine. That was twenty-three [33] years ago. The words you set down then make fleeting portraits of each of us. Neither of us was afraid of being sentimental then, lavishly so, and I believe that streak of the sentimental is still rich in us and keeps us going. Hope to be seeing you about April 17.

Faithfully yours,
Carl Sandburg

That photostat will end up in the Univ. of Ill. Library for keeps.

As a Dartmouth undergraduate, Francis Brown, later New York Times Book Review *editor, had written an impression of Sandburg on campus for* The Third Rail, *March, 1923, saying: "When Sandburg began to sing quaint American folk-songs to the accompaniment of his guitar, I seemed to see an ancient troubadour poet."*

585 | TO JAMES T. FARRELL

[Flat Rock, North Carolina]
April 14, 1956

Dear Jim Farrell:

That was a nice public letter you sent to me via The New Leader. Prizes are fifty per cent pleasant and handy to have most of the time but just about half the time prizes are a monkey business. I can't quite fathom exactly what it is that makes me feel good all over about the commentaries on the passing of Mencken. I hope to do a real memorial to Vachel Lindsay sometime. And somehow amid all the toils of circumstance I am hoping to connect with the living Jim Farrell for a glass of beer in a 3rd Avenue saloon and talk about why Ralph Chaplin, the sturdy, wobbly poet, has taken shelter under the Catholic Church. Ever good going to you—

Carl Sandburg

586 | TO MARJORIE ARNETTE BRAYE

[Flat Rock, North Carolina]
May 28, 1956

Dear Marjorie

Enclosed is United States currency to the extent of one dollar ($1.00). With this I am requesting you to purchase licorice to the amount of the enclosed currency and forward same to me by mail. I am forced to this procedure by the fact that the poor goddam drug stores of Hendersonville, one and all, as though by joint conspiratorial action, refuse to carry licorice in stock as a commodity that might be wanted by the Hendersonville consumers. . . Please overlook whatever may seem unjust or discriminatory. I mean not to impose lamentations. I merely want the doggone licorice. . . Good to hear your blessed voices yesterday. . . And I remain

Yours very truly and obstinately,
Buppong

587 | TO DAVID C. MEARNS

[Flat Rock, North Carolina]
June 21, 1956

Dear Dave:

Comes along May number Quarterly Journal Current Acquisitions and definitely the sweetest number I have ever seen. You put the Reverend Mr. Thayer in his place for all time. One lone item he had that I never met elsewhere: Lincoln being asked if the newspapers were "reliable." Replied, "Certainly, they lie and relie." The Handy article and photographs—swell. If you could send me three copies of this nice number and send me bill for same I would thank you. I can see where one of these days several of these thorough monographs of yours in the Lincoln field are going to be arrested and locked in the cell of one book. . . Have been through So Fell the Angels and this is the long wanted book on those very respectable people [Salmon P. Chase's family]. Your "Lincoln Papers" wears well as a shelf occupant. What I reread most often are the illiterates. They had qualities of rhythm and Elizabethan speech color that were in the blood of their cousin Abe. When the question is, "Where did Lincoln get his literary style?" part of the answer is that it was in his blood. I plan to do an extended thesis on this in my next reincarnation.

Ever yours,
Carl

The Quarterly Journal of Acquisitions *is published by the Library of Congress.*

588 | TO ADLAI E. STEVENSON

[Flat Rock, North Carolina]
September 25, 1956

Dear Adlai:

You would not go wrong, I would guess, if you made reference, over and over again, to those long delayed measures which the Democrats enacted which have been bulwarks against Depression. As for speeches and ideas you're throwing 'em, straight or curved, better than ever, the best since Lincoln.

Ever yours,
Carl

1957

589 | TO BRUCE CATTON

[Flat Rock, North Carolina]
December 14, 1956

Dear Bruce Catton:
Now having finished This Hallowed Ground I can't hold back
from giving you salutations; so readable, so companionable, so well-
rooted a book. The book cost; you wrote it in high tension. You were
not afraid to have sentences carry music and color. Keen of George
Ade fifty years ago to write, "A classic is a book that people refuse to
let die." Saludos!

Yrs
Carl Sandburg

590 | TO NORMAN ROSTEN

[Flat Rock, North Carolina]
[Circa early 1957]

Dear Norman—
I read your piece in Book Find News & find myself saying 'He
was always a damned sweet boy, his angels & demons so like my
own.' When in NY next March I hope to see you & exchange news.
We can go to a bar & kill one or two liquid sputniks. . . Loving
regard, my friend & brother—

Carl

*Poet and playwright Norman Rosten met Sandburg in 1942 when
he wrote a "Cavalcade of America" radio program that starred
Sandburg. They hit it off, Sandburg moving into the small Bronx
apartment of the Rostens while rehearsing. "Good homesteading
land," Sandburg called the Bronx. Commenting on* The Sandburg
Range, *a collection of poems and sections from various Sandburg
books, Rosten had written, "Whatever the future will say about
him, he will be there; like Whitman, he is one of our literary
landmarks."*

591 | TO DONNA E. WORKMAN

[Flat Rock, North Carolina]
April 17   1957

Dear Donna Workman:

I salute you all who celebrate the memory of Clarence Darrow. He was audacity and he was loneliness and he was genius. His speech was bare and simple, understandable by plain folks. He knew gobbledegook but didn't talk it. Once in a debate in the Garrick Theater of a Sunday on the question "Is the Human Race Getting Anywhere?" he said it WASN'T! He enjoyed the verb "dawdle" and spoke and wrote of how he had dawdled away too much of his life. He had contradictory color and shadow and in the story of Chicago he stands out as one of its most interesting figures of authentic genius.

With sincere salutations—
Carl Sandburg

Mrs. Workman, Chicago business executive, had asked for a Darrow tribute. Sandburg noted on a copy of this letter, "read at Memorial dinner to Darrow."

592 | TO RALPH MC GILL

[Flat Rock, North Carolina]
June 3, 1957

Dear Ralph—

Please send me three or four clips of your column on Jim Thorpe & the new Jim Thorpe City. There are certain lovers of Remembrance Rock, my novel, who wd enjoy the parallel memorial pattern. . . Your columns go on testifying you have sagacity & serenity & you are good company if only with yourself.

Ever yours,
Carl
Carl
Carl

593 | TO WILLIAM G. STRATTON

[Flat Rock, North Carolina]
[Circa July 1, 1957]

Dear Sir:

You should know that if I were writing to you just to give a personal opinion, I would not waste your time. I made a similar statement in writing to the State Parole and Pardon Board in 1952.

There are others who like myself have never before directed a communication to a board of pardons and paroles who go along with me in viewpoint and feeling.

For a long time it has been known that in the circles in which Richard Loeb and Nathan Leopold moved at the time their offense was committed that the initiative was in the hands of Loeb—that after the offense the one hardened and light-minded about it was Loeb, while those who interviewed Nathan Leopold saw him in tears and remorse.

The records of the two prisoners since confinement give further light on the two men.

I would say to you, as Governor of Illinois, either for your confidential files or for direct quotation that if I were a member of the board I would vote for immediate and unconditional pardon for Nathan Leopold.

I would add that if he were a neighbor of mine I would want to see him often if only for benefits from association with a great intellect and a rare human spirit.

I would have him on the basis of numerous reports I consider unquestionable as a guest in my house whose companionship would be valued.

Sincerely and respectfully yours,
Carl Sandburg

594 | TO ALVIN W. DREIER

[Flat Rock, North Carolina]
July 15, 1957

Dear Al:

Your announcement in a grand script arrives today almost as though with a fanfare and an adagio blast of trumpets. And how casually and neatly you give THE KEY to the situation! We will drink to Cap Streeter's ghost and maybe it will walk for us. And Jesus wept! Only three blocks from Pixley & Ehlers! I suppose the old time extra slab of pork wh[ich] was a nickel is now either a dime or two bits. Anyhow it is a place that never done me wrong and I have written and revised some of my best poems there and at Thompsons also including Hutchinson's chile joint just west of the Northwestern depot. At present negotiations not closed on a second-story job BBD & O want me to do: will report to you on progress or nix. . . Bigod it's going to be nice to join you in looking out at the old lake that has many years been our friend. Your thoughtfulness is appreciated and I'll be seeing you.

As ever
Carl

595 | TO ALLAN NEVINS

[Flat Rock, North Carolina]
August 5, 1957

Dear Allan:

Would you believe it the first thing I know I will be sewed up and tied down with so many agreeable dates hither and yon that I won't get any real work done? I would like to spend one day, two days, three days, in such a fellowship as you describe which will be there at Gettysburg in November. But my October and early November weeks are criss-crossed in such a way that as I look at it, I say, "No Gettysburg this year. I love those fellows. Allan Nevins is in my book the greatest of American historians. His company is good for me. But Jesus Christ! When and where am I going to get time to finish my unfinished works?" As my own counsel for the defense I don't know whether I am doing so good. But, my dear friend, when you reach five months from four score you will say once in a while, "By golly, they'd get along without me if I had slipped on a banana peel and fallen across to the Other Shore." With ever deep and affectionate regard—

Yrs
Carl

596 | TO GREGORY D'ALESSIO

[Flat Rock, North Carolina]
Sept. 28, 1957

Dear Gregory:

The Esteso guitar I left with you is for any purpose whatsoever that you and the officers of SCG may designate. You can sell it, you can offer it as a prize and make an award of it. I have so complete a confidence in you and Bobri that I trust you two as Lincoln did Grant and Sherman after he found them. I send you unchanging loving regard, which certainly must include Terry.

Ever yours
Carl

597 | TO MARIANNE MANTELL

[Flat Rock, North Carolina]
Dec. 5, 1957

Dear Marianne:

I shall be counting on two or three days in March of recording with you or for you or I should have said for Caedmon. I hope at that time to have a look at Stephen and possibly kiss his right and left big toes. He and I have walked in on Caedmon in the same year. When he is old enough to cast his first ballot I will be 101 years of age and when I come to see him in Peter Cooper Village I will treat him with respect knowing otherwise he will throw me in the East River. A nice old time toast goes, "May all your children be acrobats."

Love and blessings
Carl

598 | TO PAUL H. DOUGLAS

[Flat Rock, North Carolina]
June 27, 1958

Dear Senator Douglas:

You should know that I am one of the many who appreciate your toils and efforts in behalf of Indiana Dunes National Monument. I have known those dunes for more than 40 years and I give my blessing and speak earnest prayers for those who are striving for this project. Those dunes are to the Midwest what the Grand Canyon is to Arizona and the Yosemite to California. They constitute a signature of time and eternity; once lost, the loss would be irrevocable.

Good going to you.

Faithfully yours,
Carl Sandburg

599 | TO FRANKLIN J. MEINE

[Flat Rock, North Carolina]
[Spring 1958]

Brother Meine

Genuine regrets that I can not be present and join in a fellowship paying tribute to Charles Vincent Starrett, as the man sometimes signed his chaste news stories in the ole Victor Lawson's Chicago Daily News, the world's greatest afternoon newspaper, though never thus self-proclaimed. Vincent is one of those few men whom I have little difficulty in placing in most any previous era of civilized mankind. His outward look and manner, his wit and ready inner grace, his casual and debonair camaraderie that he can employ on occasion to hide his investitures of wide learning and his lore acquired by companionship with books great and little, good, bad and indifferent—you can see him at home and at ease in several former human societies, talking small talk where the easy wisecrack is approved, or making conversation on the timeless themes and queries. I am sure he could shape his own list of the Hundred Great Books and defend it against all comers. The snow of winter is on his head, as with others of us. When the time comes he shall enter Valhalla I can see him sharing confidences with A. Conan Doyle, sharing tobacco and book-talk with Charles Lamb, sipping strange green liqueurs with Francois Villon, mixing in pleasant arguments with Walter Pater, Walter Savage Landor, Walter Raleigh, and saying he will have no truck, when they arrive, with either Walter Lippmann or Walter Winchell, though in a pinch he will take Winchell as against Lippmann on account of Winchell having made bold additions to the American language. I join with you Caxtonians in your salutations to Vincent Starrett—a modern—an antique—rather timelessly human. I give the toast of Joe Jefferson years ago playing Rip Van Winkle at McVickers: "May you liff long und brosper." I add an ancient Irish toast: "The best of luck before you, bad luck behind you, and the grace of God to guard and guide you."

Carl Sandburg

Franklin J. Meine, Chicago author, wrote regarding the Caxton Club dinner honoring Charles Vincent Starrett, a Chicago Daily News *colleague of Sandburg's, whose* Book Column *was published by the Caxton Club in 1958.*

600 | TO THOMAS HORNSBY FERRIL

[Flat Rock, North Carolina]
June 27, 1958

Dear Tom:

The days and weeks go by and I get all kinds of nice little letters written to you—in my mind—which as it happens do not get put on paper and sent on to you. Meantime along comes your Herald so often having the quality of a good letter telling how the world goes with you. I still have a hunch that I'll be seeing you within a year. I still have in mind a certain anthology for two or three years from now where I may get some things said as to the poetry scene. February 14 next year I am slated in San Francisco to do the narration to the Copland Lincoln Portrait. I expect to look in on your son-in-law's book shop and your daughter whom I remember, if you will allow me, as angel-faced.

Ever and ever
Carl

601 | TO WILLIAM T. EVJUE

[Flat Rock, North Carolina]
Sept. 20, 1958

Dear Bill:

In your August 31 broadcast all of a sudden you named Frank Weber, Victor L. Berger, Henry Ohl, Jack Hanley, Fred Heath and Ed Melms. That had a breath of the past for me. I knew each of those men and wrote stories and squibs about them. . . I will phone you from Chicago hoping that we can have either the day before or the day after October 12th for a drive out to Talicsin. We have plenty to talk about and I hope you don't mind my saying to others than yourself that you are one of the best talkers in the United States.

Yours in fellowship,
Carl

Frank Weber, Victor Berger, Henry Ohl, Jack Hanley, Frederick Heath, and Edward Melms were all old Milwaukee Socialists whom both Evjue and Sandburg had known. Evjue had been a reporter on the Milwaukee Sentinel *in those days and was now editor and publisher of the* Capital Times *in Madison, Wisconsin.*

602 | TO DAVID C. MEARNS

[Flat Rock, North Carolina]
December 10, 1958

Dear Dave;

Enclosed is that there introduction what we talked about via
AT&T of which there is opinion that if you own some of the stock
the more you talk over the phone the more money you make. . . I
thought of a dozen different approaches. I stayed shy of biographical
gobbledegook. I did not fight shy of certain quotations that for
luminosity cannot be surpassed. I assumed I was writing a sort of
small curtain raiser for an elaborate enumeration of catalogue
items. . . Am not sure about spelling in next to last paragraph of
Koch: it might be Hoch. . . You are a good writer and a nice editor.
Such is my trust in you I give you sweeping license to make any
changes or deletions you consider advisable. Will be rolling in to see
you February 10 or 11 next. . . Old Scotch toast: May the road to
hell grow green waitin for you.

Yrs,
Carl

Justice W. O. Douglas is probably engaged for the evening of Feb.
12. If not, wd you tell him I covet an introduction by him. He has
done more well written & important travel books than any other
reporters & I say this having read *Aku Aku,* the title we sneeze.

*David C. Mearns had invited Sandburg to talk at the Library of
Congress on the one hundred and fiftieth anniversary of Lincoln's
birth. The Kansas Congressman Homer Hoch had spoken to the
House in 1923 about Lincoln's "grandeur of spirit." In his speech
Sandburg said, "In Lincoln's letters, speeches, state papers, running
to more than a million words, much holds good for this hour."*

603 | TO WILLIAM O. DOUGLAS

[Flat Rock, North Carolina]
Dec. 19, 1958

Dear Bill Douglas:

On reading your ninth book (or the tenth if we count Democracy and Finance, 1940), not to mention speeches and parts of decisions, also having heard your Altgeld centennial speech in Chicago and your Wesleyan University commencement speech, I am as privileged to address you as if I were Miangul Abdul Wadud the father of the Wali of Swat and speaking Pushtu. Also and furthermore you and I are the only honorary members of the Overseas Press Club. Among other things I am sure of with reference to your status: you ain't what's wrong with this country. Tom Paine termed himself "A Citizen of the World." You prove yourself so definitely as having a right to that title. Such countries and peoples, such houses, languages, laws, customs, schools, crops as you have met and seen and had fellowship with, it becomes impressive out of these thousands of pages of travel lore, vivid reporting and great readiness for understanding and fellowship. I have been with you 7,000 miles West of the Indus. Most of the book ran along as though this was to be a personal record for the refreshment of your mind and spirit at any time you wished it without reference to its ever being published as a book. I hope some time to write about you as a writer of books who is "a natural". In 1940 you nicely inscribed Democracy and Finance and later on my request you signed a photograph mentioning our box-car fraternity. . . May I ask whether you ever received a small book, now very rare, titled "A Lincoln Preface"? Anyhow it will be fun next year to send you two paperbacks, my first. . . To you and Mercedes, two stronghearts, my love and blessings.

Carl Sandburg

604 | TO SHARVEY G. UMBECK

[Flat Rock, North Carolina]
[March 3, 1959]

Dear Sharvey:

A copy of "Warden Ragen of Joliet" by Gladys Erickson has been ordered sent to you. You will find it fascinating reading. The man is of heroic stature. I may write for whatsoever use you might make of it a citation. Perhaps I should inform you that this is the first time I ever became active toward a degree being awarded someone. . . The feeling grows on me that I am more than an adopted son of Knox. Few living persons had the kind of familiarity that I had with the Knox campus and its buildings. My bare feet at seven and eight years of age knew nearly every square yard of the campus. I took a winter course in gymnastics in the old big wooden barn of a gymnasium. Across a period of some fifteen years I watched her best performers in athletics from the great Nelson Willard thru "Speedy" Gonterman and the negro halfback "Chuck" Hopkins. I heard Britt as a debater and Finley as orator, so when I meet either faculty members or students of the present generation and they think they can tell me about Knox I say to myself, "Yeah? I learned about Knox before you were born." And along this line I will reminisce for you some time when we can have a lazy hour together.

Ever good wishes,
Carl

Dr. Sharvey G. Umbeck has been president of Knox College since 1949.

605 | TO EDWARD STEICHEN

[Flat Rock, North Carolina]
October 1, 1959

Dear Ed:

We are dedicating the $2,000,000 Carl Sandburg High School in Mundelein, Illinois, just north of Chicago a little. And they are crying out loud for a photograph. We can't do better than the processional montage of six shifting phizzogs. Dedication is on October 15 and I am going out there. The member of the Board of Education who stresses the need for this great photograph is

> Richard F. Johnson
> 505 South Midlothian
> Mundelein, Illinois

I will phone you from New York on October 7 if not sooner. Our college days are not over.

> Love and two kisses on the whiskers,
> Carl

606 | TO HERB BLOCK

> [Flat Rock, North Carolina]
> June 14, 1960

Dear Herblock:

Justice Oliver Wendell Holmes said, "The novels of Henry James should have been written on white paper with WHITE INK." Nevertheless parts of what Mr. H. James wrote about Daumier have some nice spots which may rest you and please you. . . May the road to hell grow green and flowering waiting for you.

> Carl

607 | TO PAUL R. LEACH

> [Flat Rock, North Carolina]
> July 12, 1960

Dear Paul:

Regrets about delay in answering yours of January 26. My memory is not clear now on what FDR had to say and my correction. If it comes back to me I will write you. You probably can't get into cold type the intonations you put into a little commentary as you stood at my desk in that southwest corner of our local room:

"O-l-d Carl Sandburg! O-l-d-e-r than the Pyramids! Older than Jesus and the twelve Apostles." And you named other hoary ruins and vestiges out of ancient times. I have now and then given imitations of this little act of yours. The years I had in that local room are among the best in my life. Sometime when in Washington I hope we can have a session of good rememberings. That old Chicago Daily News of that particular decade is worth writing about. Ben Hecht in his book says I was sent to a labor convention and over three days sent no story back; I have clippings of those three days with my byline big as a fencepost. And Paul, here is salutation on good work done and loving regard to you.

Carl

Paul R. Leach was writing a book about his fifty years of newspaper work, mostly on the Chicago Daily News.

608 | TO ALVIN W. DREIER

[Flat Rock, North Carolina]
July 15, 1960

Dear Al:

Tell Jack Flynn that his note to you saying Connemara is "the name of a lovely, wild district in western Ireland where a lot of people still use Gaelic as their native tongue"—and Jack is correct that our place is named from that one. Oddly enough the name was given in 1900 by Ellington Adgar Smythe who came from Connemara, Ireland and who was one of those rare birds known as an Irish Presbyterian. . . All your sendings, Al, are welcome and get read and sometimes are keenly informative. I am going to back Kennedy as against Nixon but I have taken an oath not to tear my shirt. You might phone Jim to this effect. You will find the October number of Playboy with six of my poems on six pages each of different color unimportant but sweetly daffy.

Yours ever in fellowship,
Carl

609 | TO MEYER KESTNBAUM

[Flat Rock, North Carolina]
July 16, 1960

Dear Kesty:

This should be a sort of a documentary testifying that you and Hart Schaffner & Marx have supplied me with four overcoats, one going back more than 30 years, one a hummer and a Jim dandy in production of this year. And as I told you I am now proof against all kinds of cold weather for the rest of my life. I salute you and shall hold you in affectionate remembrance for the skill and the fellowship involved in this affair. A photograph I prize is one of yourself and me and the one and only Richard Nixon. I hope the Chamber remembered you with one of these prints. Whoever is elected next November I believe our conversations on the state of the Union will go on. When in Chicago I hope again to have beer and pecans while looking out on good old Lake Michigan from your home windows and I would say love and blessings to you and yours.

Carl

P.S. Steichen has had a stroke & 2 minor operations. When he is better we will try for that 4-profile photograph.

Meyer Kestnbaum, the head of the clothing firm, called Sandburg "The poet laureate of Hart Schaffner & Marx." He referred to the series of articles Sandburg had written about the company's progressive shop-steward system for the Chicago Daily News *in 1917.*

610 | TO OLIVE CARRUTHERS

[Flat Rock, North Carolina]
July 16, 1960

Dear Olive:

Suppose you put together those you refer to as "my kid poems" and let us see how it looks as a book. We might talk it over further when, as it looks at present, I shall be in Chicago on the way to or from the opening of our show with Bette Davis about September 12 in New York. I liked Kennedy's reference to Nixon as having "charity toward none and malice for all." May your good heart keep its vivid ways and luck stars be over you ever.

Yrs,
Carl

611 | TO KENNETH DODSON

[Beverly Hills, California]
July 22, 1960

Dear Ken:

You are a good fellow. You live with good fellows. And under your roof it is not a silent love. You pour it out to each other.

I am reading again your sentence about Hollywood Biblical films: "Sin attractively buried under a syrupy sundae of sex dressed to pass the Hays office, with ten thousand sweating bodies and the Pyramids as a backdrop." Understand, Ken, the fellow I am working with, this here George Stevens, who made SHANE, A PLACE IN THE SUN, GIANT, DIARY OF ANNE FRANK, he is among the foremost creative spirits that have ever come along in the cinema industry. He and I had long talks, and I feel that I am lucky to be working with a man for whom my respect runs over into reverence, a little like your and my partnership.

Luck stars be over you and yours.

Carl Sandburg

612 | TO MRS. FREMONT OLDER

[Beverly Hills, California]
July 22, 1960

Dear Cora Older:

Your letter of a while ago is before me. And it's good to hear from you. You may be sure I would like to see your History of San Francisco.

Of course I can never forget you and Fremont and the ranch and Jack Black taking me in the moonlight up to where I slept on a mountainside—and the memory includes Pauline Jacobson and her stories, that I had read in Milwaukee, about Tvietmoe and graphic figures of that time.

I may sometime get a copy of your biography of Hearst to stand alongside of four or five others that I have, along with the Hearst life serialized in Fortune. I may yet write about Hearst. I remember a certain talk with Fremont where he spoke of Hearst's independent, freegoing course of life in a way that modified my hostility.

Ever good going to you.

Yours with affectionate regard,
Carl Sandburg

P.S. I'm about half way through an autobiography titled "Ever the Winds of Chance," and there will be two or three pages about you and Fremont.

613 | TO ALAN JENKINS

[Beverly Hills, California]
September 19, 1960

Dear Alan:

I do thank you for being so thoughtful as to send me your impressions about our getting off on the wrong foot in publicity. I'm going to read your letter a couple of times more and I'm going to read slowly and carefully your talk on "The Religion of the Jews." I'm going to go over both your letter and the talk with George Stevens. I believe he goes along with your main idea of what kind of a picture of Jesus is wanted and needed. An Associated Press story of some ten days ago quoted me correctly as saying that BEN HUR is "A monument of tripe" which could also go for THE TEN COMMANDMENTS wrought by Cecil B. de Mille. You should know perhaps that George Stevens and I had long talks at our farm in North Carolina and my impression is quite definite that you, he and I are agreed on certain important basic approaches to a life of Jesus. I think we are all agreed on the charming opening sentence of the Encyclopedia Britannica article on Jesus Christ. My new book, Wind Song, has been ordered sent to you—if it does not arrive I will see to it. Health be yours and the peace of great phantoms be with you.

Yours in fellowship,
Carl

614 | TO PAULA SANDBURG

[Beverly Hills, California]
September 28, 1960

Dear buddy,

Every afternoon along 1:30 to 6:00 we hold a conference in the building of the Stevens' unit. We discuss what should be the continuity of the script. Every once in a while Stevens is joined by Ivan Moffat, who is writing the script, in memories of the war in Europe. They were close and they dig up the darndest memories. At times it seems almost scholastic, the discussions. I am sure there has never been a Bible movie come out of Hollywood that was preceded by such thorough-going research and discussion of all angles. Of evenings I have seen all of Stevens' pictures besides some interesting new ones such as INHERIT THE WIND, which is around the Scopes trial in Tennessee, and ELMER GANTRY, a far departure from Sinclair Lewis' novel—and an improvement. Where the novel was rather sleazy, this has strengths and color worth seeing. Playing Gantry is one Burt Lancaster; he collects Brancusi and at the UCLA Tribute he read my Brancusi poem. When I go to a movie of an evening I go on to dinner shortly after 6:00 with two or three of the fellows, returning to the studio to see the picture about 8:00. I'm in the hay about 12 and one way or another, what with my exercises and reading, it's about 1:00 in the afternoon when a car from the studio calls for me. Driving with Stevens one of the earlier nights I was here, we descended on Lilla Perry about 9:30 and had her out of bed to show us her netsukes and Chinese snuff bottles. She's to have a book out this fall on the Chinese snuff bottles. It's kind of pretty what bottles they kept their snuff in while it was a vogue. Betty Peterman goes shopping for me; she is a keen shopper whether it's socks or shirts.

Last night I saw for the second time Stevens first big picture of some 12 years ago, SHANE. It is a superb story, sublime with landscapes, character portrayals and quite a thesis could be done about it as a great dramatic poem. It seems now to be settled that the title will not be the horrifying, blatant THE GREATEST STORY EVER TOLD, but instead, THE LIFE OF JESUS. At the picture last night I met the little Israeli gal who played Ruth and I kissed her and told her that I would tell you and Margaret that she's as good off stage as on. Am going to a newly made picture, ALAMO, tonight. I'm just doing a babbling letter to you, sort of what I would write if I were writing a diary. I get goat milk of good quality Monday, Wednesday and Friday. After a very good start in New York our show [*The World of Carl Sandburg*] was slowed down in attendance, partly because of a flood of new shows, the Jewish holidays Rosh Hashana and Yom Kippur, and so many people going to the big show at the United Nations. So the producer, Armand Deutsch, told me yesterday that Bette and the other actors have taken a cut, so has Norman, and a Lucy Kroll telegram said the cuts were imperative, so I signed too. I guess we keep that confidential. I have a large, elegant, two room office, first time in my life I've had my name in brass letters on a door and where a good gal who was secretary to Norman Corwin, Francesca Price Solo, answers the phone in a soft voice, "Carl Sandburg's office": it's worth a nickel to hear. I found Rube Burrough still living at seventy-seven, retired, and writing the autobiography of a radical. Eric and Charlene [Sister Mary's son and daughter-in-law] are bright and strong and when I talked with Eric yesterday, he said that the day before, Charlene went to hospital and was delivered of a 6 lb. girl, at which the two elder sons are dancing around the house. It was good news you gave me that Ed is stronger and can work among the negatives and photographs he understands better than anyone else. Photographs of Stevens and myself on the front porch, each with a Nubian in his lap, are sent along with this letter. I keep meeting people who want me [because Sandburg poems were in the October issue] to autograph "Playboy." This is a scoopful of a letter, not very precious but in spots nicely gossipy, and make no mistake, I love you a million bushels.

Carl

1960

615 | TO PAULA SANDBURG

[Beverly Hills, California]
[Circa October, 1960]

Paula dear—

Give this enclosure to whoever shd send me a ballot to mark for
JFK—

Ever,
Carl

616 | TO EDWARD STEICHEN

[Beverly Hills, California]
December 7, 1960

Dear Ed:

A letter from Ivan Kashkeen dated October 20 in Moscow
arrives. He has "been ill and out of town for a long time." A postscript says, "Until now we did not see anywhere any of the photos
Mr. Steichen had done here. We wonder are they all so unworthy
of his attention. We'd be glad to get some of them nevertheless. We
highly esteem his work." Another postscript says, "I hope to send
you in some months the Russian translation of the abridged version
of your life of Abraham Lincoln! (It's done not by me but at my
urgent request.)" Therefore take notice that you are not forgotten
in Moscow.

It is damn sweet news that you are up and around and working
to the good, according to Paula. Love to you and to the extraordinary
and beautiful Joanna.

Carl

*Kashkeen had translated Sandburg's work into Russian. Steichen
and Sandburg had seen him in Moscow when they traveled there
for the "Family of Man" exhibit in 1959.*

[Beverly Hills, California]
December 7, 1960

Dear Ralph:

"Tusen Tack" which is Swedish for a thousand thanks for your letter and the poems and particularly the poems of Ralph McGill, Jr. A boy is beautifully alive who could have in him the simplicity and the vision in that little eight line poem titled IF. It is going to be fun to watch him grow. The comment up front, "His imagery is superb and his haiku almost correct," I go along with that. I remember a critic some thirty years ago writing that, "Sandburg can turn a good hokku and that is about all." The spacing of his haikus was fine and could be a challenge to young Ralph to go on and on. I hope he has given a slow and deliberate reading of my "Notes for a Preface" up front in my COMPLETE POEMS.

I have read aloud on three or four occasions your short, short story around "My mule is dead. I am drowned in this pond." It is history woven with contemplations you didn't know you had till you started to write that piece. Your health and your humor and your analytical insights keep going on. Sometime I may try to figure out who are the ten richest men in the country. You would be one of them along with Steichen, Ed Murrow, Stevenson, Oppenheimer, S. L. A. Marshall, Harry Golden and a few more. As I look at the vast stream of oratory this year, two fellows stand out for language and delivery: Eugene McCarthy and Herbert Lehman nominating Stevenson for president.

Take care, Ralph, watch your step. Live long.

Ever yours,
Carl

618 | TO PAULA SANDBURG

[Beverly Hills, California]
December 30, 1960

Dearest Paula,

I'm glad you call it an ailment and not a disease. All along the Steichens always have had ailments and not diseases with the single exception of Oma at her end. It interests me that this comes to you at the Christmas holiday season. In Elmhurst, across the 1920's when Ed would come on from New York and you and Oma were lighted like Christmas trees about his coming, the rushing around and the hullabaloo nearly got you down. You were warned. I have warned you several times in your office as I found you there, concentrating on this and that. You have a rare, high-power mind. Something of your nervous system operates along with that mind. Now you have ease from pain only when you move about or lie down. You can't now sit those long hours at your desk working on various problems. Anyhow, it's nice that I'm going to be back in February and we'll have a morning walk and an evening walk—holding hands. I look on Jennifer II, along with some of the most beautiful Nubians, as creations of yours, creations as definitely as either photographs or delphiniums created by Ed plus God. It will be fun to tell you about Stevens and our "unit." Give Marn a kiss for me and tell Janet when I am home again I expect every day she will tell me (never failed me yet) what the temperature is.

As ever,
Buddy

P.S. Remember your great grandfather who went through all of the hunger and cold and deep snow out of Moscow with Napoleon and living to be 102. I had a nice talk with Dr. Max Cutler who fixed Opa's nose cancer. Look how tough and nice Ed has been coming through his late ailments. You ain't been nicely lazy in these later years.

Jennifer II was the Toggenburg doe which, in an official test that topped all breeds, made a world record of 5,750 pounds of milk.

619 | TO SOPHOCLES PAPAS

[Beverly Hills, California]
19 January 1961

Dear Sophocles:

Your letter about you and John and me is lovely to have! When I see you I will give you some sweet anecdotes about his earlier years. He tried to say "Grandpa" and it came out "Buppong." Among a few persons that name Buppong clings. Marjorie and Bill [Braye] always use it. He and his sister and I formed a trio that could sing certain songs; once we went before an audience of United Presbyterians who had a camp near us in Connemara. I gave him and his sister that lute-shaped guitar, a brother to the one that Marje had, and I suppose he fooled with it and became fascinated. You should have him sleep sometime, or at least have a nap, in the bed where Segovia has slept; you can call that corner of your house Saints' Rest.

Please know my heart is soft about what you see with such certainty in my grandson. Love to you and Mercia.

Ever yours,
Carl

Sophocles Papas, one of the leading teachers of the classical guitar, owned the Columbia Music Company in Washington, D.C., was a close friend of Segovia, and taught Sandburg's grandson.

620 | TO FRANCES ARVOLD

[Beverly Hills, California]
April 21, 1961

Dear Frances:

At any one moment when our show was on the TV screen I expected to see you step up and apply Kleenex below my nose. And they probably said, "We'll put that one in the next one for pleasant comedy." Send along more than one poem. And please don't fail me on photographs. Send along one that includes your own good face.

We worked on what is generally agreed to be a TV classic which will be around when we are all under the grass roots unless cremated. I designated the one or two quarts of cinders from my body to go to the house where I was born. Write me about your poems and about your work. Everybody loved you. There was a warm and keen fellowship about our crew, all of it good for me. Norman Corwin and I have finished a manuscript of a book we will co-sign when published next fall and its titled, "The World of

Carl Sandburg"

Frances Arvold, out of Fargo, S.D., was the make-up artist for two television documentaries, "Carl Sandburg at Gettysburg" and "Carl Sandburg—The Prairie Years."

621 | TO ELIZABETH STEVENSON IVES

[Beverly Hills, California]
May 3, 1961

Dear Buffy:

From across the continent here I have to report to you that I am sewed up by contract and what little time I can get to spend in North Carolina must be at Connemara Farm over near Hendersonville. Your face and your voice sort of go with your letter. The first time we met was at the Governor's mansion in Springfield and the last time we met was on the lower floor of Madison Square Garden the night I made a three minute speech and Adlai thirty minutes. One of these days maybe in 1962 I may get to Paint Hill Farm at Southern Pines. Adlai is on a tough spot and showing fine form. Destiny has made that spot terribly important.

With loving regard,
Carl

Adlai Stevenson was U.N. Ambassador when Buffy, his sister, Elizabeth Ives, invited Sandburg to a Civil War dedication ceremony in Durham, N.C.

622 | TO EDWARD STEICHEN

[Los Angeles, California]
May 25, 1961

Dear Ed:

You should know that for some of us who have known you more than fifty years your program on Accent was nothing short of wonderful, having definitely wisdom and majesty. It was moving to me because it sort of accented knowledge, wisdom, training, guidance, that I have had from you. Now I have read every line and word of the book the Museum got out. It is a sweet and keen book. I can see you and Joanna as a wonderful team, making it both informative and lovable. A man who has worked nobly and with originality across many years is lucky to have so many of the best details set forth as in this book. I put my arms around the both of you.

Ever yours,
Carl

623 | TO PHILIP A. HART

[Beverly Hills, California]
June 6, 1961

Dear Senator Hart:

In the person of Frederick Douglass we have a figure who baffles the "White Supremacists." His story has charm. As you probably know. He was a fugitive slave out of Baltimore who in the North saved his wages and bought the freedom of his fiancee in Baltimore. She came north and they were married and in the passing of years she died and Frederick Douglass took to himself another wife, a white woman. There was hullabaloo about this here and there and Douglass replied in effect, "I don't see what they are troubled about. My first wife was the color of my mother. My second wife is the color of my father." Douglass was welcomed by Lincoln at the White House and what he wrote about those meetings was interesting. He wrote something to the effect that in the presence of Lincoln he was not conscious of the color line. Good going to you in your efforts.

Ever good wishes,
Carl Sandburg

Senator Philip A. Hart, of Michigan, had introduced a bill to restore the home of Douglass and asked Sandburg for comment.

624 | TO HARRY GOLDEN

[Beverly Hills, California]
June 14, 1961

Dear Harry:

The photograph of Bette [Davis] and me was made frontstage at the end of the opening of the show in the Henry Miller Theatre in New York. What they were playing was titled, "The World of Carl Sandburg," as you know. There was a standing ovation to me but in the pitch-black beyond the footlights I could not see it. Norman Corwin and I are signing contracts today for the publication next fall of "The World of Carl Sandburg" by Norman Corwin as author. There'll be cheap paperback reprints by Samuel French who publishes for stock and amateurs. If you get a photograph of Bette and me from the Associated Press please get a duplicate for me. I send you these things with no concrete suggestions at all and if nothing comes of them you will never hear no demurs from me. Your book is going to be a nice hayride. I am ready anytime to read proofs or to welcome your good face out here. I am not sure I understand it but long ago I met some mathematician saying, "Make the sign of infinity and pass on."

P.S. On my 75th birthday dinner at Knox College Steichen journeyed from his Umpawaug Farm in Connecticut to be present and to say among other remarks when called on to speak, "On the day that God made Carl He didn't do anything else." When I am naming important teachers and personal forces in my life I must name Steichen and his sister. They have been a faculty of many professors in several fields whether the fine arts, genetics or healthy and wholesome mysticism. No man was ever more lucky in a brother-in-law. When I look at his brilliant record in two world wars, his depth of love and devotion to his country added to his immense performances in the field of photography and the fine arts, he has definitely a kind of majesty in my book.

CS

625 | TO JOHN F. KENNEDY

[Beverly Hills, California]
[Circa mid-June, 1961]

Dear Mr. President:

This book is too long, with more than a half million words about the rise and movement of the American Dream, too long for you to read amidst your time pressures. However, the speech on pages 18-22 this volume may be worth your reading. It embodies in some degree, the consecration of spirit you have in this fateful hour. I beg to salute you on wonderfully appropriate appointments made and two speeches that are to become American classics.

Faithfully yours,
Carl Sandburg

This is the dedicatory letter Sandburg presented to President John F. Kennedy with a copy of Remembrance Rock. *Sandburg referred to the President's inauguration and U.N. speeches.*

626 | TO HARRY GOLDEN

[Beverly Hills, California]
June 20, 1961

Dear Harry

Please send me four or five copies of the May-June Israelite. I have now read three times the page one piece titled, "The Freedom

Riders in Alabama." You are going a little better than ever in your role which I term, "Apostle of Liberty." The book reviews by R. G. [Richard Goldhurst, Golden's eldest son] are keen. As I ramble through this current number I get a definite impression it is one of the best you have ever done. You should send a marked copy to Senator Hart of Michigan who has a bill in Congress providing for purchase of a memorial home of Frederick Douglass. I sent him a letter that he can throw into the Congressional Record, saying incidentally that Douglass proves baffling to the White Supremacists. He was a Negro whom Lincoln welcomed at the White House.

A phone call came today from Gwynn Steinbeck saying she has done music to eight poems of mine and that music people who have heard the discs say they are great. She is bringing the discs out here next week and I will hear them and we will discuss them.

Did I send you Sam Marshall's Detroit News story about one angle that I have never met before. A calculation has been made that in order to produce the deaths of six million Jews, the Nazis had to subtract 600,000 men from their armed forces. This, of course, gives an angle on the contribution of the Jews to the destruction of the Nazi armed forces. I have an impression that I mailed to you this Marshall report.

. . . They are elated and jumping with joy at Connemara over a three week visit in July that they will have from one of the loveliest and brightest eighteen year old girls in this country, the granddaughter Karlen Paula. . . I may have told you that Harcourt Brace will publish, "The World of Carl Sandburg" by Norman Corwin next fall, and it will be fun to see what kind of a race it runs with Carl Sandburg by Harry Golden by God. . . You may have missed this clipping which shows that you and Ralph McGill is comrades. . . Do you have a complete list of the high schools and elementary schools named after me? Two elementary schools in the Detroit area have popped up in the last month. On word from you I will send you a complete list. You are free to use if you like the enclosed poem by Charles Hamblett from his book, "A Letter to the Living.". . . At the annual meeting of the Friars last January, a dinner honoring Gary Cooper, I made a five minute speech saying at the end, "I believe we are correct in saying that Gary Cooper is the most beloved illiterate to appear in American history." Then I turned and walked three steps to Gary Cooper and kissed him on the forehead, the first time I have ever done such a thing. Gary, who one time studied cartooning, went to work on a message and a cartoon for me and it was passed on down to where I sat next to Audrey Hepburn. I enclose it for you and howsoever you may wish to use it. But for Christ's sake don't lose it. . . Do I recall your saying that J. F. Kennedy recited "Cool Tombs" or did he merely mention that he was familiar with it? I had a nice letter from him acknowledging warm appreciation of a two-volume deluxe "Remembrance Rock" I sent him. In my inscription in "Remembrance Rock" I wrote, "I am one of the many who register to your Inaugural Address as an American Classic." He closed his letter, "I have been an admirer of yours for many years and therefore I am extremely pleased to have this inscribed book.". . . As I have told you before, you are always in my prayers.

Faithfully,
Carl

627 | TO PAULA SANDBURG

[Beverly Hills, California]
July 6, 1961

Dear Paula:

I am sending you here a copy of a letter from John. He is beautifully sober and so lovable. His sentence in his letter, "I quit work to attend school and felt guilty in doing so." At any time that you should feel that he is short of funds, and a little funds from us would help, you may send him whatever you think is wise, judicious, nice and pretty. He is a love of a boy, and he's got some of the best of the Steichen and Sandburg breeds. I remember when you were in tears over that first marriage, and I said, "I think it means we are going to have grandchildren, and it may be that they will be exactly what we want." Now it has happened. You have done well all the way through, and I kiss you a salute to our progeny.

Carl

Of course, show the letter to Marn who will enjoy it & be proud.

628 | TO EDWARD R. MURROW

[Beverly Hills, California]
July 10, 1961

Dear Ed:

At the end of a preface to my one-volume Lincoln published in 1954, I used four sentences from a speech of Brazilian Ambassador Joaquim Nabuco at a dinner on the 100th Birthday Anniversary of Lincoln. He said, "With the increased velocity of modern changes, we do not know what the world will be a hundred years hence. For sure, the ideals of the generation of the year 2000 will not be the same of the generation of the year 1900. Nations will then be governed by currents of political thought which we can no more anticipate than the seventeenth century could anticipate the political currents of the eighteenth, which still in part sway us. But whether the spirit of authority, or that of freedom, increases, Lincoln's legend will ever appear more luminous in the amalgamation of centuries, because he supremely incarnated both those spirits."

Now comes along last week a translation of a biography of Joaquim Nabuco by his daughter Dona Carolina Nabuco. Now, Ed, this Nabuco was an agitator, a self designated abolitionist, writing sometimes under the pseudonym Garrison, terming slavery "The Great Crime." As you probably know, they ended slavery by a series of transitions. Says the close of the book, "His embalmed body, lying in state on the deck, guarded night and day by United States Marines, crossed the desolate expanses of the ocean aboard the cruiser, 'North Carolina,' which was escorted by another warship . . . flying the Brazilian standard. . . . In Rio, glorious last rites were solemnly held under the auspices of the government, and the old torn standards of the abolitionist associations were removed from the museums and symbolically paraded through the streets."

And what has smote me, Ed, is that here is a great traditional figure in the fight for liberty for all men. There ought to be a 16-page or 32-page pamphlet story of the life of this man sent all across South America. Perhaps there should be millions of sheets given away that tell on the two sides about this figure who is in Latin America the figure nearest approaching Lincoln. In one Washington speech he said, "We are all but drops in the ocean. Yet we all want to have the consciousness of the ocean and not just of a drop." In the course of politics in Brazil he wrote that it was strange to find himself "at the head of the Monarchist Coalition." And why? "I must fight for the Princess, who is our Lincoln, as I fought for abolition." At another time he was writing: "The Liberty party entered this battle under the protection of the abolitionist movement. . . . We are all preparing ourselves with the same feeling of individual liberty with which Cromwell's soldiers steeled themselves for the great religious battles that established the supremacy of Parliament, and with the same unselfishness and abnegation with which the first Puritans left the shores of old England to found New England in America. Knowing what we want and holding our hearts high, we are making ourselves ready, Mr. President, to give some day to this nation a government in which, as in the Roman consuls and tribunes, the world may see both the sanctity of the country and the inviolability of the people represented." On page 18 is a letter signed Joaquim to his father. It is a 3-exclamation point sentence reading, "I dream of no other glory for you than that of Abraham Lincoln!!!" His defense of a slave murderer was terrific drama, and he did save the man from the death penalty; he was as good as Clarence Darrow. Now, Ed, I am hard pressed with duties, but there is something here that I believe can be of great educational use in the Latin American countries. He loved liberty for all men in a way that the Communists don't.

And, Ed, your Sunday afternoon half hours are good work. You get that fine, reasonable personality of yours across to millions of folks, and across the years you should have at least one Sunday a month—and maybe all Sundays.

Your old college chum,
Carl

P.S. My copy of this biography in English translation came to me from Carolina Nabuco herself down in Rio. It was published by the nearby Stanford University Press, but I think they don't know about me and Nabuco.

Edward R. Murrow, as director of the United States Information Agency, enthusiastically supported Sandburg's proposal.

629 | TO ALICIA PATTERSON

[Los Angeles, California]
July 11, 1961

Dear Alicia:

I have too long put off sending you a message about Newsday. As a newspaper, it is beautifully affirmative about life. It is sweet, keen, strong and quiveringly alive. It is in terrific contrast to the Los Angeles Times. Sometimes when I ask myself, "What in the hell is wrong with this paper?", I find myself answering, "Somehow it seems to try to love people and life and can't quite make it." Often I clip and read more than once such editorials as many months back, "The Need For Urgency" and the one recently on the television-radio lobby in Congress.

I am going along here with a tentative title of "Creative Consultant" to George Stevens, the only man who could have lured me to Hollywood. The four pictures which he made when he came home from the war, SHANE, A PLACE IN THE SUN, GIANT and THE DIARY OF ANNE FRANK I take as assured classics of the cinema, and I refer to Stevens as "a Michaelangelo of the cinema." I am keenly enjoying Virginia as a book editor. I salute with reverence the shadow of your father and hope sometime to write about why I do so.

With salutations and ever loving regard.

Carl

Alicia Patterson was editor and publisher of Newsday. *The book editor, Virginia Pasley, was also a friend of Sandburg's.*

630 | TO JOHN M. ELLIOTT

[Beverly Hills, California]
July, 11, 1961

Dear Mr. Elliott:

Please know that I have regrets that all my time is being contracted for out here. It would definitely be a pleasure to meet the
representatives at this time of the good old Amalgamated. Sometime when finishing a book that I am now on I shall write about
a strike in Milwaukee and another in Chicago when I came to
know rather closely Bill Mahone, Ed Murrow and Dick Bland,
your editor whom I saw often in his office when on the Chicago
Day Book and later on the Chicago Daily News.

My salutations to you and your associates.

Fraternally yours,
Carl Sandburg

*John M. Elliott was international president of the Amalgamated
Association of Street, Electric Railway and Motor Coach Employes
of America.*

631 | TO PAULA SANDBURG

[Beverly Hills, California]
July 14, 1961

Dearest Paula:

Today came those two photographs of Jennifer II. Profile and
rear. I tell people you are a champion breeder of a champion, that
you are a geneticist, a naturalist, an ornithologist, Phi Beta Kappa
and a sweet gal. This is so near a real love letter that I'm going
to quit here and sign.

Carlo

632 | TO PAULA SANDBURG

[Beverly Hills, California]
July 17, 1961

MEMO *for my Paula.*

Last Saturday night went for the first time in my life to the Hollywood Bowl, the guest of Mr. and Mrs. Andre Kostelanitz, taking with me as fellow guests Lilla Perry and Betty Peterman. It was a kind of a Grand Canyon of an audience, every seat taken, twenty thousand people, to hear an all-Gershwin program. A master of ceremonies named Cassidy at the intermission, before reporting coming events, suddenly was saying, "We have present with us this evening a man who has become a legend in his own time, Carl Sandburg." On the instant a spotlight played on me and I stood up and stretched my right arm to this announcer and then to the twenty thousand innocent people assembled. So there we are, "A legend in our own time." And what you and I have to say is, "Jesus, it could be worse!"

Carl

633 | TO HARRY GOLDEN

[Beverly Hills, California]
July 28, 1961

Dear Harry:

I never brought a guitar to Darrow's office and sang. I never met Mrs. Hillman till years after the second and later strike, the strike in 1915. During the fifteen weeks the strike lasted I wrote a story about it every day in the Day Book, with sometimes a front page story. It was on Darrow's return from Los Angeles after his trial and acquittal that we became close thru news stories and an editorial on his announcement that he was for the Allies and against Germany in the first World War. Also he liked my review of his book "Farmington" which the Chicago Daily News book editor had printed as a booklet with a fine photograph of Darrow on the cover. He had occasion once to write me a lead pencil note which ended, "I don't want you to step out of my life," signed merely Darrow. I believe no one ever called him Clarence. He rates for me as being somewhat to Chicago what Diogenes was to Athens. Harry, you may use the foregoing if it can serve, but you are nearly as fantastic as Ben Hecht in having me in Chicago in 1910 and reporting the garment strike and bringing a guitar to Darrow's office and singing for him and Mrs. Hillman.

It is false testimony and borders on fantastic to say: "Sometimes he would go to a convention and not show up for days." I covered five days of a convention of the AF of L in Atlantic City and several other conventions, usually labor, and never failed to show with a story and a byline in Milwaukee and Chicago papers. To show you that I may have a thicker skin than you have, I am willing, if you say so, to go to print with the whole kit and kaboodle as it now stands in gold print on the galley proofs. If what I am writing seems to you overanxious and meticulous, then you fail to understand in the long run I am protecting you as well as myself. I still think there is extraordinary writing and portraiture in the Pack Memorial pieces by James Thurber, Herb Block and Ed Murrow.

July 31, 1961

In 1915 came the Amalgamated Clothing Workers fifteen week strike. I wrote a story, long or short, about it every day in the Day Book, with sometimes a front page story. During two weeks Sidney Hillman conducted the strike in bed with flu and I came to his bedside nearly every day and gave him the latest reports that I had. In one way and another I kept in touch with Hillman and his lovely wife, Bessy, and in the 1944 campaign I wrote part of a leaflet widely distributed in Los Angeles. In this leaflet I replied to Hearst's vicious interpretations to the line, "Clear it with Sidney." Like David Dubinsky, Hillman had integrity and constructive abilities all too rare in the world of organized labor.

Carl

[Beverly Hills, California]
August 3, 1961

Dear Kitty:

Out of the toil and intelligence that you gave to our one-volume Lincoln I would trust you to do whatever your good mind dictates with regard to the alleged discrepancies in STORM OVER THE LAND, the One Volume Lincoln, and the 4 Volume Lincoln. I doubt whether I want to please one of these new come Civil War buffs who finds it highly important that there is a difference in the mental picture of a major general who "fell from his saddle a corpse," and "dismounted, mortally wounded." I favor not accommodating the buff. You gave my word for him, "a nuisance," and we will "file and forget." You have the words for it, " 'inaction' sounds insipid!" There have been plenty of mildly erroneous statements in BATTLES AND LEADERS OF THE CIVIL WAR. Your readiness to be scrupulously correct I appreciate. One thing we can be sure of —if they re-enact the Battle of Antietam the general will be shot with a paper bullet and fall to the ground with beet juice flowing from the imaginary mortal wound.

I speak for the Mrs. and Margaret and Janet as well as myself when at any time in the years to come that you or you and Ann would like a week or two at Connemara you will have a warm welcome and some pretty good fun. They have a Sardinian donkey there now, a European version of our western burro, you might like to ride up Big Glassy. It is good I shall be working with Rita, always reminded me somewhat of my friend Lillian Gish. Her smile is good for the blues.

Again the promotion man writes using the adjective, "disparate" which I refuse to use, and I'll bet not one book seller in ten is sure of its meaning. Those two copies of LINCOLN COLLECTOR arrived and I thank you. Where would I be sending your copy of Harry Golden's book? . . . Our old standby Helene seems to be moving out from where she has been for so many years. . . . What this octogenarian has to say is, "It's rather lovely that we are all ambulant and in our right minds."

As ever,
Carl

635 | TO MARY HEMINGWAY

[Los Angeles, California]
August 31, 1961

Dear Mary,

You are one of the most beautiful children of God to ever walk the earth. That story of yours with the marvelous photographs in LOOK is one of the finest love stories ever written. The sonnets of Shakespeare and of Elizabeth Barrett Browning don't compare with it. I am proud that I have known you. In Harry Golden's book next November you will see I have done my best at salutations to you and to the great fellow you knew so close and deep. I say all this with deep thanks to you whom I knew when we were on the dear old Chicago Daily News.

Carl Sandburg

P.S. The color photo of you and E.H. [Ernest Hemingway] and the Kudu, with your note about it is one of the sweetest graphic things ever caught in a picture.

636 | TO HERBERT MITGANG

[Flat Rock, North Carolina]
September 25, 1961

Dear Herb:

My good and learned and skilled friend herewith and hereby I give you thanks for your work on our Illinois tour. You have done some nice basic work touching on nearly everything. We can discuss later whether my feeling about the umbrella and the hat of Lincoln and other relics and materials I don't recall now in the

Chicago Historical Society [should be filmed for the program]. Tell my old college chum Windburn Williams it looks good to me now and I solemnly say, God help us all including the brave and forthright Jack Kennedy.

Yours always,

Carl

The groundwork for Sandburg's television documentary tour of Lincoln's "Prairie Years" was prepared by Herbert Mitgang of the New York Times *and Palmer Williams of CBS Reports.*

637 | TO MARY HEMINGWAY

[Flat Rock, North Carolina]
October 5, 1961

Dear Mary:

I find I have a carbon of the piece I did on request of Harry Golden for his book. In this letter from Ernest your writing interrupted his. You saw he had already done well and was going too far for his own good at the moment. Also at the time your "heartcry" had not come along in Look. It couples beautifully with the poem of praise he gave you in Look some years back. We should keep in touch. Sometime I would like to make a day or so stopover in Ketchum. You have strengths, deep quiet strengths along with awareness, sensitivity and wisdom gathered out of years wonderfully mingled with storm and peace. Yours with admiration and love,

Carl

In the enclosure for Mary Hemingway, Sandburg began, "Hemingway throws a long shadow over the pages of American literary history." She invited Sandburg to see Ketchum, Idaho; she wrote, "There is very little room here for pettiness, with the earth's huge careless majesty outside every window." Mary Hemingway had been a reporter on the Chicago Daily News.

638 | TO S. L. A. MARSHALL

[Flat Rock, North Carolina]
January 23, 1962.

Dear SLAM:

Something like thirty-two years ago I was joined with Hemingway in our affection for the Desplains River which ran between his home town Oak Park and my home town Maywood. Far later he was the first and only recipient of the Nobel prize to say to the Associated Press that if the decision had been with him he would have named me. His third wife lasted to the end and was perfection. I knew her well at The Chicago Daily News for two or three years and we keep up a close friendship, lately with letters and phone conversations. I am sure that your American Heritage piece will be a hummer and will stand as an able minority report of importance to any in the future who work on a definitive biography. You have done a classic of a book on war. I gave NIGHT DROP two days of reading and three days of writing. I move across the next three or four months into the end of contracted pieces of work when I will be able to say, "I'se a free man now, Massa." Yours with ever loving regard,

Carl

Among the books written by S. L. A. Marshall, military editor of the Detroit News, *was* Night Drop, *for which Sandburg wrote the preface.*

639 | TO MRS. CHARLES J. BEDNAR

[Flat Rock, North Carolina]
4 February 62

Dear Juanita:

I have to write you in response to your long letter about enlarging the birthplace. My feeling is definite that any enlargement of the space it now occupies would be risky, would be taking chances. You are doing rather wonderfully with the place as it is. I don't like to think of it being larger with the added amount of supervision then required. I love you for the keen and intelligent way you have handled a responsibility that has been incessant and not easy. Please keep it simple like the life of old August Sandburg who married Clara Matilda Anderson. And please know I salute you on being so thoughtful and so loyal. I doubt whether at seventy-three or even at eighty-three you will have a worthy successor.

Ever yours,
Carl

Mrs. Charles Bednar (Juanita) was one of the moving spirits behind the Carl Sandburg Association, for the preservation of the Sandburg birthplace cottage in Galesburg.

640 | TO ZEEV Z. DOVER

[Flat Rock, North Carolina]
July 1, 1962

Dear Consul Dover:

I have your kind letter of June 15, suggesting an invitation to visit Israel in the near future. I should like very much to see the country, visit with their leaders, and have some fellowship with the students at the university.

My feeling in the matter is that I would probably be able to come along later this Fall, depending also upon the plans of Harry Golden who will be my companion. After the receipt of the invitation itself we shall then set the dates, somewhere between the middle of October and the first part of December. But we shall give you ample notice of course of the dates selected.

Thanking you for your kindness, you shall be welcome at Connemara when you pass through this part of the country. When you come, please do so in the late afternoon. With my esteem,

Sincerely yours,
Carl Sandburg

1963

Sandburg had been invited to speak to the students at Hebrew University, in Jerusalem. But by the end of 1962 he was beginning to stay close to home.

641 | TO LEO ORSO

[Flat Rock, North Carolina]
July 3, 1963

Dear Mr. Orso:

I appreciated very much all the interesting clippings that you sent us a month ago and so did Mr. Sandburg.

We were hoping that you would come to see us in July, after we returned home from a trip to Tampa, Florida where Carl had an engagement June 25. We really expected to be at home all of July when we received word from George Stevens that Carl is needed there to help edit the film on which he was script writer: "The Greatest Story Ever Told." We leave for Los Angeles July 12th and expect to be gone about two weeks. As soon as I know definitely when we will be home again, I shall write you and hope that you will then be able to come for a visit here. Carl would enjoy so much hearing your tapes, especially the 1963 Birthday Party and other tapes that you have done. You have done so much to make permanent records of events that otherwise would have "gone with the wind."

Carl is in very good health but he simply does not write letters, hasn't written one for a year, for he thinks he is entitled to a vacation. He always reminds us that he has written twenty-three books. He sends you his love.

With love from us all
Lilian Paula Sandburg

Paula Sandburg handled Carl's correspondence after 1963. Otherwise, Sandburg continued to follow the literary and news currents in the United States and the world keenly until his death in his Flat Rock home on July 22, 1967.

Acknowledgments

A number of individuals and libraries loaned or copied letters, provided information for notes about persons and events, and steered the editor to sources in the United States and abroad. In addition, several friends and associates helped in the research and chores of assembling this book.

Special gratitude goes to Robert Halsband, biographer and adjunct professor of English, Columbia University, for stylistic and bibliographic guidance; Victoria Heller, for her skillful research and cheerful presence; Alfred Rice, for his counsel in literary affairs; my son, Lee Mitgang, for Latin translations from Catullus, in Ezra Pound's letters, and my daughters, Esther and Laura Mitgang, for filing, stapling, and rubber-banding.

Allegheny College Library (Ida M. Tarbell Collection); Paul Angle, secretary, Chicago Historical Society, for letters and data; Robert O. Anthony, curator, The Walter Lippmann Collection, Yale University; Mrs. David Aultfather; Frederic Babcock; John Baggerley, for guidance to Fremont Older letters; Dr. F. Clever Bald, Michigan Historical Collections, University of Michigan; Roger W. Barrett, for the letters of his father, Oliver Barrett; Roland Baughman, special collections, Columbia University; Mrs. Charles Bednar, of the Sandburg Birthplace, for sources in Galesburg; Barbara Bekeza, for research in the files of the Galesburg *Evening Mail;* Paul Benjamin, for letters; Senator William Benton, for letters and recollections; Mrs. Caroll Binder; Herbert L. Block (Herblock), for letters; Mrs. Richard D. Bokum (Fanny Butcher), for letters and recollections; Reuben W. Borough, for copies of his valuable collection of early Sandburg letters, and memories of Social Democratic party days; Mrs. Herbert Bradley; Dr. and Mrs. William Braye; John Mason Brown, for Sandburg reflections; Mrs. Hazel Buchbinder; Witter Bynner; Carl Carmer; Olive Carruthers; Margaret Haley Carpenter, for letter to Sara Teasdale; Bruce Catton; Helene Champlain; Henry A. Christian, Rutgers Library; Cecil B. Chase, Bancroft Library, University of California.

Norman Corwin, for his exchange of letters and astute interpretation of Sandburg's creative life; Mary A. Creighton, editor, the Galesburg

Acknowledgments

Post; Robert Cromie, Chicago *Tribune* book editor, for scholarly assistance; Gregory d'Alessio, for letters and guitar reminiscences; Jonathan Daniels; Edward Davison; Mrs. Mitchell Dawson, for information; Clarence Decker; Floyd Dell; Kenneth M. Dodson, for letters and memories of a friendship; John Dos Passos; Senator Paul Douglas; Associate Justice William O. Douglas; Alvin W. Dreier, for Chicago memories and letters; R. L. Duffus, for California reminiscences; Max Eastman, for Sandburg background; William T. Evjue, editor of the *Capitol Times,* Madison, Wisconsin; Frederic Fadner; Mrs. A. R. Faver, for guidance to South Carolina sources; Daniel Fitzpatrick, for St. Louis memories; Thomas Hornsby Ferril, for letters; Margaret A. Flint, Assistant State Librarian, Illinois State Historical Library; Mrs. Douglas S. Freeman, for permission to use her husband's letters in the Library of Congress; Donald Gallup, curator, American Collection, Yale University; Wayne Gard, for letters; Elmer Gertz; Cliff Gessler; Harry Golden, for letters and helpful guidance to sources; Max Goodsill, Knox College sage, for letters and Galesburg guidance; Harry F. Guggenheim, *Newsday;* Harry Hansen, for Chicago memories.

Mrs. Alfred Harcourt, for Harcourt-Sandburg correspondence; Peter Heggie, executive secretary, The Authors Guild; Mrs. Ernest Hemingway, for letters and recollections; Ken Holden, for letters and Michigan memories; Dr. Alan Jenkins, for generous sharing of letters and written observations; Walter Johnson, editor of the Adlai Stevenson Papers; Louis Clark Jones; Gene Kelly; Herman Kahn, Assistant Archivist for Presidential Libraries, Washington, D.C.; Mrs. Meyer Kestnbaum; Lucy Kroll, for letters and anecdotal memories; James Laughlin, New Directions; Mrs. Lloyd Lewis, for letters and facts of a long friendship; Lilly Library, Indiana University; Walter Lippmann; Alan Lomax; Amy Lowell Library, Harvard University; Harriet Monroe Collection, University of Chicago; Catherine McCarthy, Sandburg's editor at Harcourt before her retirement; Ralph McGill, Atlanta *Constitution;* Marianne Mantell, Caedmon Records; General S. L. A. Marshall; Grace M. Mayer, Museum of Modern Art, New York.

David C. Mearns, ex-chief of the manuscript division, reference department, The Library of Congress, an indispensable Lincoln scholar, Sandburg friend, and public servant; Mrs. Edward R. Murrow, for access to Murrow-Sandburg letters; Mrs. John Murray (Lois Smith Douglas) of the Armstrong-Browning Library at Baylor University; Leo Orso, for letters and memories; Dr. John G. Neihardt; Dr. Allan Nevins; Amy Nyholm of the Newberry Library; William Peterkin, for letters to

Acknowledgments

Julia Peterkin; Mrs. Granville T. Prior, South Carolina Historical Society; Principessa Mary de Rachewiltz, daughter of Ezra Pound; Warden Joseph Ragen, Joliet Prison, Illinois; Isadora Bennett Reed, for a store of South Carolina and Chicago memories; Mrs. Ole E. Rölvaag; Mrs. Edgar L. Rossin, for letters to and from her mother, Alice Corbin Henderson; Sophocles Papas, for memories and links to Andres Segovia and the guitar circle; Margaret Parton; Mrs. Lilla Perry, for letters and recollections; Mrs. Betty Peterman (Gole), Sandburg secretary at the Chicago *Daily News;* Professor Max Putzell, University of Connecticut; Dr. Richard V. Sandburg; Mrs. Lew Sarett, for letters to her and her husband; Andres Segovia, for reminiscences of Sandburg guitar chords.

Don Shoemaker, editor of the Miami *Herald,* for letters and explanations; Upton Sinclair; William Small; Vincent Starrett, Chicago *Tribune;* Edward Steichen; John Steichen; Paula Steichen; George Stevens; Adlai Stevenson III; Walter B. Stroesser; University of Texas Library; Mrs. William H. Townsend; Clyde C. Tull, for his letters and memories; Brenda Ueland, for letters; Dr. Sharvey G. Umbeck, president of Knox College, Galesburg; Louis Untermeyer, for letters and explanations; Irita Van Doren; Mrs. Arthur Wachs, sister of Carl Sandburg; Clyde C. Walton, Illinois State Historical Library; Professor John C. Weigel, for letters and Sandburg information; Evelyn Wells; Harriet Welling; Joseph Wershba, CBS News producer, trusted friend of the Sandburg family, for guidance; Mrs. George P. West; Mrs. Neda Westlake of the University of Pennsylvania for the letters to Theodore Dreiser; Dr. Quincy Wright, for essential letters to and from Sandburg and his father, Professor Philip Green Wright, and memories of The Asgard Press; Jake Zeitlin, for his letters.

Index

Index

Index

Index

Index

Index

Index

Index

Index

Index

Index

Index

Index

Index

Index

Index

Index

Index

Index

Index

Index